Shojo Beat

Rasetsu

Vol. 1

WANT SOMETHING SWEET? ♡
NOPE.

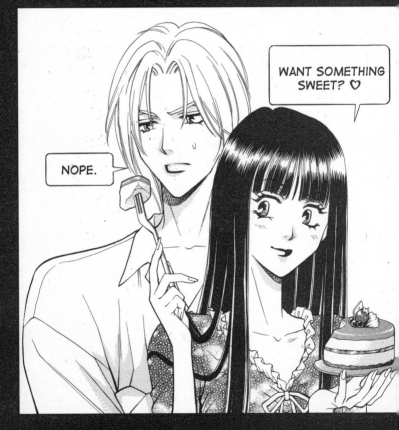

Story & Art by

Chika Shiomi

Rasetsu

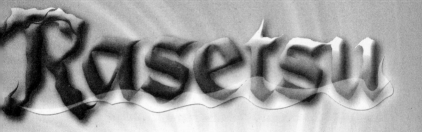

Volume 1
Contents

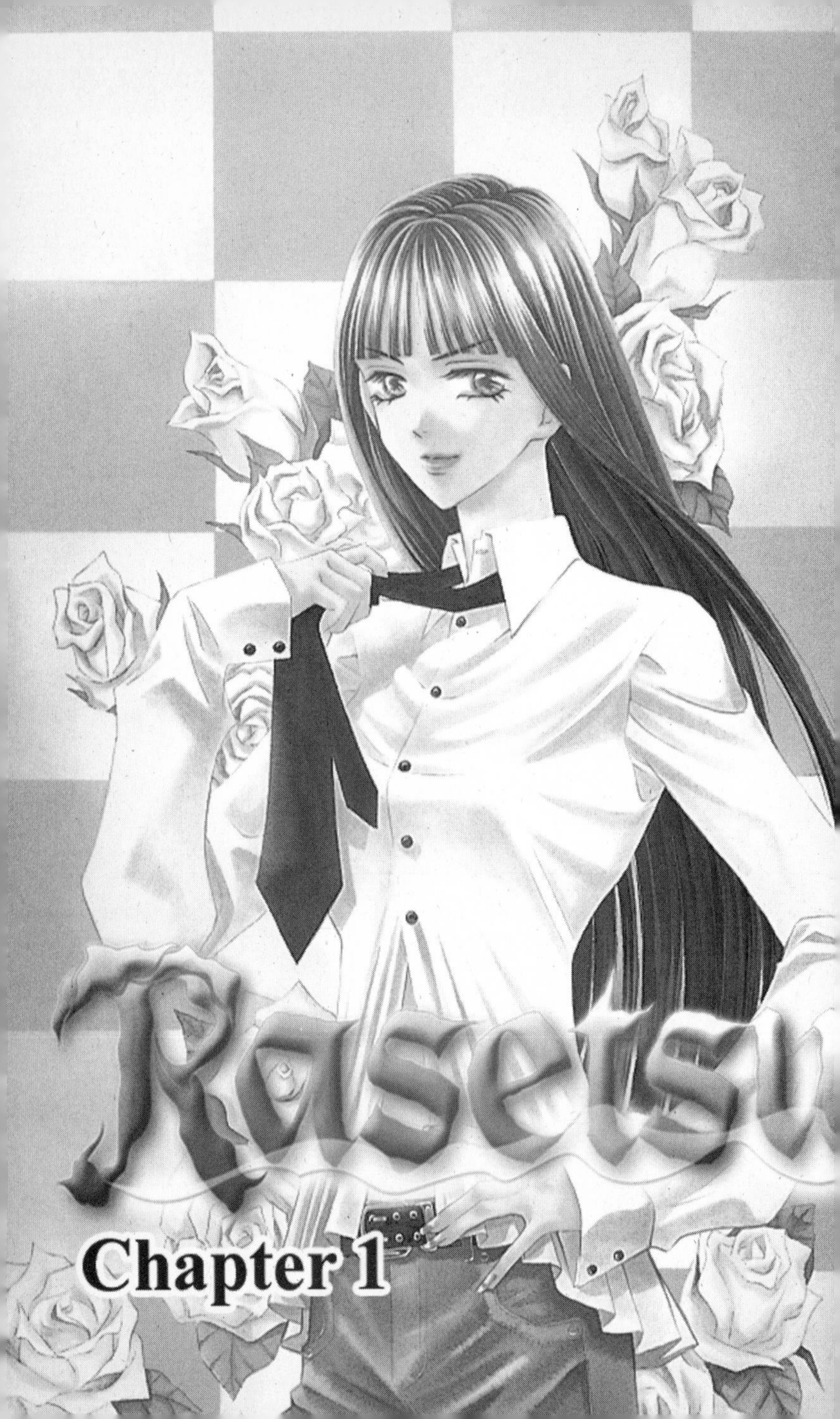
Rasetsu
Chapter 1

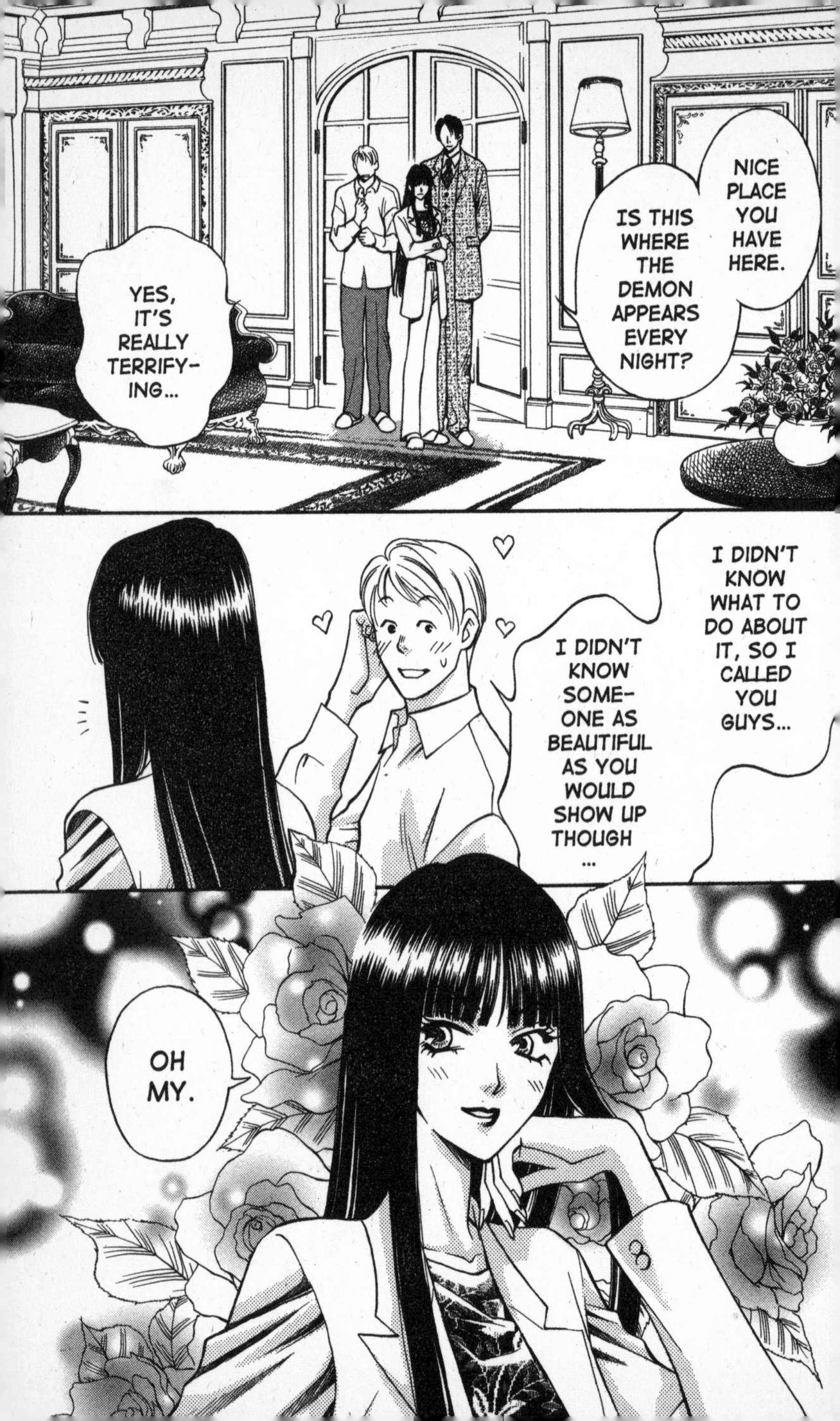
NICE PLACE YOU HAVE HERE.
IS THIS WHERE THE DEMON APPEARS EVERY NIGHT?
YES, IT'S REALLY TERRIFY-ING...
I DIDN'T KNOW WHAT TO DO ABOUT IT, SO I CALLED YOU GUYS...
I DIDN'T KNOW SOME-ONE AS BEAUTIFUL AS YOU WOULD SHOW UP THOUGH...
OH MY.

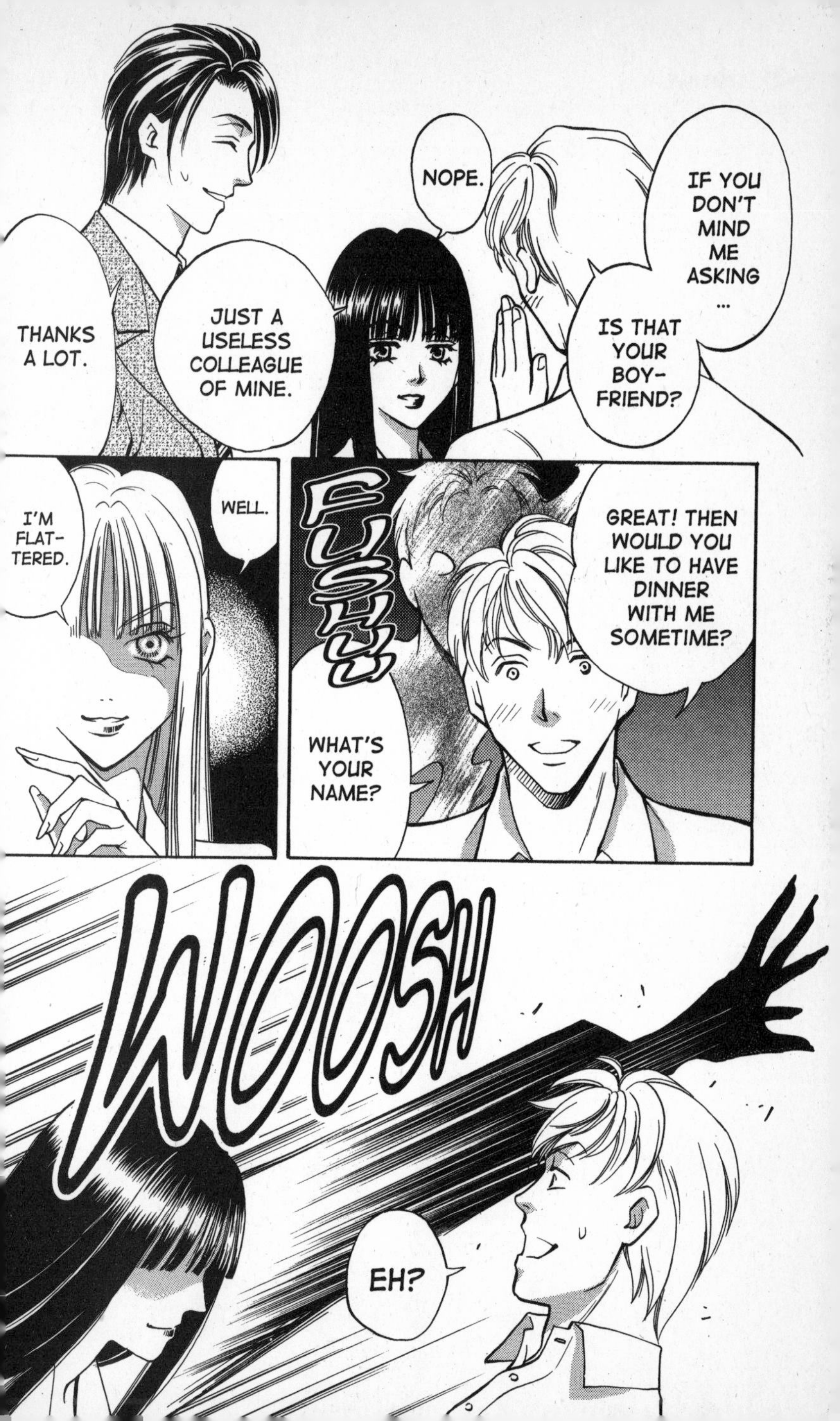
IF YOU DON'T MIND ME ASKING ...
IS THAT YOUR BOY-FRIEND?
NOPE.
JUST A USELESS COLLEAGUE OF MINE.
THANKS A LOT.
GREAT! THEN WOULD YOU LIKE TO HAVE DINNER WITH ME SOMETIME?
FUSHU
WHAT'S YOUR NAME?
WELL.
I'M FLAT-TERED.
WOOSH
EH?

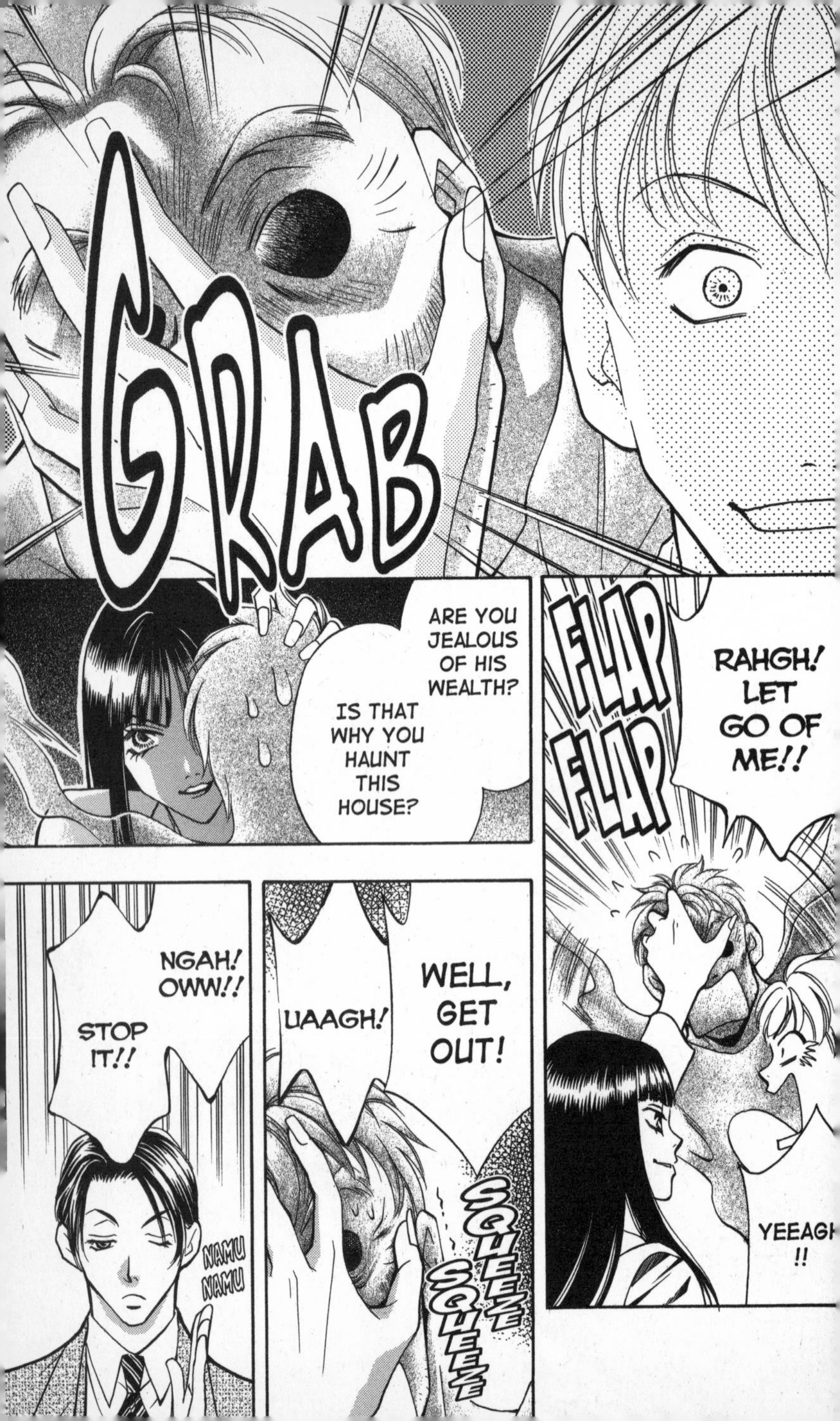
GRAB
FLAP FLAP
RAHGH! LET GO OF ME!!
YEEAGH!!
ARE YOU JEALOUS OF HIS WEALTH?
IS THAT WHY YOU HAUNT THIS HOUSE?
WELL, GET OUT!
UAAGH!
SQUEEZE SQUEEZE
NGAH! OWW!!
STOP IT!!
NAMU NAMU

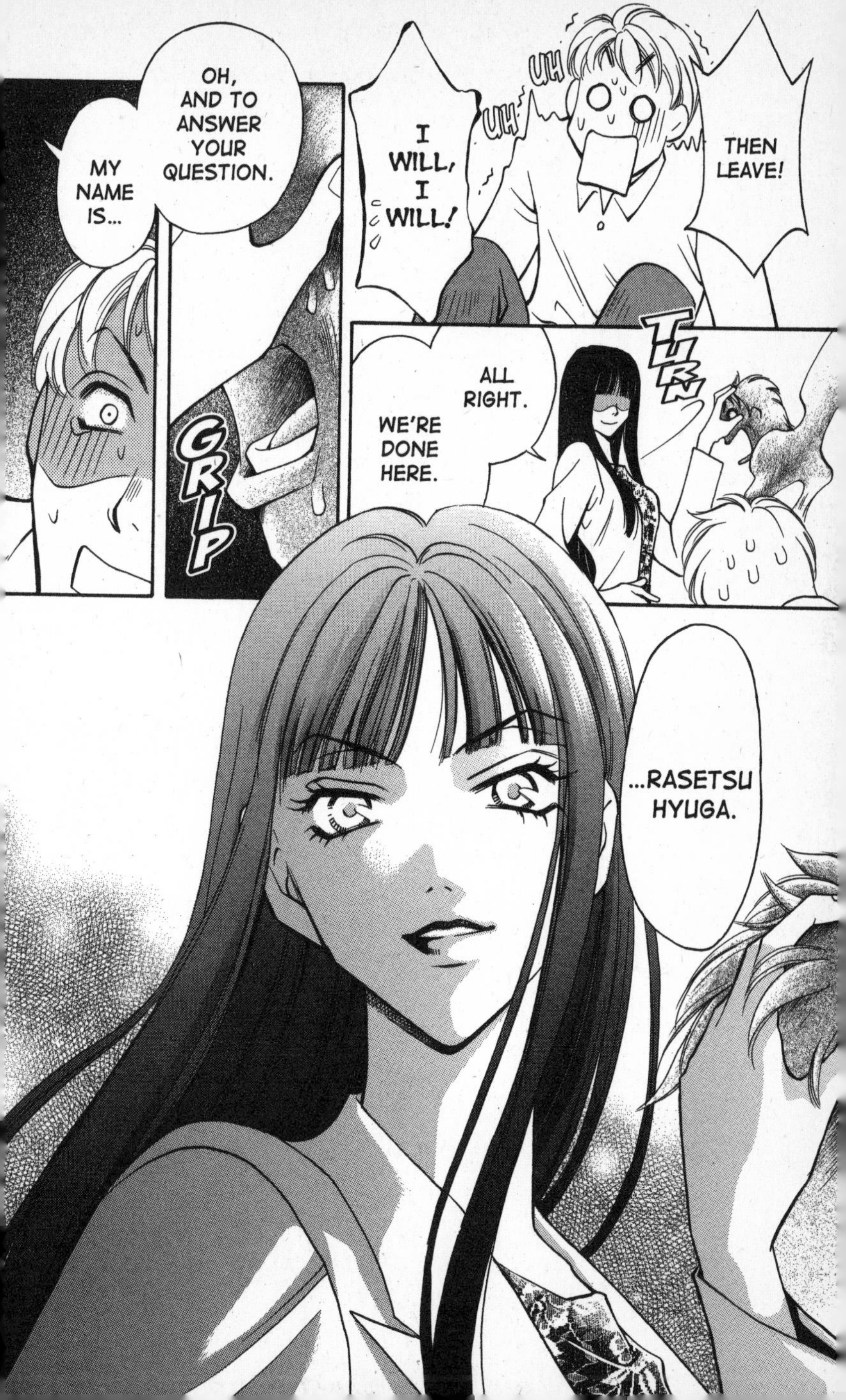
THEN LEAVE!
UH UH
I WILL, I WILL!
TURN
ALL RIGHT.
WE'RE DONE HERE.
GRIP
OH, AND TO ANSWER YOUR QUESTION.
MY NAME IS...
...RASETSU HYUGA.

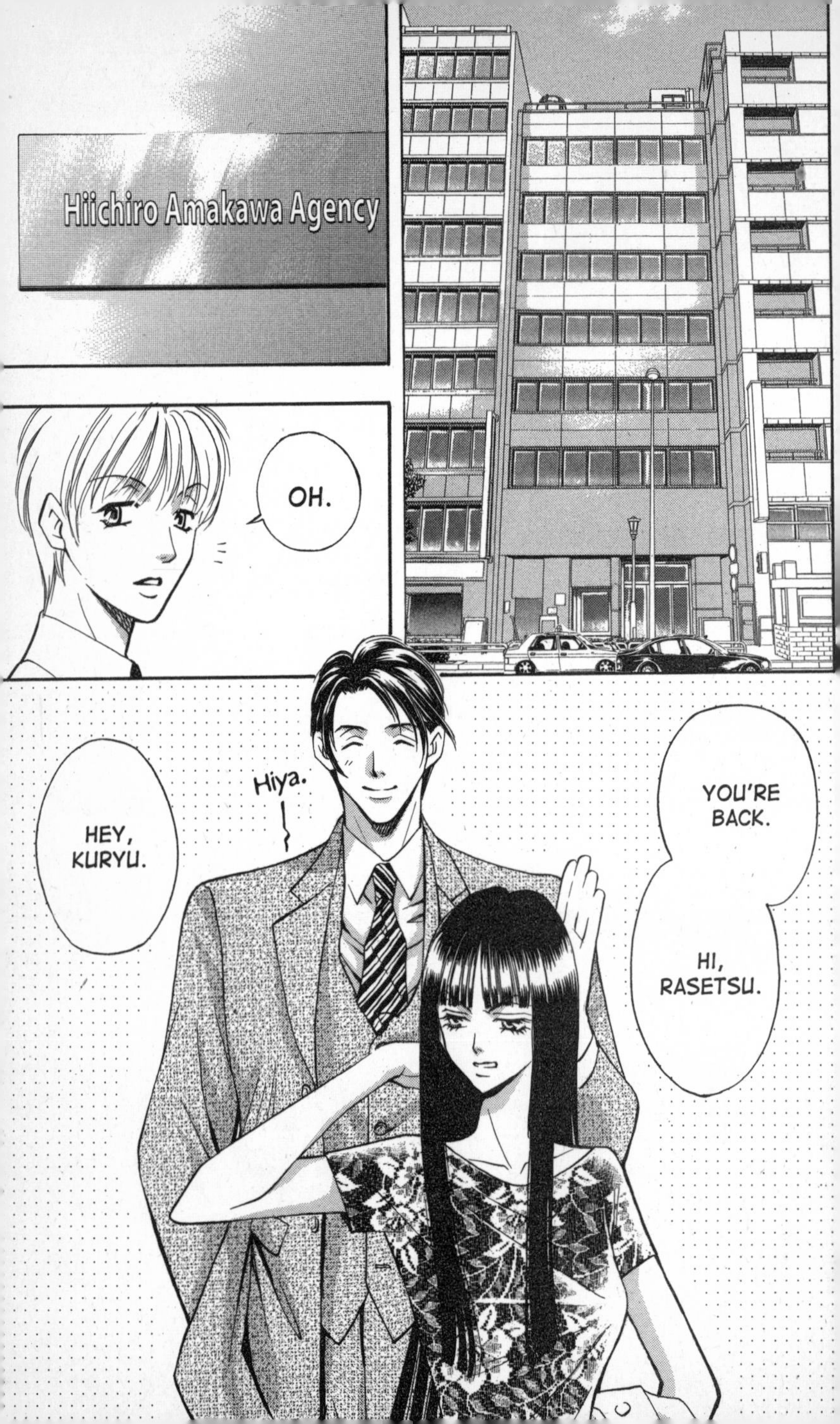
Hiichiro Amakawa Agency
OH.
YOU'RE BACK.
HI, RASETSU.
Hiya.
HEY, KURYU.

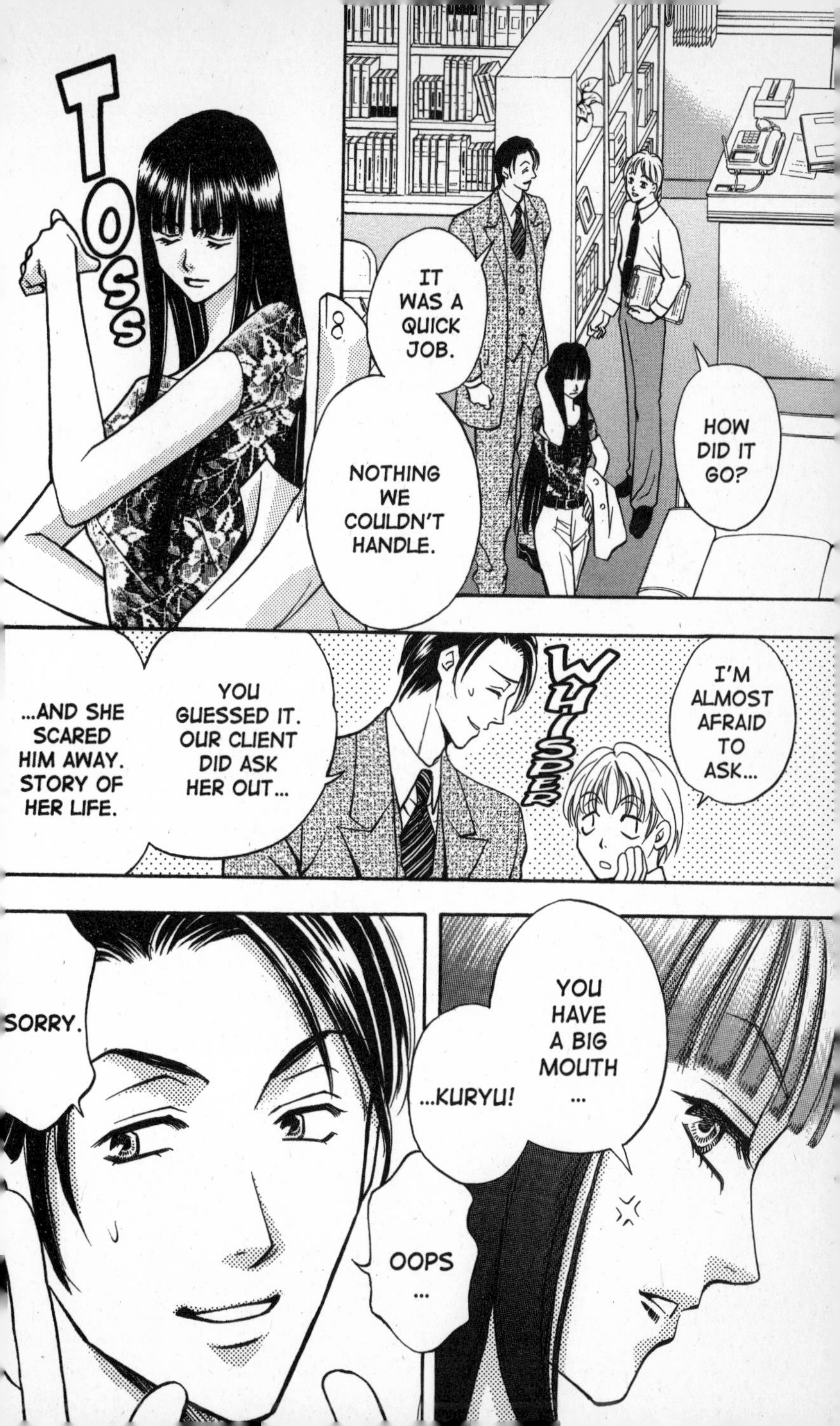
HOW DID IT GO?
IT WAS A QUICK JOB.
NOTHING WE COULDN'T HANDLE.
TOSS
I'M ALMOST AFRAID TO ASK...
WHISPER
YOU GUESSED IT. OUR CLIENT DID ASK HER OUT...
...AND SHE SCARED HIM AWAY. STORY OF HER LIFE.
YOU HAVE A BIG MOUTH ...
...KURYU!
OOPS ...
SORRY.

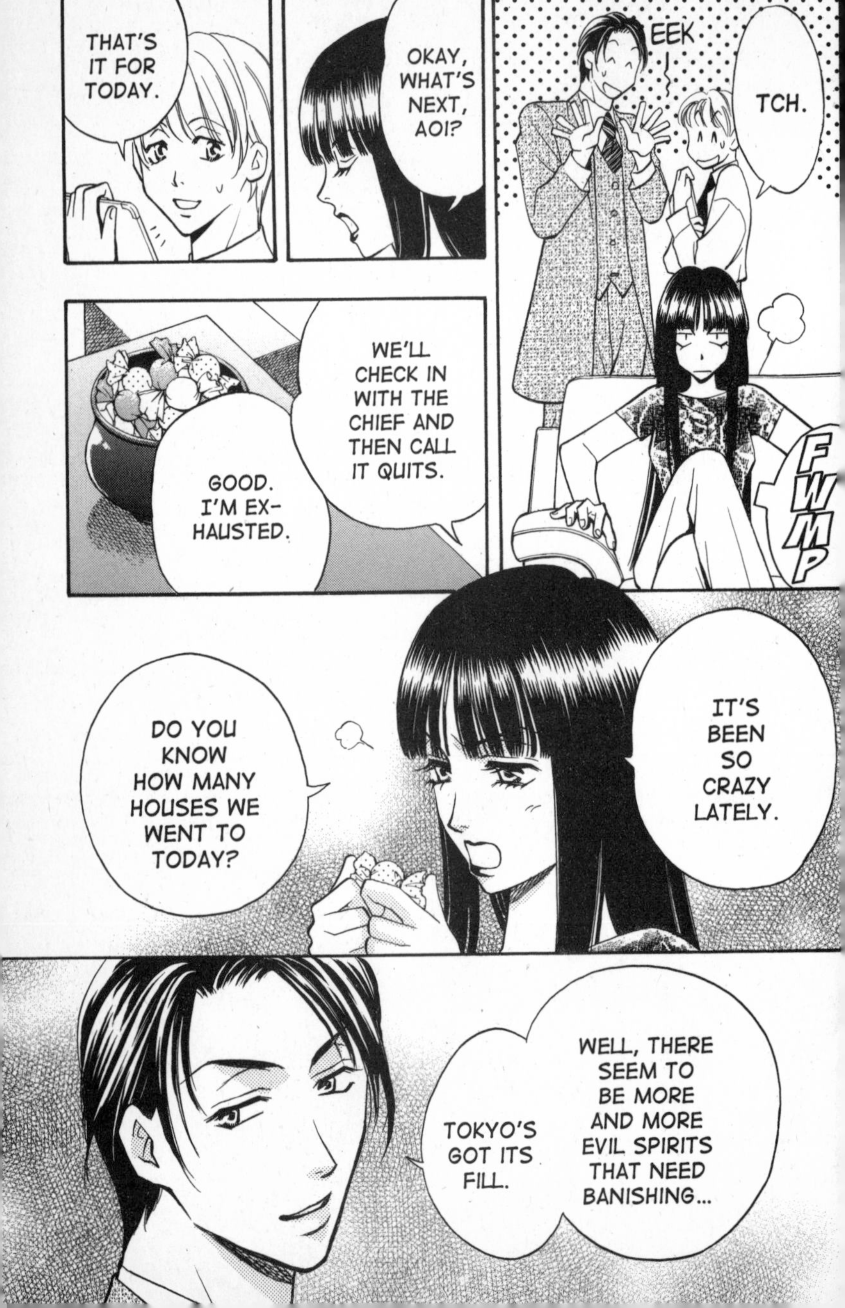
TCH.
EEK
FWMP
OKAY, WHAT'S NEXT, AOI?
THAT'S IT FOR TODAY.
WE'LL CHECK IN WITH THE CHIEF AND THEN CALL IT QUITS.
GOOD. I'M EX-HAUSTED.
IT'S BEEN SO CRAZY LATELY.
DO YOU KNOW HOW MANY HOUSES WE WENT TO TODAY?
WELL, THERE SEEM TO BE MORE AND MORE EVIL SPIRITS THAT NEED BANISHING...
TOKYO'S GOT ITS FILL.

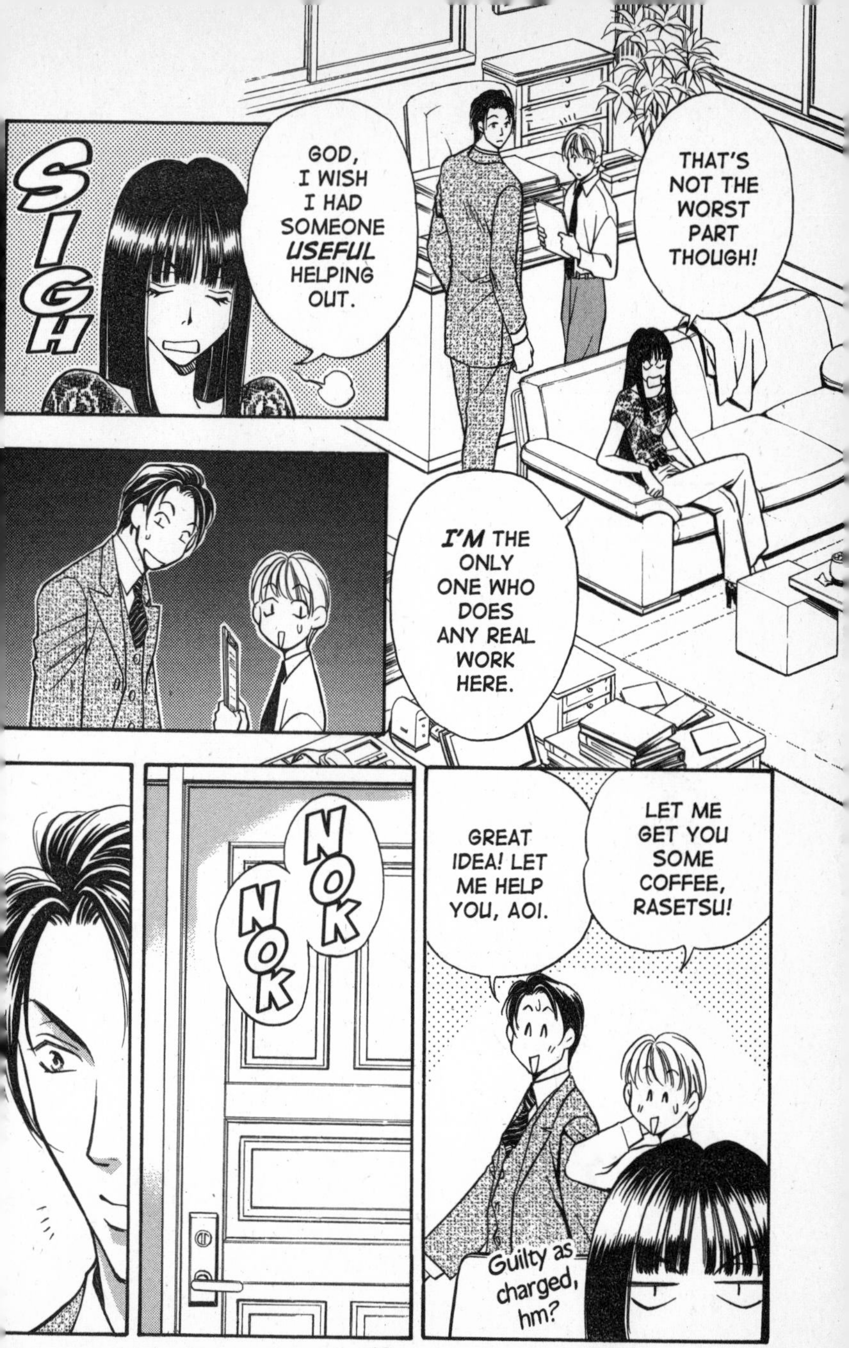
THAT'S NOT THE WORST PART THOUGH!
I'M THE ONLY ONE WHO DOES ANY REAL WORK HERE.
SIGH
GOD, I WISH I HAD SOMEONE USEFUL HELPING OUT.
LET ME GET YOU SOME COFFEE, RASETSU!
GREAT IDEA! LET ME HELP YOU, AOI.
Guilty as charged, hm?
NOK
NOK

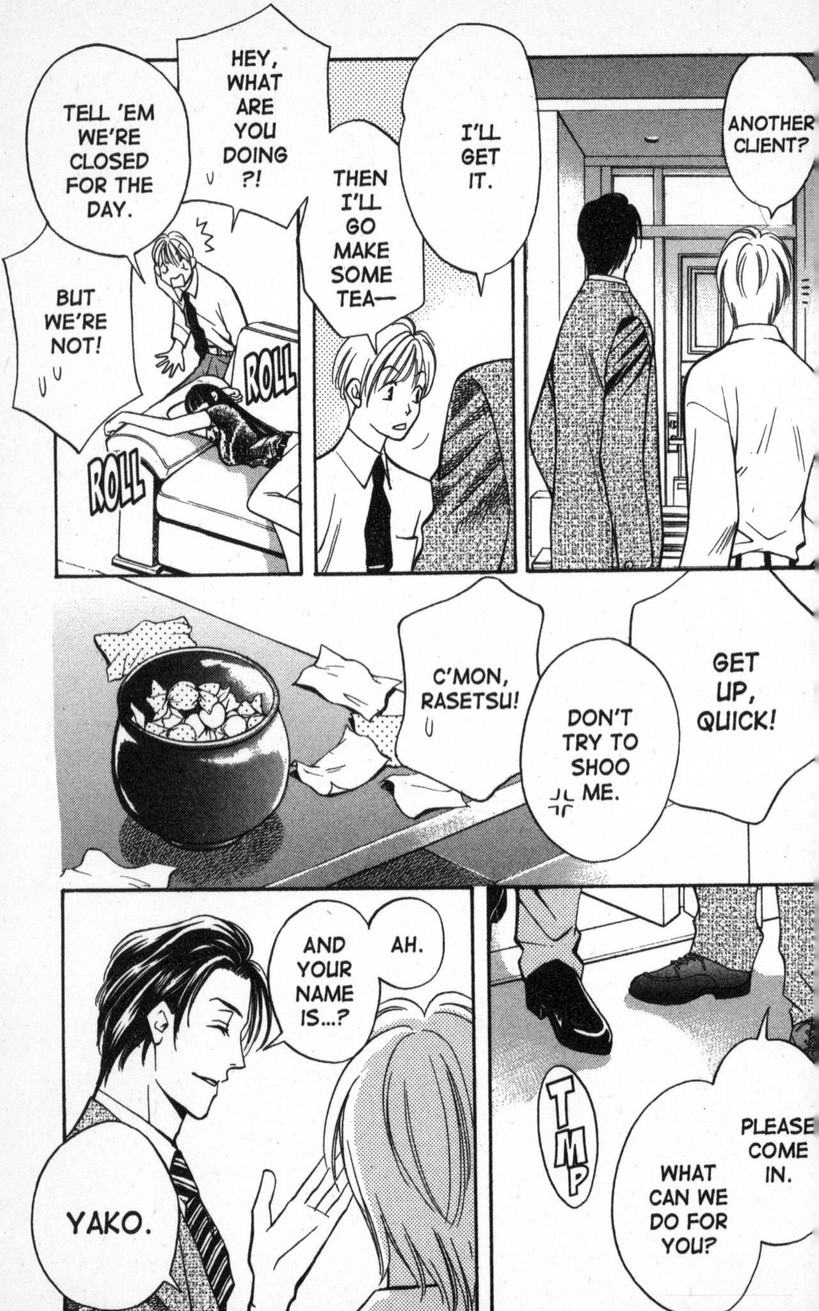
ANOTHER CLIENT?
I'LL GET IT.
THEN I'LL GO MAKE SOME TEA—
HEY, WHAT ARE YOU DOING?!
TELL 'EM WE'RE CLOSED FOR THE DAY.
ROLL
BUT WE'RE NOT!
ROLL
GET UP, QUICK!
DON'T TRY TO SHOO ME.
C'MON, RASETSU!
PLEASE COME IN.
WHAT CAN WE DO FOR YOU?
TMP
AH.
AND YOUR NAME IS...?
YAKO.

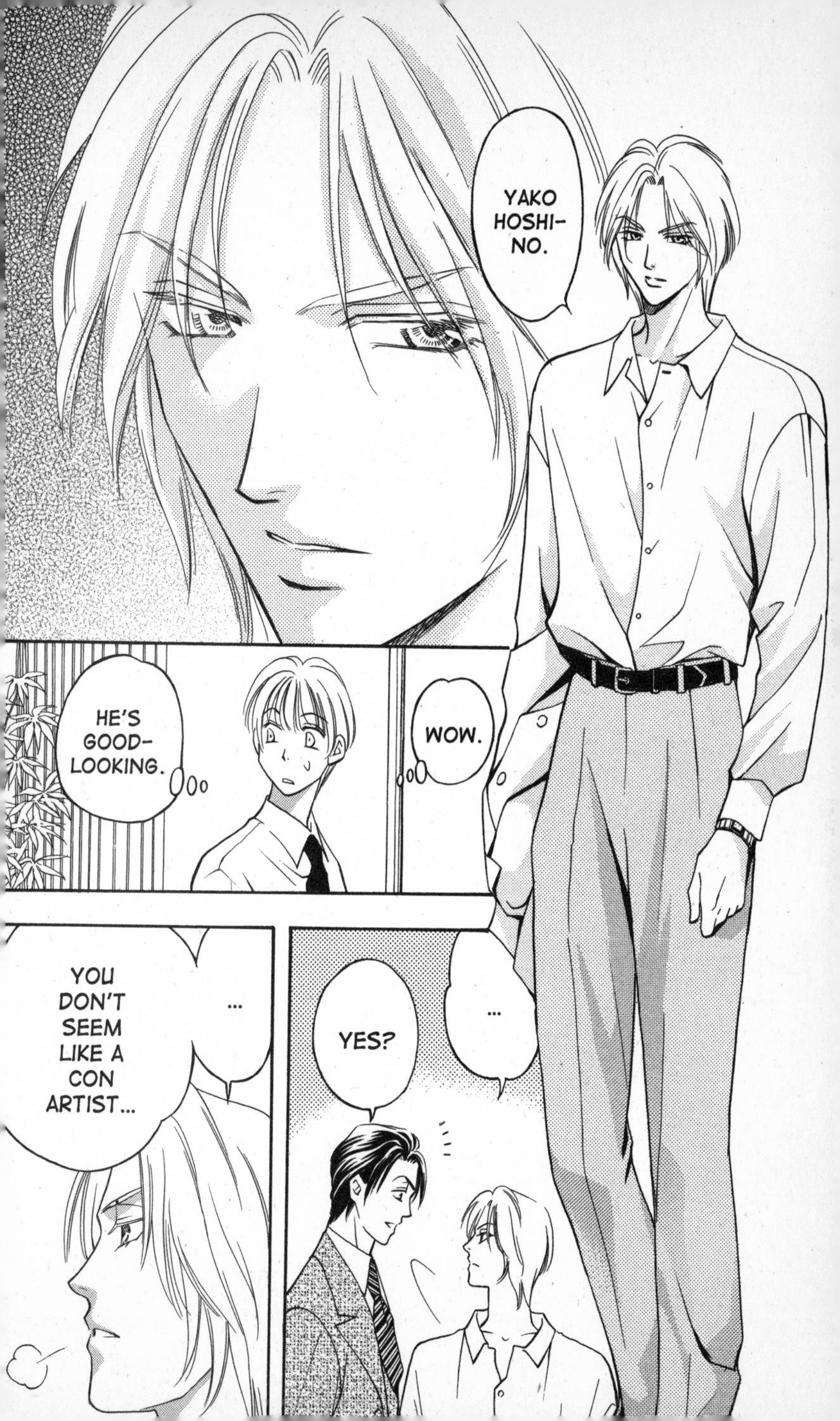

YAKO HOSHI-NO.
WOW.
HE'S GOOD-LOOKING.
...
YES?
...
YOU DON'T SEEM LIKE A CON ARTIST...

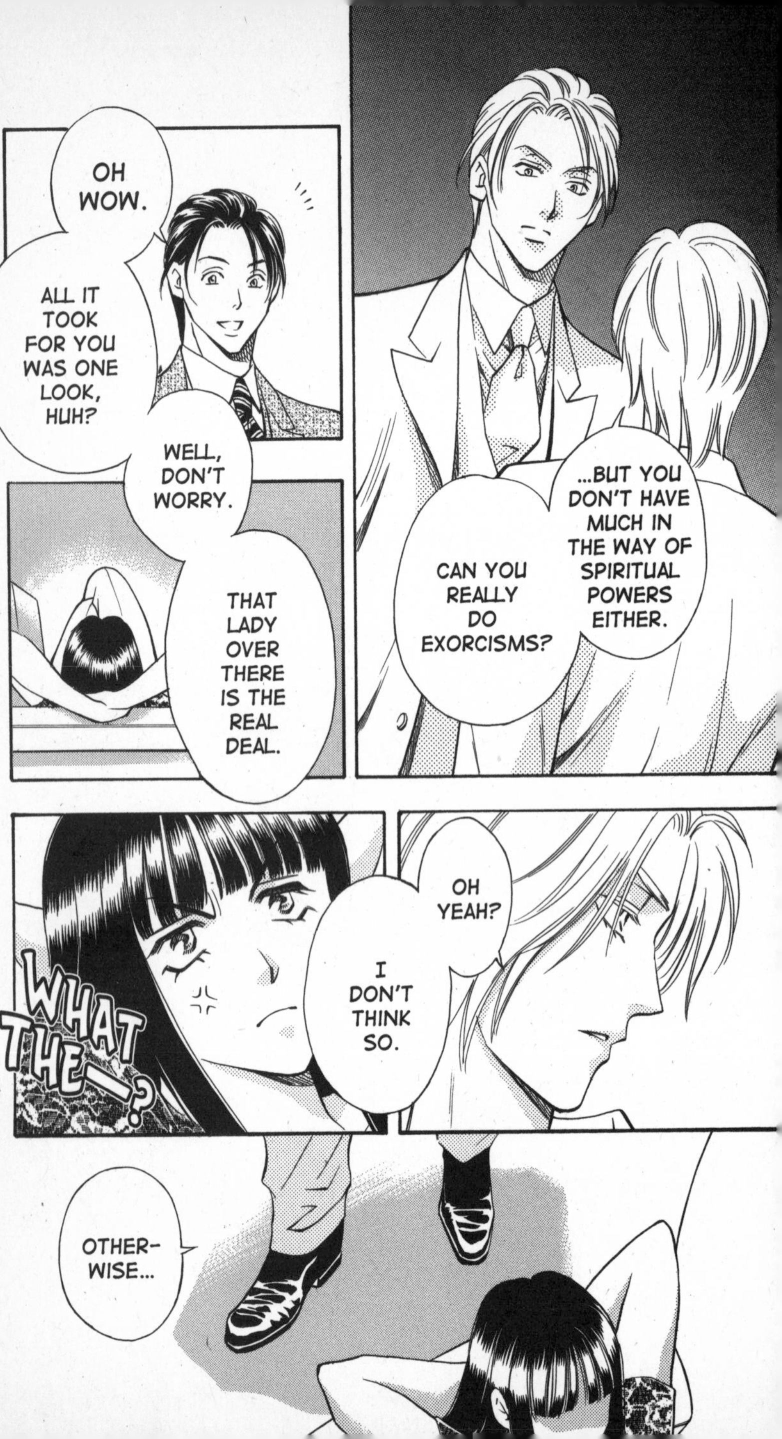

...BUT YOU DON'T HAVE MUCH IN THE WAY OF SPIRITUAL POWERS EITHER.
CAN YOU REALLY DO EXORCISMS?
OH WOW.
ALL IT TOOK FOR YOU WAS ONE LOOK, HUH?
WELL, DON'T WORRY.
THAT LADY OVER THERE IS THE REAL DEAL.
OH YEAH?
I DON'T THINK SO.
WHAT THE—?
OTHER-WISE...

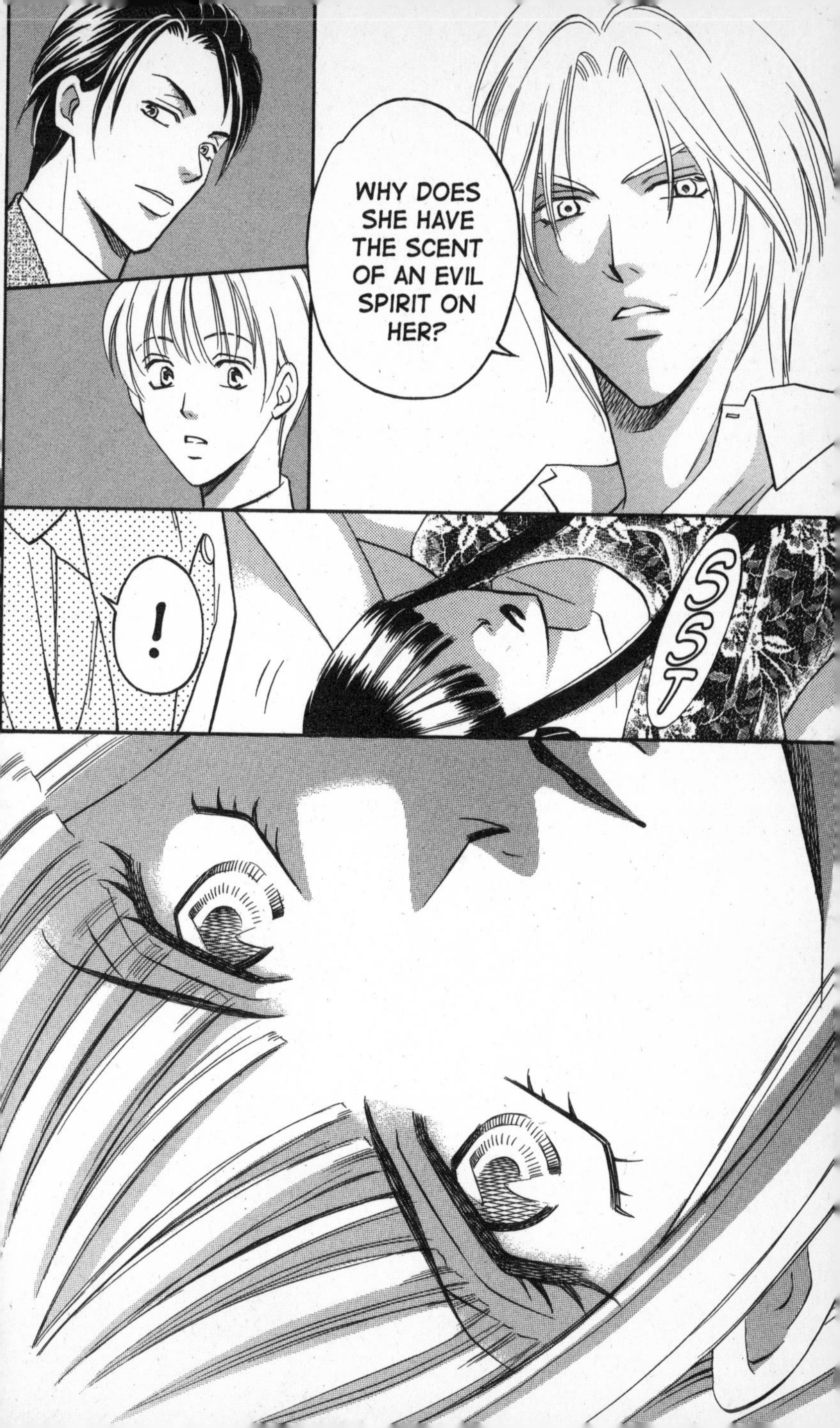
WHY DOES SHE HAVE THE SCENT OF AN EVIL SPIRIT ON HER?
SSST
!

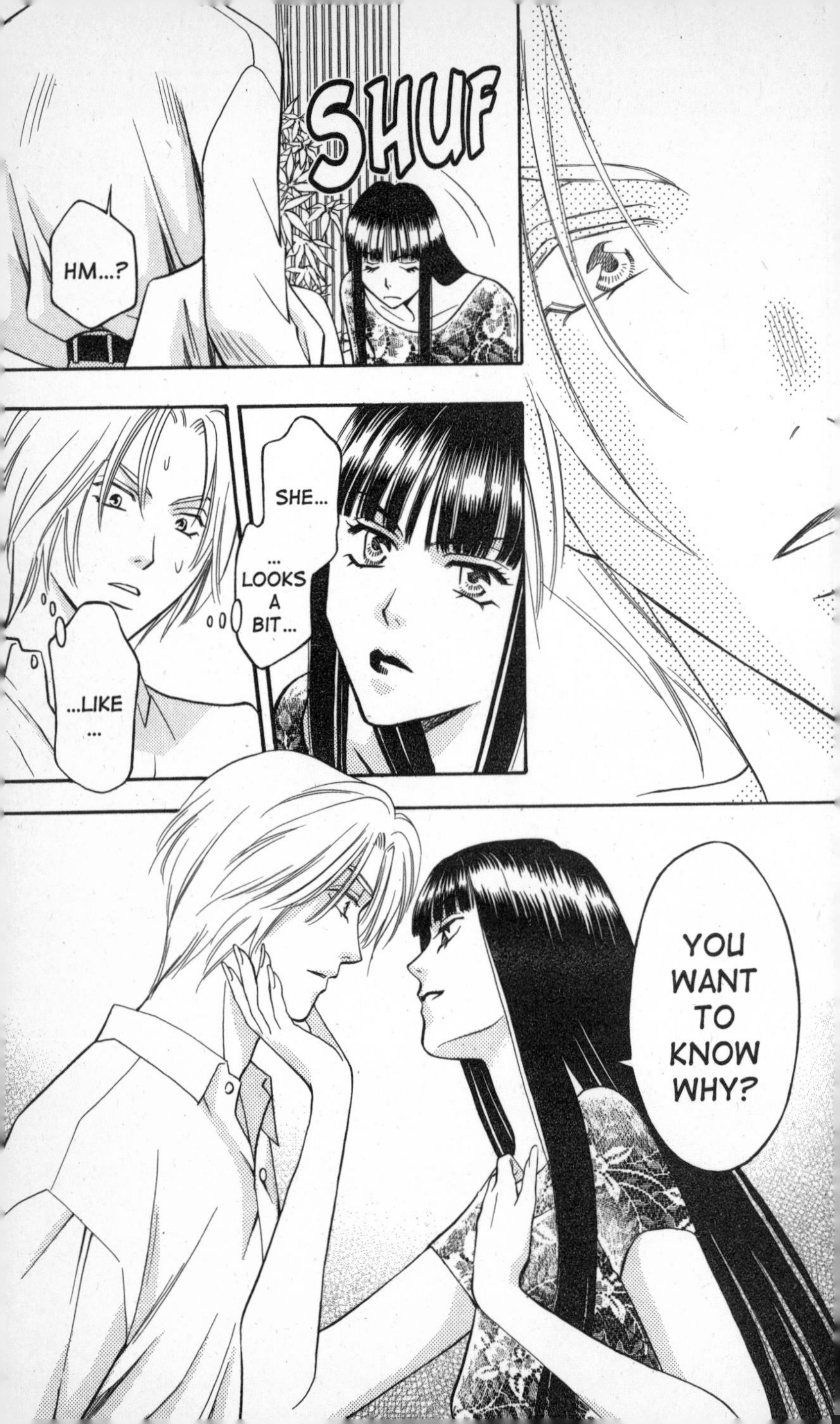
SHUF
HM...?
SHE...
... LOOKS A BIT...
...LIKE ...
YOU WANT TO KNOW WHY?

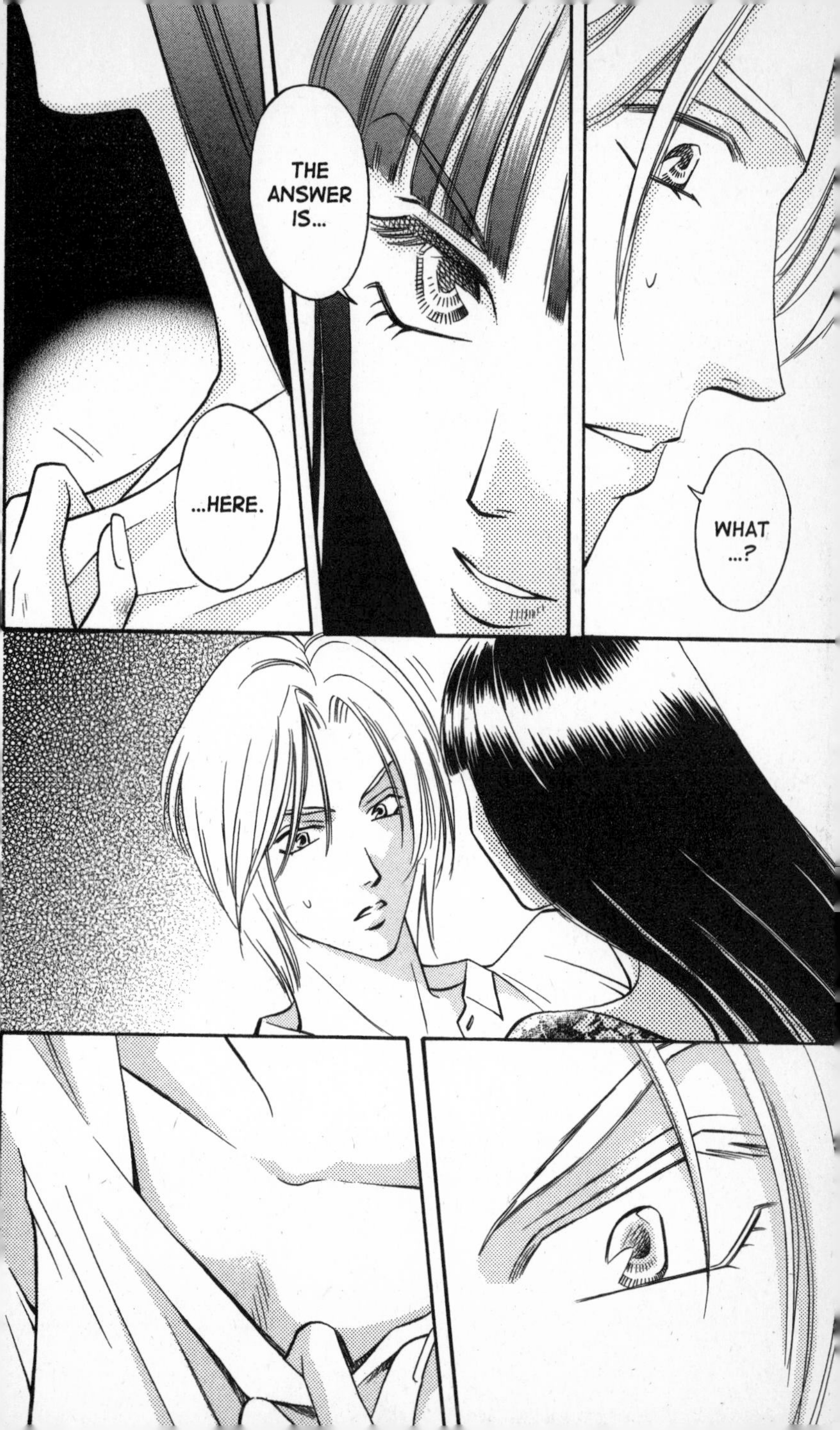
WHAT ...?
THE ANSWER IS...
...HERE.

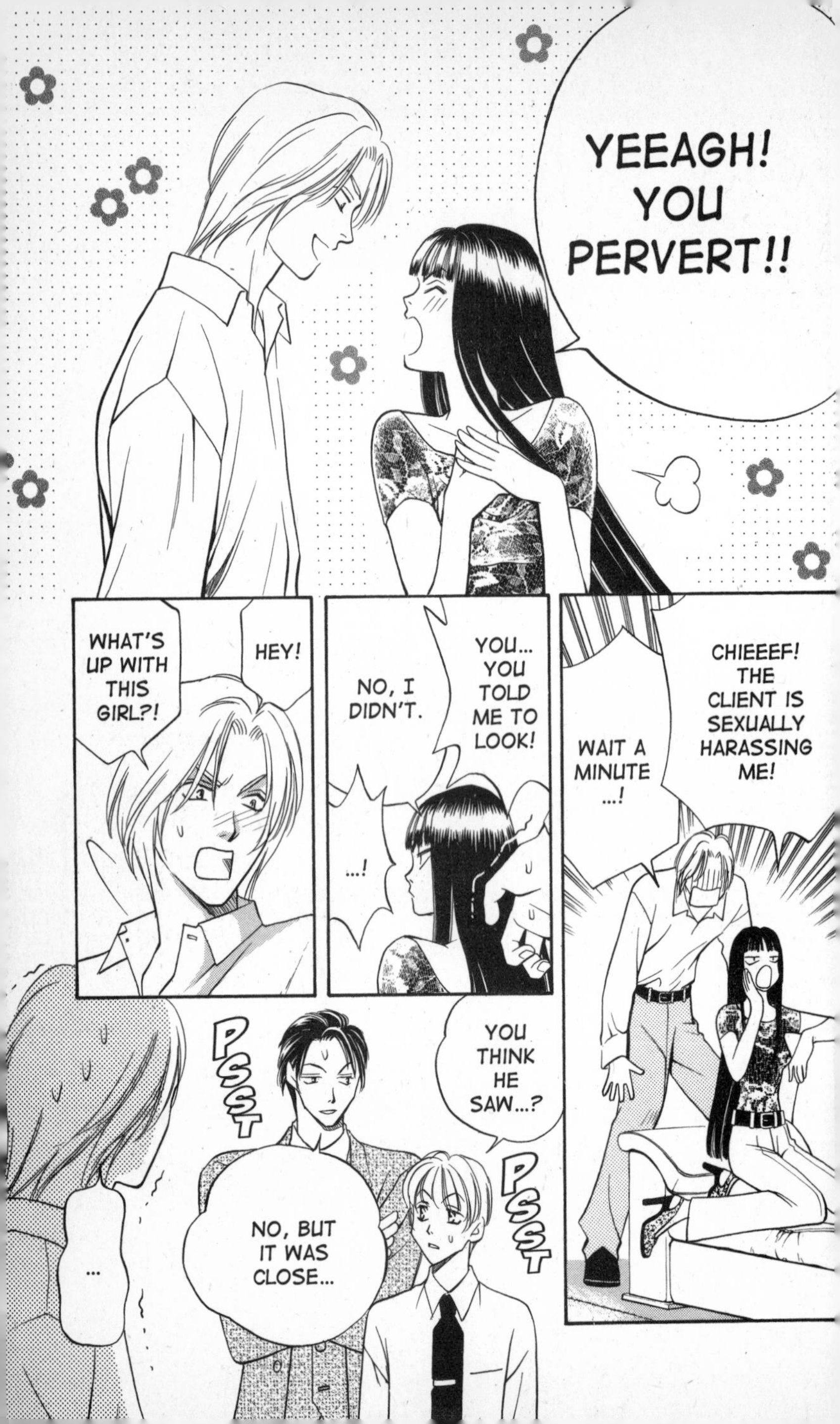
YEEAGH! YOU PERVERT!!
CHIEEEF! THE CLIENT IS SEXUALLY HARASSING ME!
WAIT A MINUTE ...!
YOU... YOU TOLD ME TO LOOK!
NO, I DIDN'T.
...!
HEY!
WHAT'S UP WITH THIS GIRL?!
PSST
YOU THINK HE SAW...?
PSST
NO, BUT IT WAS CLOSE...
...

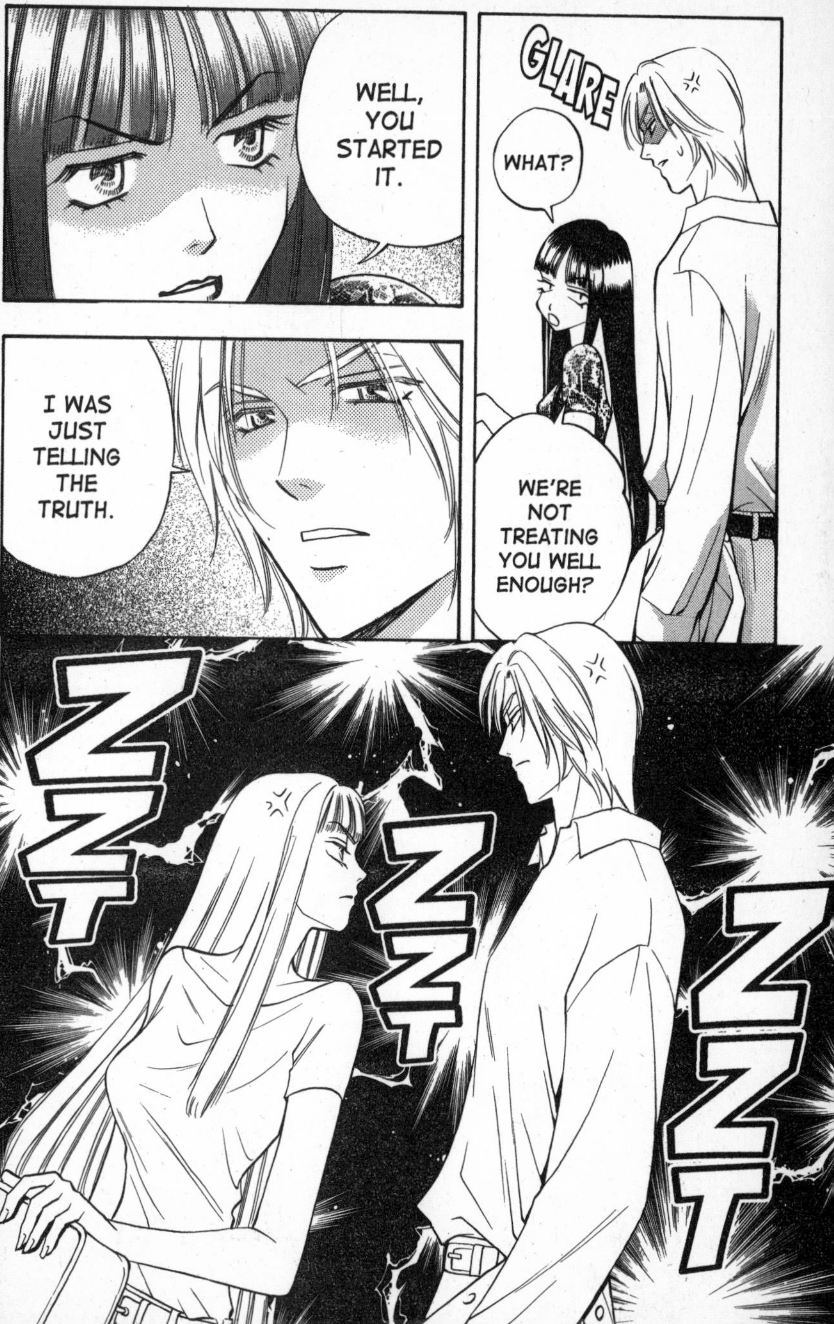
GLARE
WHAT?
WE'RE NOT TREATING YOU WELL ENOUGH?
WELL, YOU STARTED IT.
I WAS JUST TELLING THE TRUTH.
ZZZT
ZZZT
ZZZT

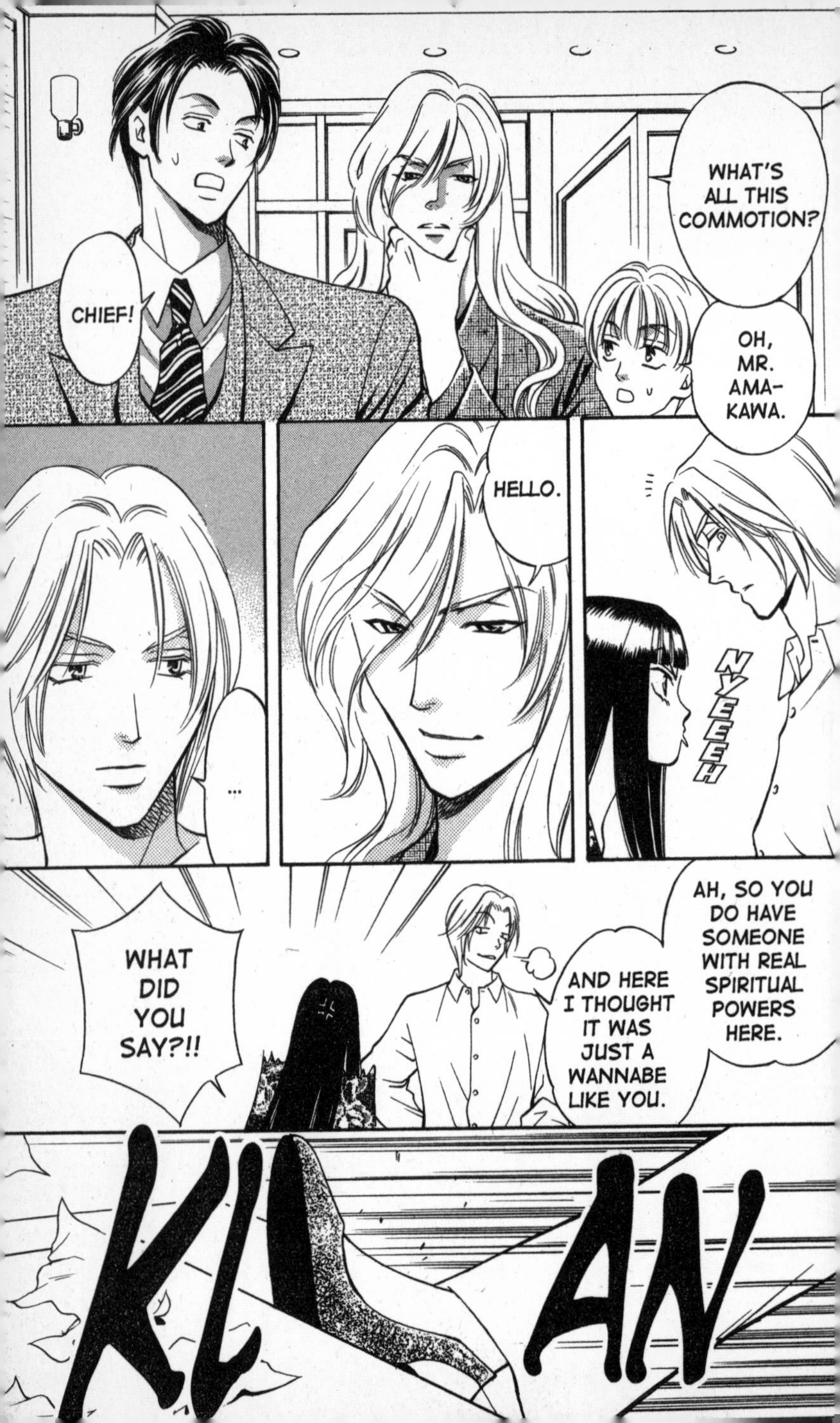
WHAT'S ALL THIS COMMOTION?
OH, MR. AMA-KAWA.
CHIEF!
NYEEEH
HELLO.
...
AH, SO YOU DO HAVE SOMEONE WITH REAL SPIRITUAL POWERS HERE.
AND HERE I THOUGHT IT WAS JUST A WANNABE LIKE YOU.
WHAT DID YOU SAY?!!
KLAN

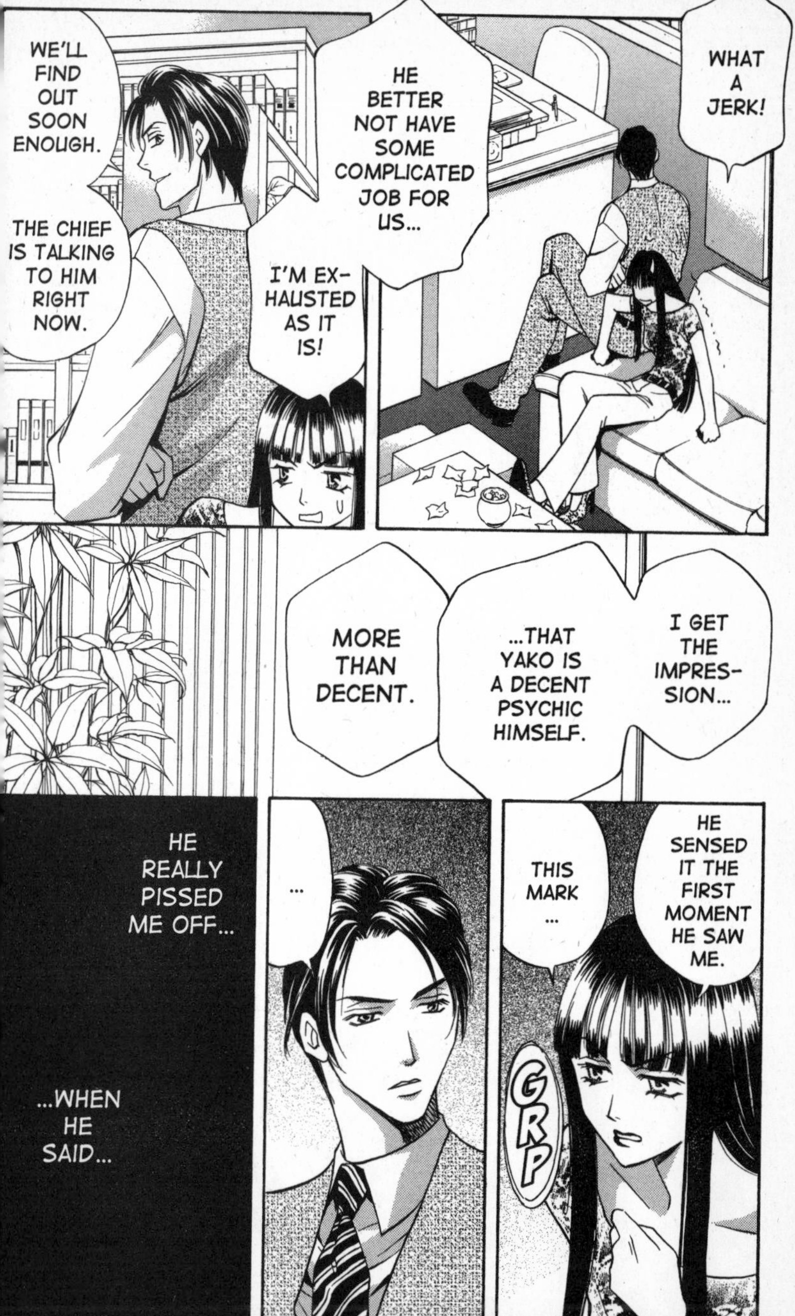
WHAT A JERK!
HE BETTER NOT HAVE SOME COMPLICATED JOB FOR US...
I'M EX-HAUSTED AS IT IS!
WE'LL FIND OUT SOON ENOUGH.
THE CHIEF IS TALKING TO HIM RIGHT NOW.
I GET THE IMPRES-SION...
...THAT YAKO IS A DECENT PSYCHIC HIMSELF.
MORE THAN DECENT.
HE SENSED IT THE FIRST MOMENT HE SAW ME.
THIS MARK ...
GRP
...
HE REALLY PISSED ME OFF...
...WHEN HE SAID...

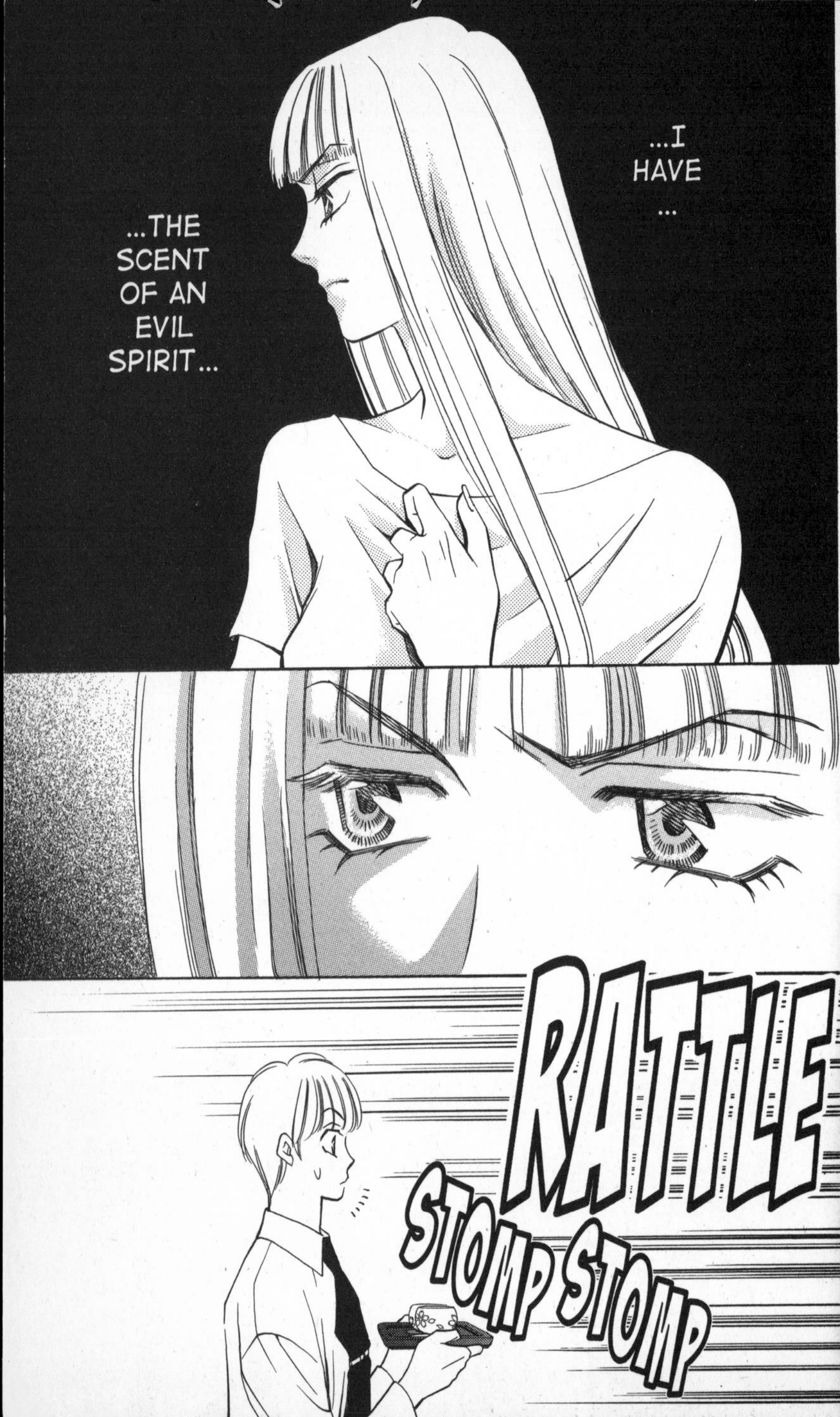
...I HAVE ...
...THE SCENT OF AN EVIL SPIRIT...
RATTLE
STOMP STOMP

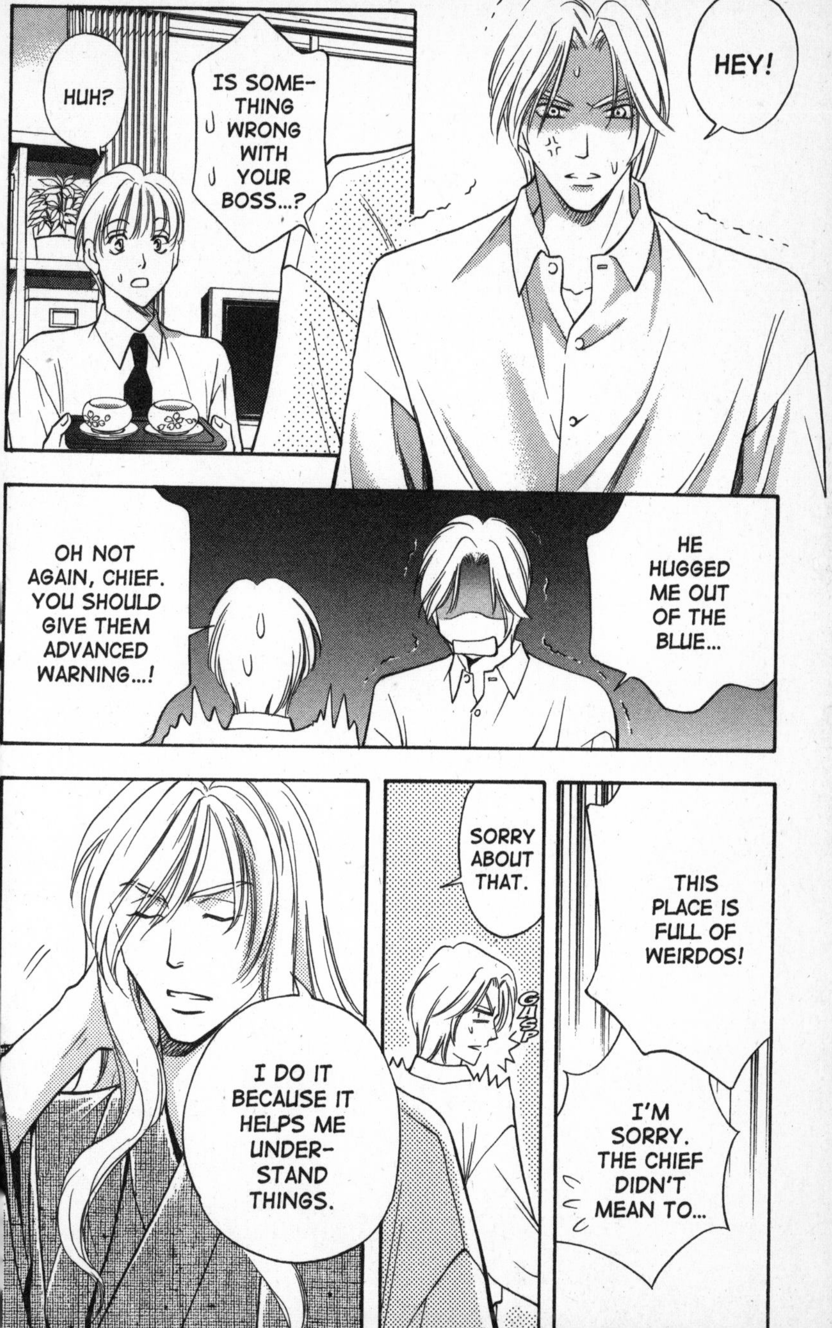
HEY!
IS SOMETHING WRONG WITH YOUR BOSS...?
HUH?
HE HUGGED ME OUT OF THE BLUE...
OH NOT AGAIN, CHIEF. YOU SHOULD GIVE THEM ADVANCED WARNING...!
THIS PLACE IS FULL OF WEIRDOS!
I'M SORRY. THE CHIEF DIDN'T MEAN TO...
SORRY ABOUT THAT.
GASP
I DO IT BECAUSE IT HELPS ME UNDERSTAND THINGS.

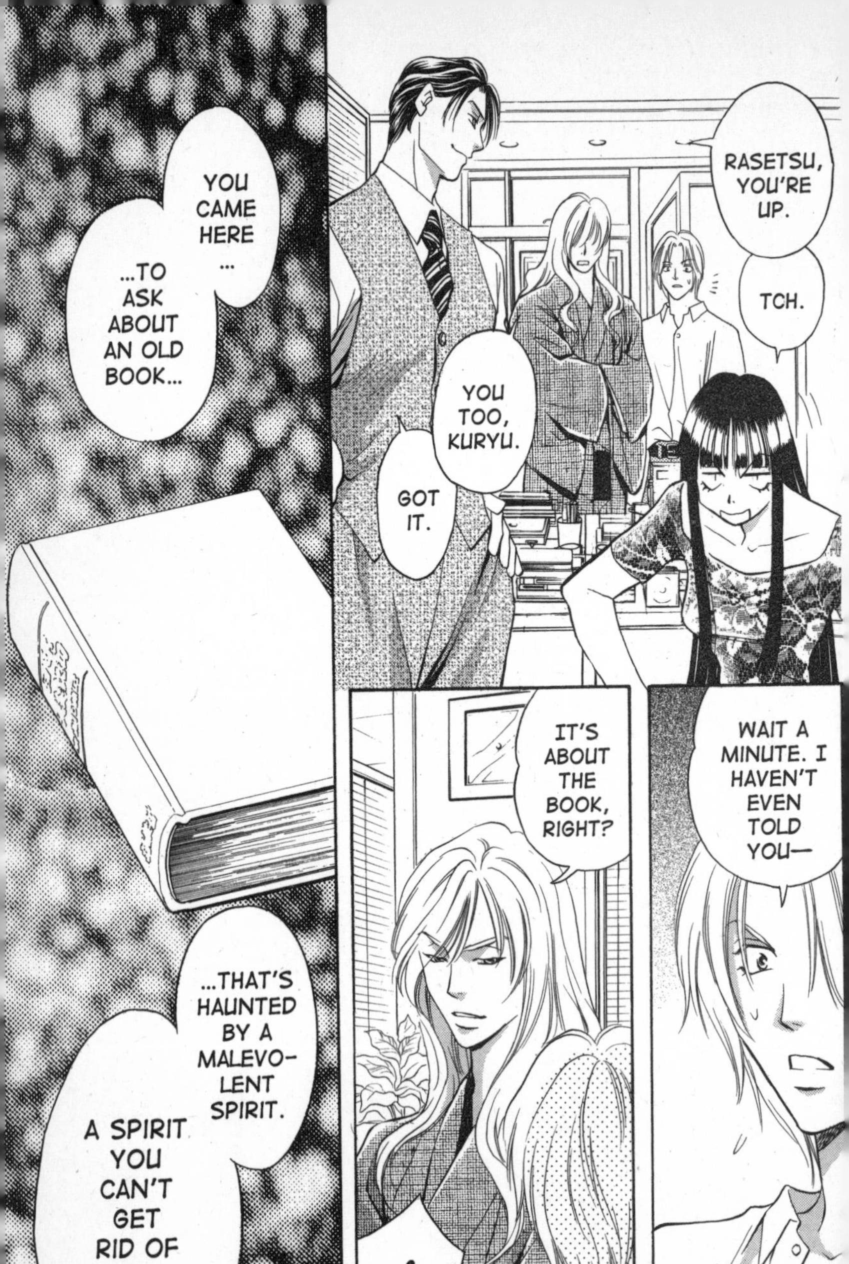
RASETSU, YOU'RE UP.
TCH.
YOU TOO, KURYU.
GOT IT.
WAIT A MINUTE. I HAVEN'T EVEN TOLD YOU—
IT'S ABOUT THE BOOK, RIGHT?
!
YOU CAME HERE ...
...TO ASK ABOUT AN OLD BOOK...
...THAT'S HAUNTED BY A MALEVO-LENT SPIRIT.
A SPIRIT YOU CAN'T GET RID OF YOUR-SELF.

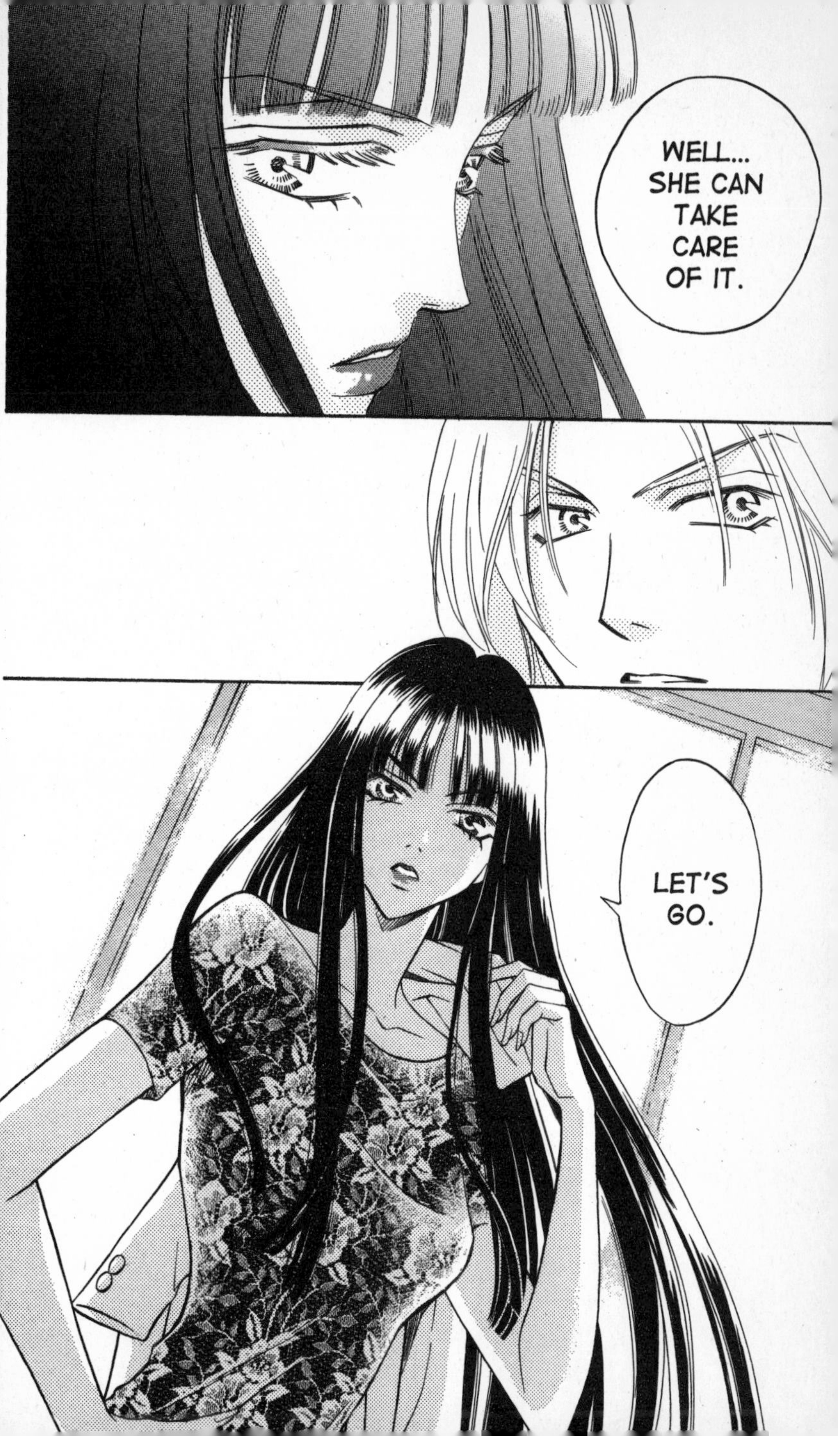
WELL... SHE CAN TAKE CARE OF IT.
LET'S GO.

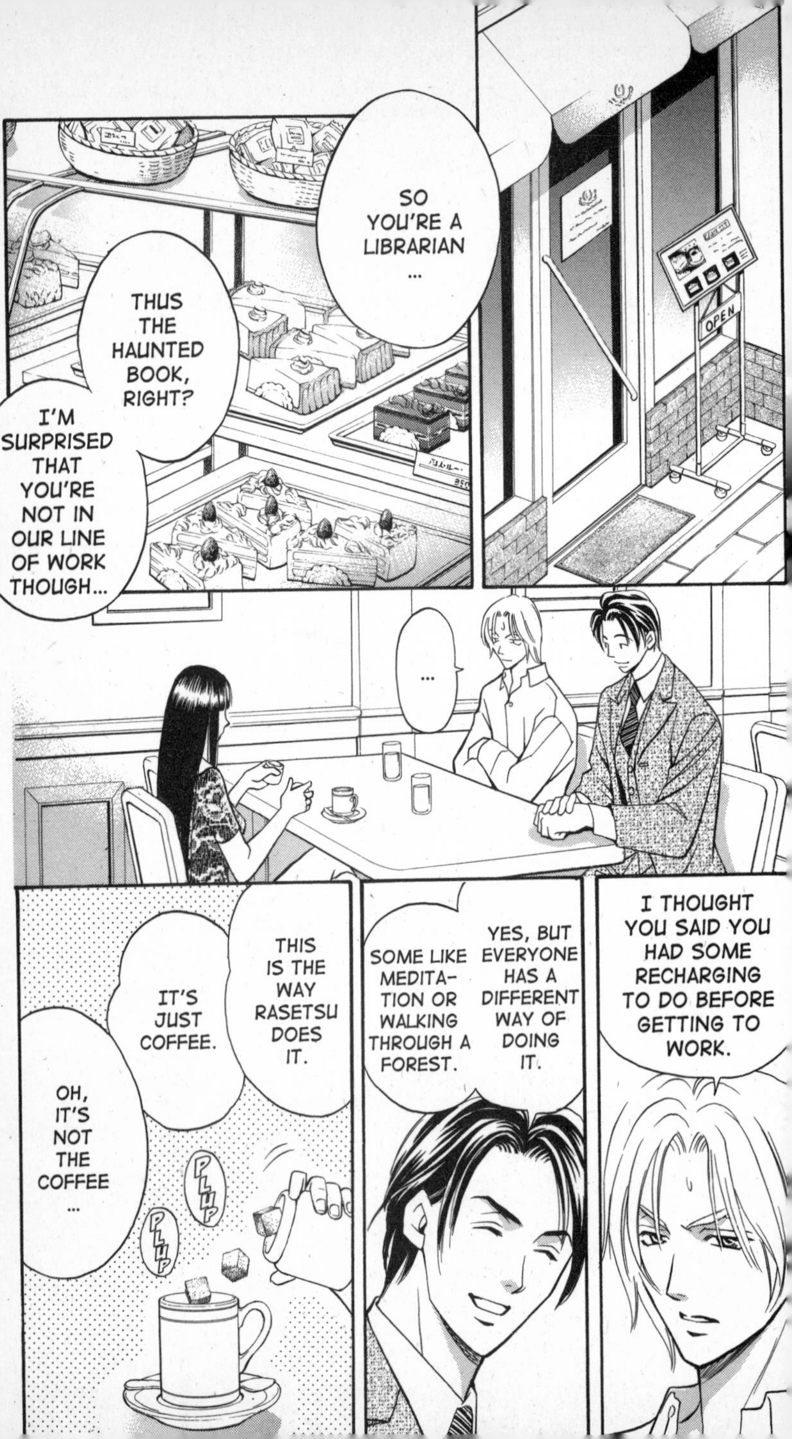
OPEN
SO YOU'RE A LIBRARIAN ...
THUS THE HAUNTED BOOK, RIGHT?
I'M SURPRISED THAT YOU'RE NOT IN OUR LINE OF WORK THOUGH...
...
I THOUGHT YOU SAID YOU HAD SOME RECHARGING TO DO BEFORE GETTING TO WORK.
YES, BUT EVERYONE HAS A DIFFERENT WAY OF DOING IT.
SOME LIKE MEDITATION OR WALKING THROUGH A FOREST.
THIS IS THE WAY RASETSU DOES IT.
IT'S JUST COFFEE.
OH, IT'S NOT THE COFFEE ...
PLUP
PLUP

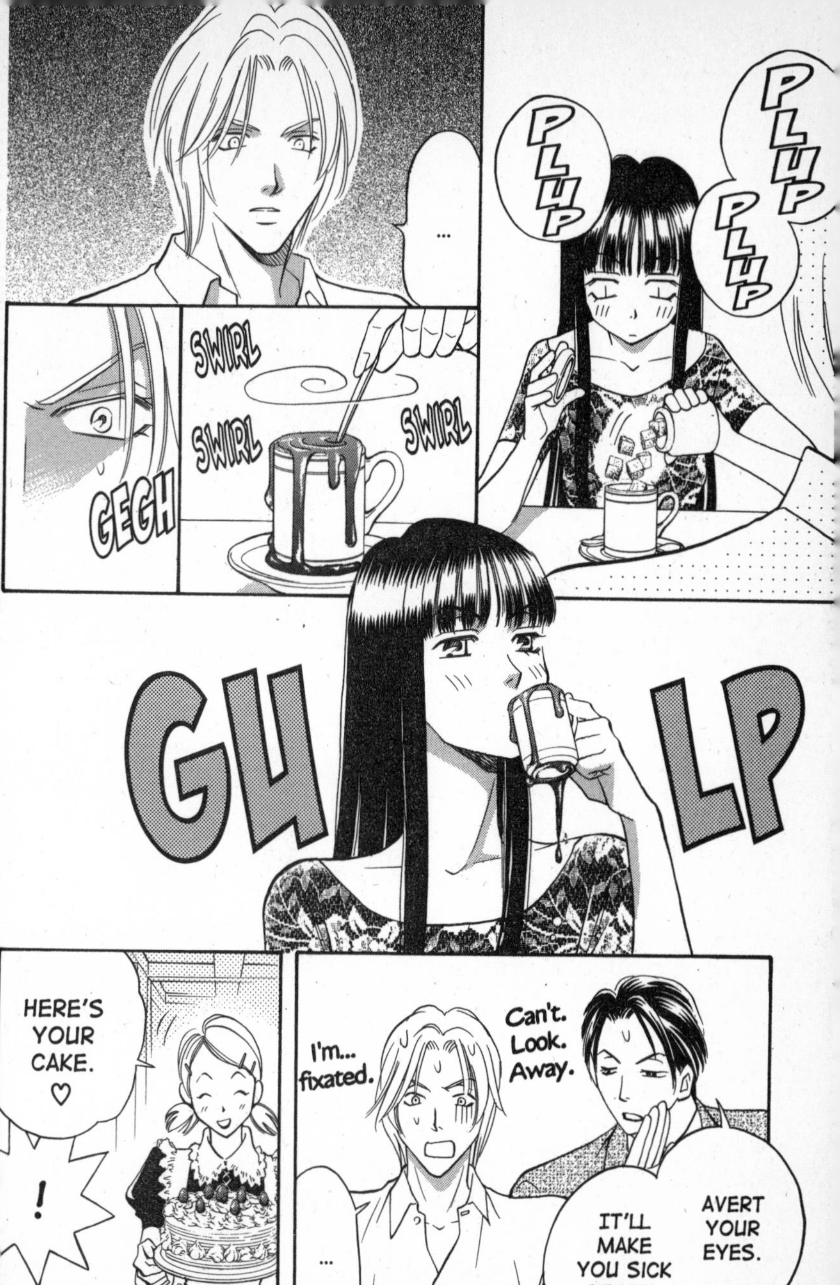
PLUP
PLUP
PLUP
...
SWIRL
SWIRL
SWIRL
GEGH
GULP
Can't. Look. Away.
I'm... fixated.
AVERT YOUR EYES.
IT'LL MAKE YOU SICK OTHERWISE.
...
HERE'S YOUR CAKE. ♡
!

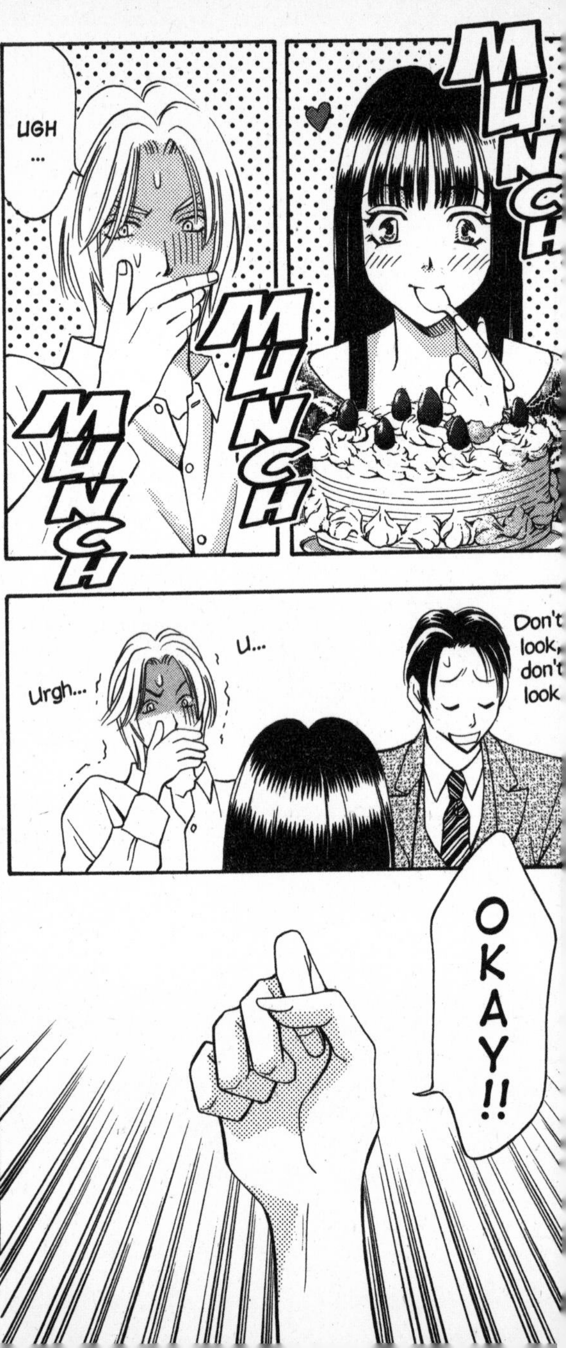
MUNCH
MUNCH
MUNCH
UGH ...
Don't look, don't look
U...
Urgh...
OKAY!!

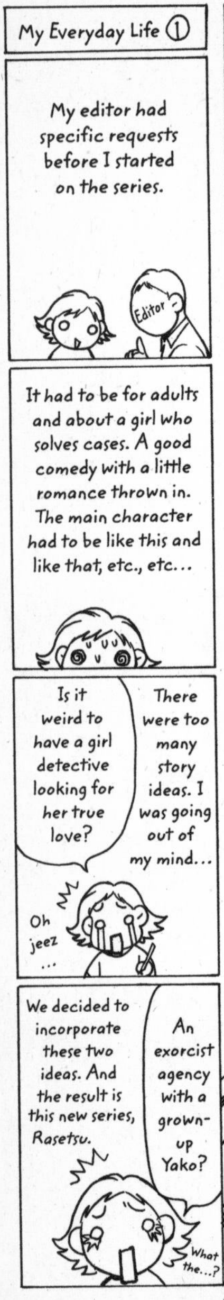
My Everyday Life ①
My editor had specific requests before I started on the series.
Editor
It had to be for adults and about a girl who solves cases. A good comedy with a little romance thrown in. The main character had to be like this and like that, etc., etc...
There were too many story ideas. I was going out of my mind...
Is it weird to have a girl detective looking for her true love?
Oh jeez...
An exorcist agency with a grown-up Yako?
We decided to incorporate these two ideas. And the result is this new series, Rasetsu.
What the...?

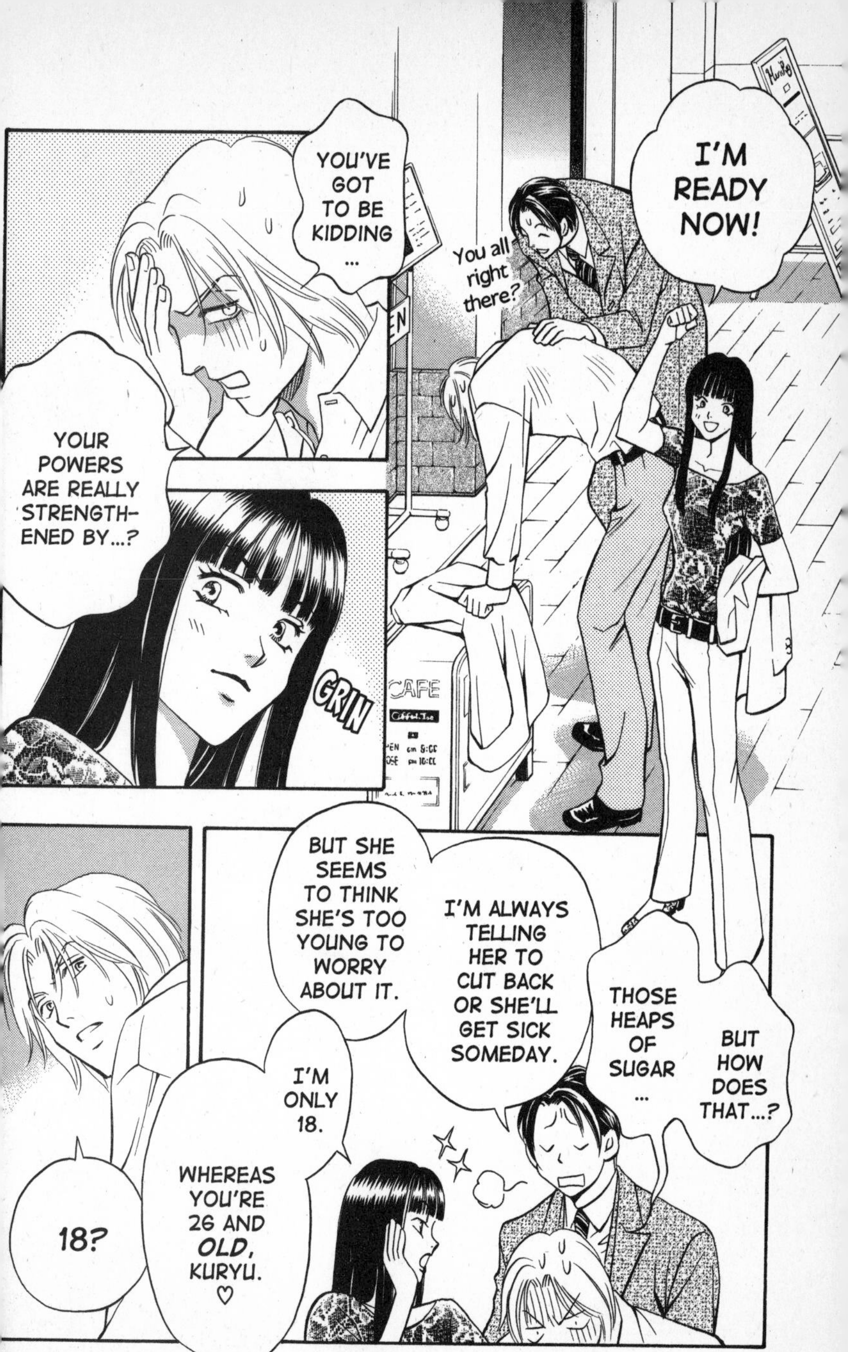
I'M READY NOW!
You all right there?
YOU'VE GOT TO BE KIDDING ...
YOUR POWERS ARE REALLY STRENGTH-ENED BY...?
GRIN
BUT HOW DOES THAT...?
THOSE HEAPS OF SUGAR ...
I'M ALWAYS TELLING HER TO CUT BACK OR SHE'LL GET SICK SOMEDAY.
BUT SHE SEEMS TO THINK SHE'S TOO YOUNG TO WORRY ABOUT IT.
I'M ONLY 18.
WHEREAS YOU'RE 26 AND OLD, KURYU. ♡
18?

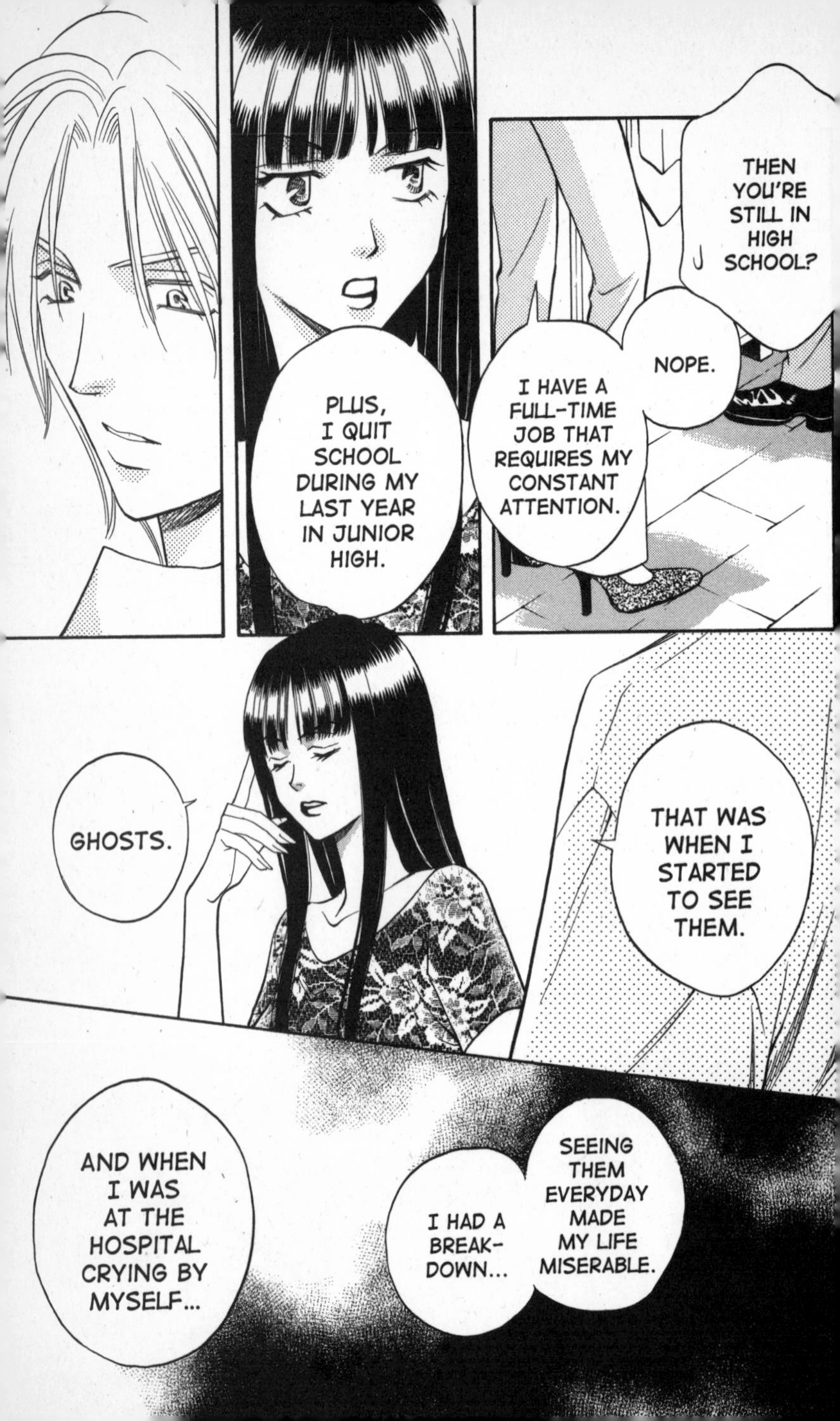
THEN YOU'RE STILL IN HIGH SCHOOL?
NOPE.
I HAVE A FULL-TIME JOB THAT REQUIRES MY CONSTANT ATTENTION.
PLUS, I QUIT SCHOOL DURING MY LAST YEAR IN JUNIOR HIGH.
THAT WAS WHEN I STARTED TO SEE THEM.
GHOSTS.
SEEING THEM EVERYDAY MADE MY LIFE MISERABLE.
I HAD A BREAK-DOWN...
AND WHEN I WAS AT THE HOSPITAL CRYING BY MYSELF...

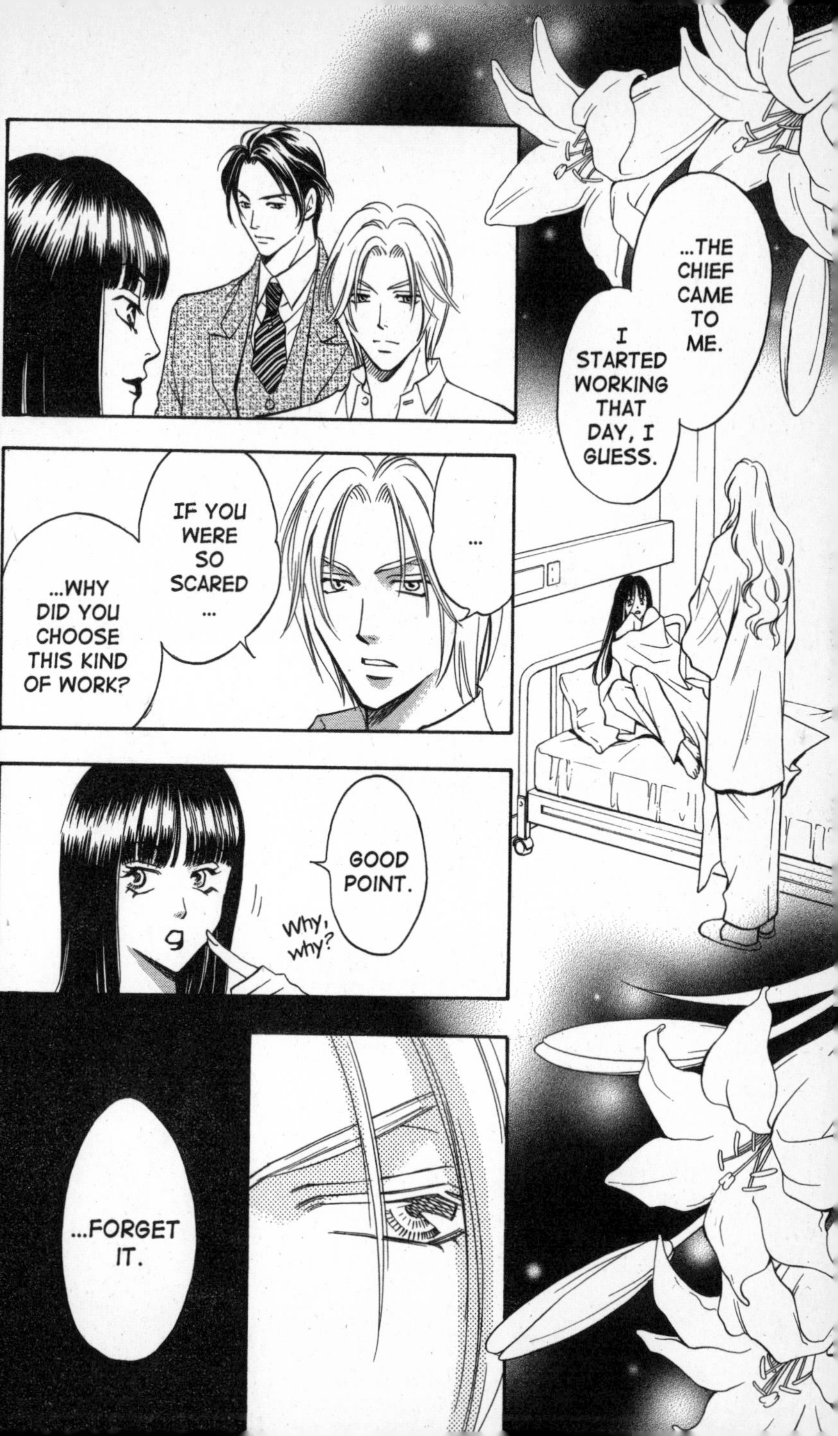
...THE CHIEF CAME TO ME.
I STARTED WORKING THAT DAY, I GUESS.
...
IF YOU WERE SO SCARED ...
...WHY DID YOU CHOOSE THIS KIND OF WORK?
GOOD POINT.
Why, why?
...FORGET IT.

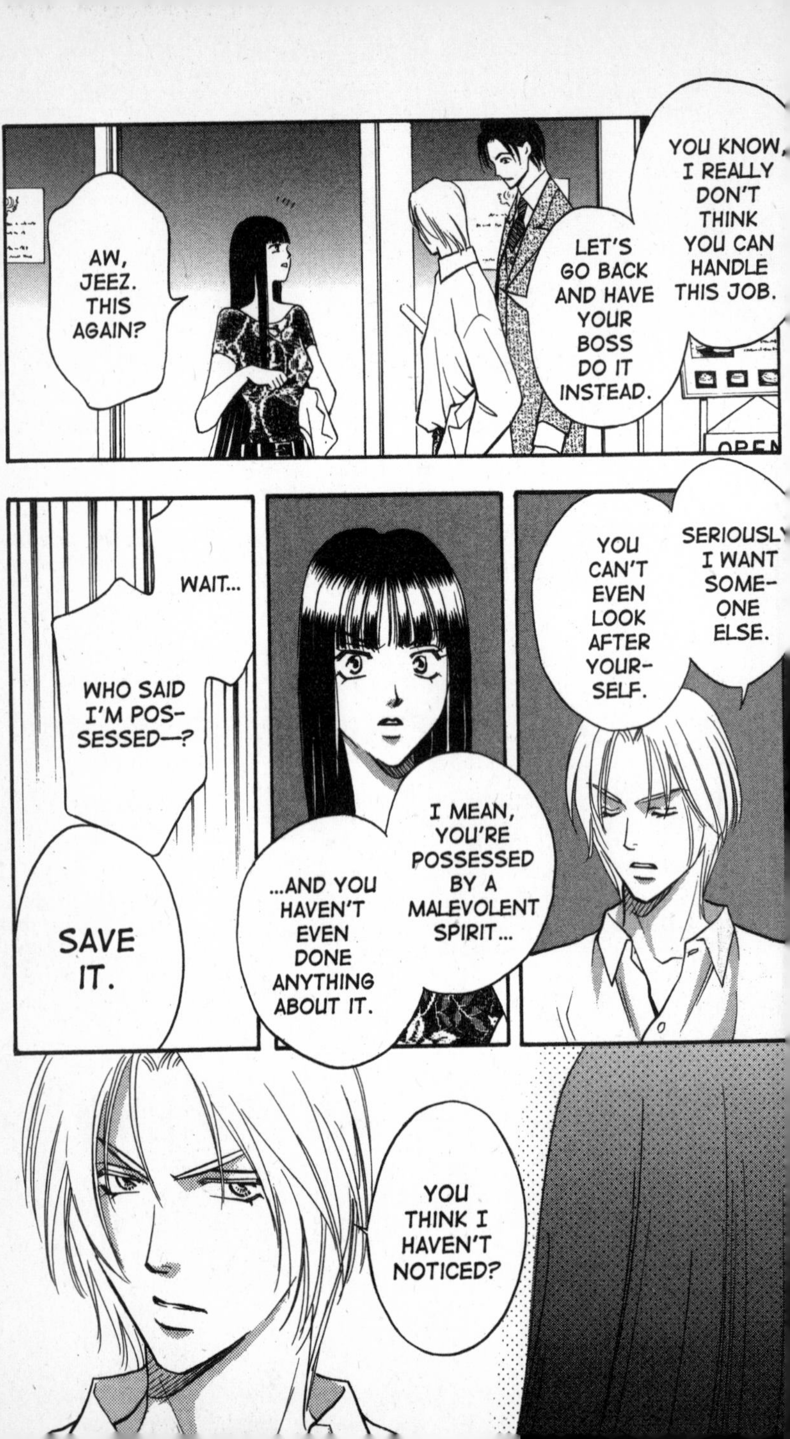
YOU KNOW, I REALLY DON'T THINK YOU CAN HANDLE THIS JOB.
LET'S GO BACK AND HAVE YOUR BOSS DO IT INSTEAD.
AW, JEEZ. THIS AGAIN?
SERIOUSLY I WANT SOME-ONE ELSE.
YOU CAN'T EVEN LOOK AFTER YOUR-SELF.
I MEAN, YOU'RE POSSESSED BY A MALEVOLENT SPIRIT...
...AND YOU HAVEN'T EVEN DONE ANYTHING ABOUT IT.
WAIT...
WHO SAID I'M POS-SESSED—?
SAVE IT.
YOU THINK I HAVEN'T NOTICED?

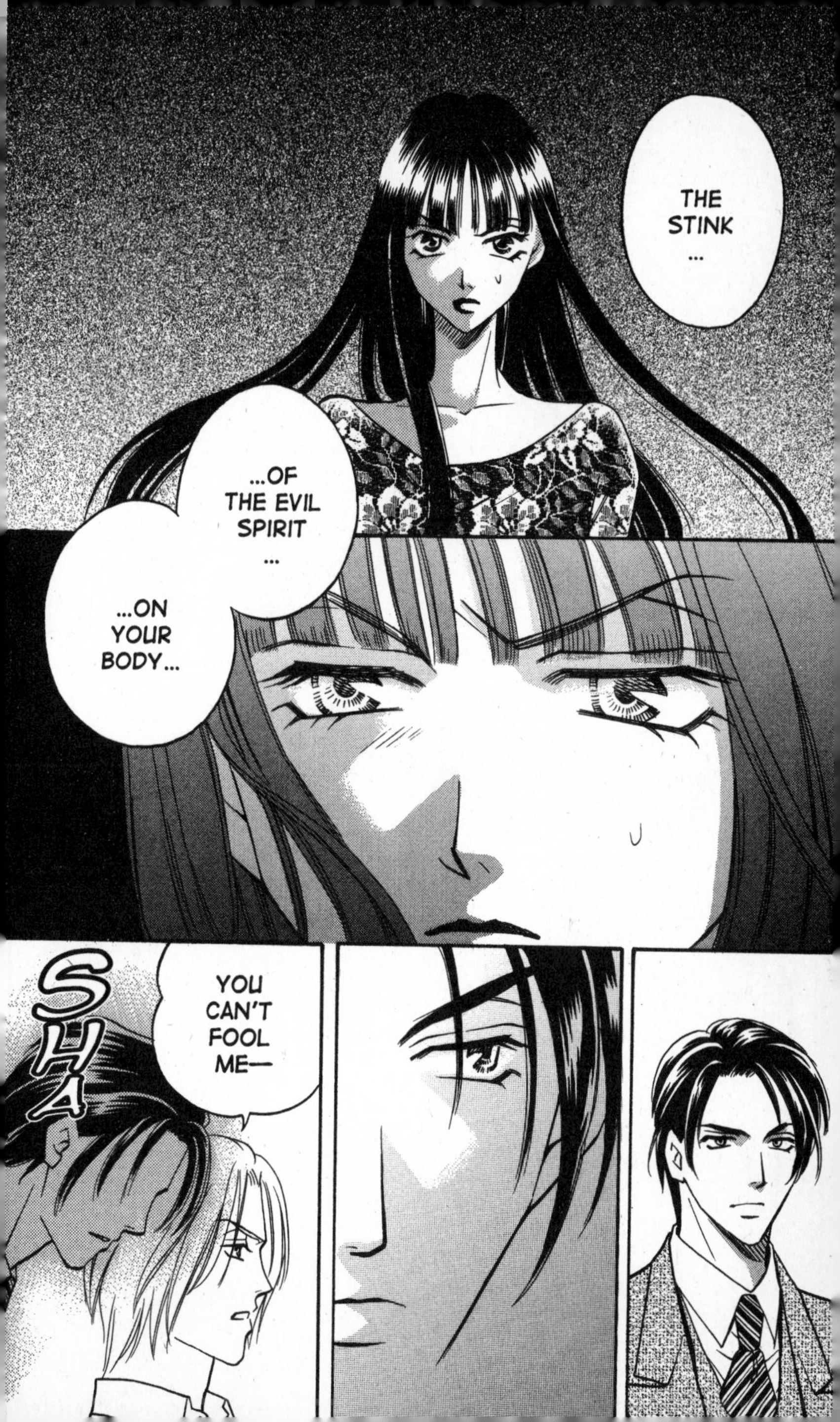
THE STINK ...
...OF THE EVIL SPIRIT ...
...ON YOUR BODY...
YOU CAN'T FOOL ME—
SHA

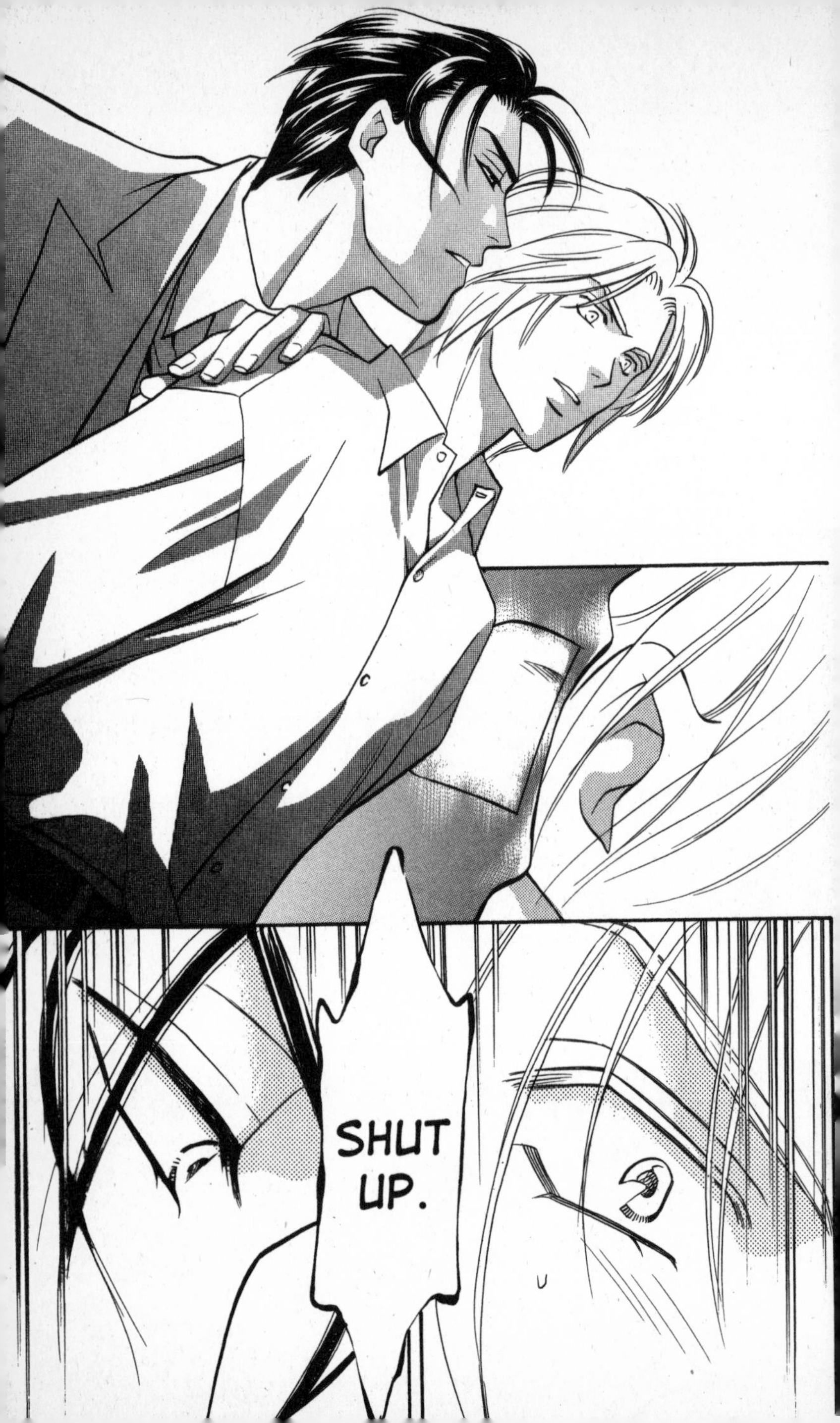
SHUT UP.

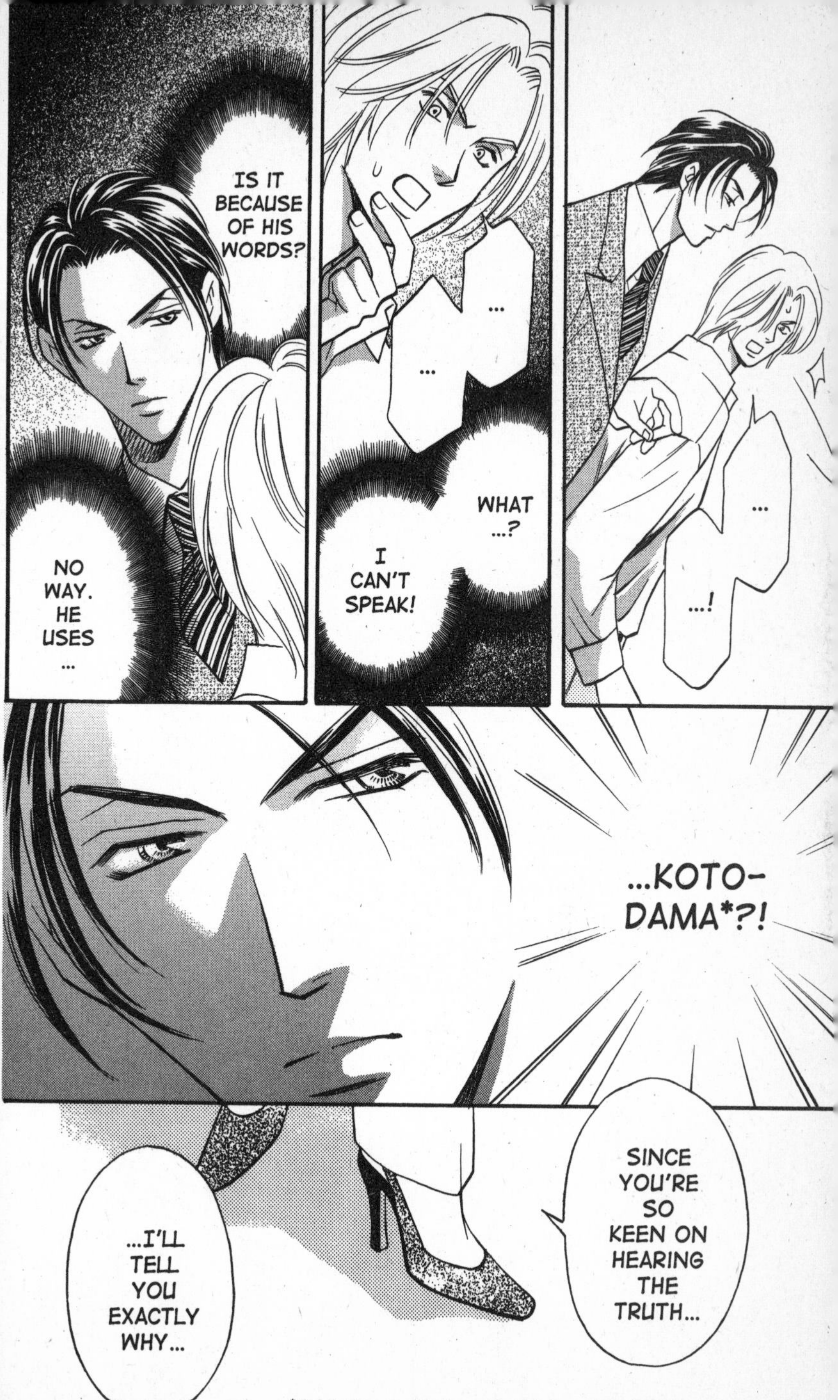
...
...!
...
...
WHAT ...?
I CAN'T SPEAK!
IS IT BECAUSE OF HIS WORDS?
NO WAY. HE USES ...
...KOTO-DAMA*?!
SINCE YOU'RE SO KEEN ON HEARING THE TRUTH...
...I'LL TELL YOU EXACTLY WHY...

*Spiritual power that is manifested through the intonation of words.

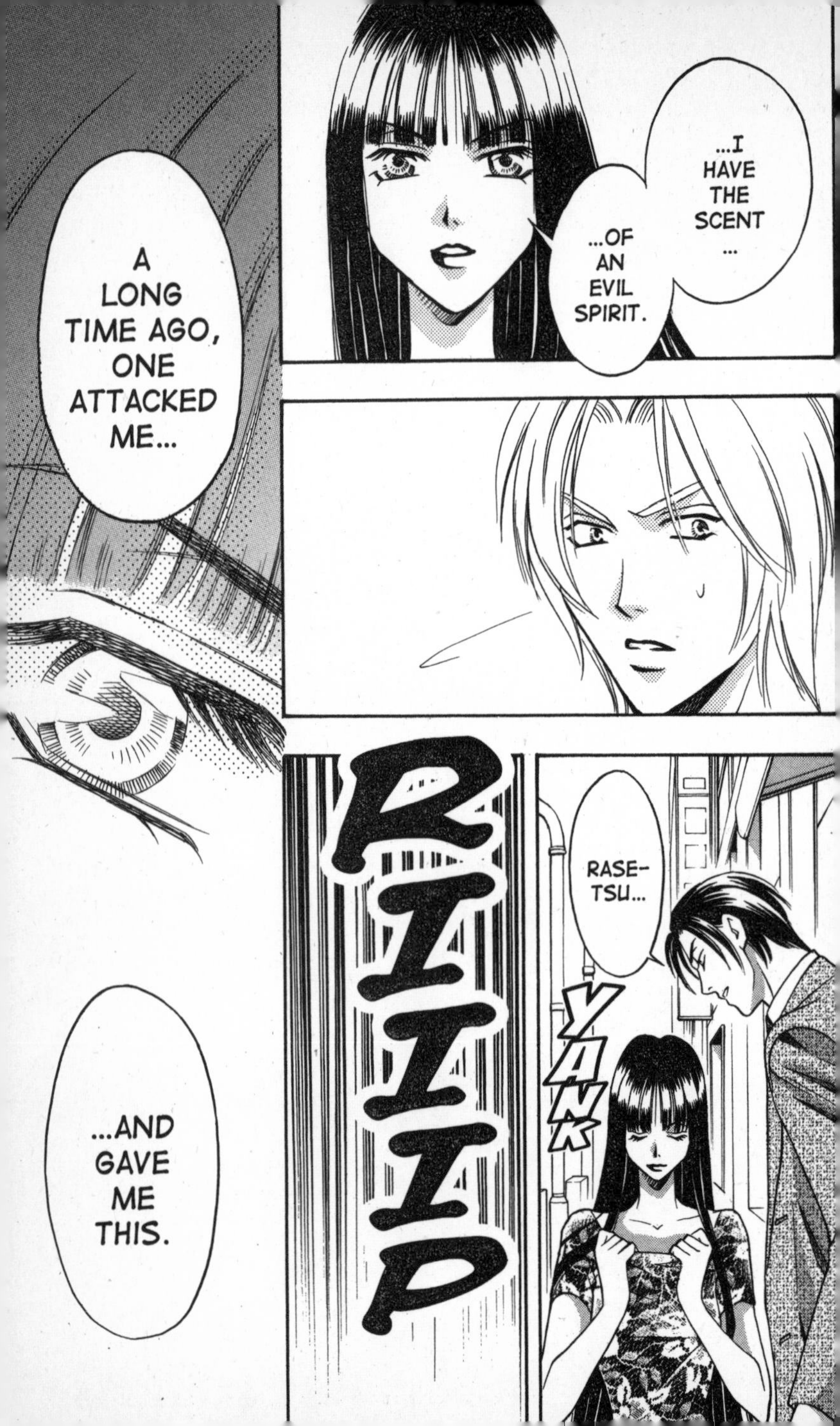
...I HAVE THE SCENT ...
...OF AN EVIL SPIRIT.
RASE-TSU...
YANK
RIIIP
A LONG TIME AGO, ONE ATTACKED ME...
...AND GAVE ME THIS.

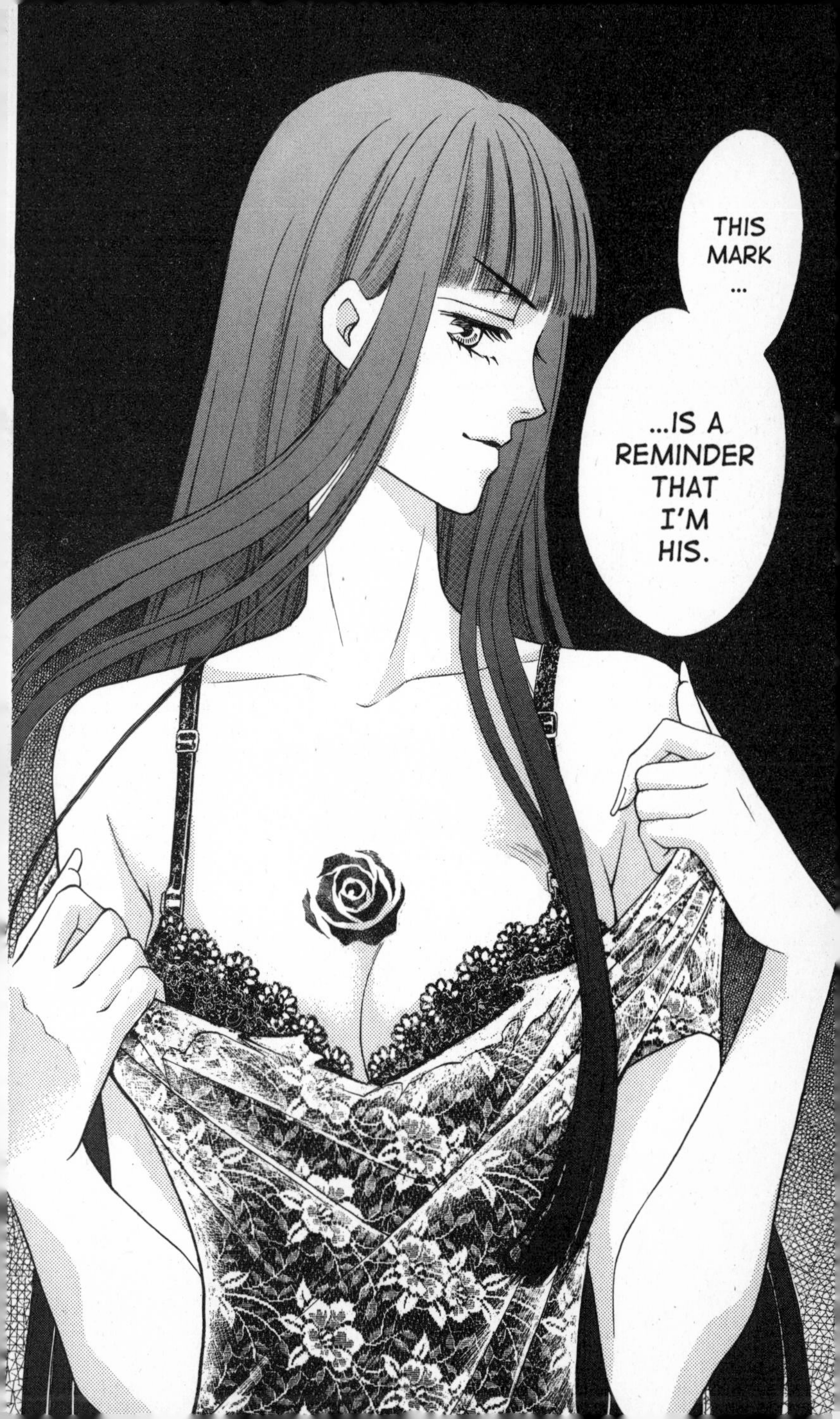
THIS MARK ...
...IS A REMINDER THAT I'M HIS.

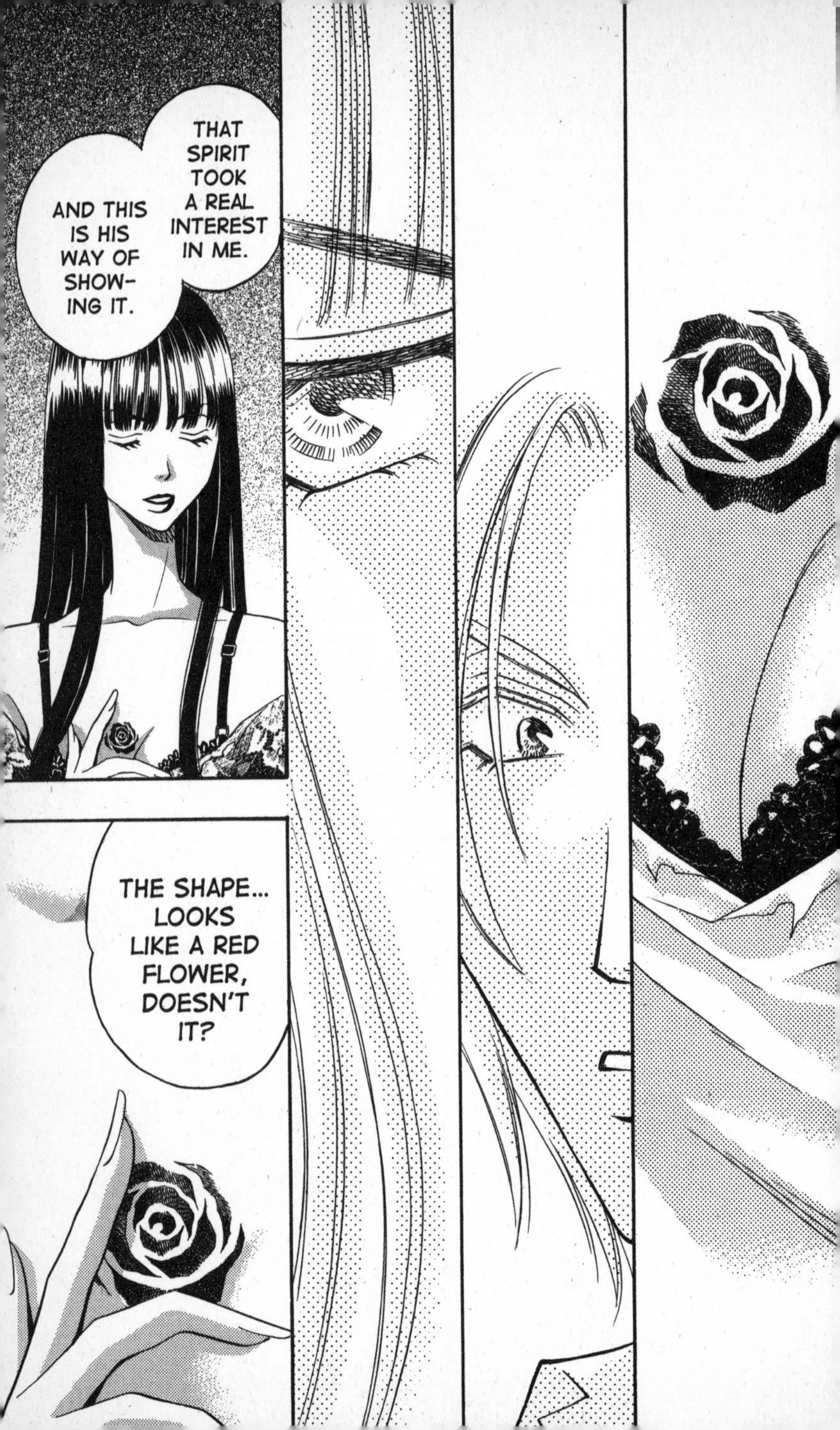
THAT SPIRIT TOOK A REAL INTEREST IN ME.
AND THIS IS HIS WAY OF SHOWING IT.
THE SHAPE... LOOKS LIKE A RED FLOWER, DOESN'T IT?

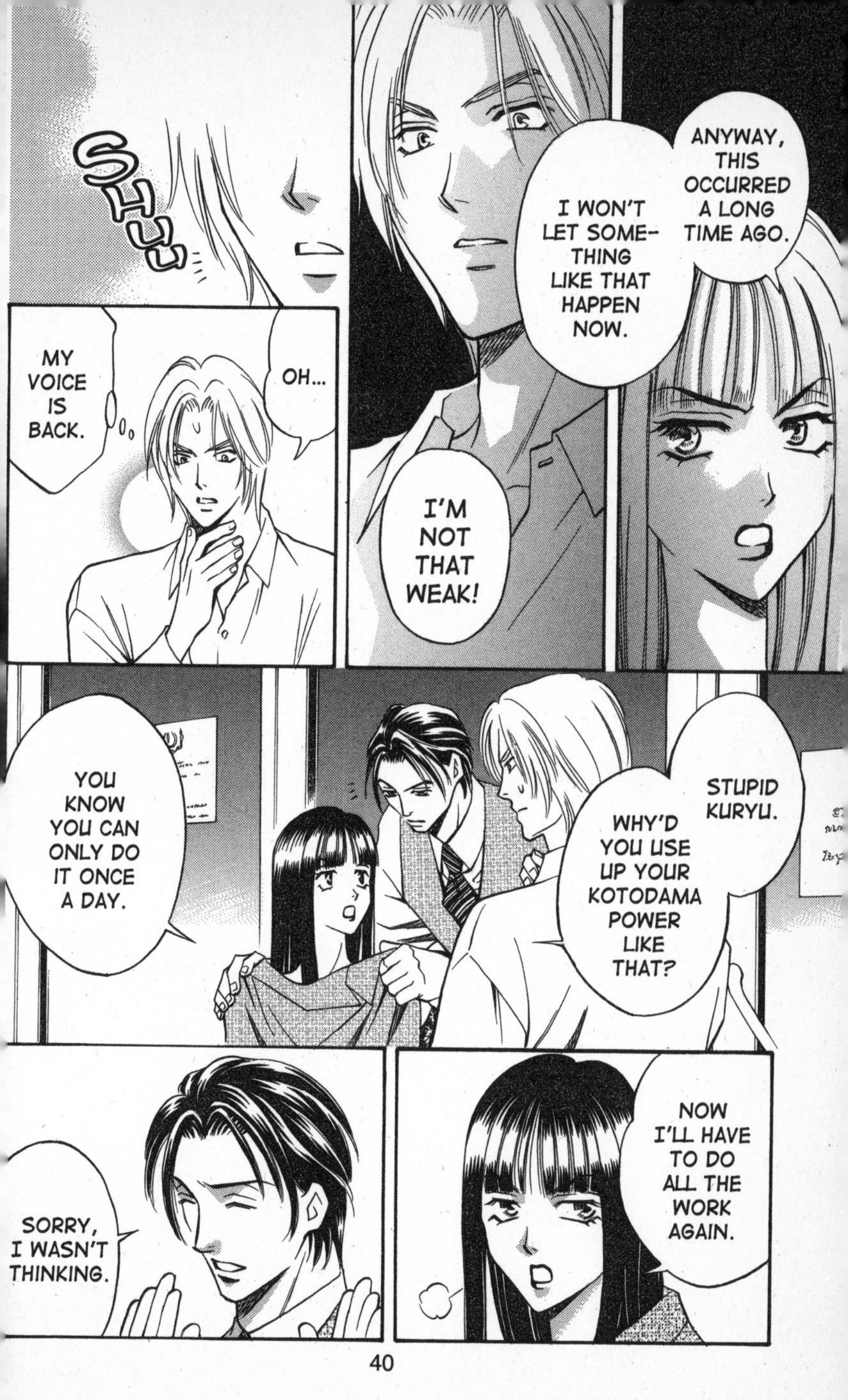
ANYWAY, THIS OCCURRED A LONG TIME AGO.
I WON'T LET SOME-THING LIKE THAT HAPPEN NOW.
I'M NOT THAT WEAK!
SHUU
OH...
MY VOICE IS BACK.
STUPID KURYU.
WHY'D YOU USE UP YOUR KOTODAMA POWER LIKE THAT?
YOU KNOW YOU CAN ONLY DO IT ONCE A DAY.
NOW I'LL HAVE TO DO ALL THE WORK AGAIN.
SORRY, I WASN'T THINKING.

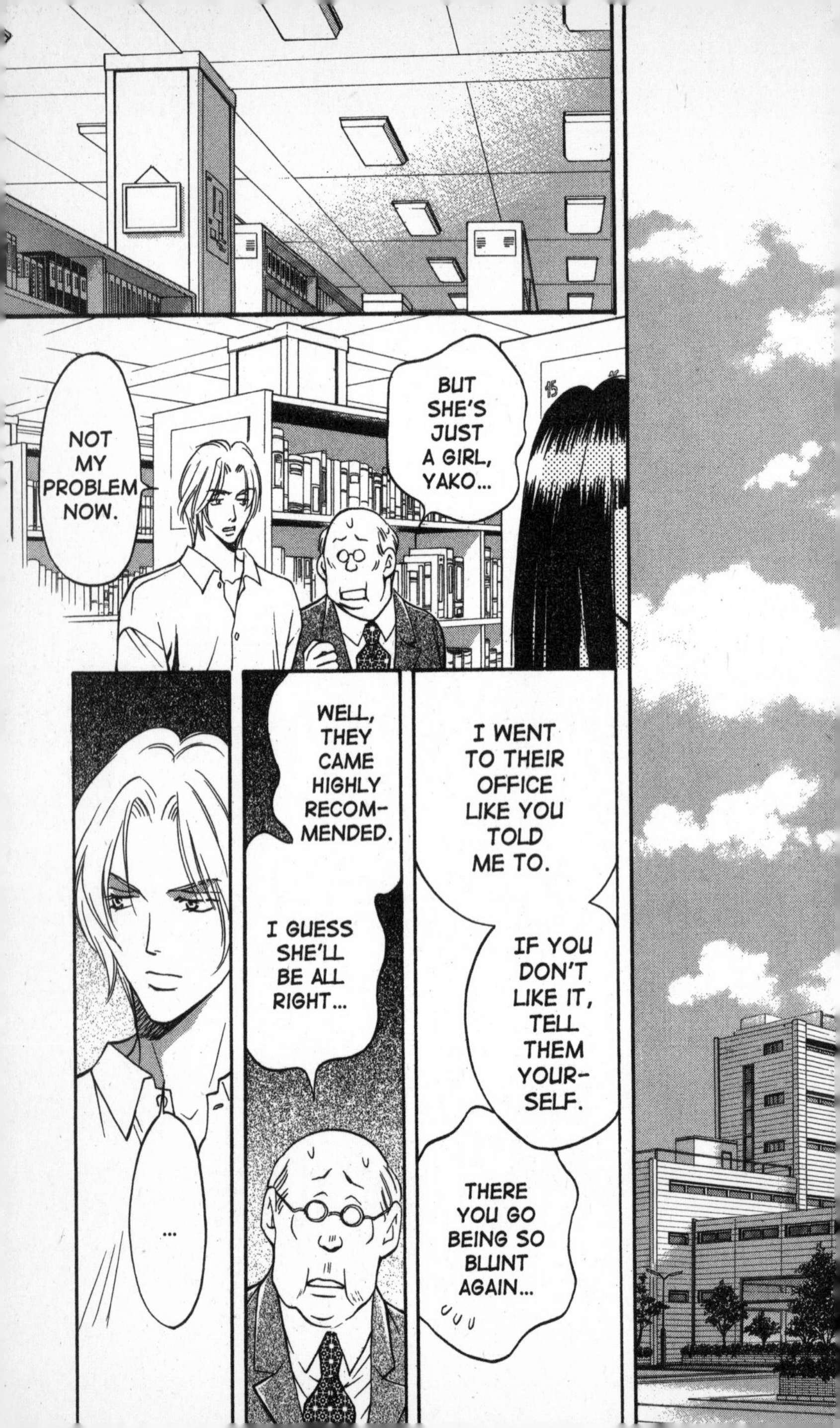
BUT SHE'S JUST A GIRL, YAKO...
NOT MY PROBLEM NOW.
I WENT TO THEIR OFFICE LIKE YOU TOLD ME TO.
IF YOU DON'T LIKE IT, TELL THEM YOURSELF.
THERE YOU GO BEING SO BLUNT AGAIN...
WELL, THEY CAME HIGHLY RECOMMENDED.
I GUESS SHE'LL BE ALL RIGHT...
...

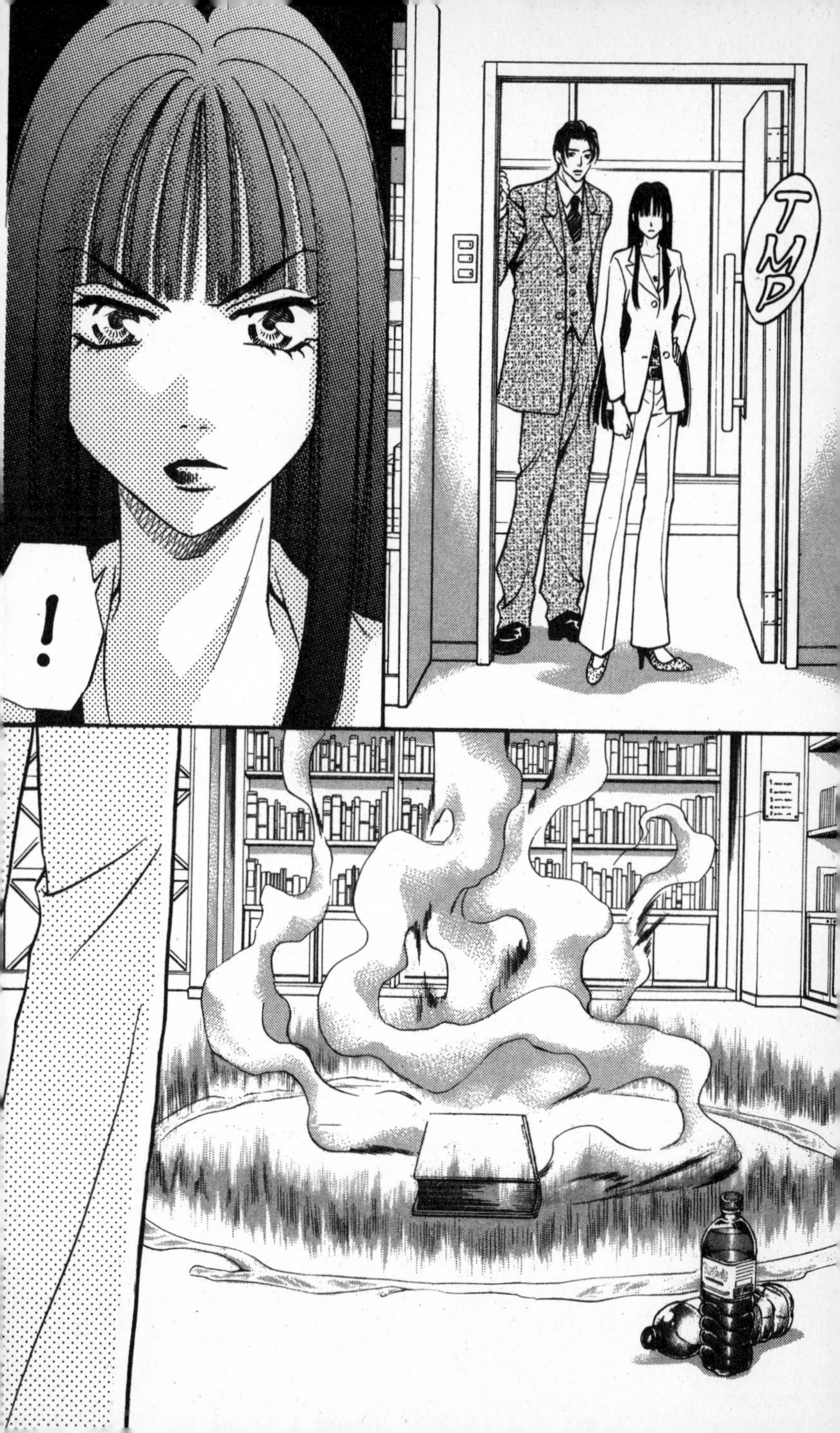
TMD
!

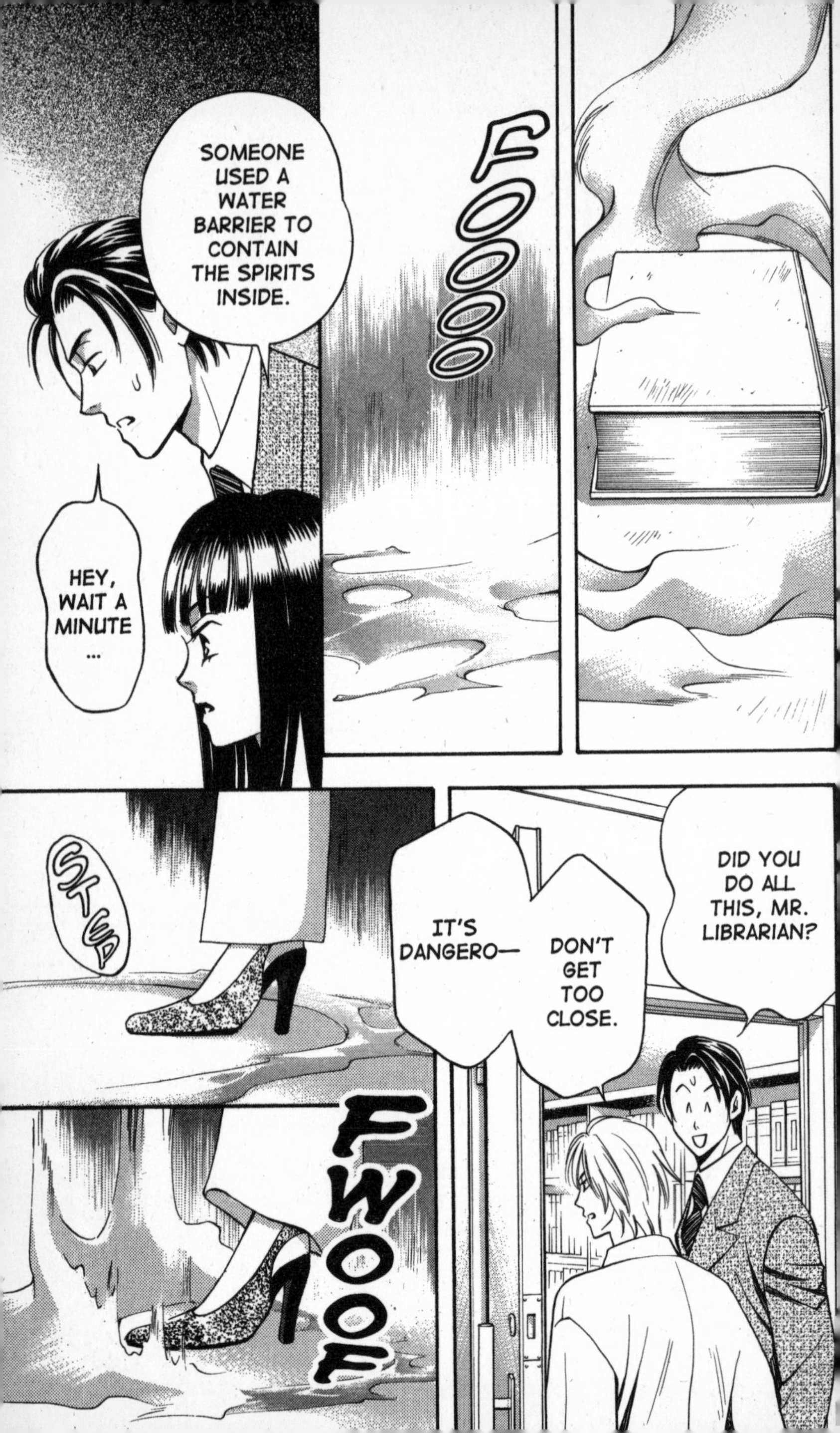
FOOOOO
SOMEONE USED A WATER BARRIER TO CONTAIN THE SPIRITS INSIDE.
HEY, WAIT A MINUTE ...
DID YOU DO ALL THIS, MR. LIBRARIAN?
DON'T GET TOO CLOSE.
IT'S DANGERO—
STEP
FWOOF

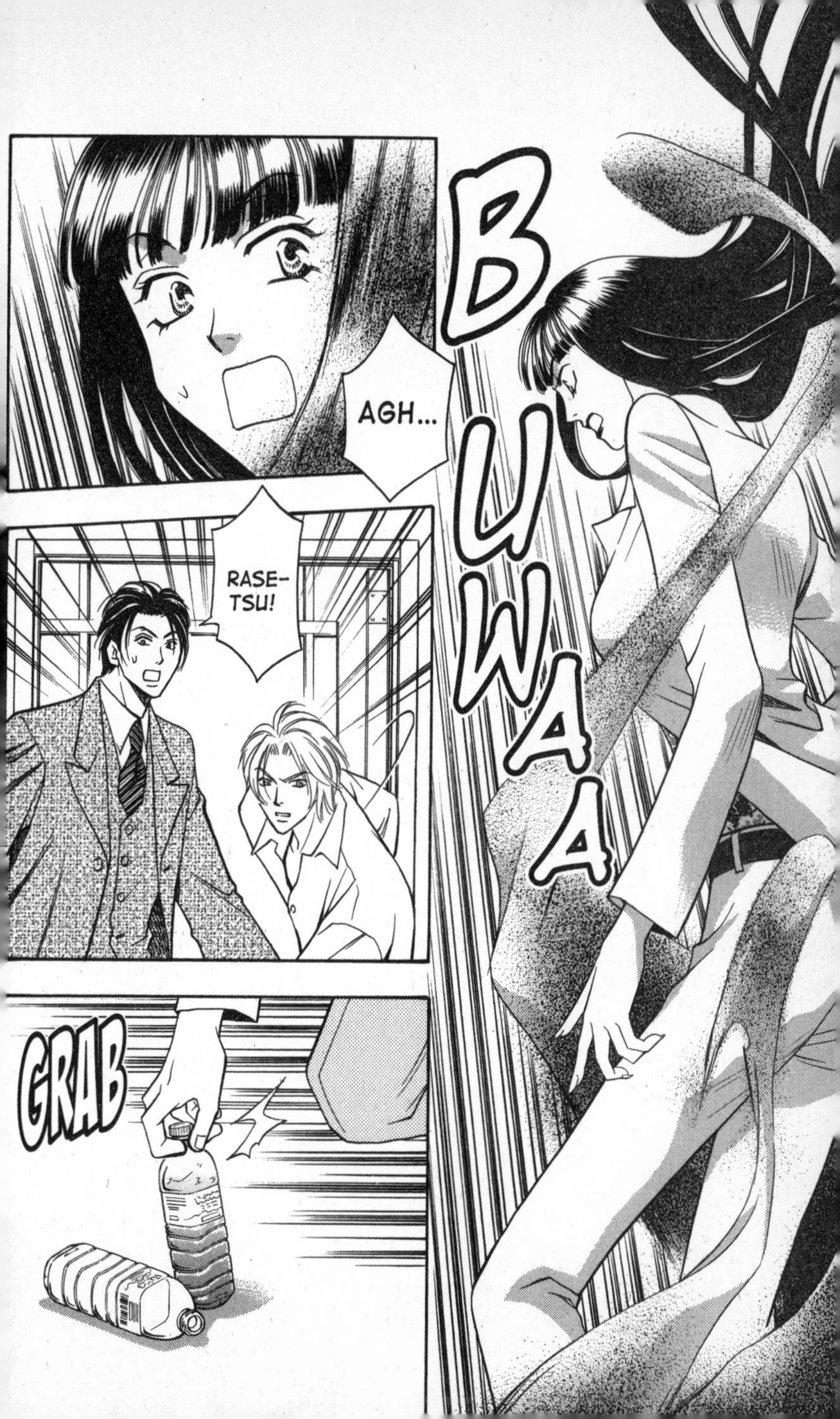
BUWAA
AGH...
RASE-TSU!
GRAB

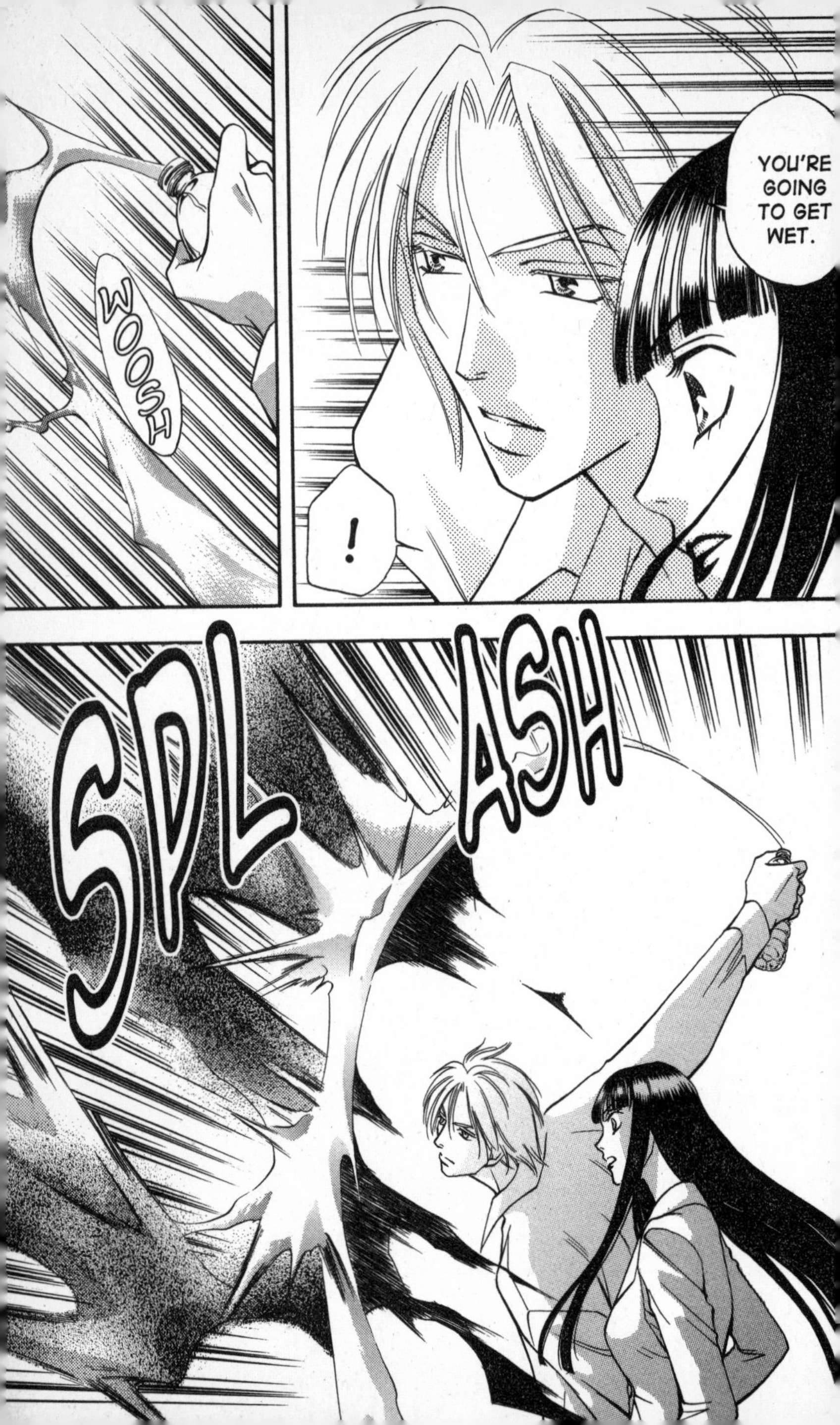
YOU'RE GOING TO GET WET.
!
WOOSH
SPLASH

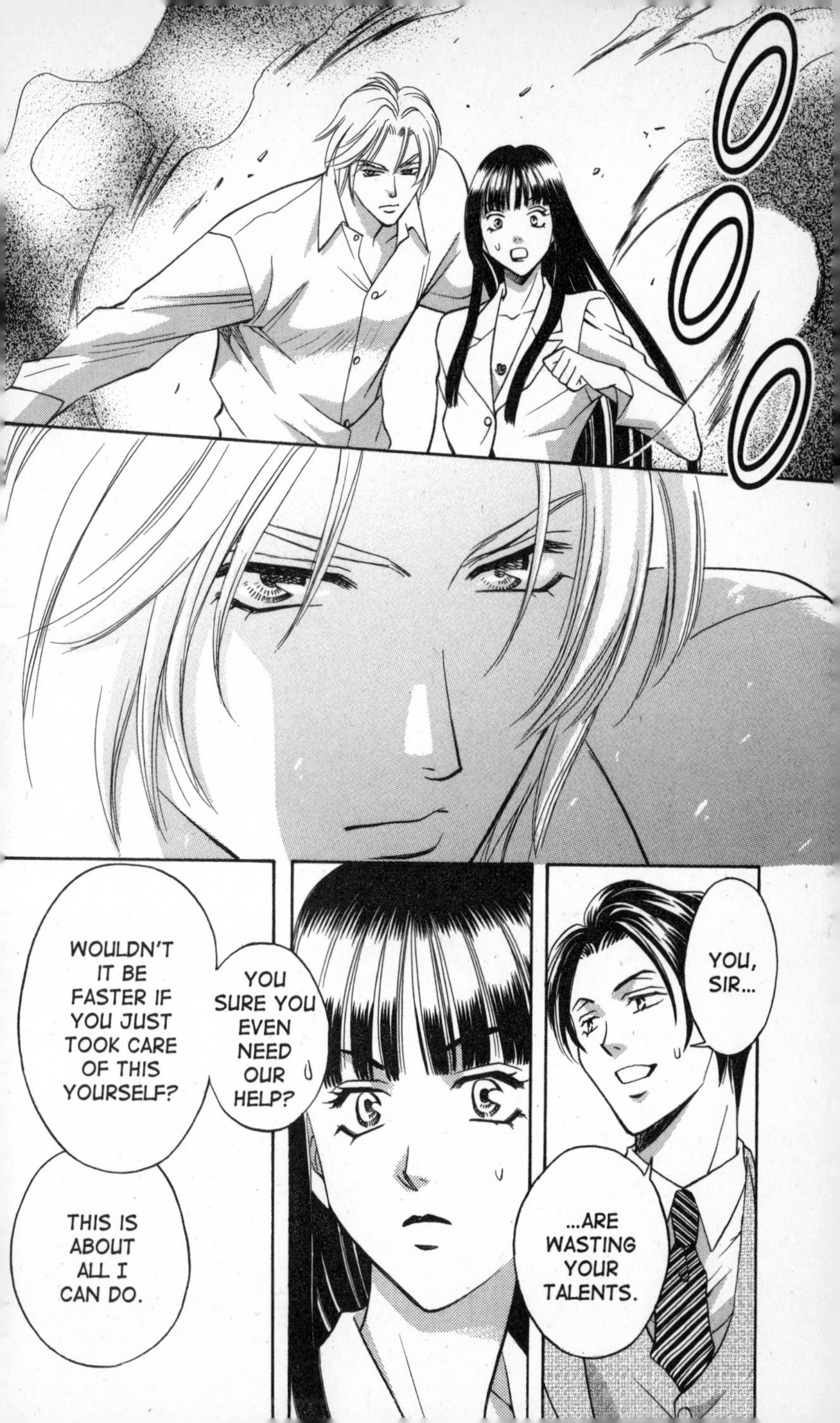
YOU, SIR...
...ARE WASTING YOUR TALENTS.
YOU SURE YOU EVEN NEED OUR HELP?
WOULDN'T IT BE FASTER IF YOU JUST TOOK CARE OF THIS YOURSELF?
THIS IS ABOUT ALL I CAN DO.

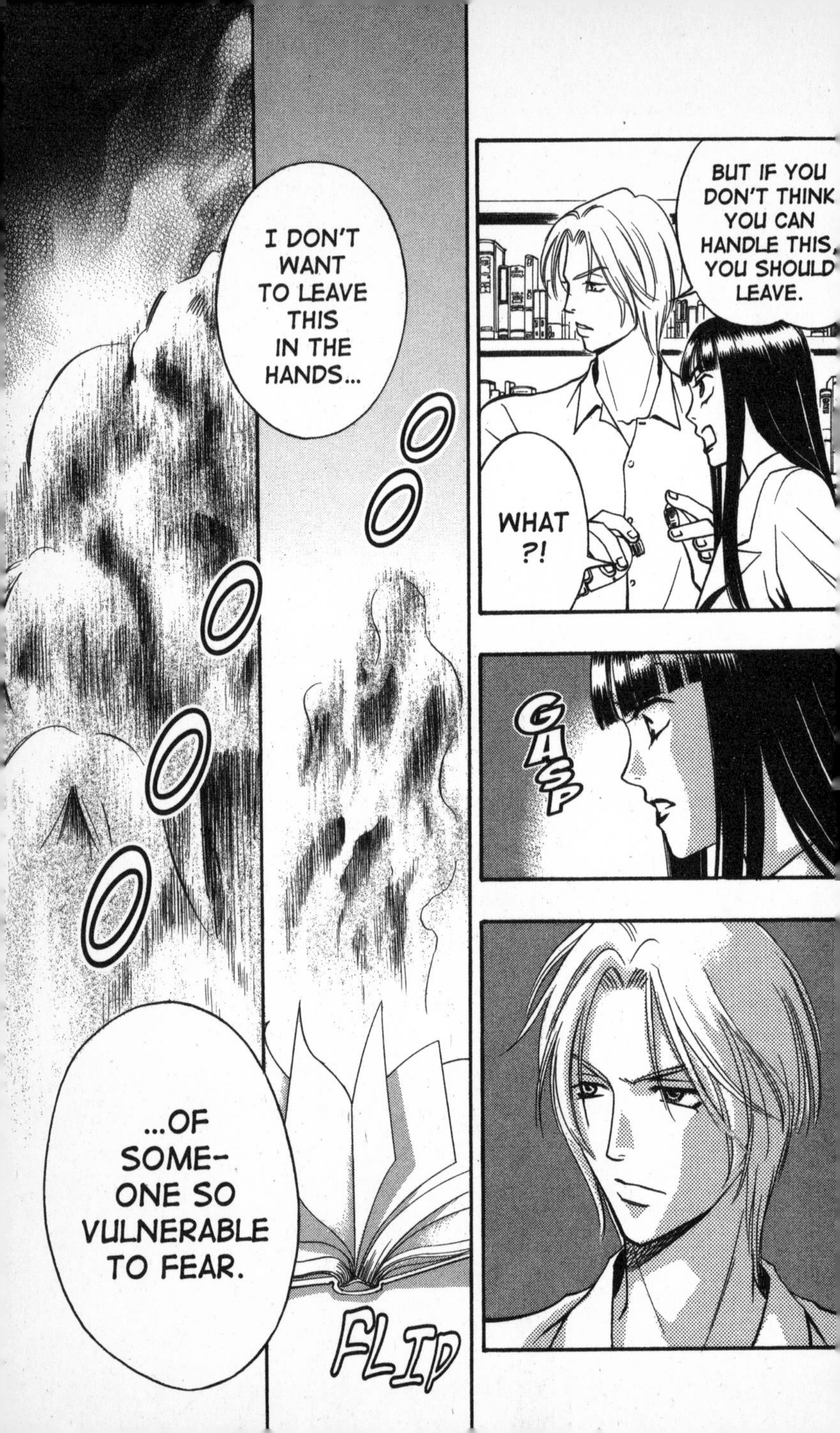
BUT IF YOU DON'T THINK YOU CAN HANDLE THIS, YOU SHOULD LEAVE.
WHAT ?!
GASP
I DON'T WANT TO LEAVE THIS IN THE HANDS...
...OF SOME-ONE SO VULNERABLE TO FEAR.
FLIP

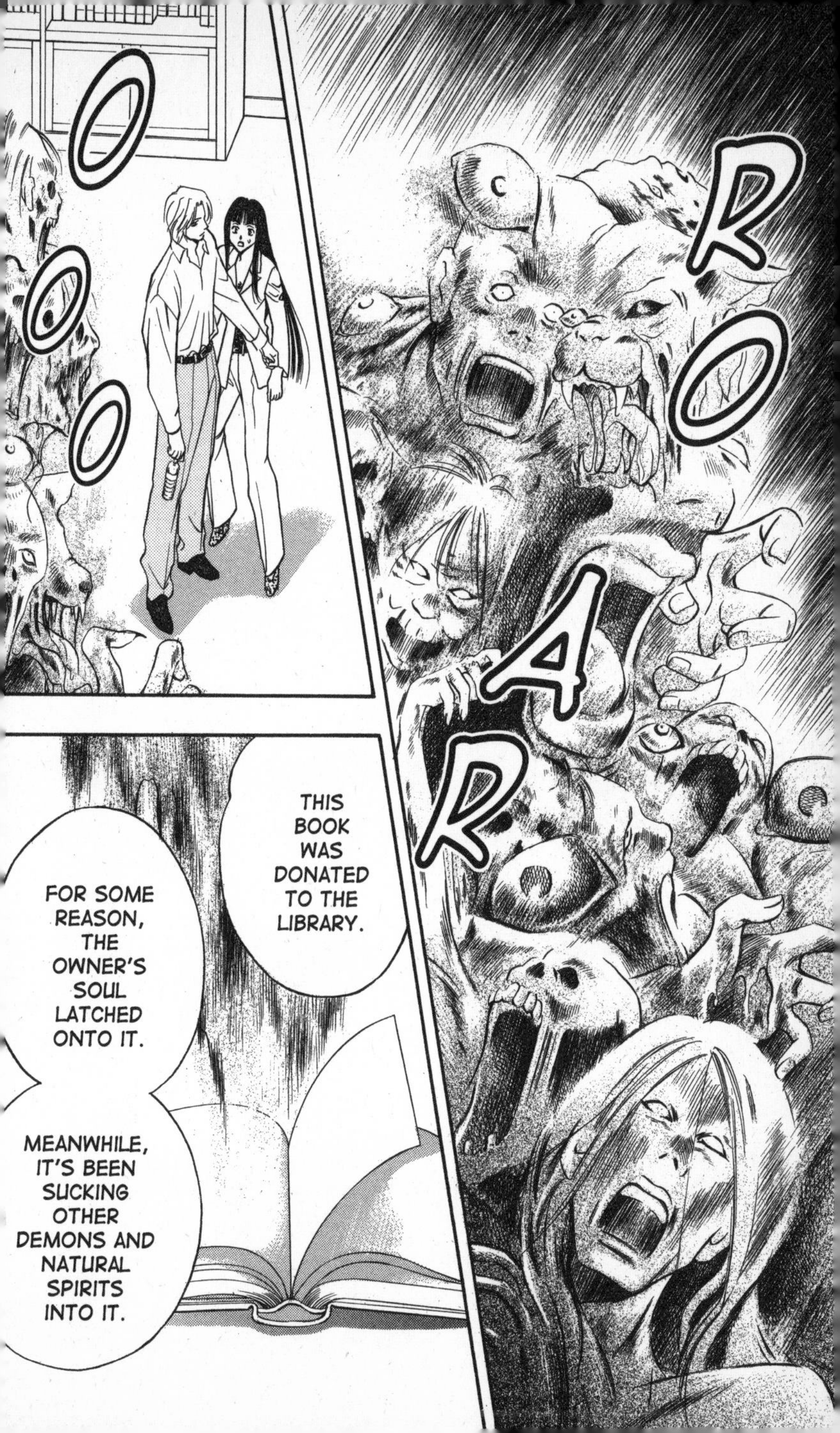
ROAR
OOO
THIS BOOK WAS DONATED TO THE LIBRARY.
FOR SOME REASON, THE OWNER'S SOUL LATCHED ONTO IT.
MEANWHILE, IT'S BEEN SUCKING OTHER DEMONS AND NATURAL SPIRITS INTO IT.

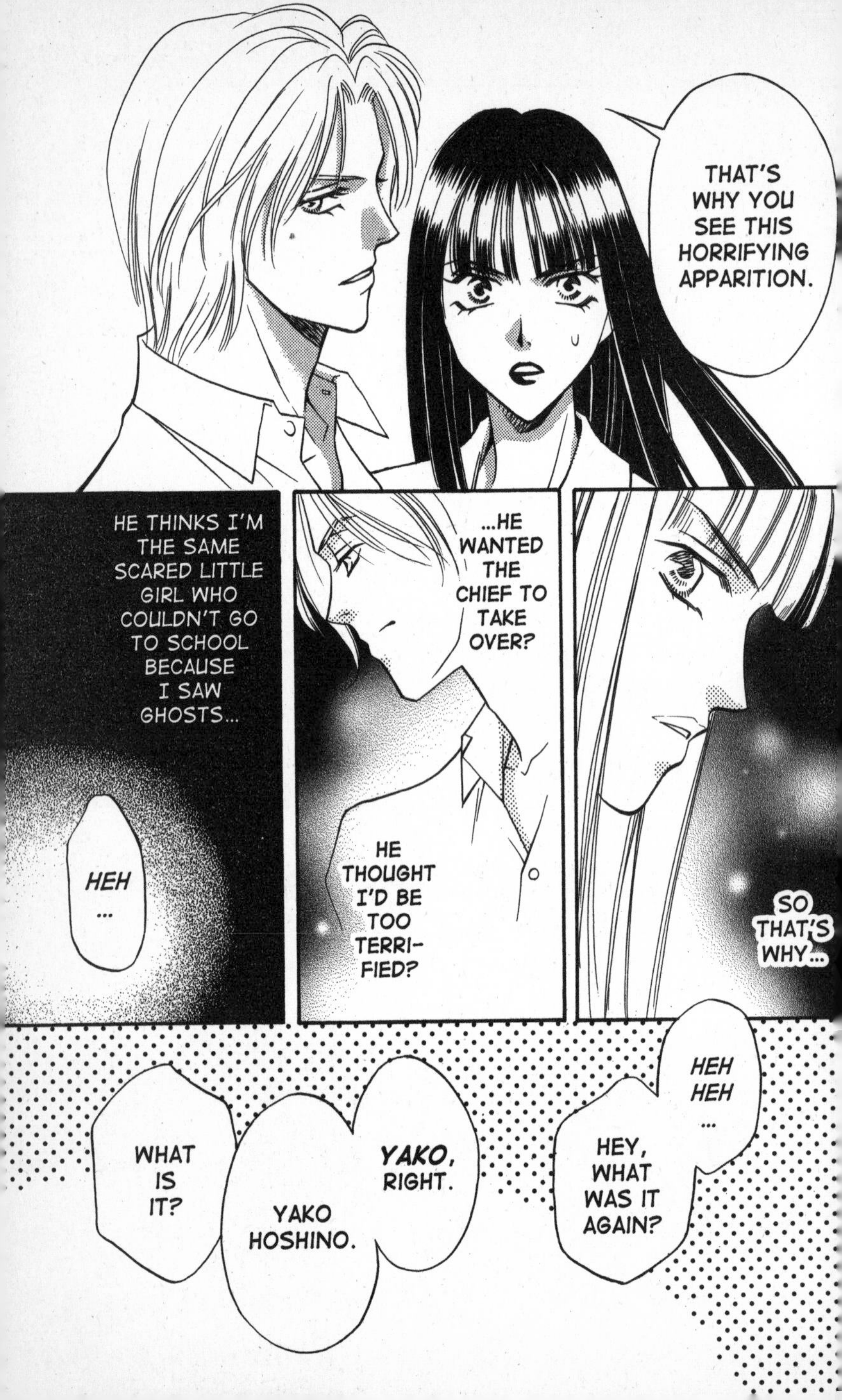
THAT'S WHY YOU SEE THIS HORRIFYING APPARITION.
SO THAT'S WHY...
...HE WANTED THE CHIEF TO TAKE OVER?
HE THOUGHT I'D BE TOO TERRIFIED?
HE THINKS I'M THE SAME SCARED LITTLE GIRL WHO COULDN'T GO TO SCHOOL BECAUSE I SAW GHOSTS...
HEH ...
HEH HEH ...
HEY, WHAT WAS IT AGAIN?
YAKO, RIGHT.
YAKO HOSHINO.
WHAT IS IT?

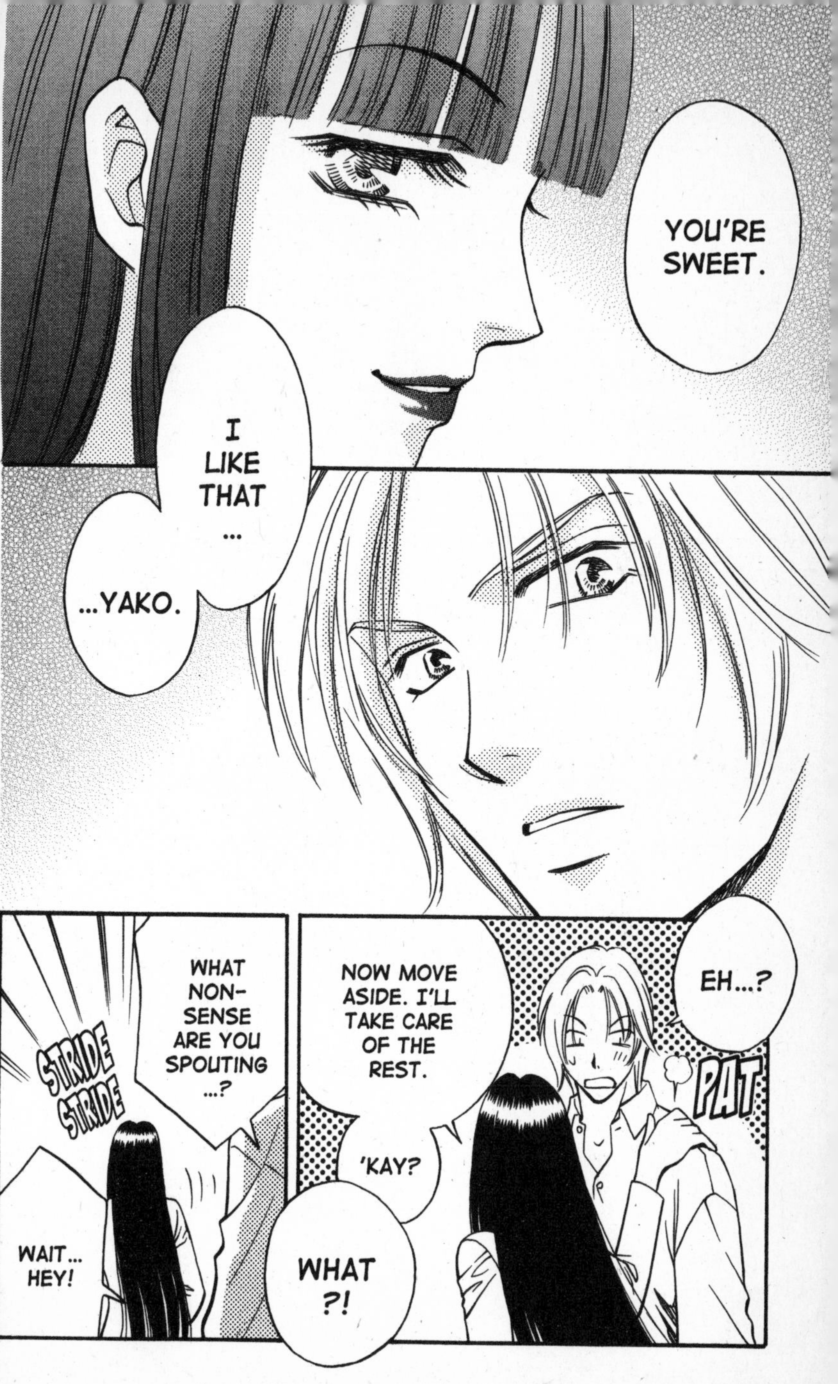
YOU'RE SWEET.
I LIKE THAT ...
...YAKO.
EH...?
PAT
NOW MOVE ASIDE. I'LL TAKE CARE OF THE REST.
'KAY?
WHAT?!
WHAT NON-SENSE ARE YOU SPOUTING ...?
STRIDE STRIDE
WAIT... HEY!

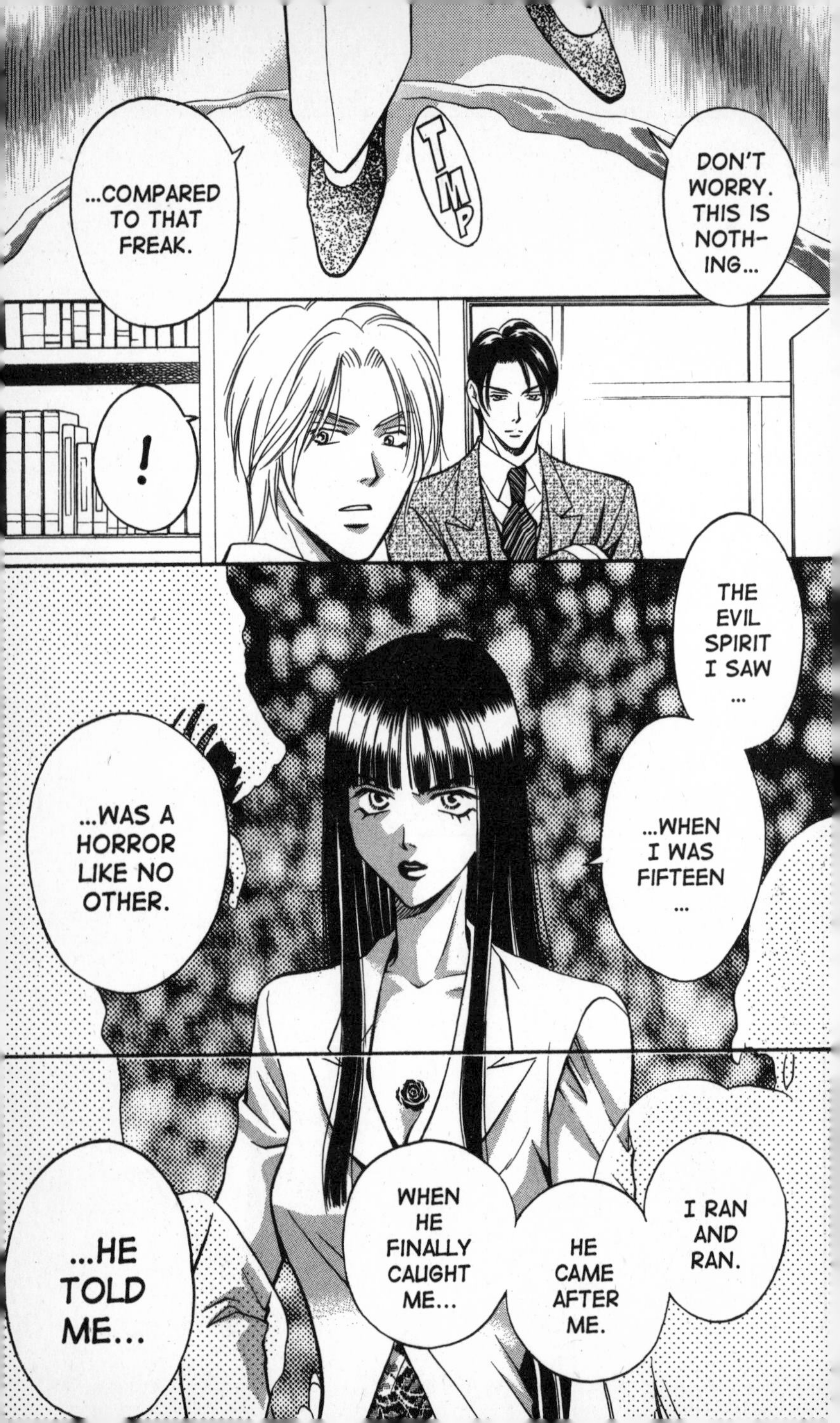
DON'T WORRY. THIS IS NOTH-ING...
TMP
...COMPARED TO THAT FREAK.
!
THE EVIL SPIRIT I SAW ...
...WHEN I WAS FIFTEEN ...
...WAS A HORROR LIKE NO OTHER.
I RAN AND RAN.
HE CAME AFTER ME.
WHEN HE FINALLY CAUGHT ME...
...HE TOLD ME...

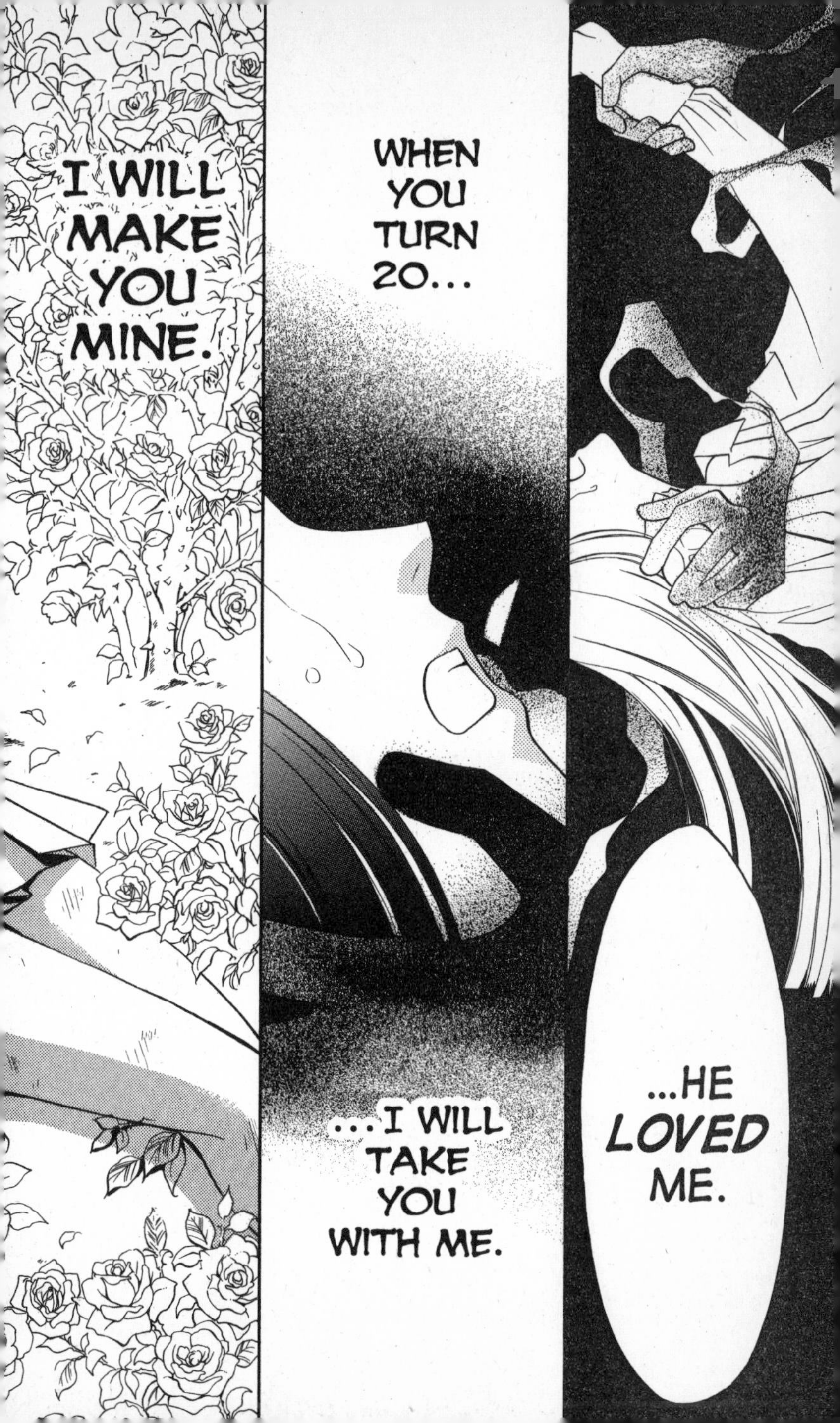
...HE *LOVED* ME.
WHEN YOU TURN 20...
...I WILL TAKE YOU WITH ME.
I WILL MAKE YOU MINE.

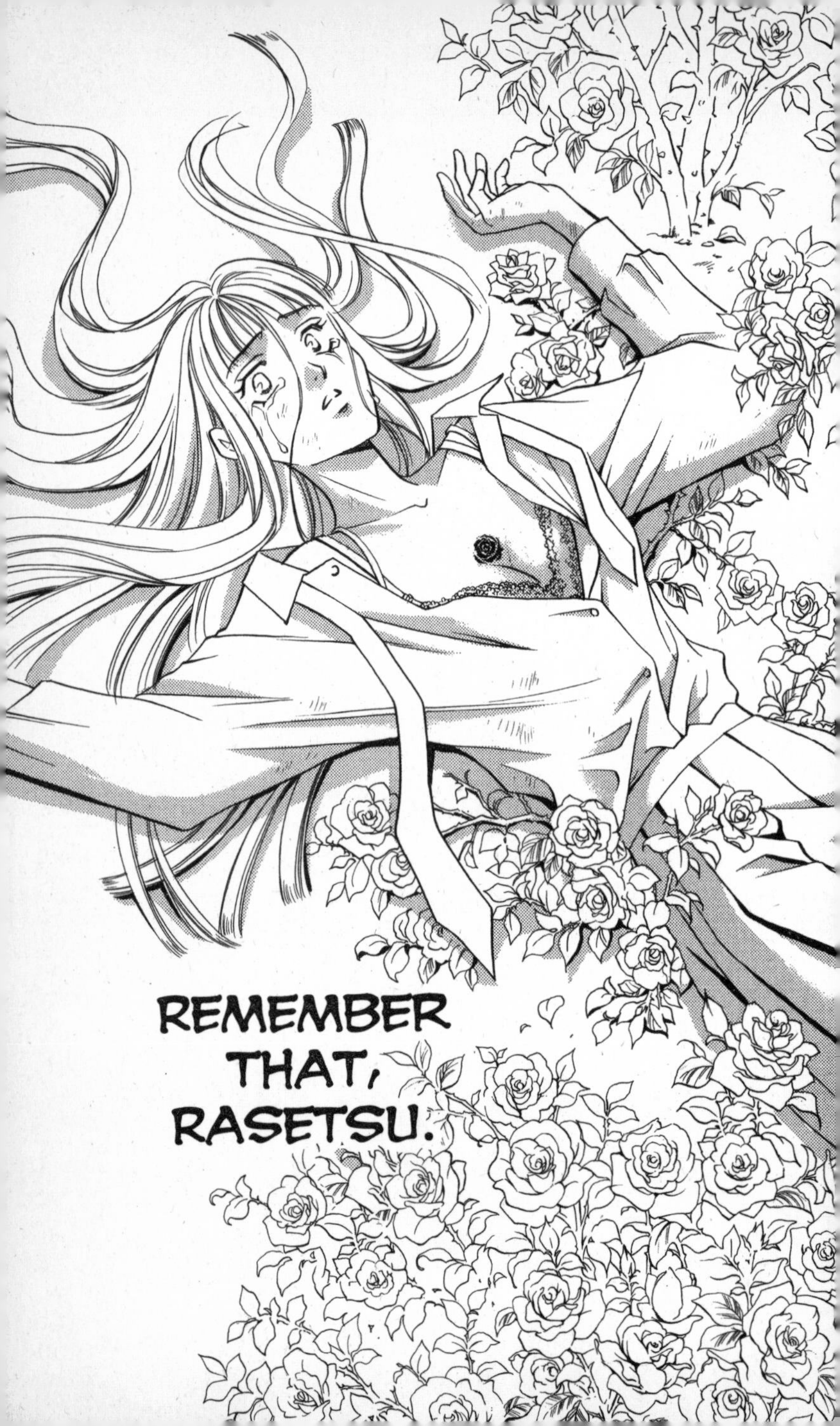
REMEMBER THAT, RASETSU.

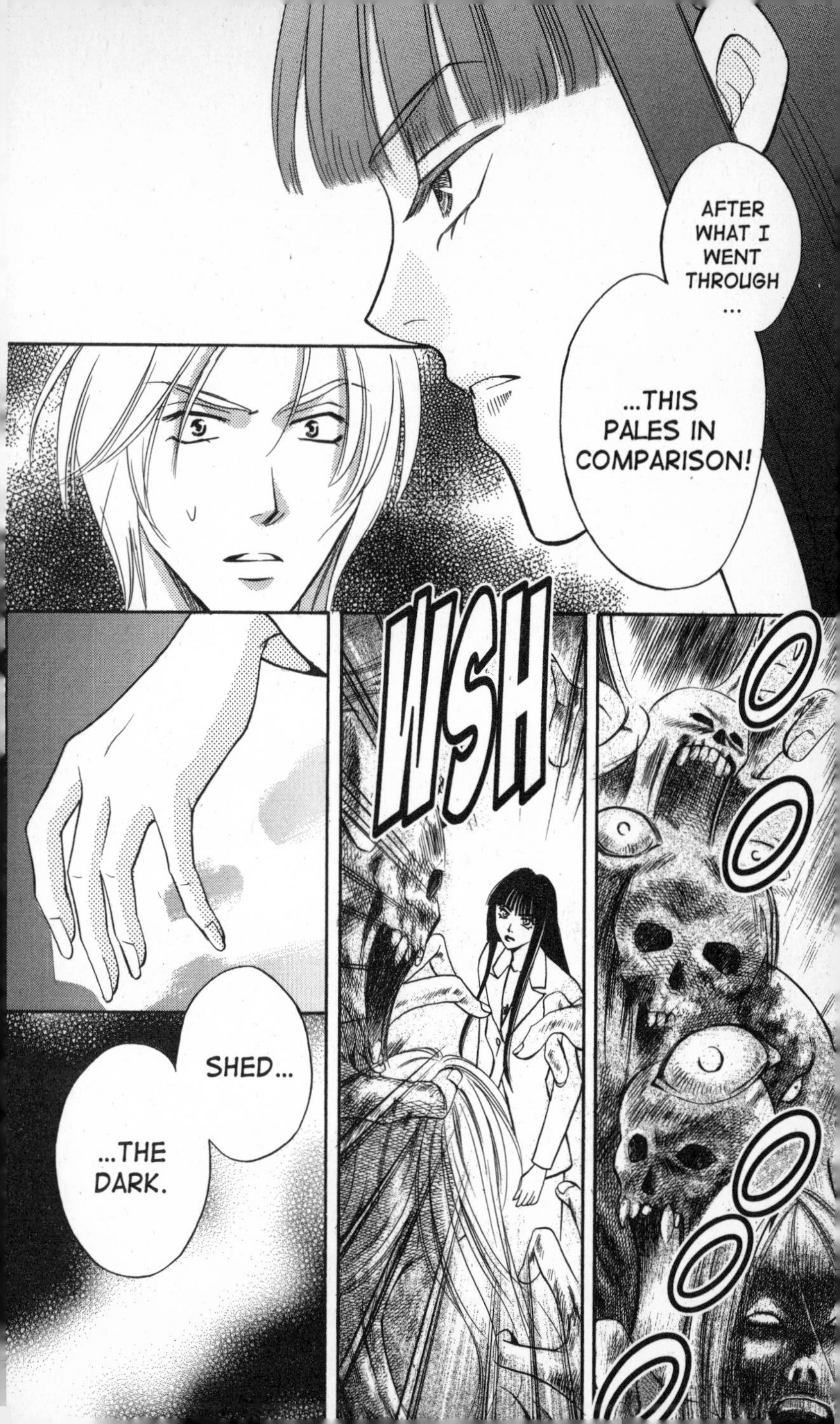
AFTER WHAT I WENT THROUGH ...
...THIS PALES IN COMPARISON!
OOOOOOO
WSH
SHED...
...THE DARK.

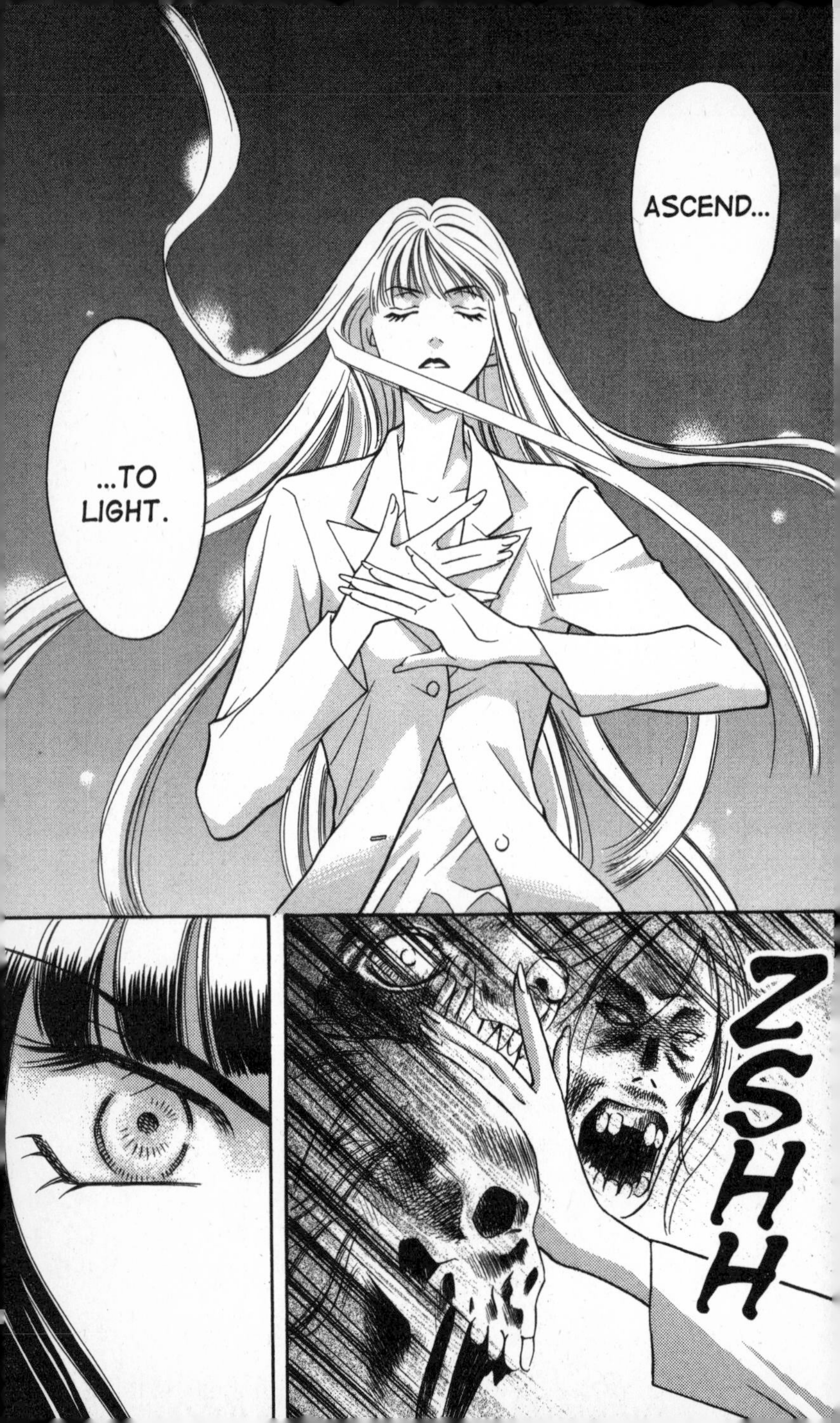
ASCEND...
...TO LIGHT.
ZSHH

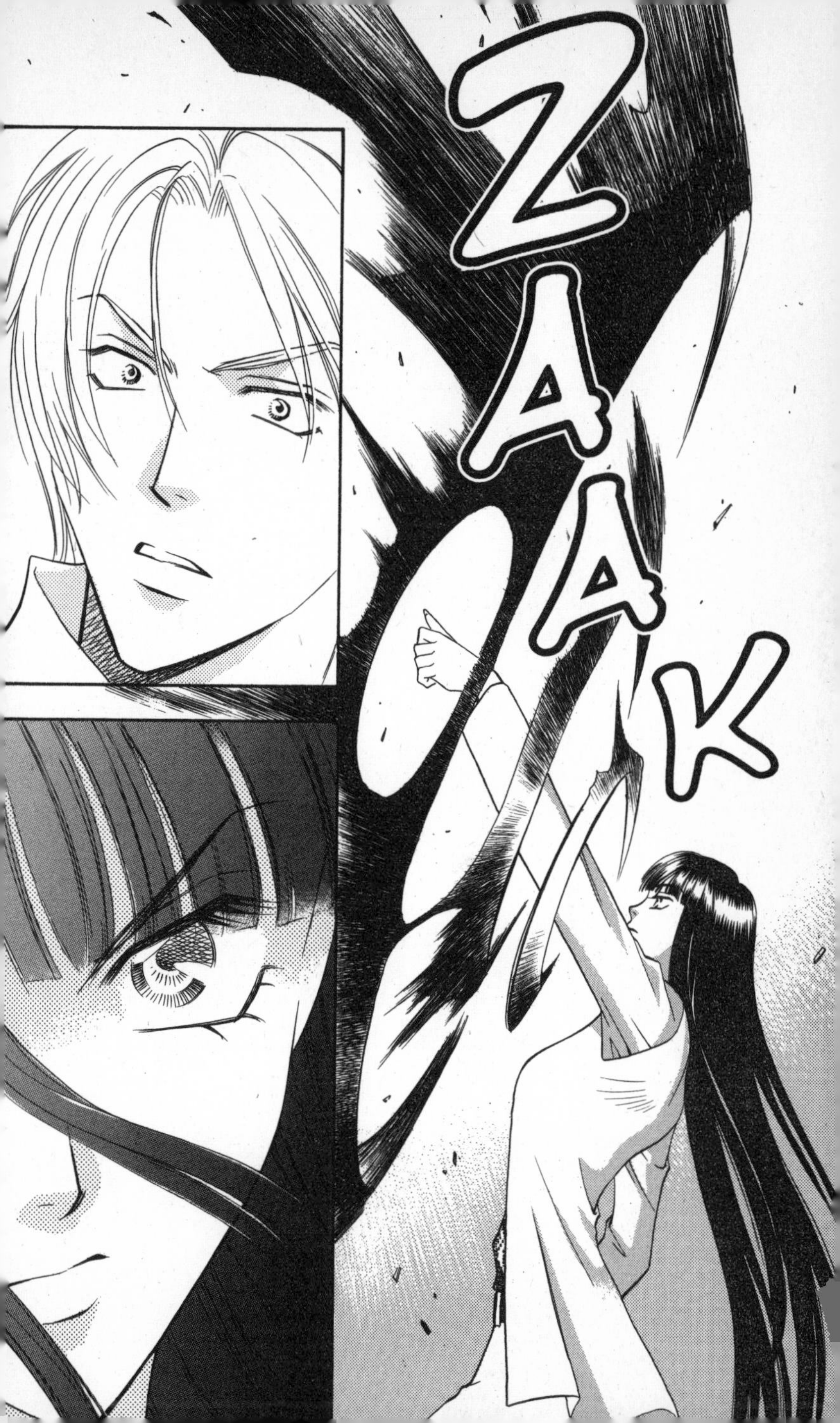
ZAAK

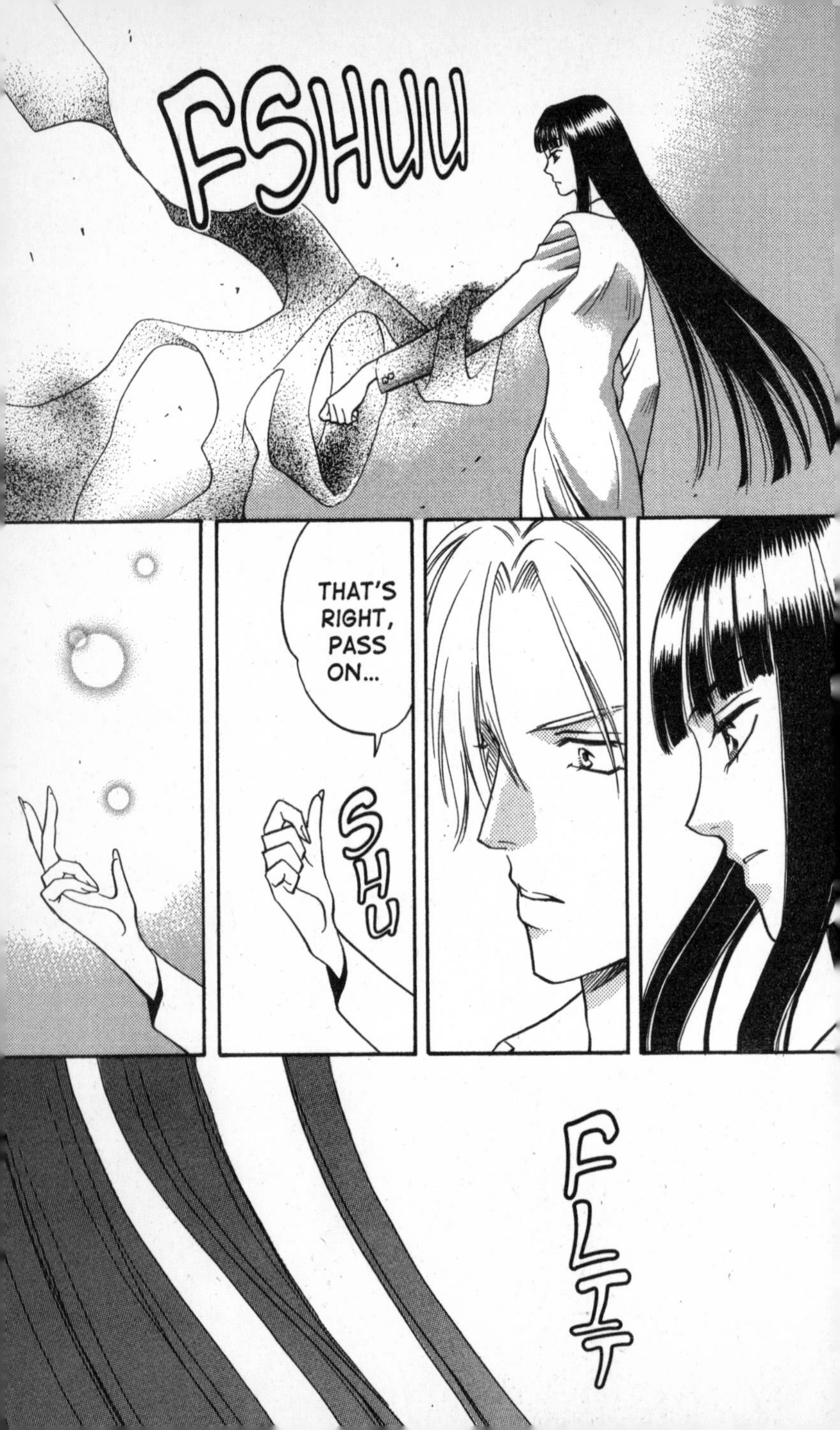
FSHUU
THAT'S RIGHT, PASS ON...
SHU
FLIT

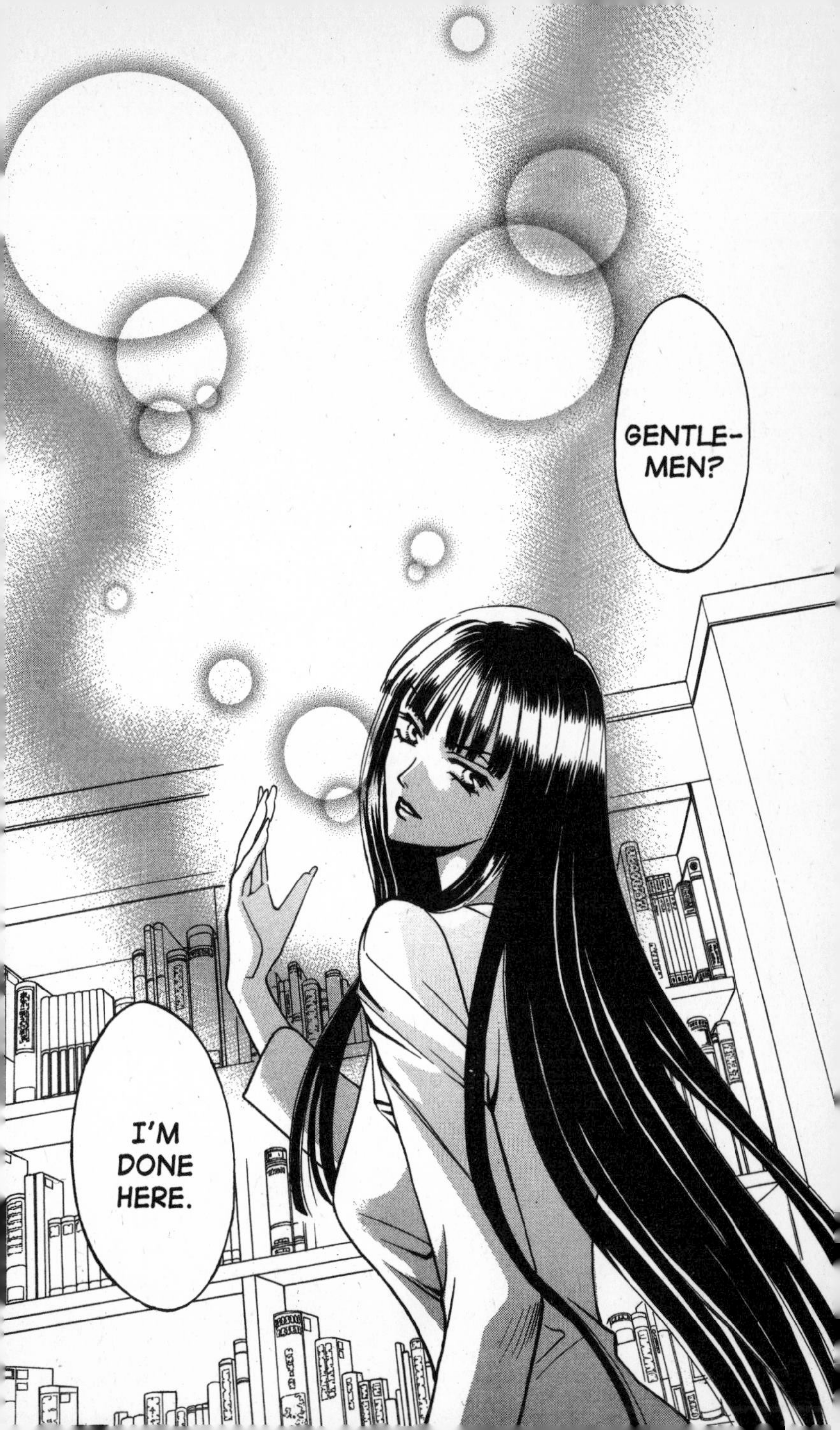
GENTLE- MEN?
I'M DONE HERE.

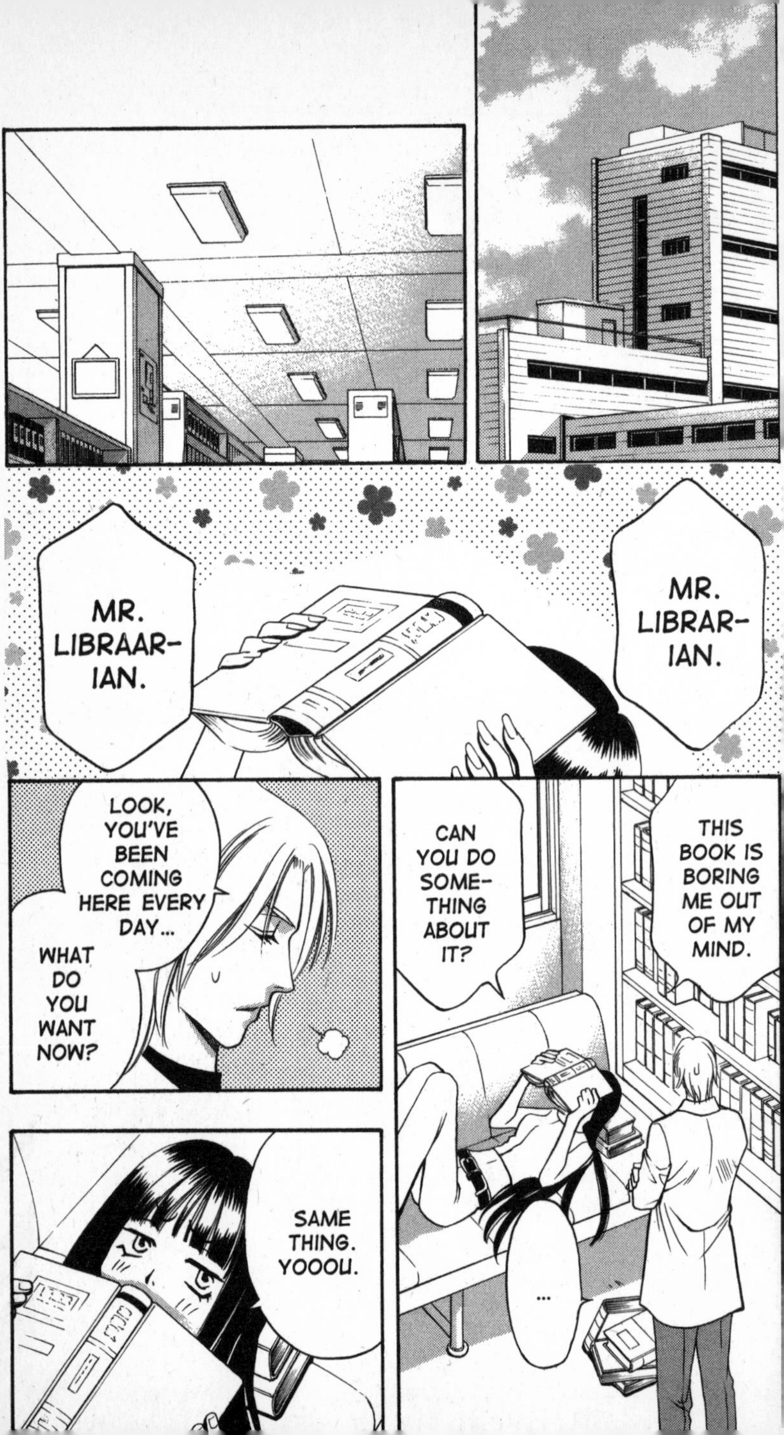
MR. LIBRAR- IAN.
MR. LIBRAAR- IAN.
THIS BOOK IS BORING ME OUT OF MY MIND.
CAN YOU DO SOME- THING ABOUT IT?
...
LOOK, YOU'VE BEEN COMING HERE EVERY DAY...
WHAT DO YOU WANT NOW?
SAME THING. YOOOU.

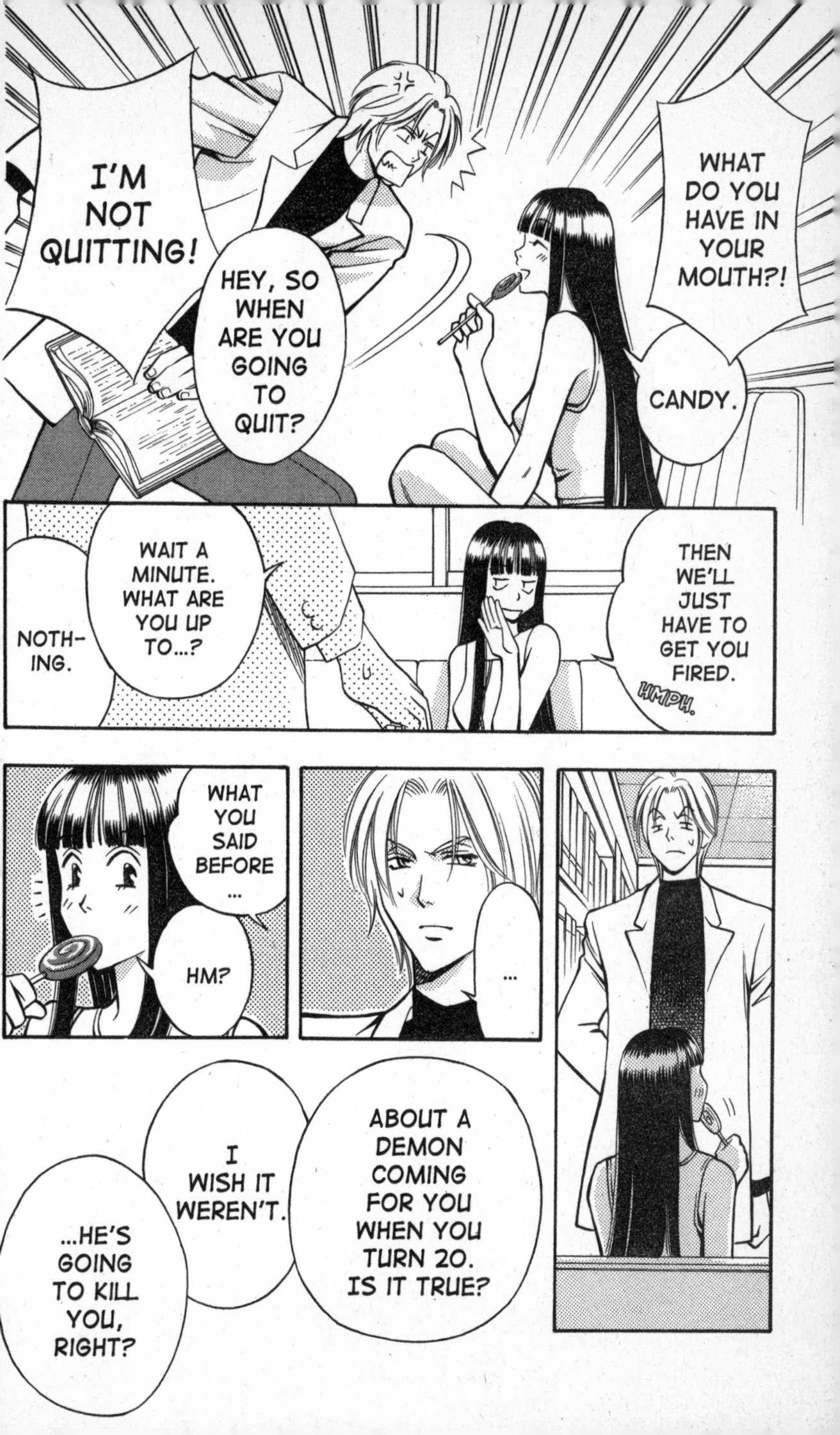
WHAT DO YOU HAVE IN YOUR MOUTH?!
CANDY.
HEY, SO WHEN ARE YOU GOING TO QUIT?
I'M NOT QUITTING!
THEN WE'LL JUST HAVE TO GET YOU FIRED.
HMPH.
WAIT A MINUTE. WHAT ARE YOU UP TO...?
NOTH-ING.
...
WHAT YOU SAID BEFORE ...
HM?
ABOUT A DEMON COMING FOR YOU WHEN YOU TURN 20. IS IT TRUE?
I WISH IT WEREN'T.
...HE'S GOING TO KILL YOU, RIGHT?

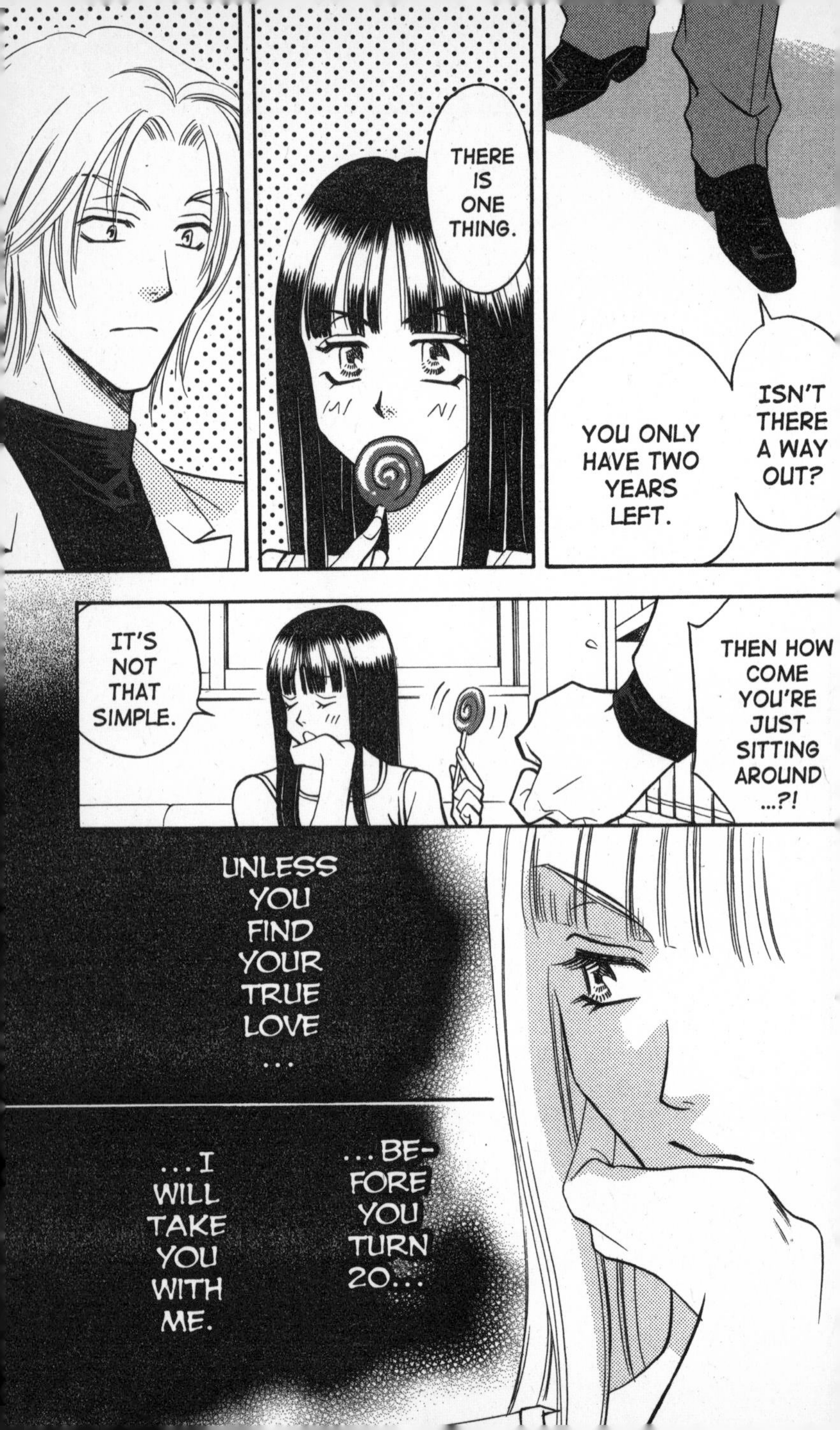

ISN'T THERE A WAY OUT?
YOU ONLY HAVE TWO YEARS LEFT.
THERE IS ONE THING.
THEN HOW COME YOU'RE JUST SITTING AROUND ...?!
IT'S NOT THAT SIMPLE.
UNLESS YOU FIND YOUR TRUE LOVE ...
...BE-FORE YOU TURN 20...
...I WILL TAKE YOU WITH ME.

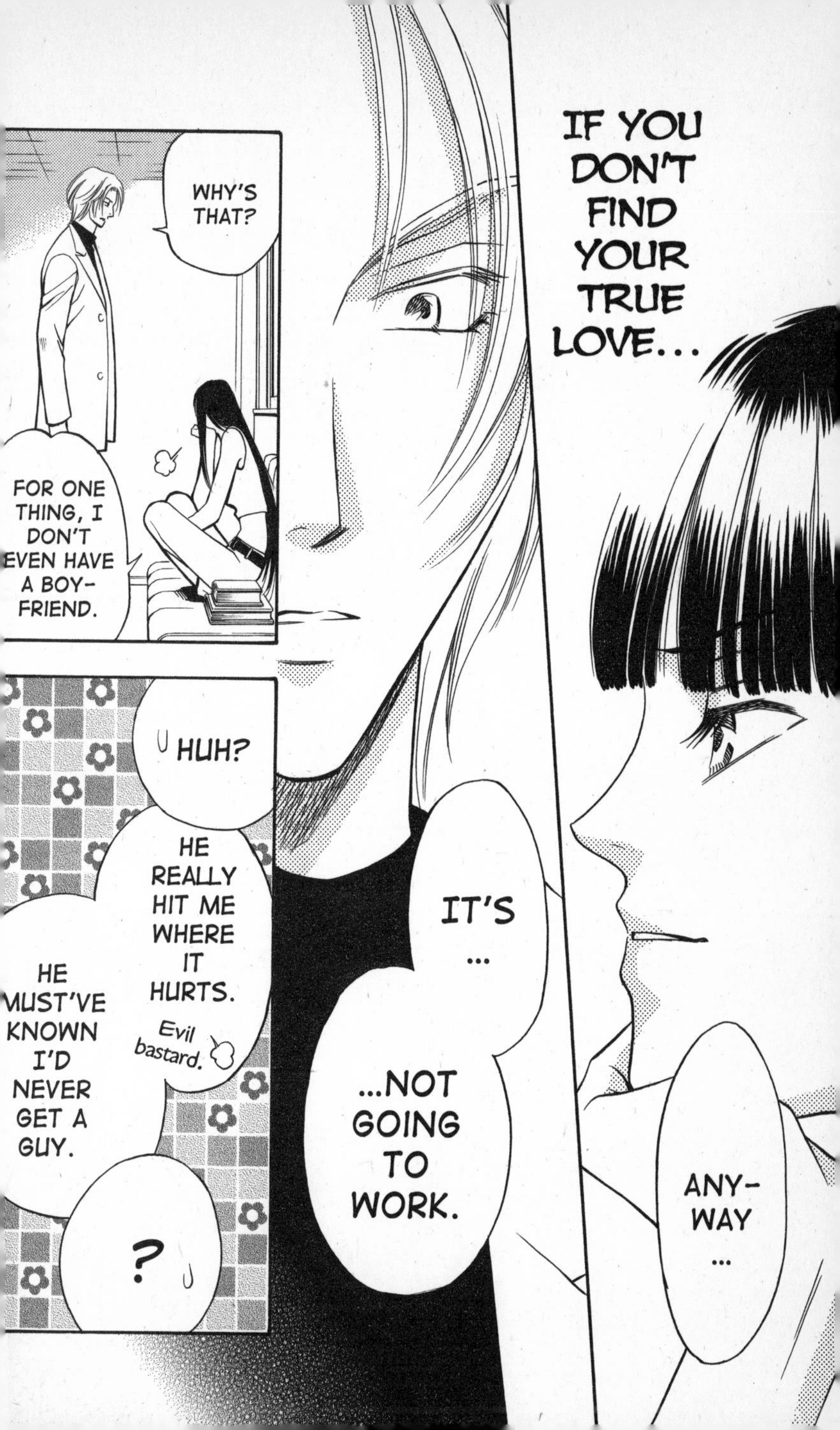
IF YOU DON'T FIND YOUR TRUE LOVE...
ANYWAY...
IT'S...
...NOT GOING TO WORK.
WHY'S THAT?
FOR ONE THING, I DON'T EVEN HAVE A BOYFRIEND.
HUH?
HE REALLY HIT ME WHERE IT HURTS.
Evil bastard.
HE MUST'VE KNOWN I'D NEVER GET A GUY.
?

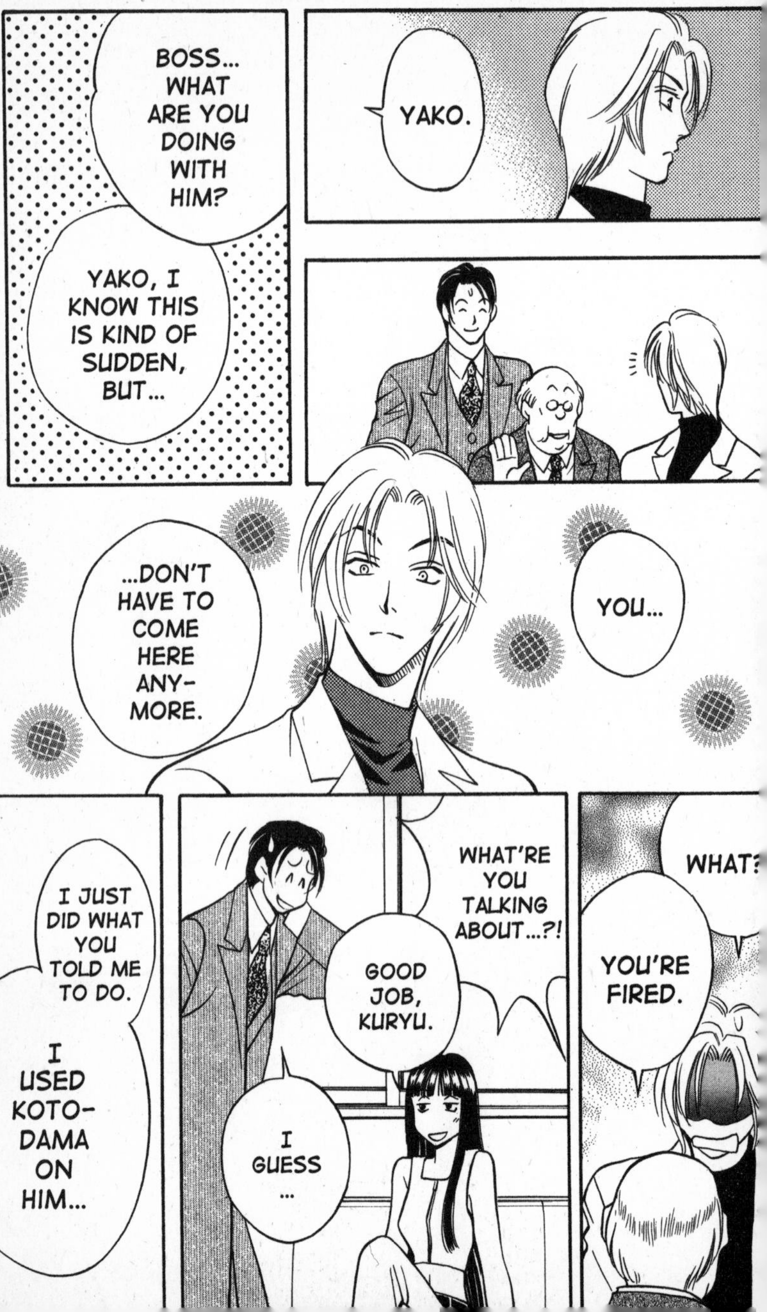
YAKO.
BOSS... WHAT ARE YOU DOING WITH HIM?
YAKO, I KNOW THIS IS KIND OF SUDDEN, BUT...
YOU...
...DON'T HAVE TO COME HERE ANY-MORE.
WHAT?
YOU'RE FIRED.
WHAT'RE YOU TALKING ABOUT...?!
GOOD JOB, KURYU.
I GUESS...
I JUST DID WHAT YOU TOLD ME TO DO.
I USED KOTO-DAMA ON HIM...

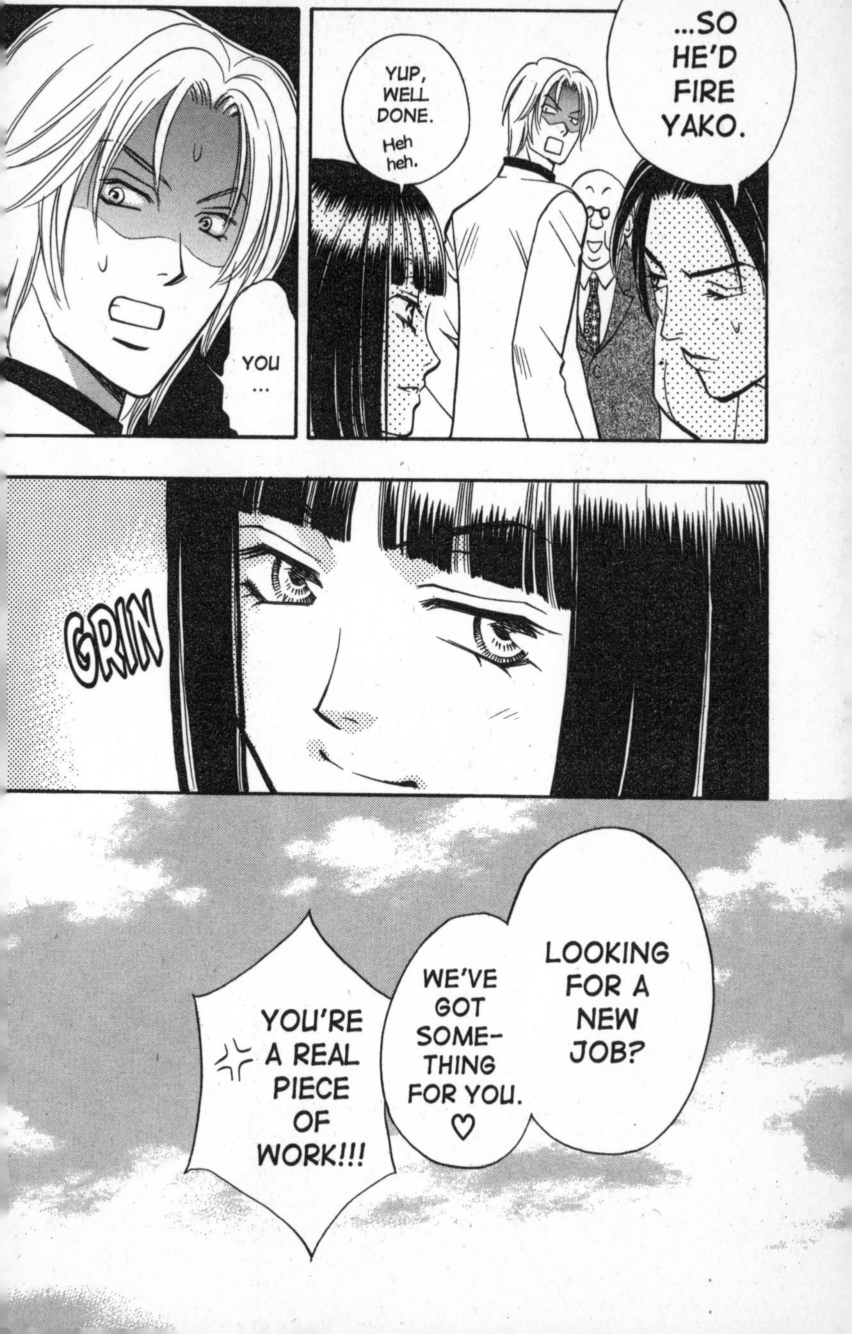
...SO HE'D FIRE YAKO.
YUP, WELL DONE.
Heh heh.
YOU ...
GRIN
LOOKING FOR A NEW JOB?
WE'VE GOT SOME-THING FOR YOU. ♡
YOU'RE A REAL PIECE OF WORK!!!

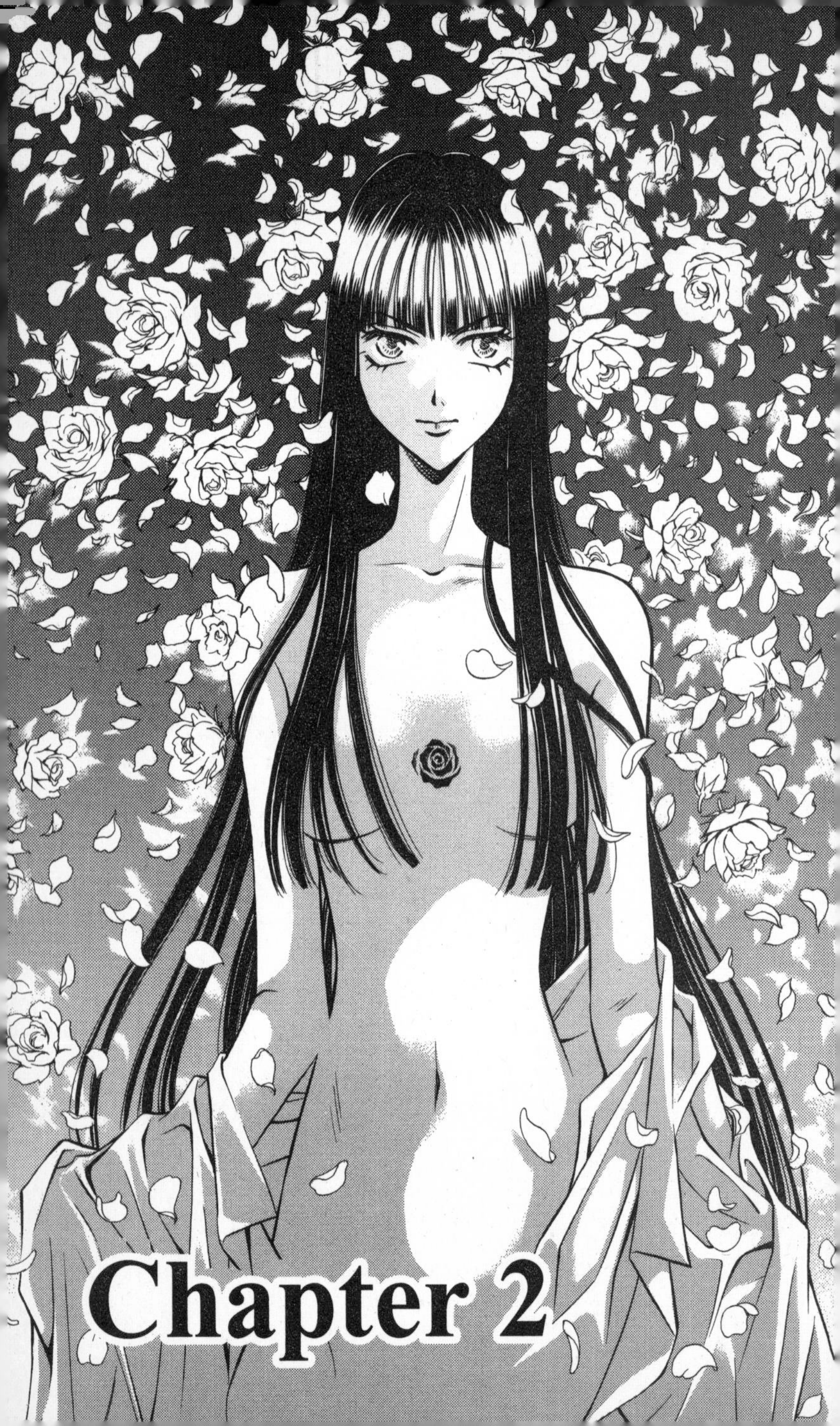
Chapter 2

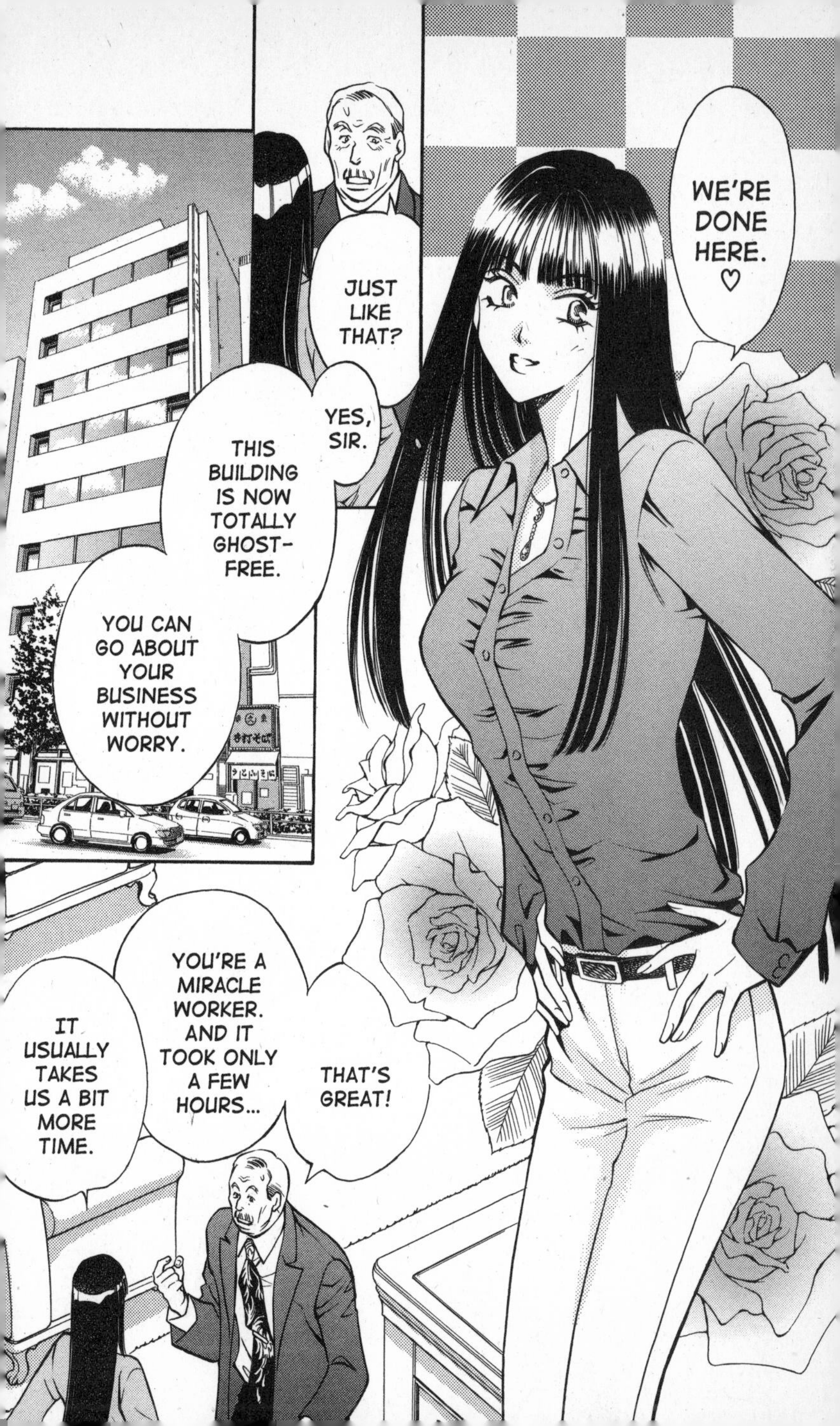
WE'RE DONE HERE. ♡
JUST LIKE THAT?
YES, SIR.
THIS BUILDING IS NOW TOTALLY GHOST-FREE.
YOU CAN GO ABOUT YOUR BUSINESS WITHOUT WORRY.
THAT'S GREAT!
YOU'RE A MIRACLE WORKER. AND IT TOOK ONLY A FEW HOURS...
IT USUALLY TAKES US A BIT MORE TIME.

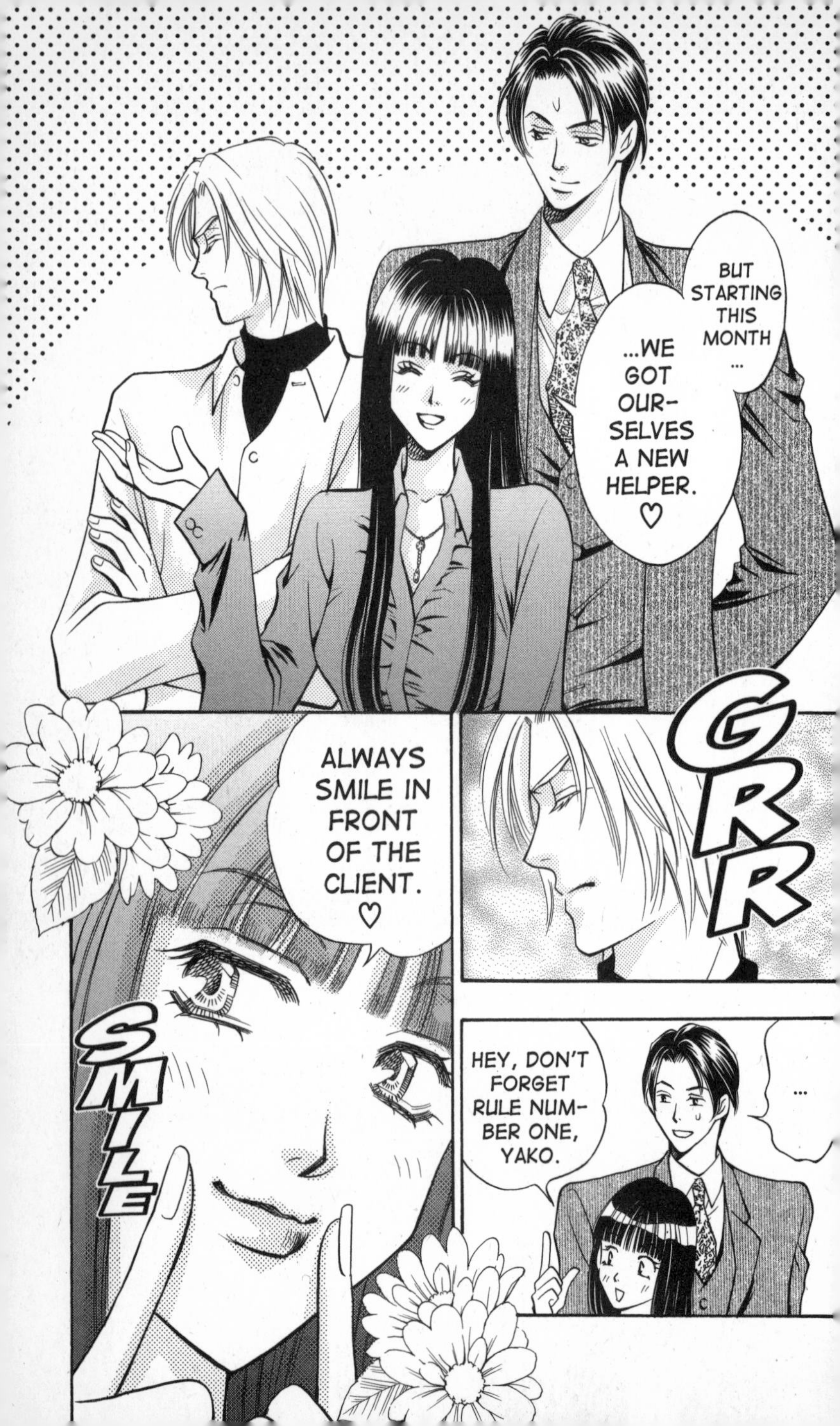
BUT STARTING THIS MONTH...
...WE GOT OUR-SELVES A NEW HELPER. ♡
GRR
ALWAYS SMILE IN FRONT OF THE CLIENT. ♡
SMILE
...
HEY, DON'T FORGET RULE NUM-BER ONE, YAKO.

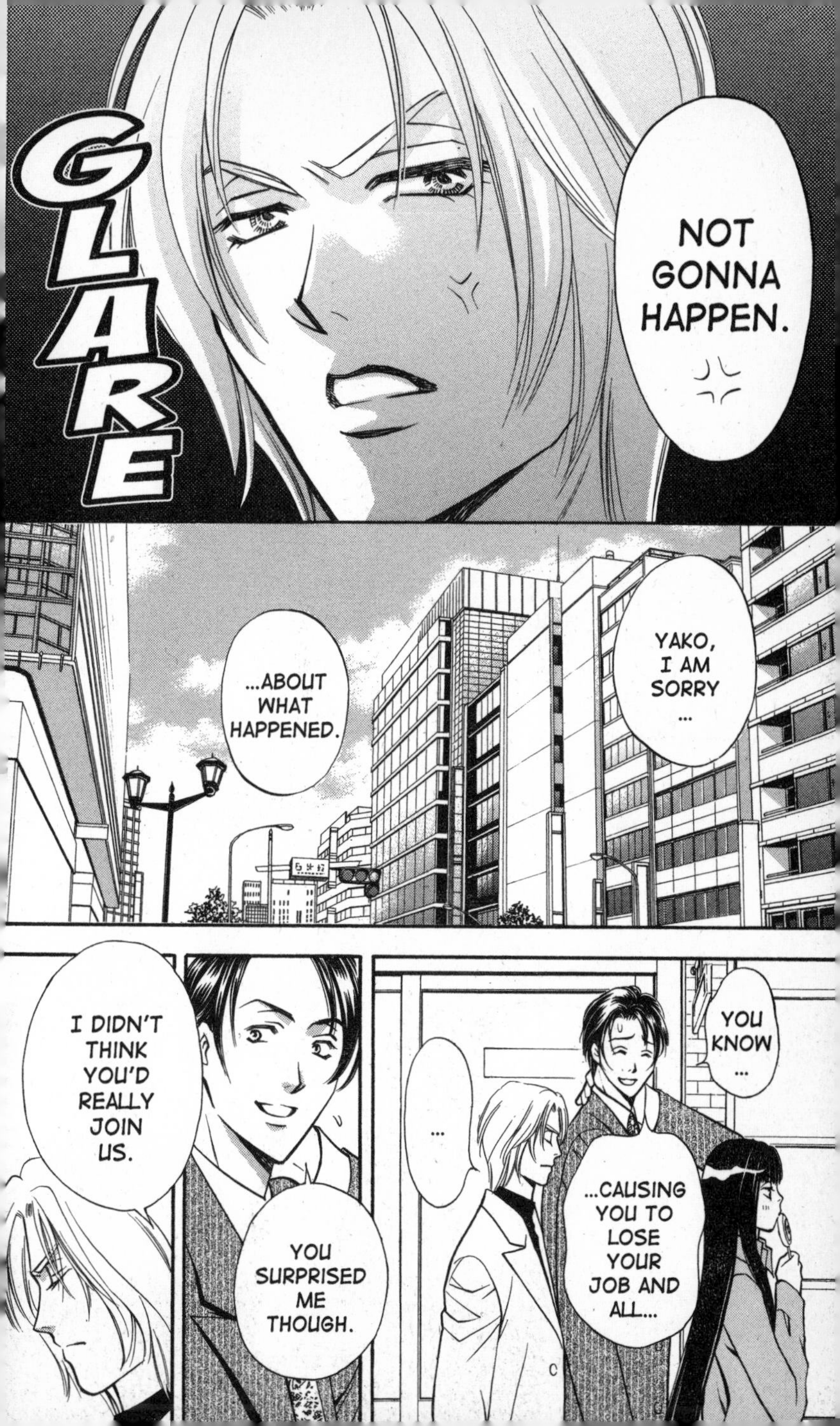
NOT GONNA HAPPEN.
GLARE
YAKO, I AM SORRY ...
...ABOUT WHAT HAPPENED.
YOU KNOW ...
...CAUSING YOU TO LOSE YOUR JOB AND ALL...
...
I DIDN'T THINK YOU'D REALLY JOIN US.
YOU SURPRISED ME THOUGH.

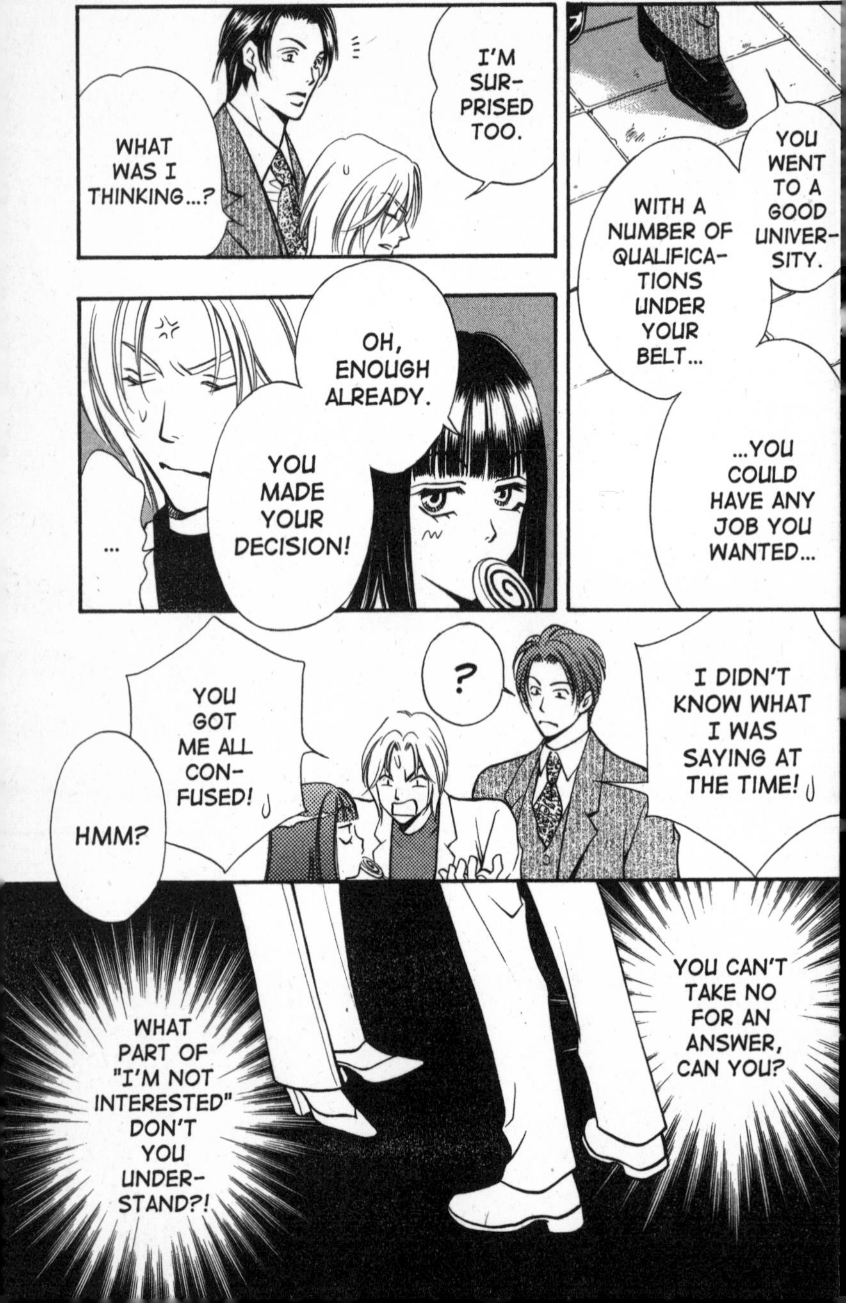
YOU WENT TO A GOOD UNIVERSITY.
WITH A NUMBER OF QUALIFICATIONS UNDER YOUR BELT...
...YOU COULD HAVE ANY JOB YOU WANTED...
I'M SURPRISED TOO.
WHAT WAS I THINKING...?
OH, ENOUGH ALREADY.
YOU MADE YOUR DECISION!
...
I DIDN'T KNOW WHAT I WAS SAYING AT THE TIME!
?
YOU GOT ME ALL CONFUSED!
HMM?
YOU CAN'T TAKE NO FOR AN ANSWER, CAN YOU?
WHAT PART OF "I'M NOT INTERESTED" DON'T YOU UNDERSTAND?!

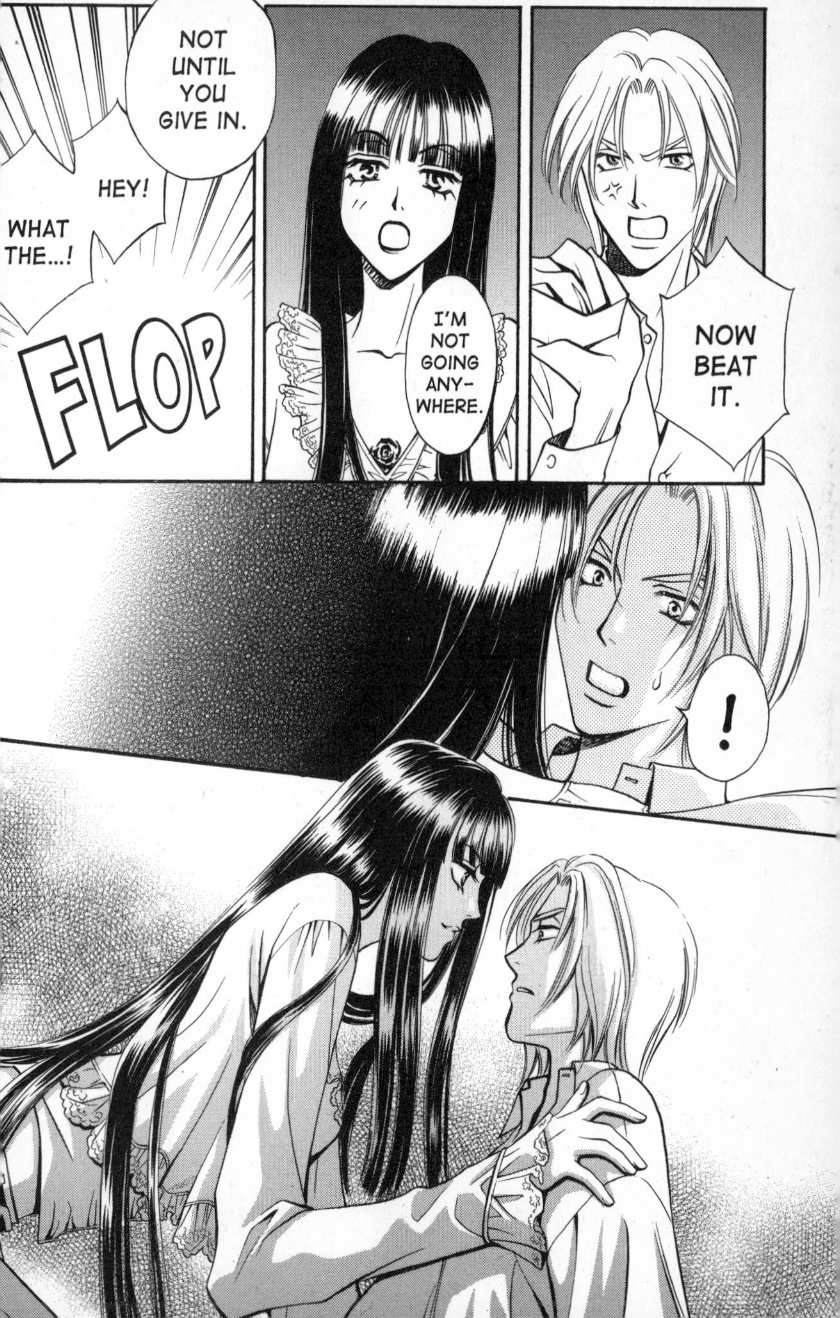
NOW BEAT IT.
I'M NOT GOING ANY-WHERE.
NOT UNTIL YOU GIVE IN.
HEY!
WHAT THE...!
FLOP
!

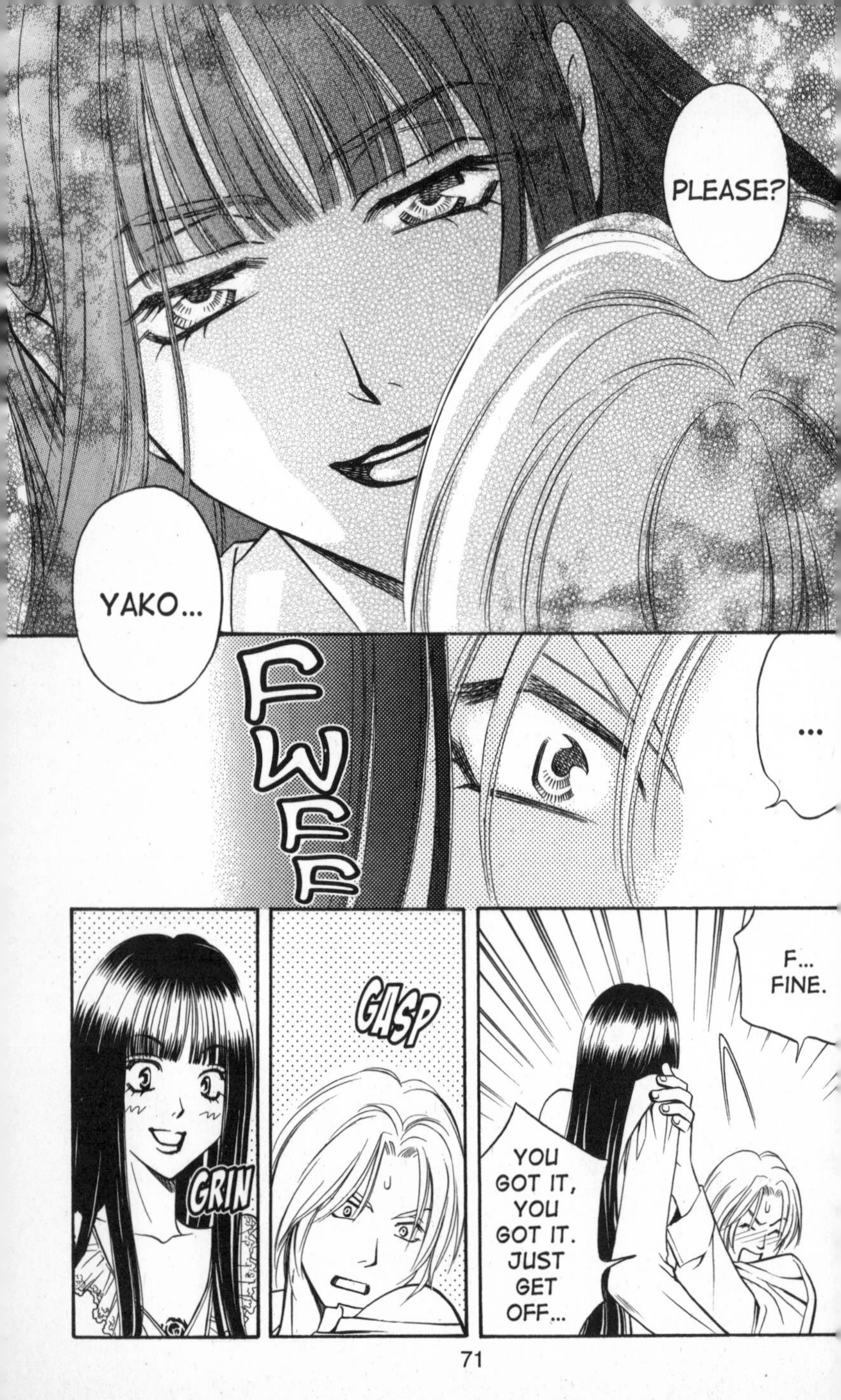
PLEASE?
YAKO...
...
FWFF
F... FINE.
YOU GOT IT, YOU GOT IT. JUST GET OFF...
GASP
GRIN

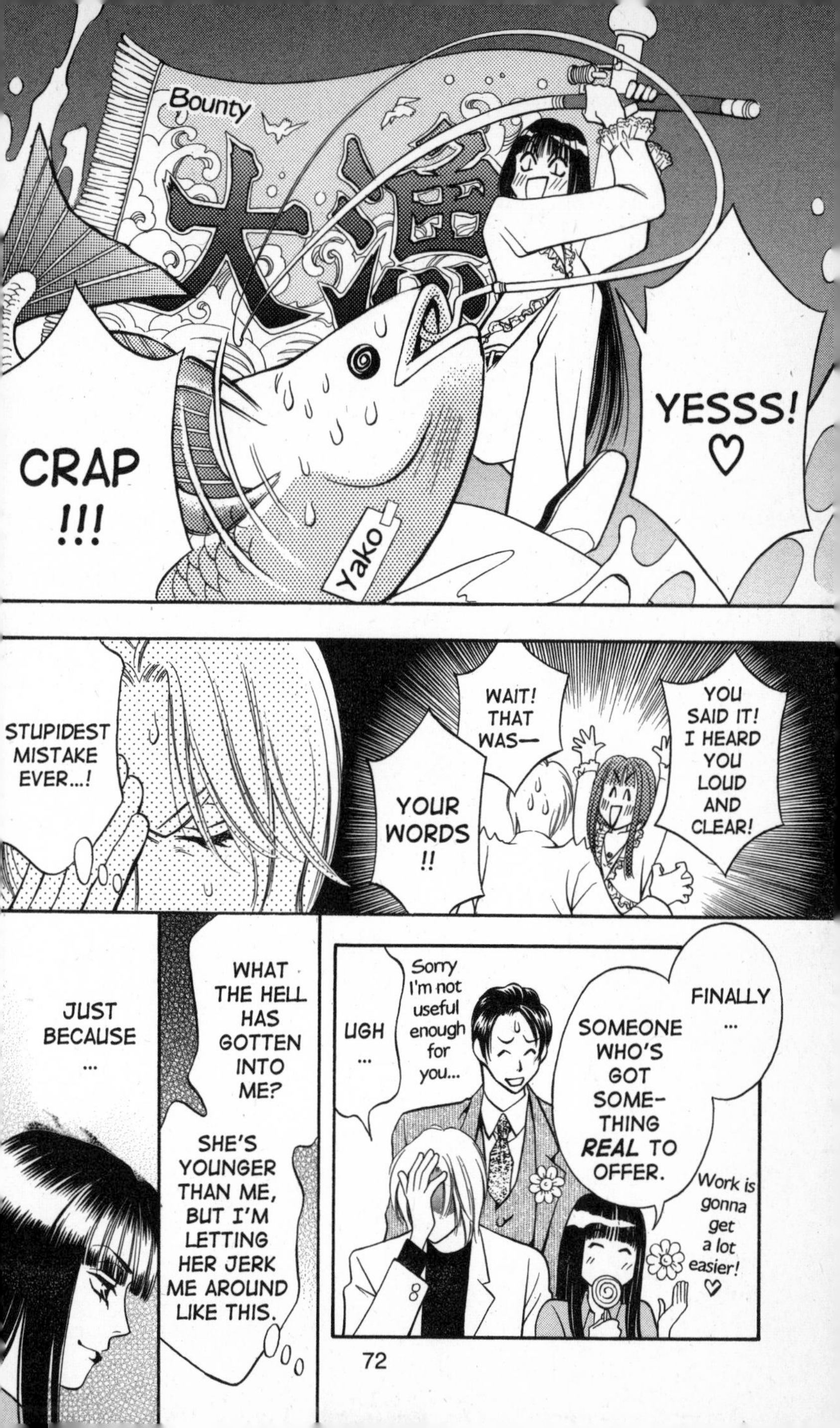
YESSS! ♡
Bounty
Yako
CRAP!!!
YOU SAID IT! I HEARD YOU LOUD AND CLEAR!
WAIT! THAT WAS—
YOUR WORDS!!
STUPIDEST MISTAKE EVER...!
FINALLY...
SOMEONE WHO'S GOT SOMETHING *REAL* TO OFFER.
Work is gonna get a lot easier! ♡
Sorry I'm not useful enough for you...
UGH...
WHAT THE HELL HAS GOTTEN INTO ME?
SHE'S YOUNGER THAN ME, BUT I'M LETTING HER JERK ME AROUND LIKE THIS.
JUST BECAUSE...

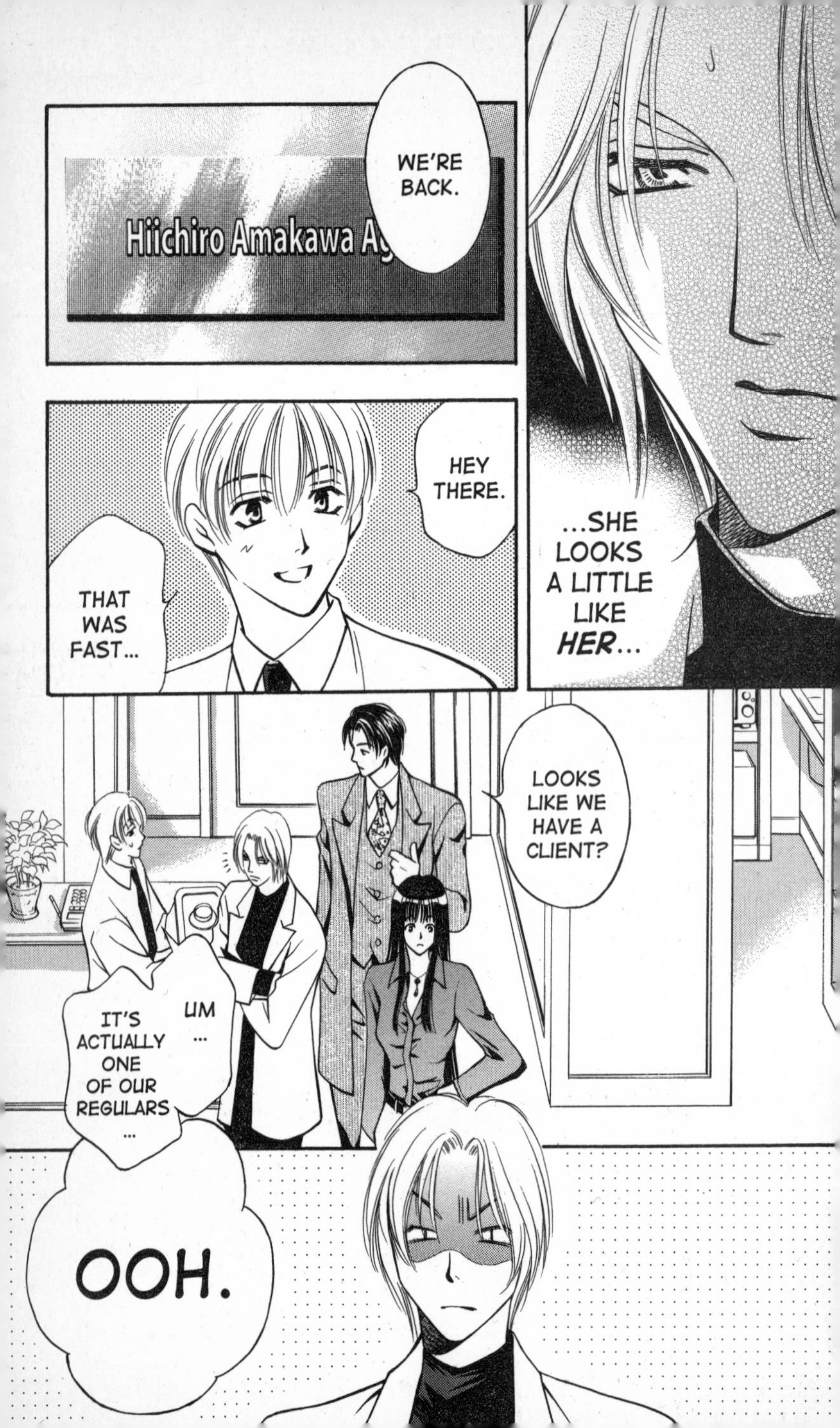
...SHE LOOKS A LITTLE LIKE *HER*...
Hiichiro Amakawa Ag
WE'RE BACK.
HEY THERE.
THAT WAS FAST...
LOOKS LIKE WE HAVE A CLIENT?
UM ...
IT'S ACTUALLY ONE OF OUR REGULARS ...
OOH.

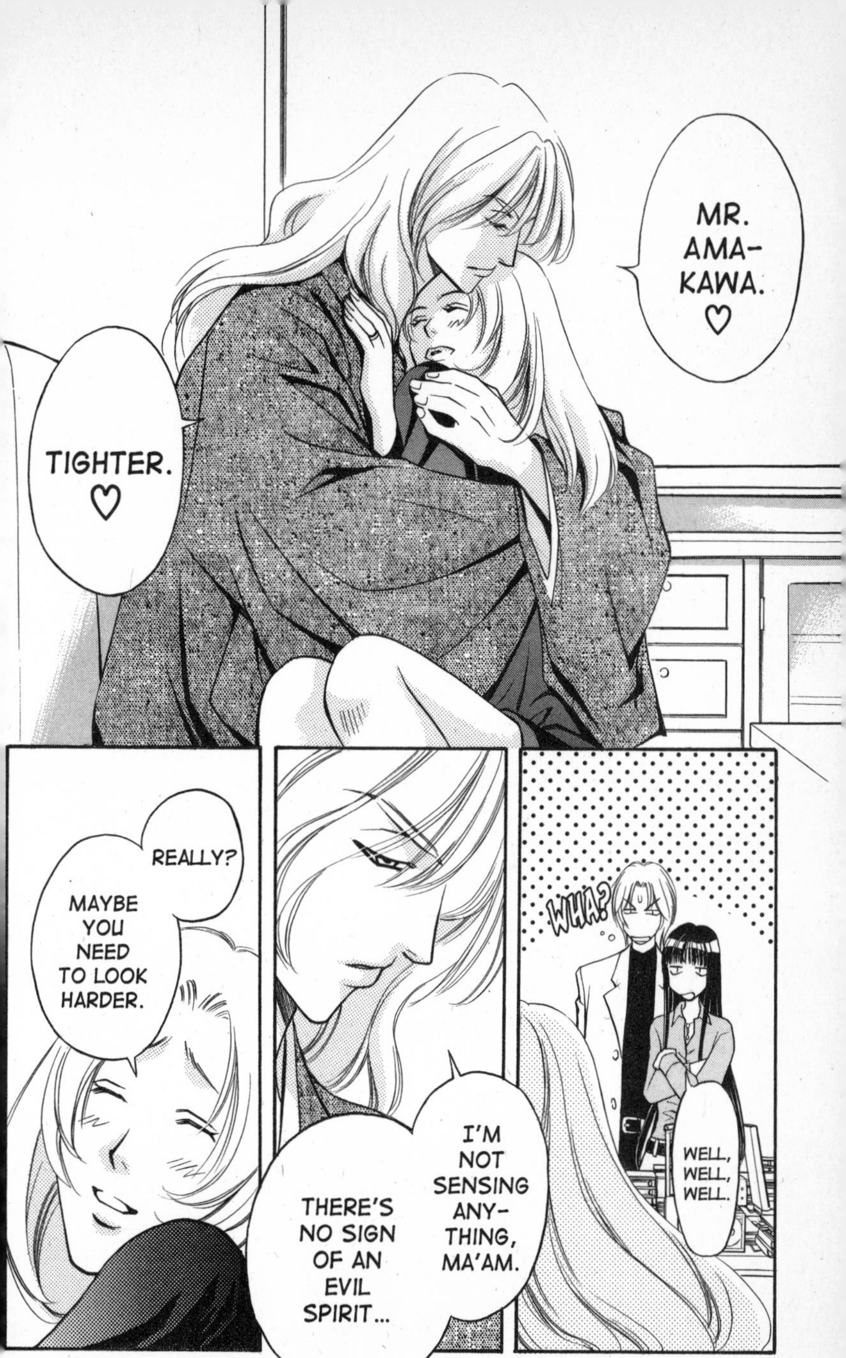
MR. AMA-KAWA. ♡
TIGHTER. ♡
WHA?
WELL, WELL, WELL.
I'M NOT SENSING ANY-THING, MA'AM.
THERE'S NO SIGN OF AN EVIL SPIRIT...
REALLY?
MAYBE YOU NEED TO LOOK HARDER.

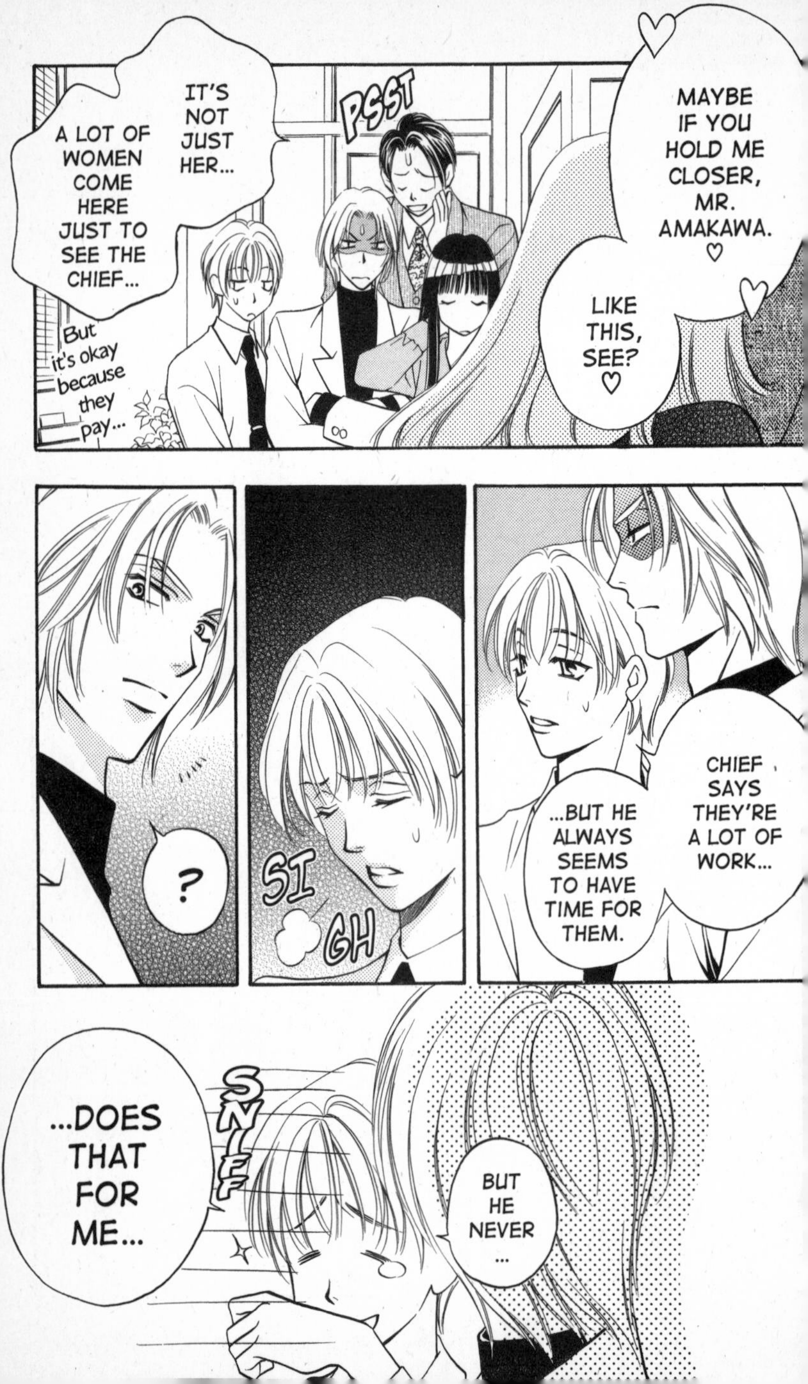
MAYBE IF YOU HOLD ME CLOSER, MR. AMAKAWA. ♡
LIKE THIS, SEE? ♡
PSST
IT'S NOT JUST HER...
A LOT OF WOMEN COME HERE JUST TO SEE THE CHIEF...
But it's okay because they pay...
CHIEF SAYS THEY'RE A LOT OF WORK...
...BUT HE ALWAYS SEEMS TO HAVE TIME FOR THEM.
SIGH
?
BUT HE NEVER ...
SNIFF
...DOES THAT FOR ME...

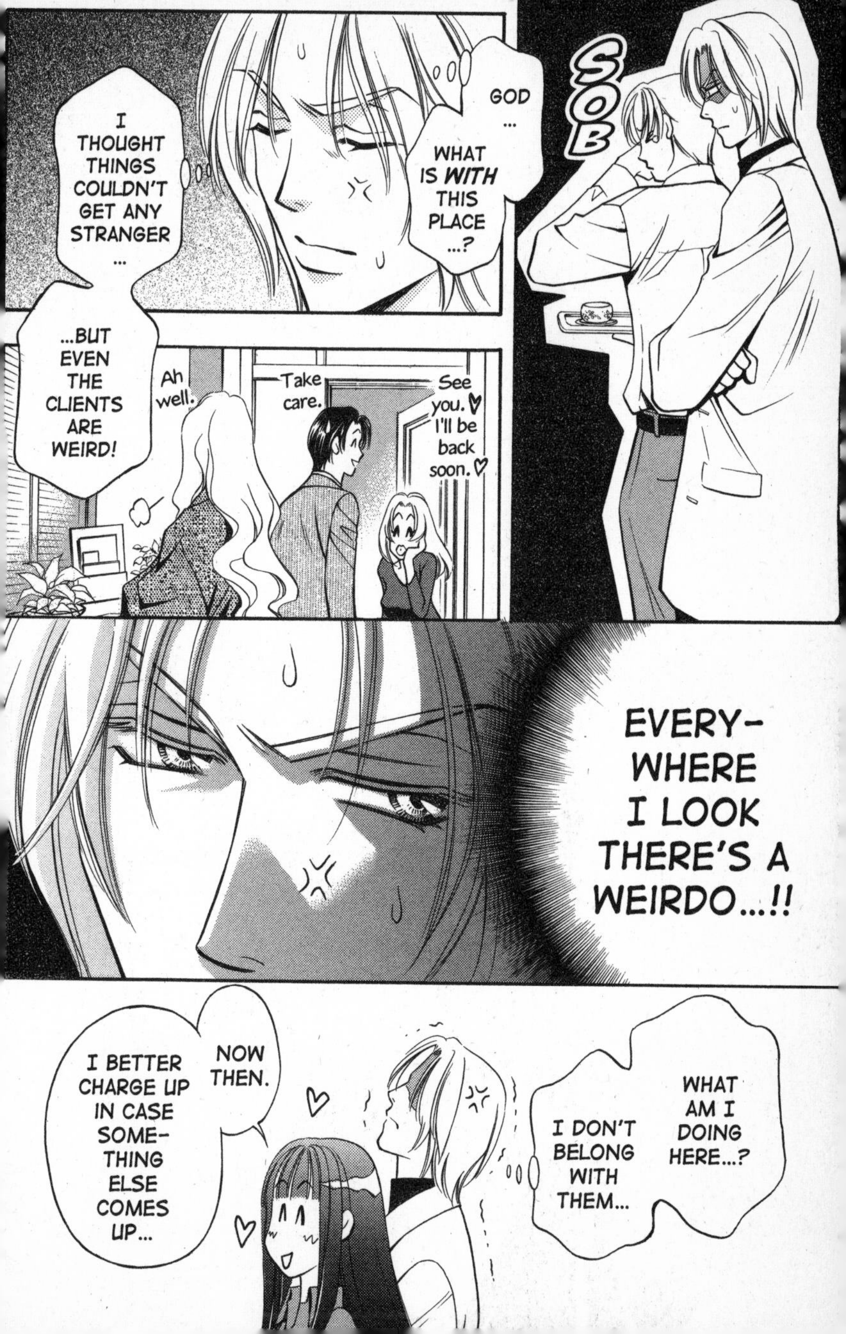
SOB
GOD ...
WHAT IS *WITH* THIS PLACE ...?
I THOUGHT THINGS COULDN'T GET ANY STRANGER ...
...BUT EVEN THE CLIENTS ARE WEIRD!
See you. ♡ I'll be back soon. ♡
Take care.
Ah well.
EVERY-WHERE I LOOK THERE'S A WEIRDO...!!
WHAT AM I DOING HERE...?
I DON'T BELONG WITH THEM...
NOW THEN.
I BETTER CHARGE UP IN CASE SOME-THING ELSE COMES UP...

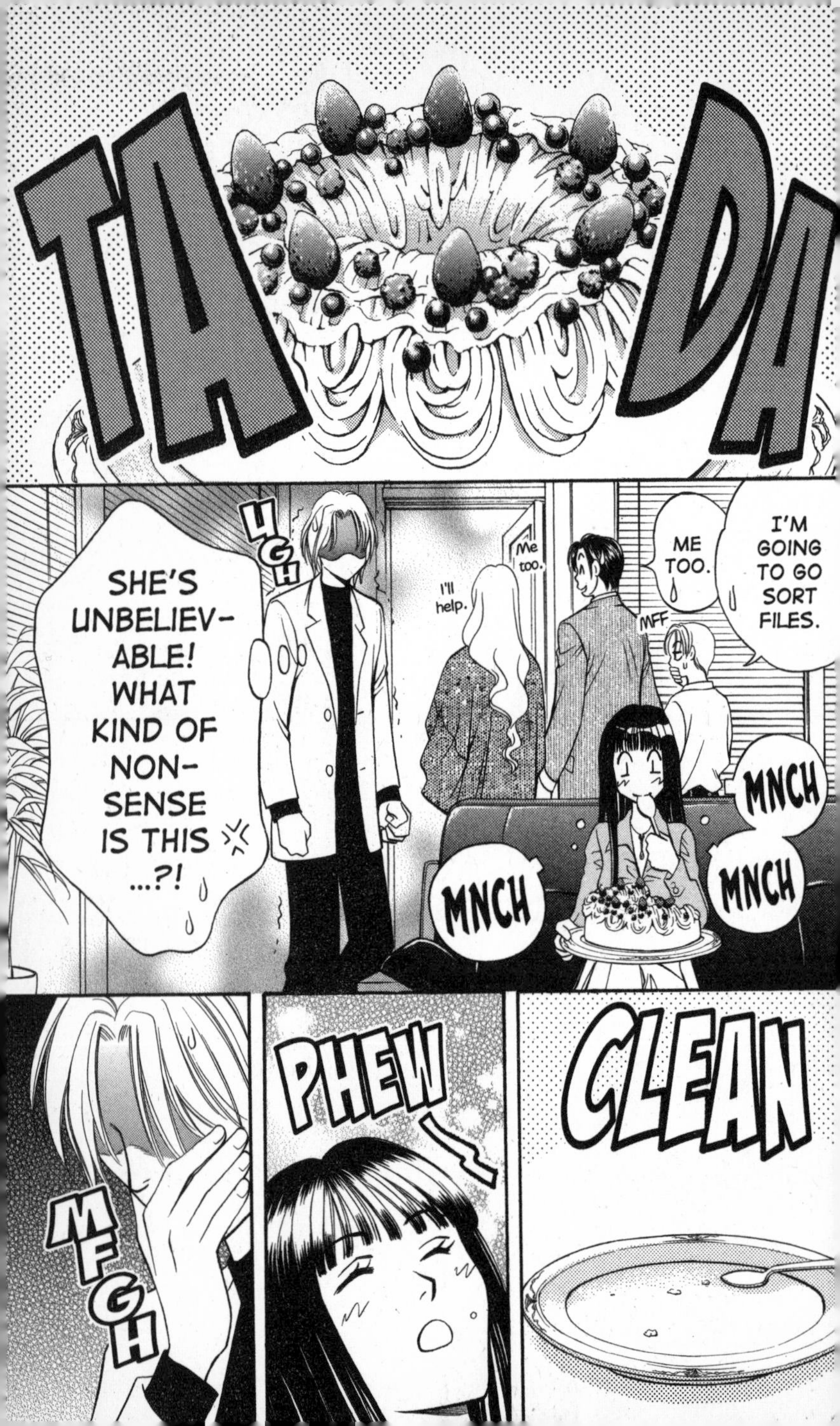
TA DA
I'M GOING TO GO SORT FILES.
ME TOO.
MFF
Me too.
I'll help.
UGH
SHE'S UNBELIEV-ABLE! WHAT KIND OF NON-SENSE IS THIS ...?!
MNCH
MNCH
MNCH
CLEAN
PHEW
MFGH

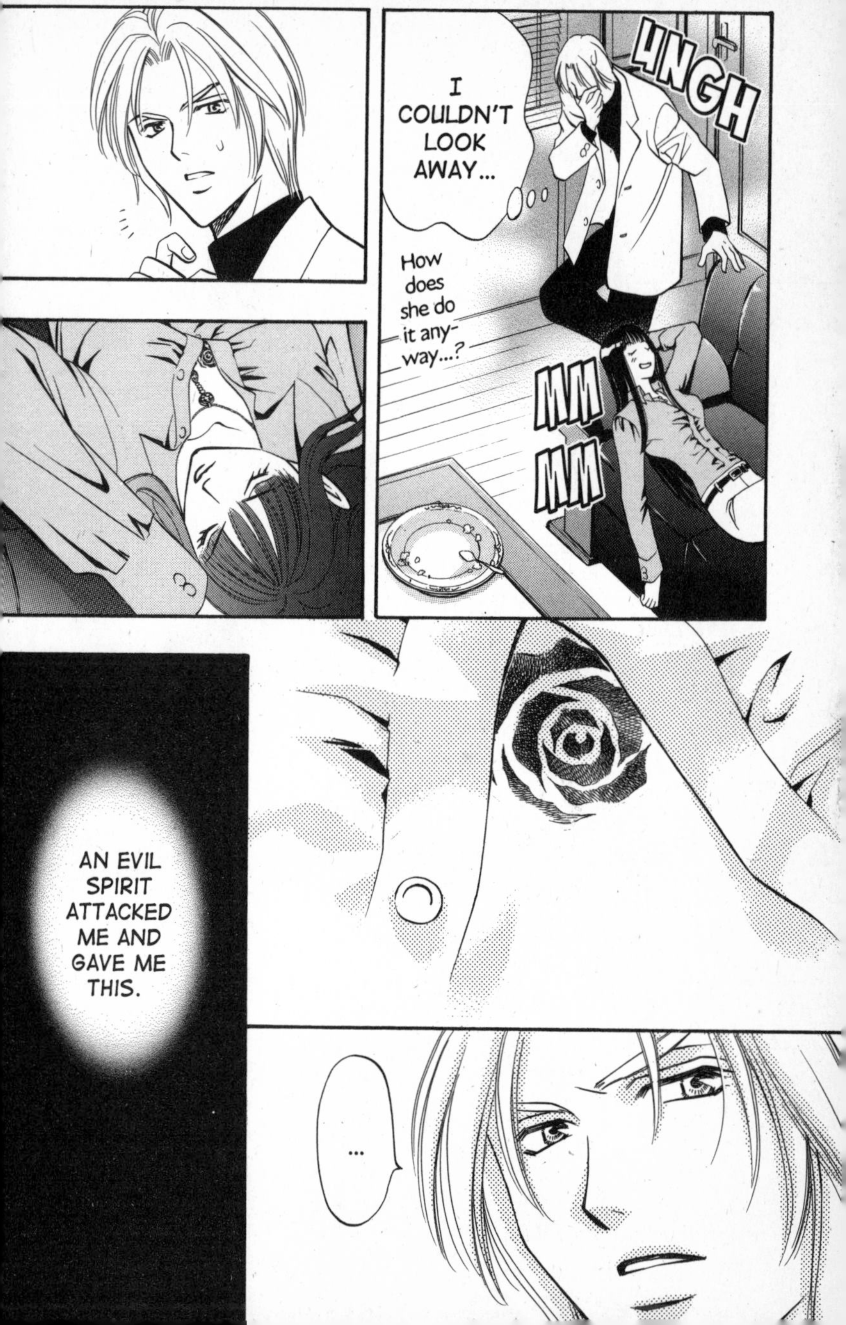
UNGH
I COULDN'T LOOK AWAY...
How does she do it any-way...?
MM MM
AN EVIL SPIRIT ATTACKED ME AND GAVE ME THIS.
...

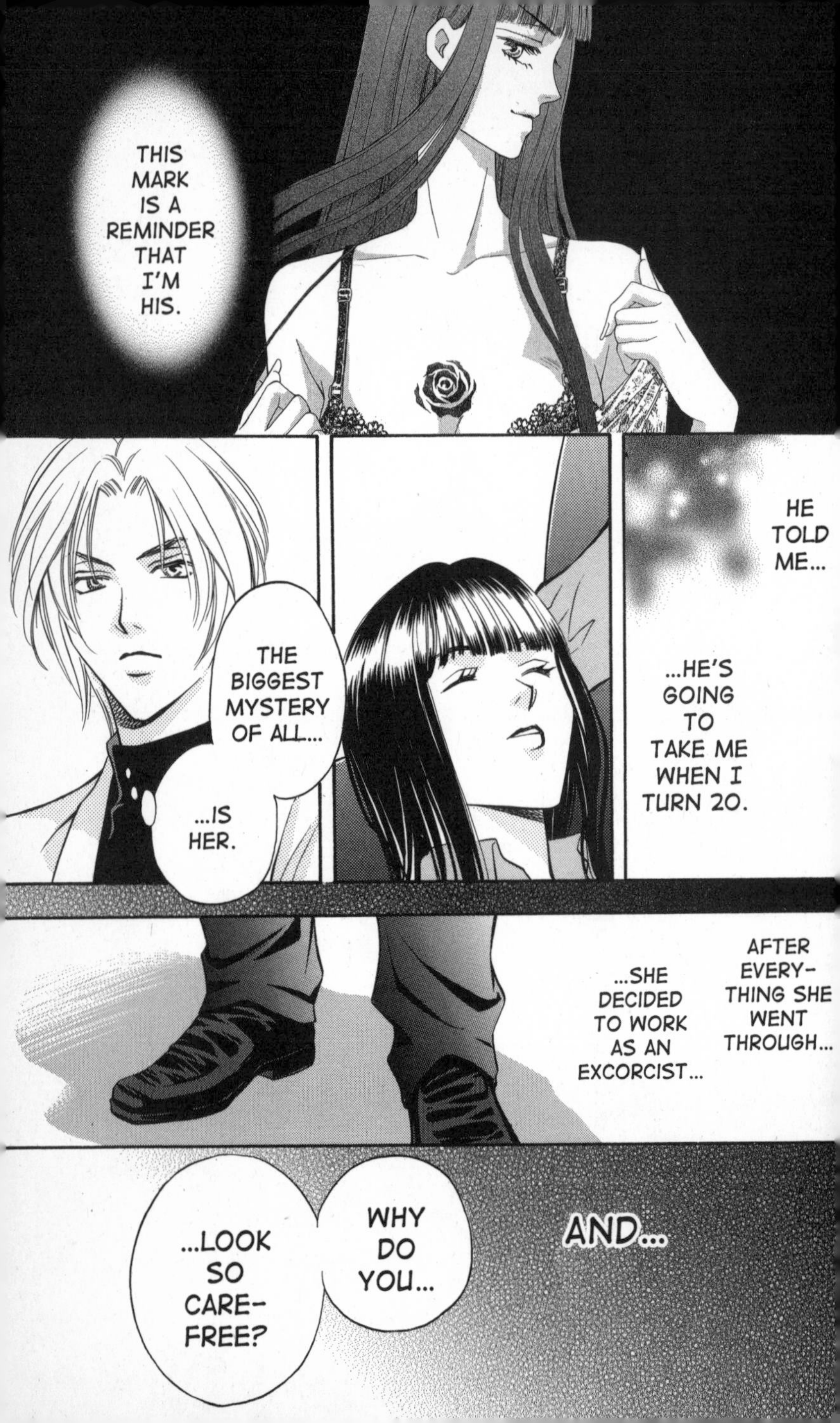
THIS MARK IS A REMINDER THAT I'M HIS.
HE TOLD ME...
...HE'S GOING TO TAKE ME WHEN I TURN 20.
THE BIGGEST MYSTERY OF ALL...
...IS HER.
AFTER EVERY-THING SHE WENT THROUGH...
...SHE DECIDED TO WORK AS AN EXCORCIST...
AND...
WHY DO YOU...
...LOOK SO CARE-FREE?

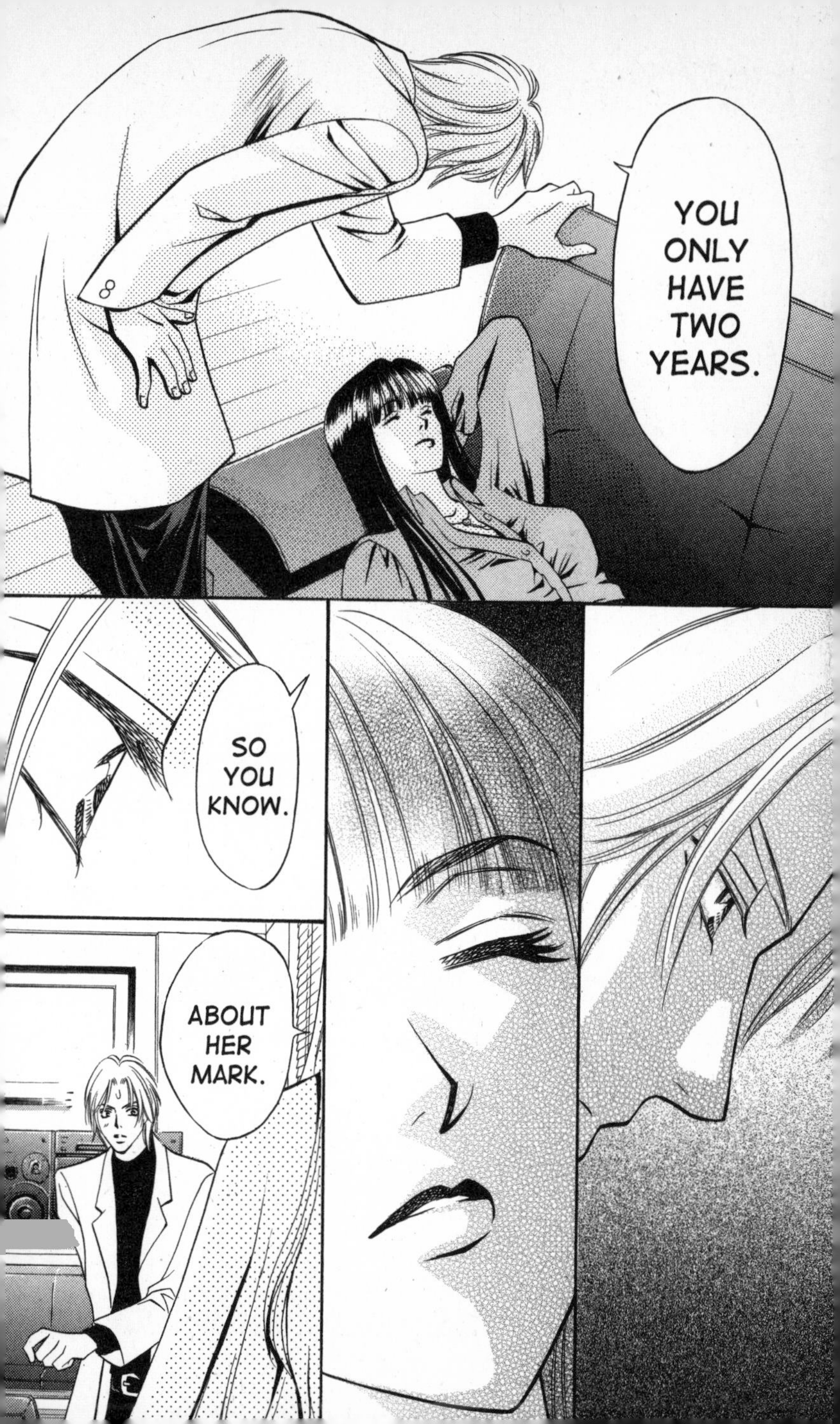
YOU ONLY HAVE TWO YEARS.
SO YOU KNOW.
ABOUT HER MARK.

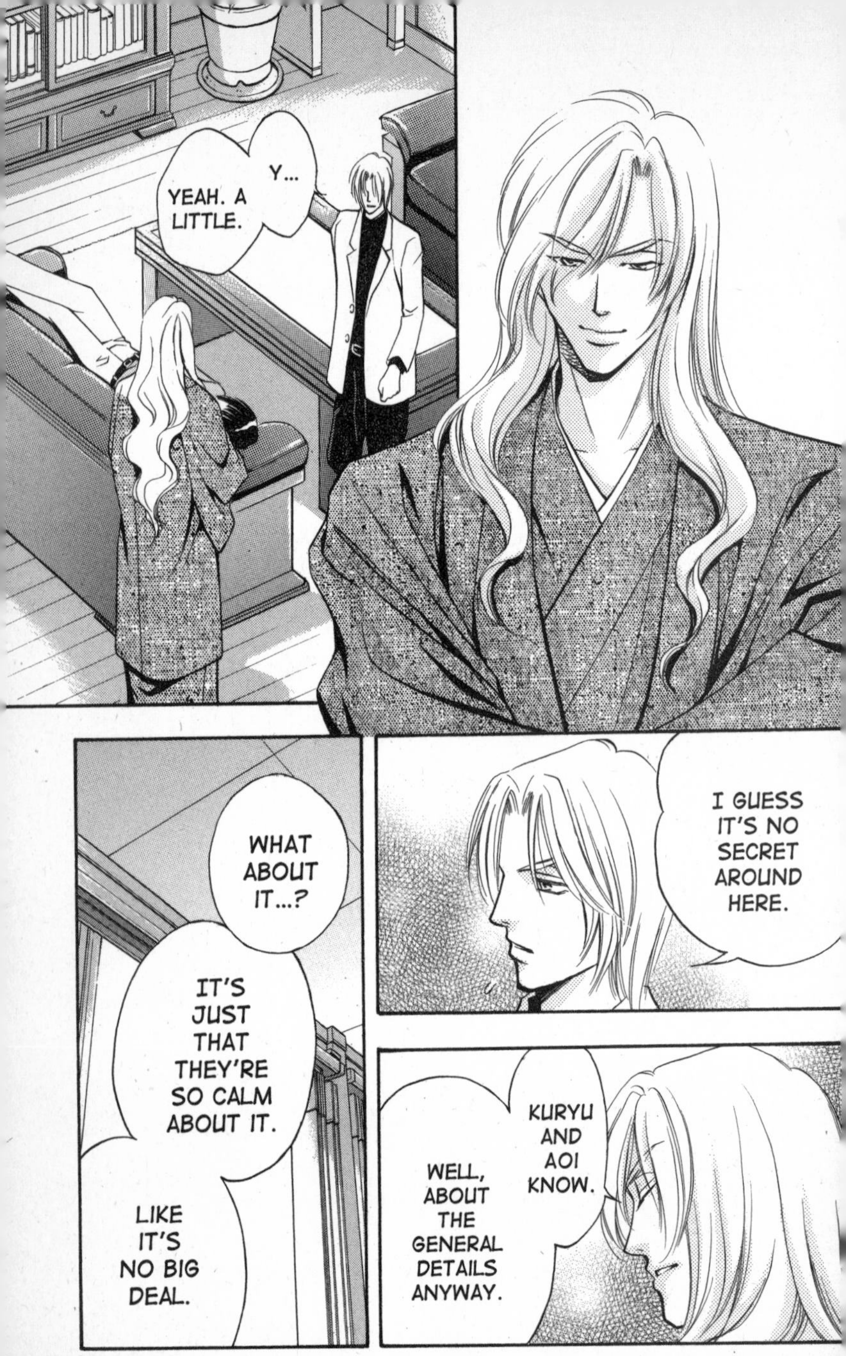
Y... YEAH. A LITTLE.
I GUESS IT'S NO SECRET AROUND HERE.
KURYU AND AOI KNOW.
WELL, ABOUT THE GENERAL DETAILS ANYWAY.
WHAT ABOUT IT...?
IT'S JUST THAT THEY'RE SO CALM ABOUT IT.
LIKE IT'S NO BIG DEAL.

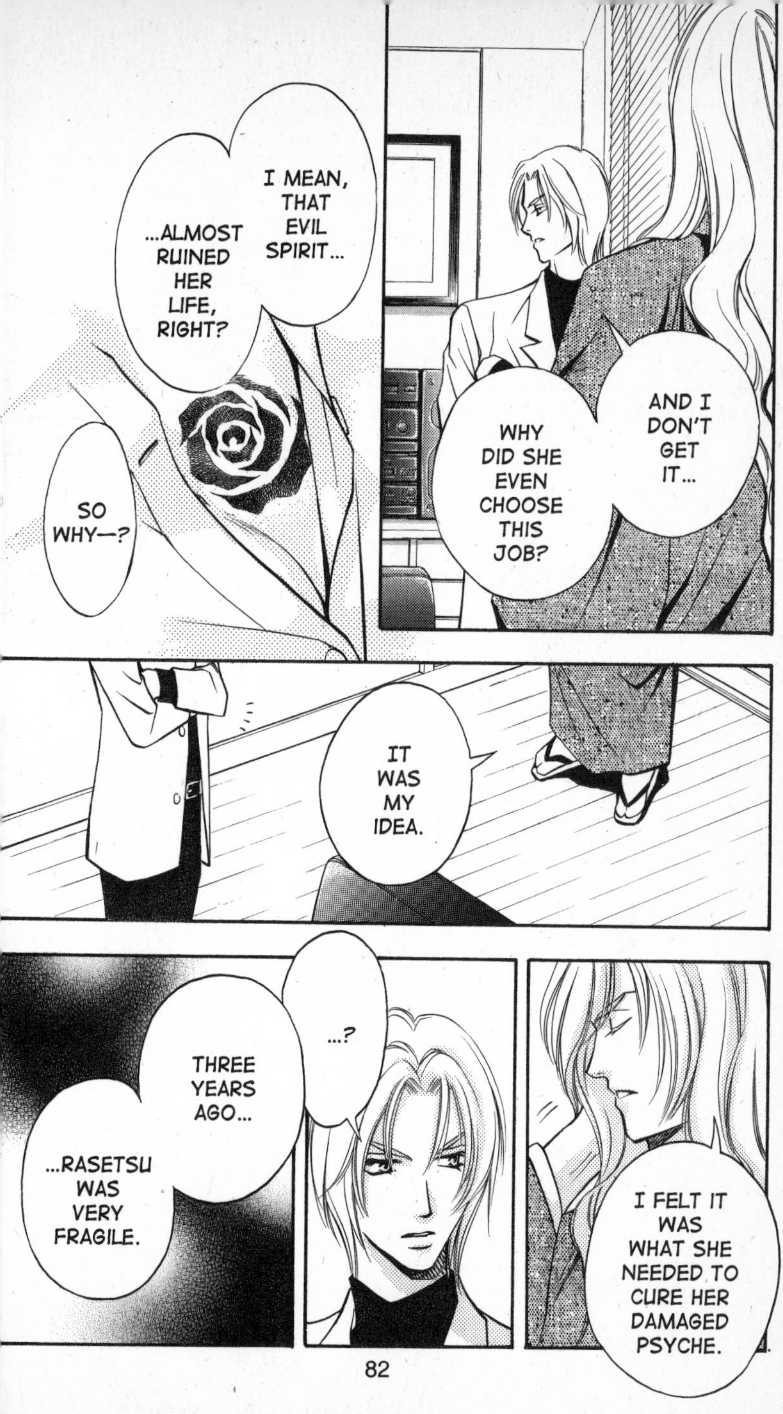
AND I DON'T GET IT...
WHY DID SHE EVEN CHOOSE THIS JOB?
I MEAN, THAT EVIL SPIRIT...
...ALMOST RUINED HER LIFE, RIGHT?
SO WHY—?
IT WAS MY IDEA.
I FELT IT WAS WHAT SHE NEEDED TO CURE HER DAMAGED PSYCHE.
...?
THREE YEARS AGO...
...RASETSU WAS VERY FRAGILE.

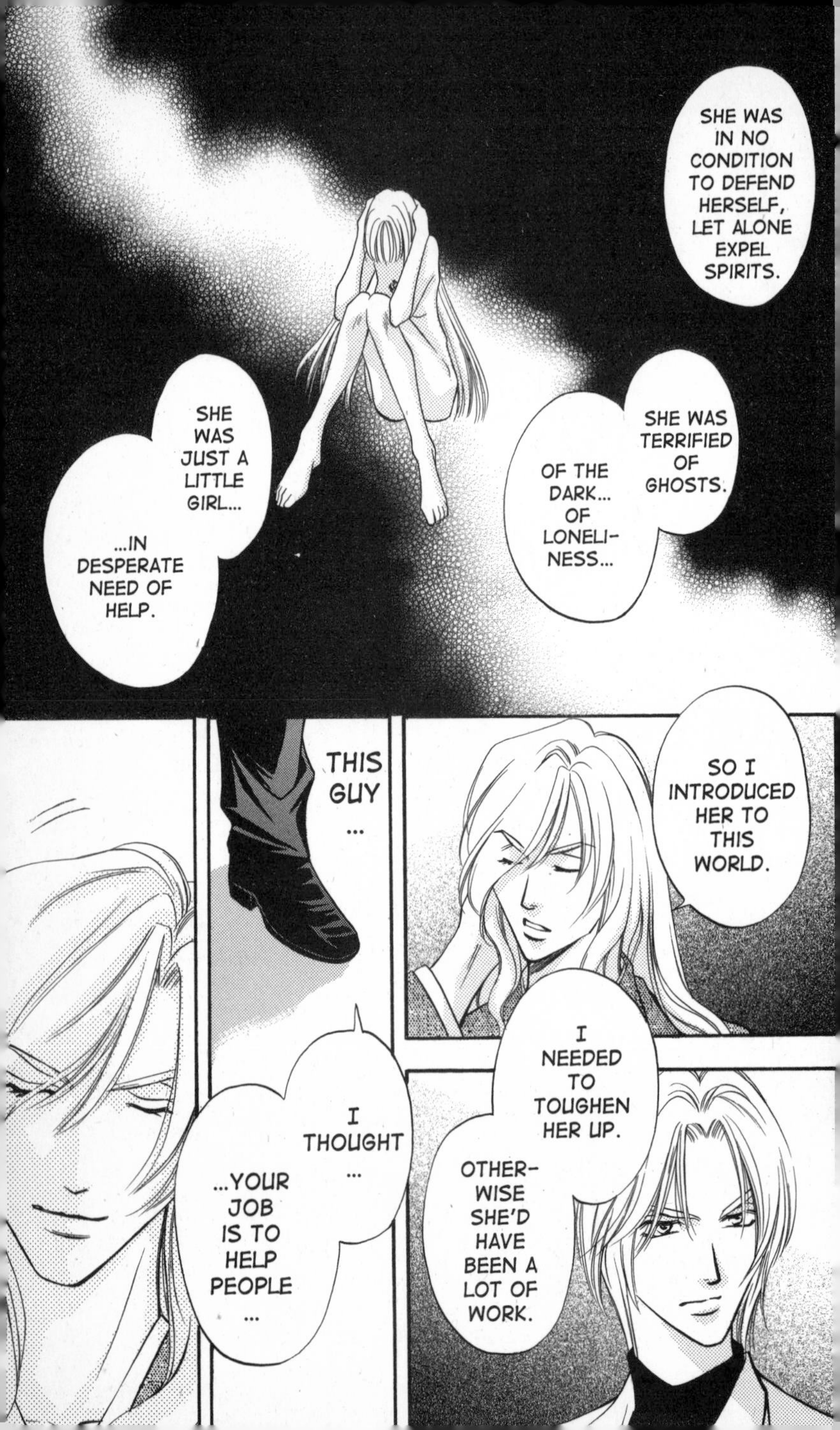
SHE WAS IN NO CONDITION TO DEFEND HERSELF, LET ALONE EXPEL SPIRITS.
SHE WAS TERRIFIED OF GHOSTS.
OF THE DARK... OF LONELI-NESS...
SHE WAS JUST A LITTLE GIRL...
...IN DESPERATE NEED OF HELP.
SO I INTRODUCED HER TO THIS WORLD.
I NEEDED TO TOUGHEN HER UP.
OTHER-WISE SHE'D HAVE BEEN A LOT OF WORK.
THIS GUY...
I THOUGHT...
...YOUR JOB IS TO HELP PEOPLE...

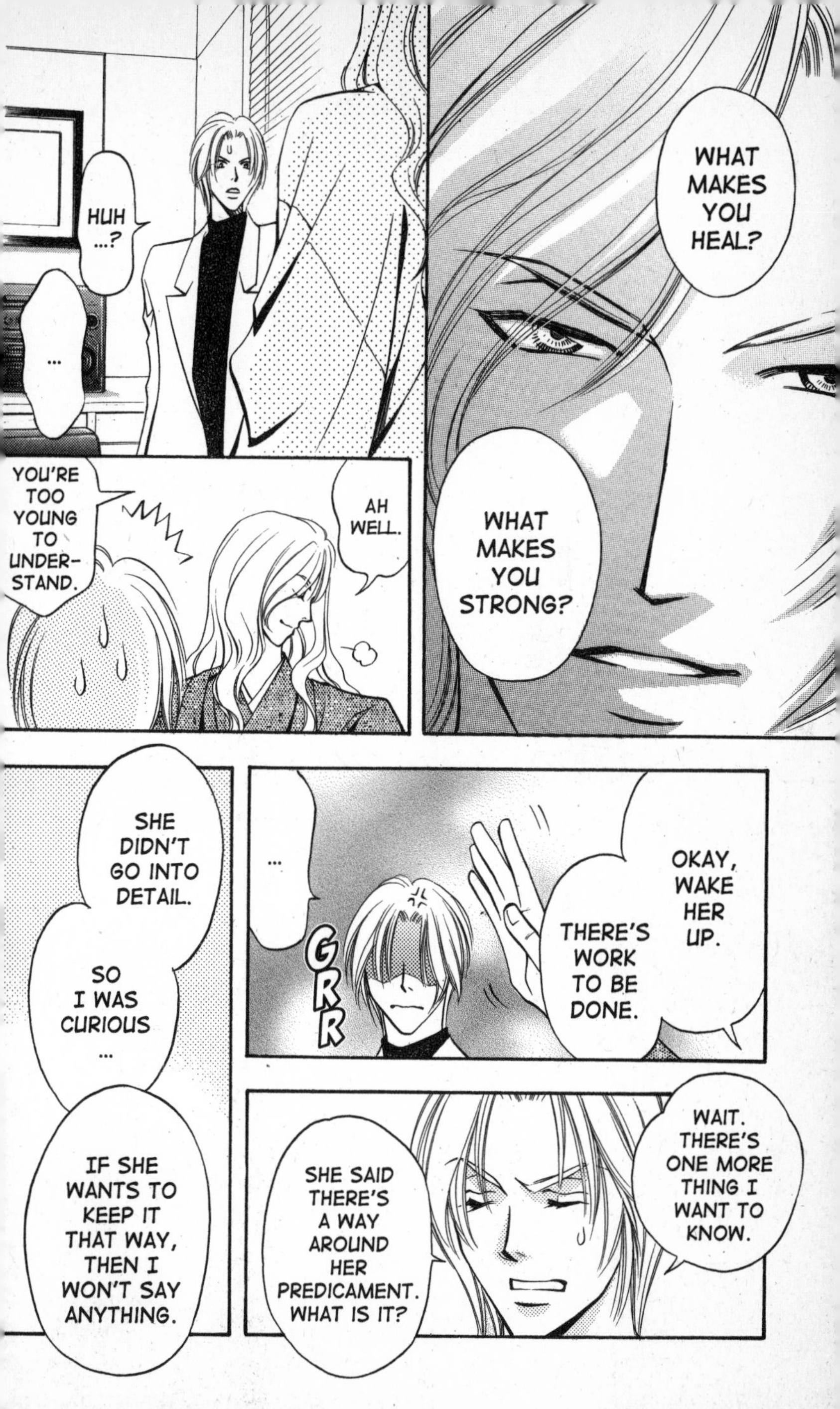
WHAT MAKES YOU HEAL?
WHAT MAKES YOU STRONG?
HUH ...?
...
AH WELL.
YOU'RE TOO YOUNG TO UNDER-STAND.
OKAY, WAKE HER UP.
THERE'S WORK TO BE DONE.
...
GRR
WAIT. THERE'S ONE MORE THING I WANT TO KNOW.
SHE SAID THERE'S A WAY AROUND HER PREDICAMENT. WHAT IS IT?
SHE DIDN'T GO INTO DETAIL.
SO I WAS CURIOUS ...
IF SHE WANTS TO KEEP IT THAT WAY, THEN I WON'T SAY ANYTHING.

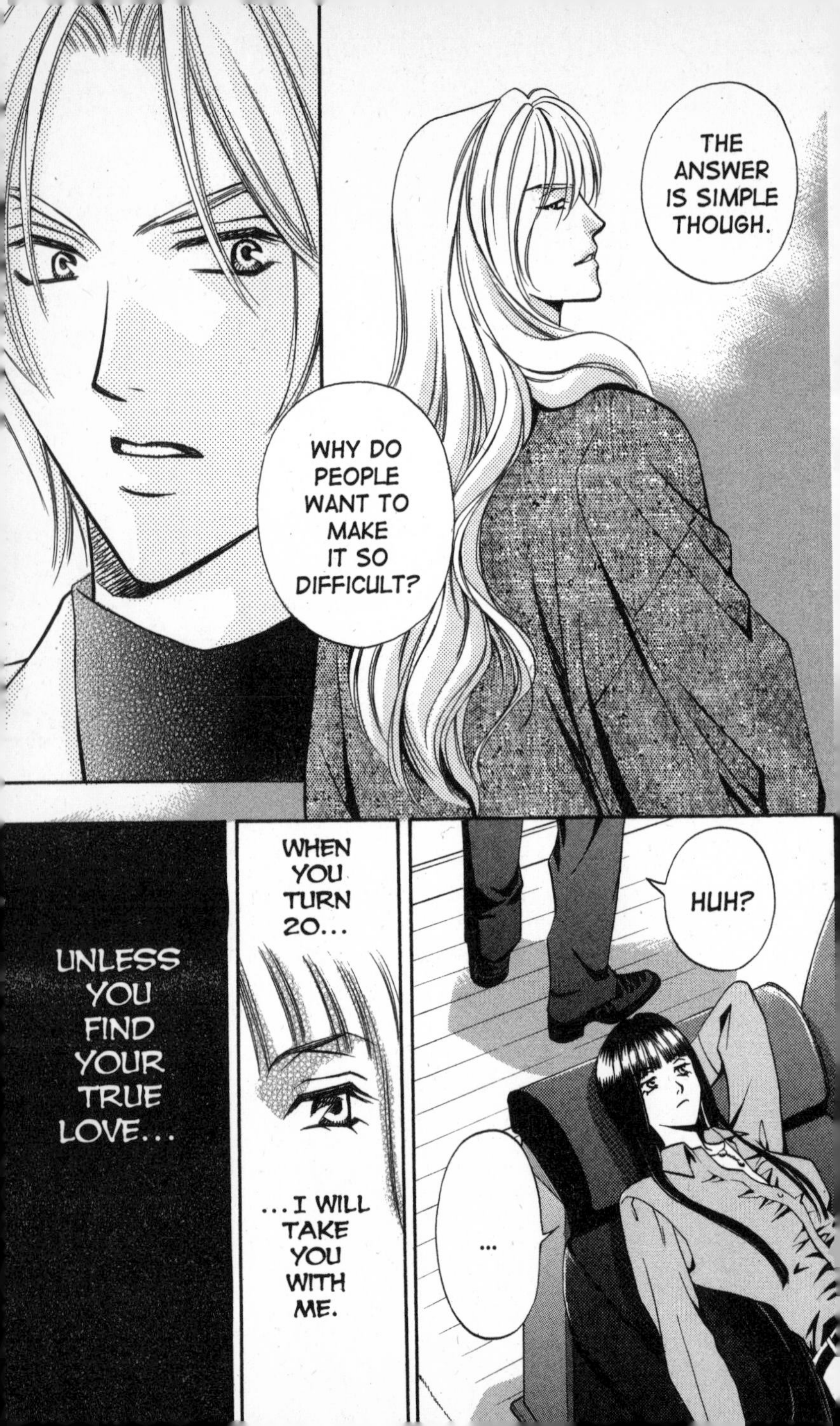
THE ANSWER IS SIMPLE THOUGH.
WHY DO PEOPLE WANT TO MAKE IT SO DIFFICULT?
HUH?
...
WHEN YOU TURN 20...
...I WILL TAKE YOU WITH ME.
UNLESS YOU FIND YOUR TRUE LOVE...

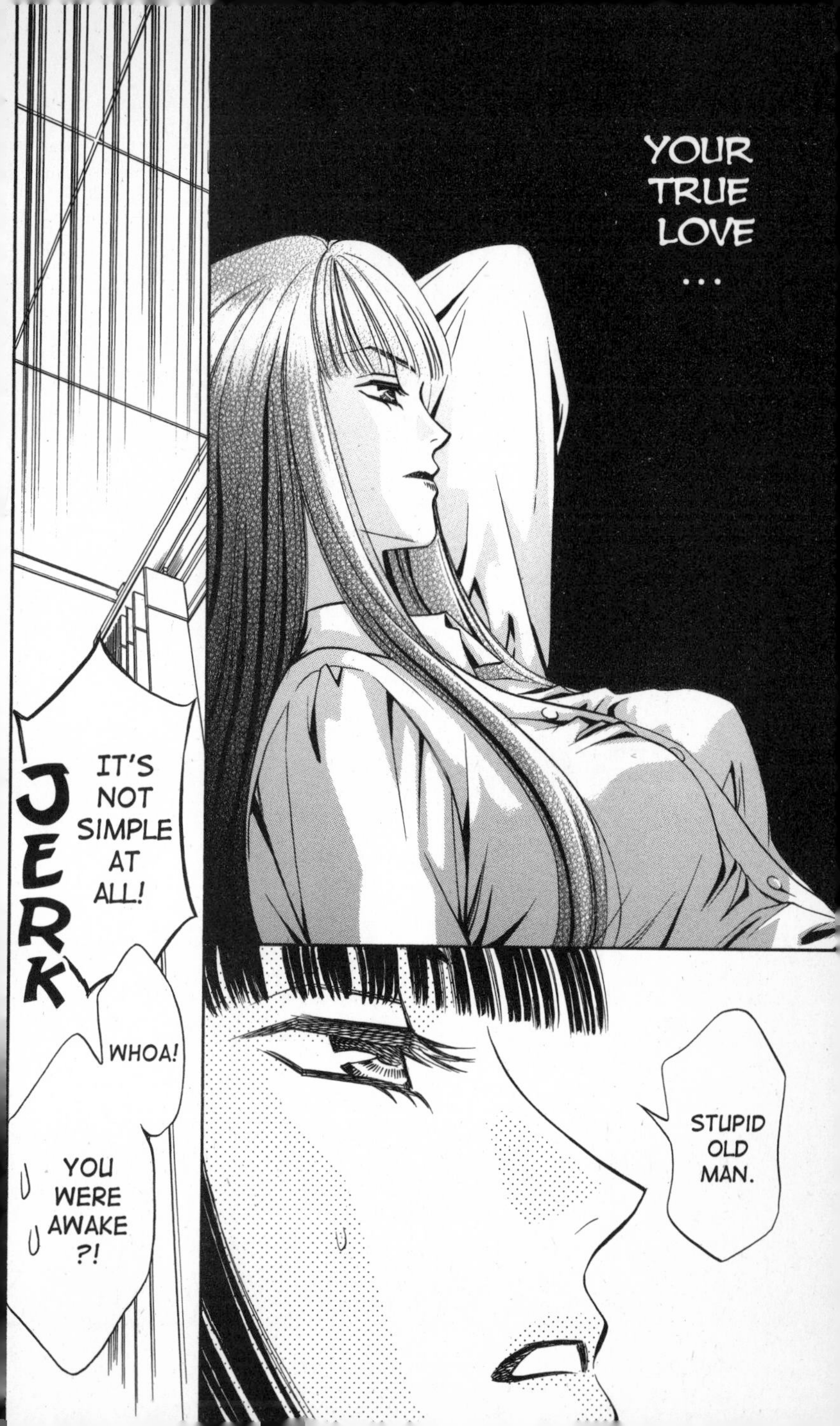
YOUR TRUE LOVE ...
STUPID OLD MAN.
IT'S NOT SIMPLE AT ALL!
JERK
WHOA!
YOU WERE AWAKE ?!

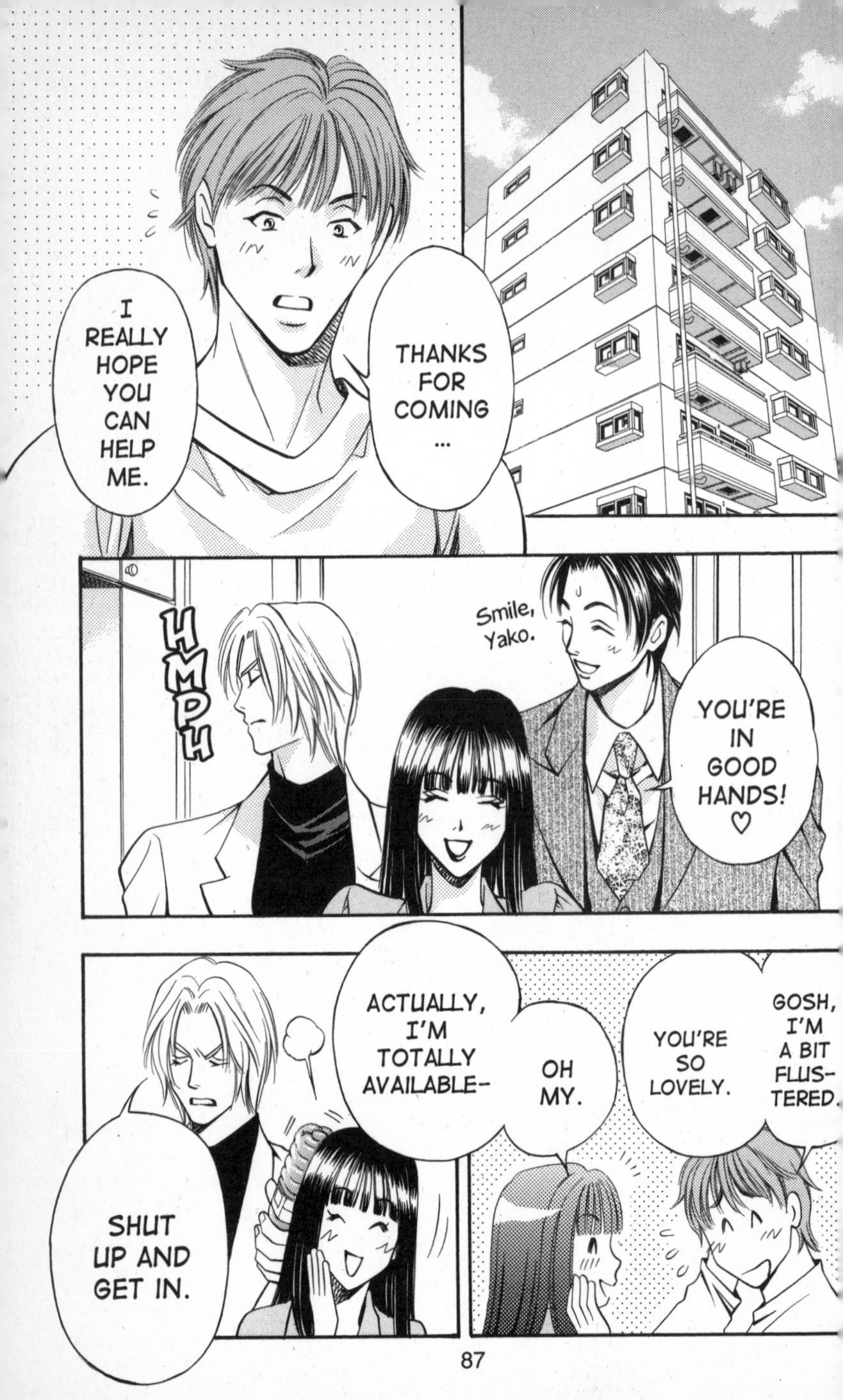
THANKS FOR COMING ...
I REALLY HOPE YOU CAN HELP ME.
Smile, Yako.
YOU'RE IN GOOD HANDS! ♡
HMPH
GOSH, I'M A BIT FLUSTERED.
YOU'RE SO LOVELY.
OH MY.
ACTUALLY, I'M TOTALLY AVAILABLE-
SHUT UP AND GET IN.

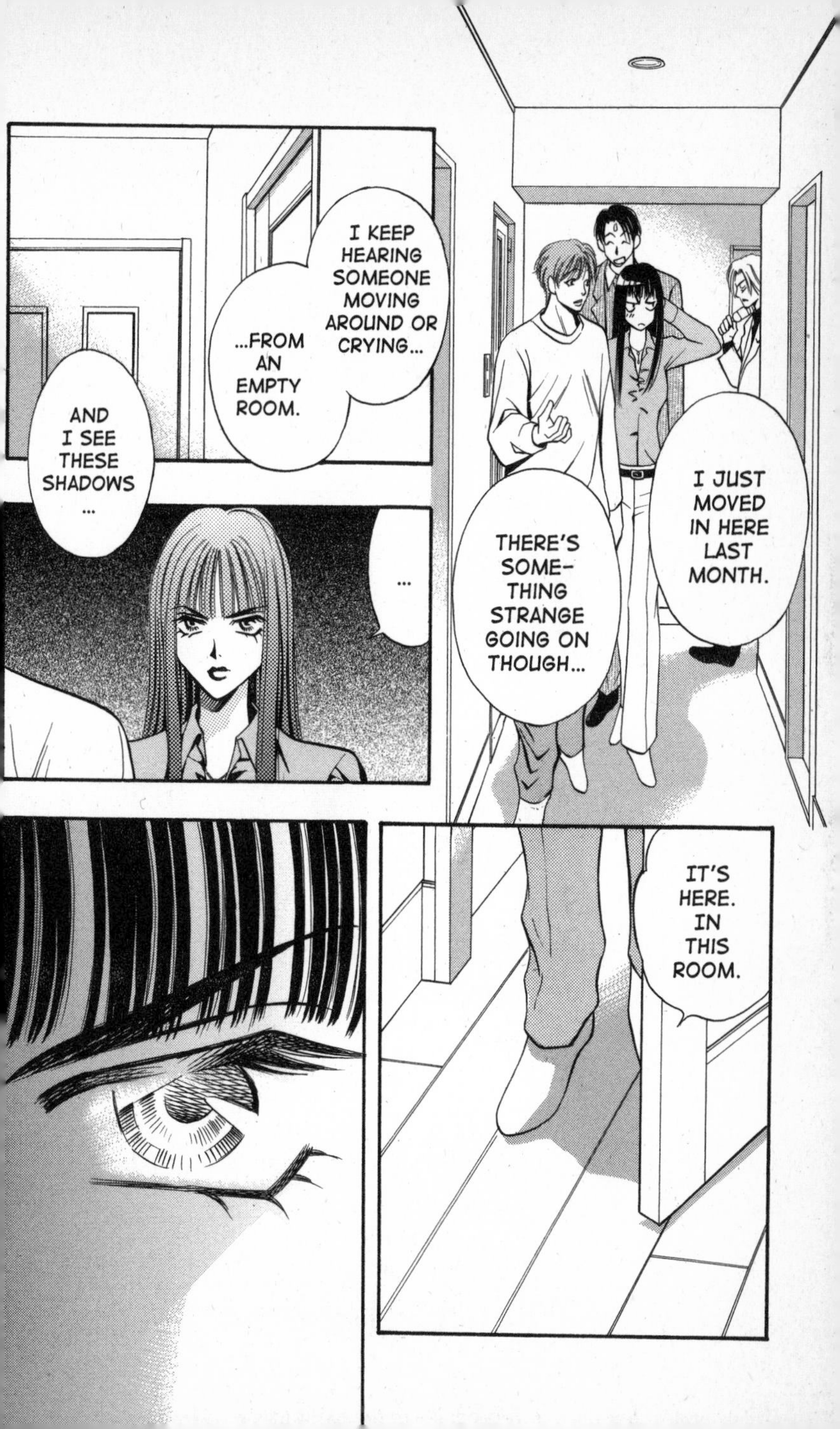
I JUST MOVED IN HERE LAST MONTH.
THERE'S SOME-THING STRANGE GOING ON THOUGH...
I KEEP HEARING SOMEONE MOVING AROUND OR CRYING...
...FROM AN EMPTY ROOM.
AND I SEE THESE SHADOWS...
...
IT'S HERE. IN THIS ROOM.

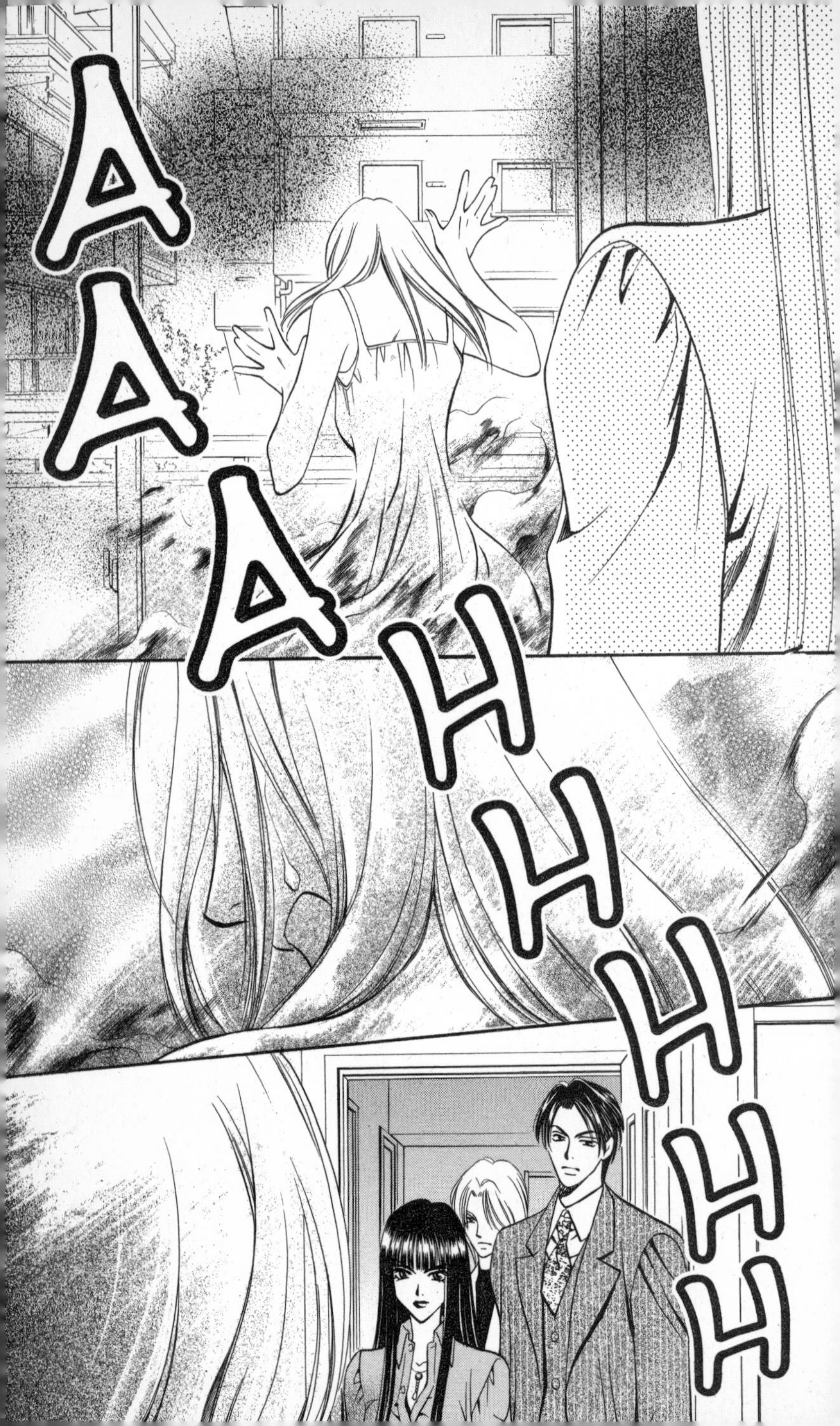
AAAHHHHHH

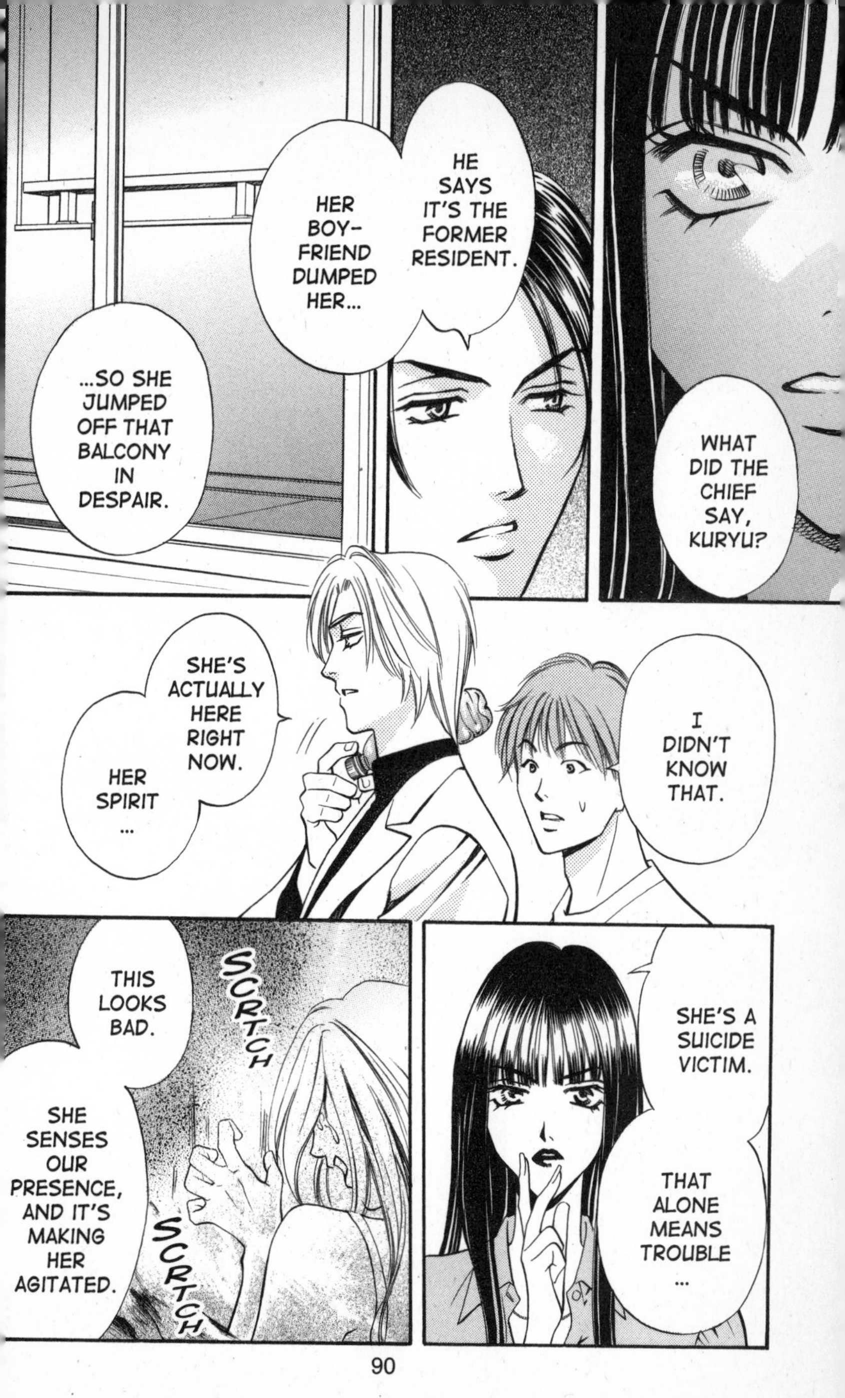
WHAT DID THE CHIEF SAY, KURYU?
HE SAYS IT'S THE FORMER RESIDENT.
HER BOY-FRIEND DUMPED HER...
...SO SHE JUMPED OFF THAT BALCONY IN DESPAIR.
I DIDN'T KNOW THAT.
SHE'S ACTUALLY HERE RIGHT NOW.
HER SPIRIT ...
SHE'S A SUICIDE VICTIM.
THAT ALONE MEANS TROUBLE ...
THIS LOOKS BAD.
SCRTCH
SHE SENSES OUR PRESENCE, AND IT'S MAKING HER AGITATED.
SCRTCH

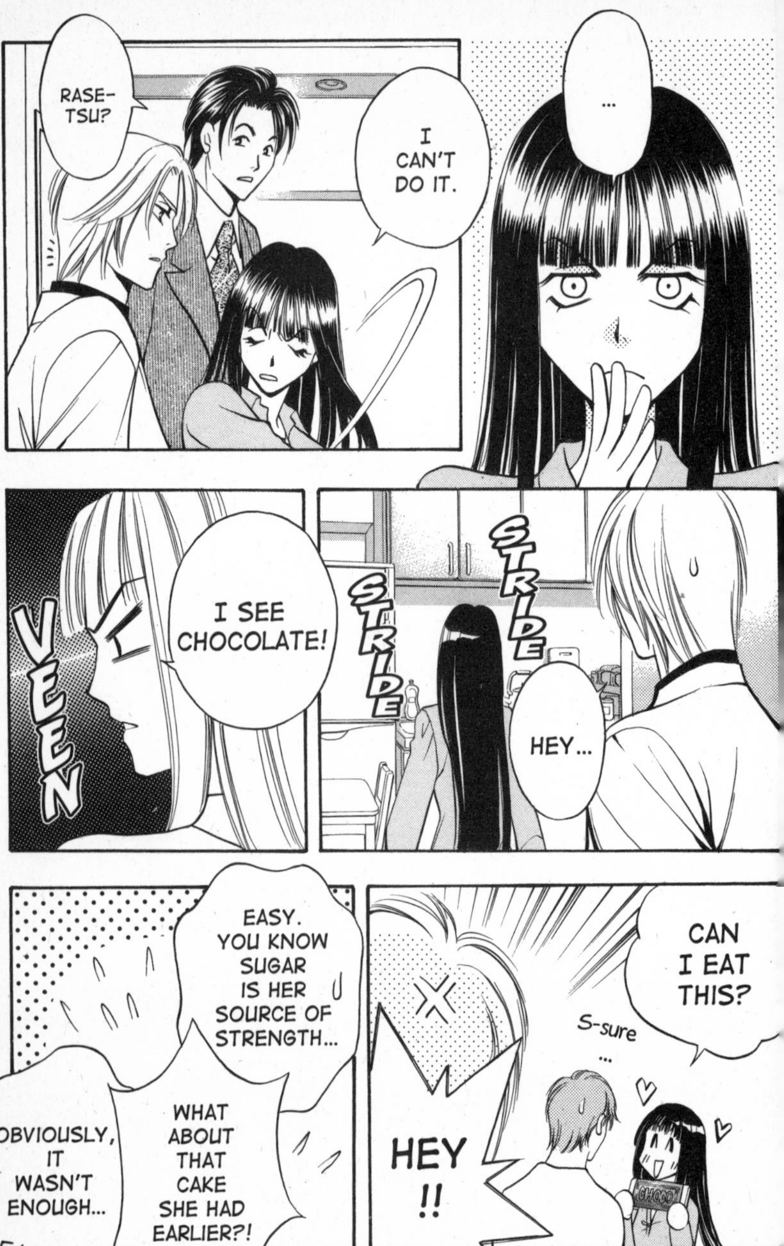
...
I CAN'T DO IT.
RASE-TSU?
STRIDE STRIDE
HEY...
I SEE CHOCOLATE!
VEEN
CAN I EAT THIS?
S-sure ...
HEY !!
CHOCO
EASY. YOU KNOW SUGAR IS HER SOURCE OF STRENGTH...
WHAT ABOUT THAT CAKE SHE HAD EARLIER?!
OBVIOUSLY, IT WASN'T ENOUGH...
Frightening...

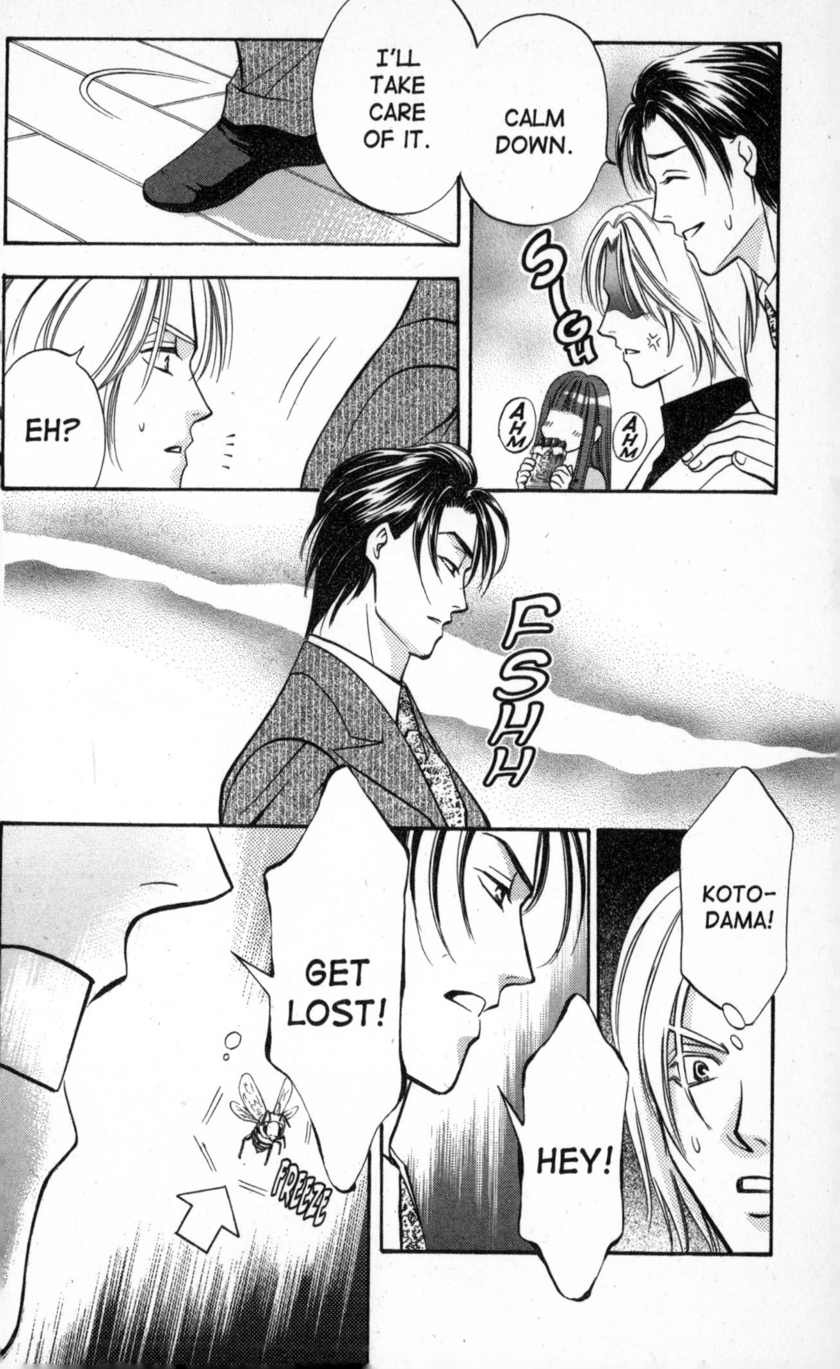
CALM DOWN.
SIGH
AHM
AHM
I'LL TAKE CARE OF IT.
EH?
FSHH
KOTO-DAMA!
HEY!
GET LOST!
FREEZE

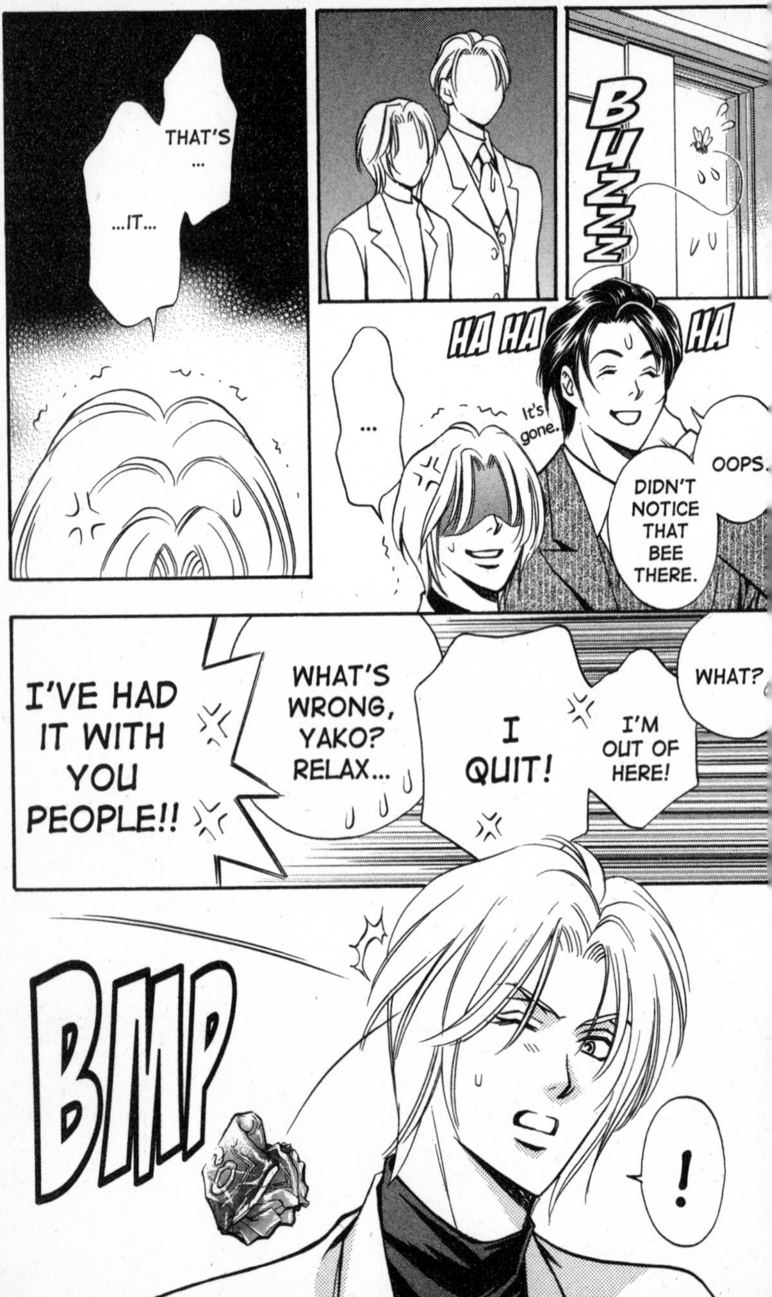
BUZZZ
HA HA HA
OOPS.
DIDN'T NOTICE THAT BEE THERE.
It's gone.
...
THAT'S ...
...IT...
WHAT?
I'M OUT OF HERE!
I QUIT!
WHAT'S WRONG, YAKO? RELAX...
I'VE HAD IT WITH YOU PEOPLE!!
BMP
!

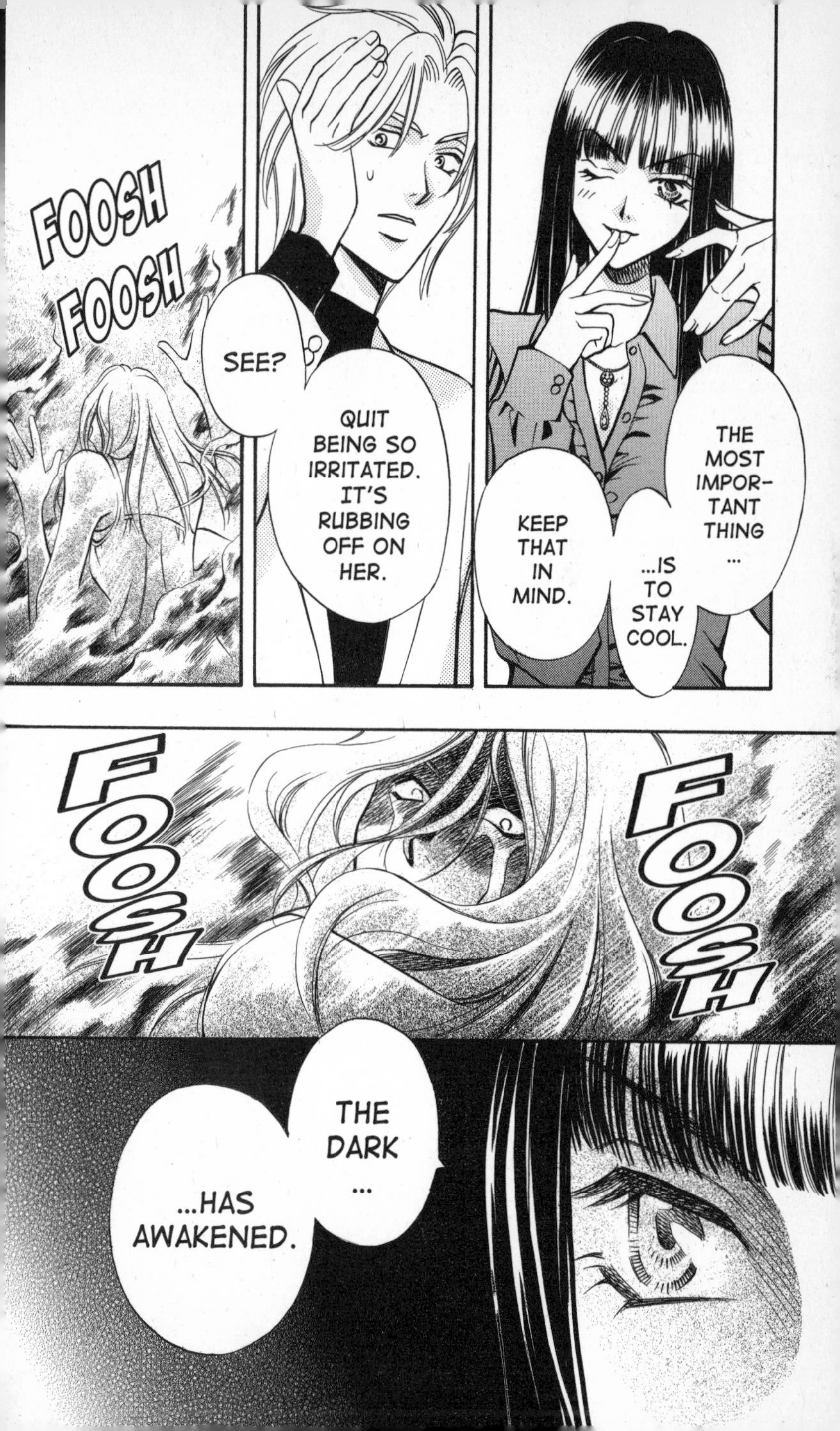
THE MOST IMPOR-TANT THING ...
...IS TO STAY COOL.
KEEP THAT IN MIND.
QUIT BEING SO IRRITATED. IT'S RUBBING OFF ON HER.
SEE?
FOOSH FOOSH
FOOSH
FOOSH
THE DARK ...
...HAS AWAKENED.

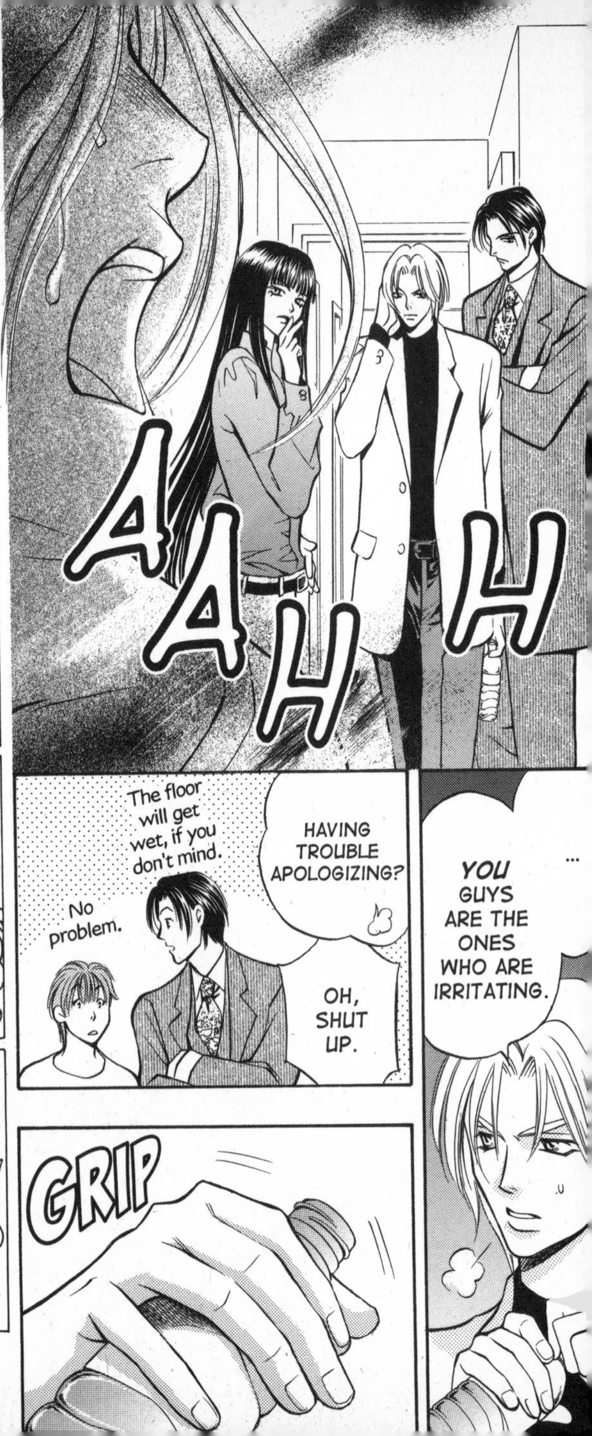
AAHH
...
YOU GUYS ARE THE ONES WHO ARE IRRITATING.
HAVING TROUBLE APOLOGIZING?
OH, SHUT UP.
The floor will get wet, if you don't mind.
No problem.
GRIP

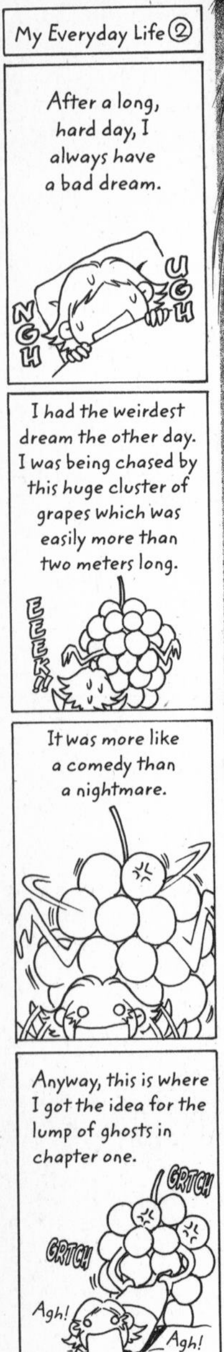
My Everyday Life ②
After a long, hard day, I always have a bad dream.
UGH
NGH
I had the weirdest dream the other day. I was being chased by this huge cluster of grapes which was easily more than two meters long.
EEEK!!
It was more like a comedy than a nightmare.
Anyway, this is where I got the idea for the lump of ghosts in chapter one.
GRTCH
GRTCH
Agh!
Agh!

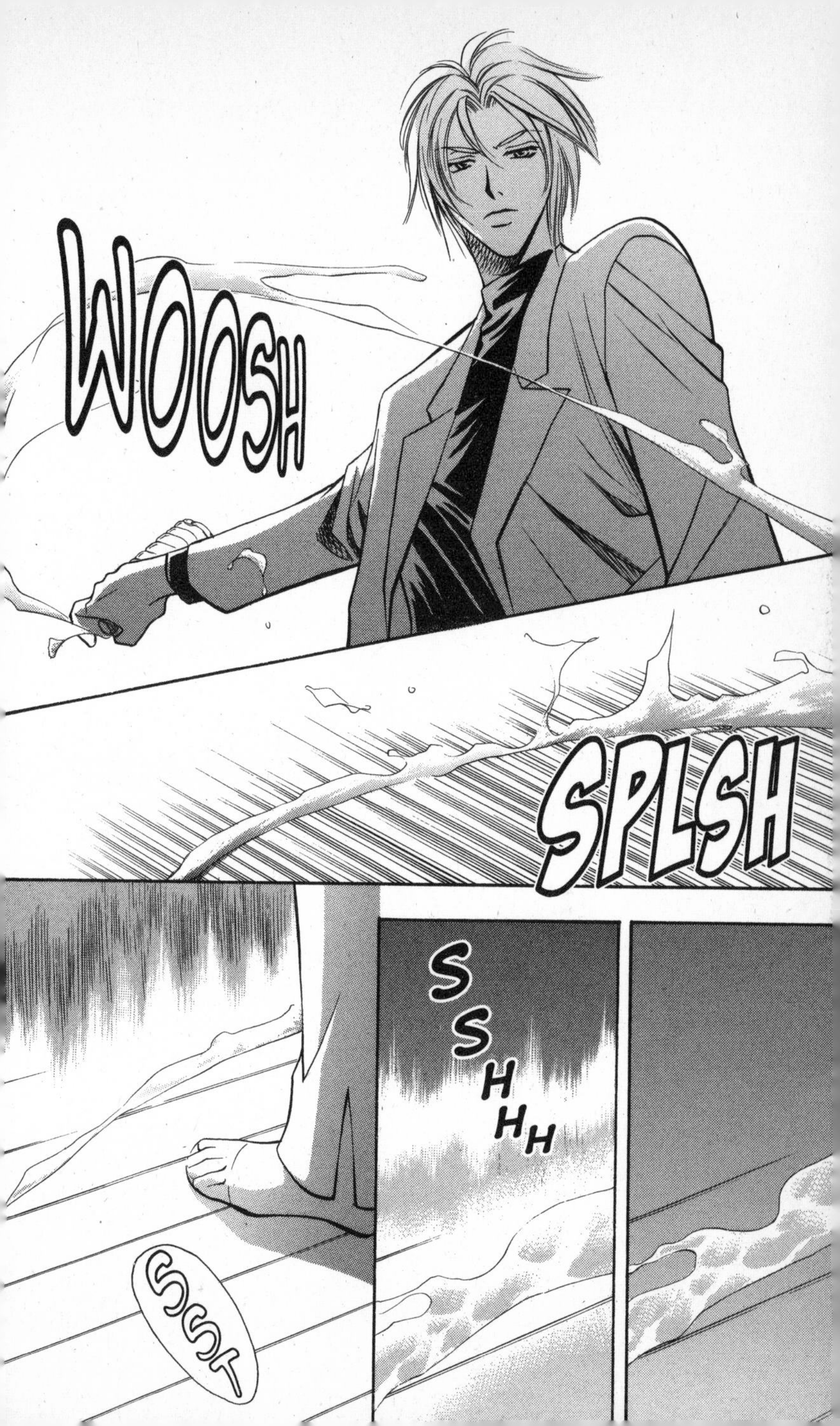
WOOSH
SPLSH
SSHHH
SSST

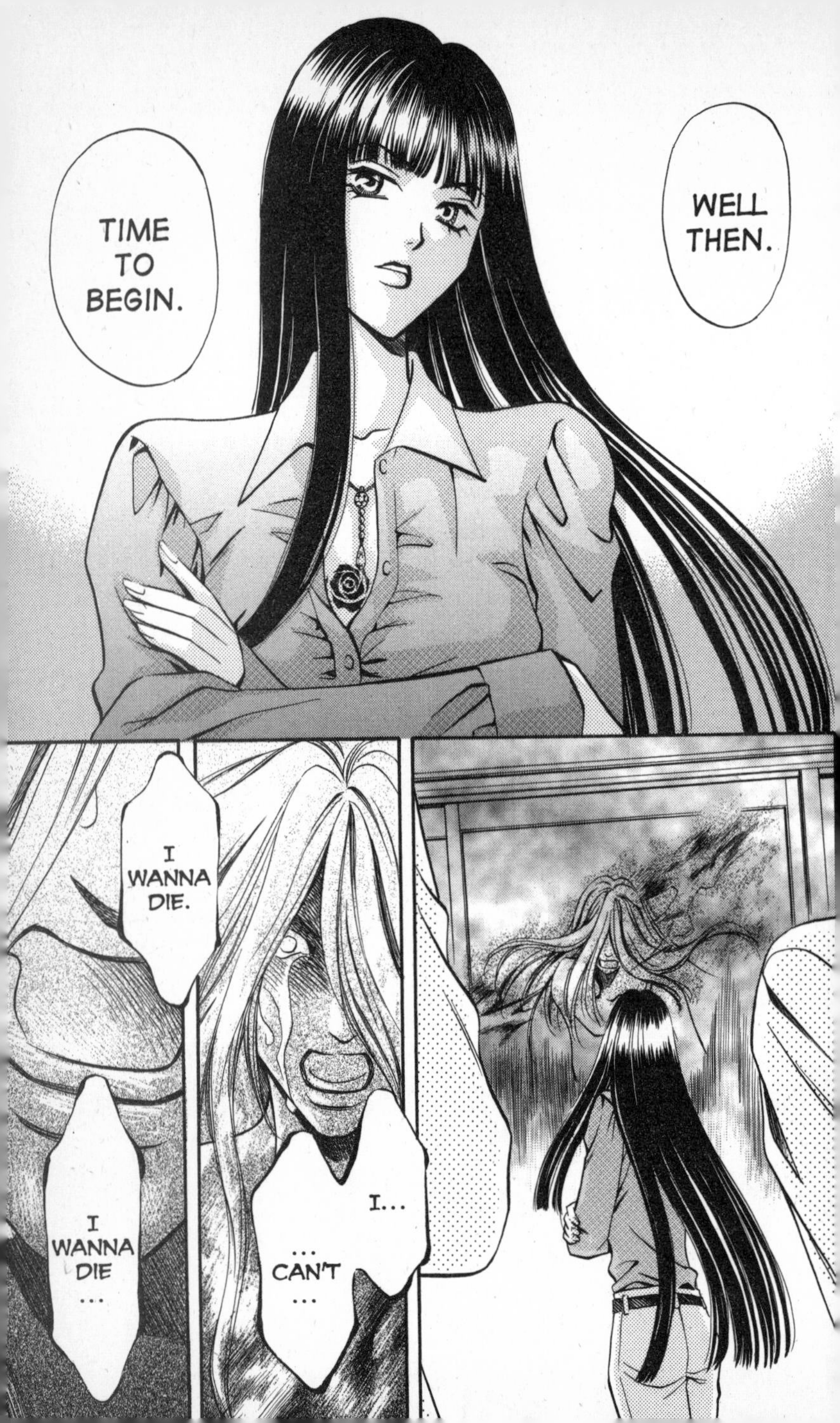
WELL THEN.
TIME TO BEGIN.
I... ...CAN'T ...
I WANNA DIE.
I WANNA DIE ...

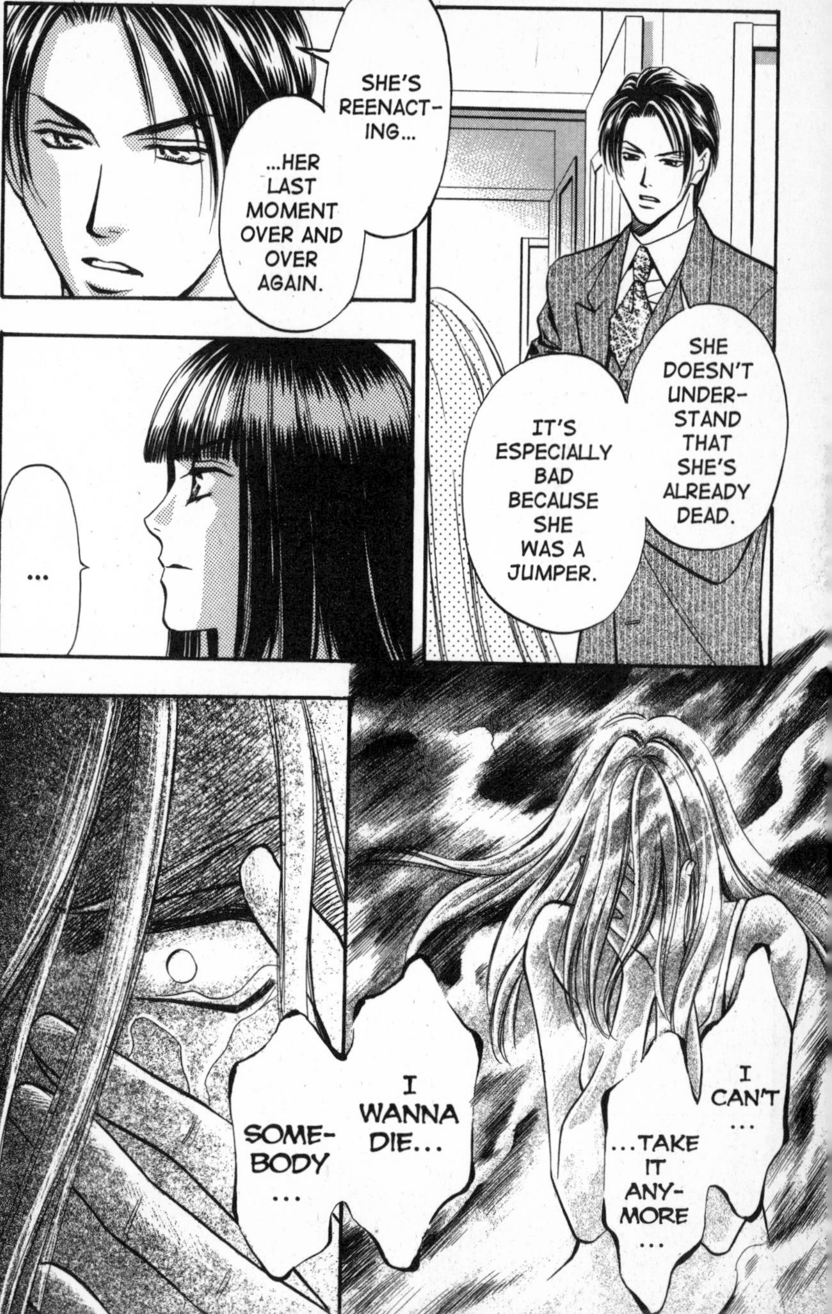
SHE'S REENACTING...
...HER LAST MOMENT OVER AND OVER AGAIN.
SHE DOESN'T UNDERSTAND THAT SHE'S ALREADY DEAD.
IT'S ESPECIALLY BAD BECAUSE SHE WAS A JUMPER.
...
I CAN'T...
...TAKE IT ANYMORE...
I WANNA DIE...
SOMEBODY...

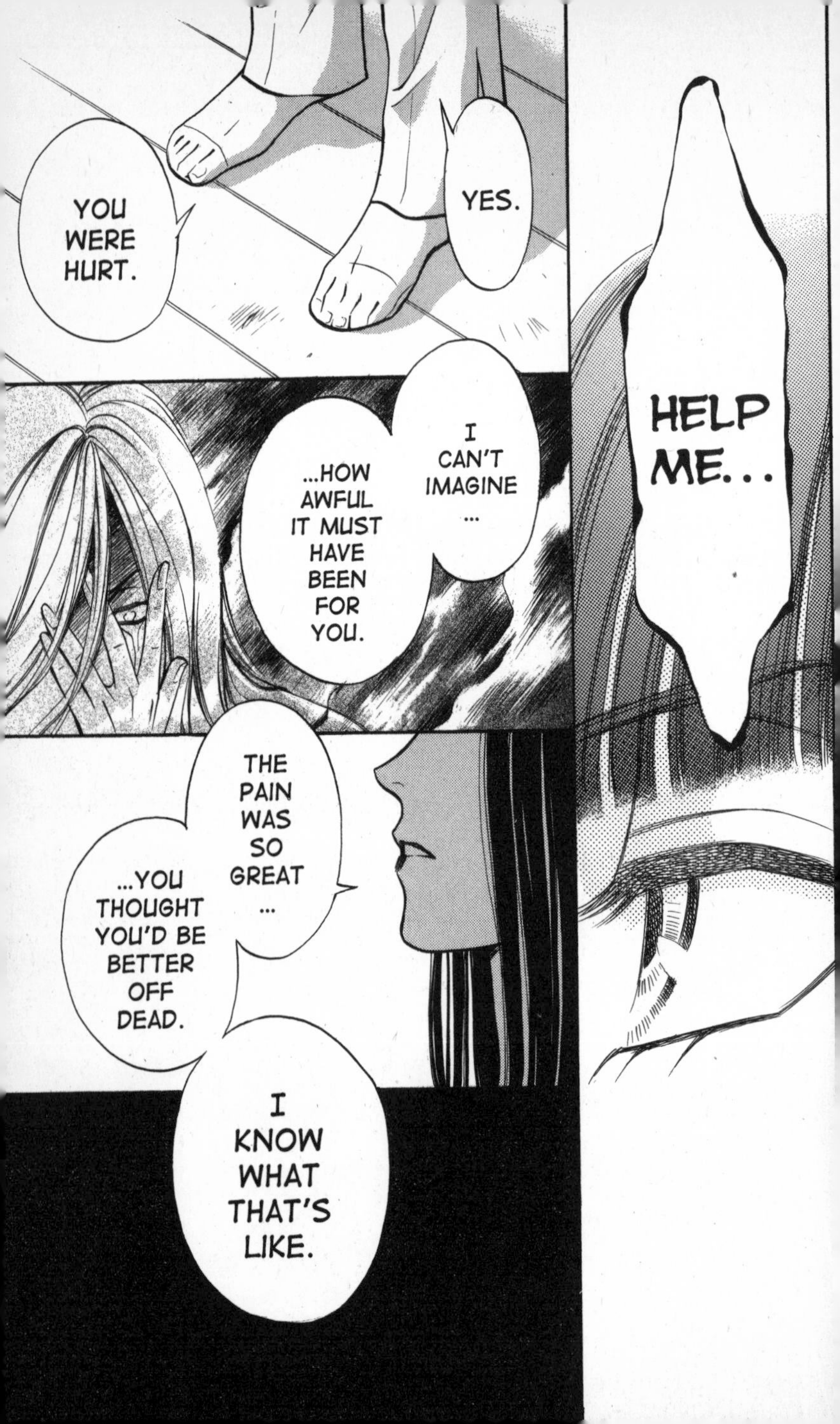
HELP ME...
YES.
YOU WERE HURT.
I CAN'T IMAGINE...
...HOW AWFUL IT MUST HAVE BEEN FOR YOU.
THE PAIN WAS SO GREAT...
...YOU THOUGHT YOU'D BE BETTER OFF DEAD.
I KNOW WHAT THAT'S LIKE.

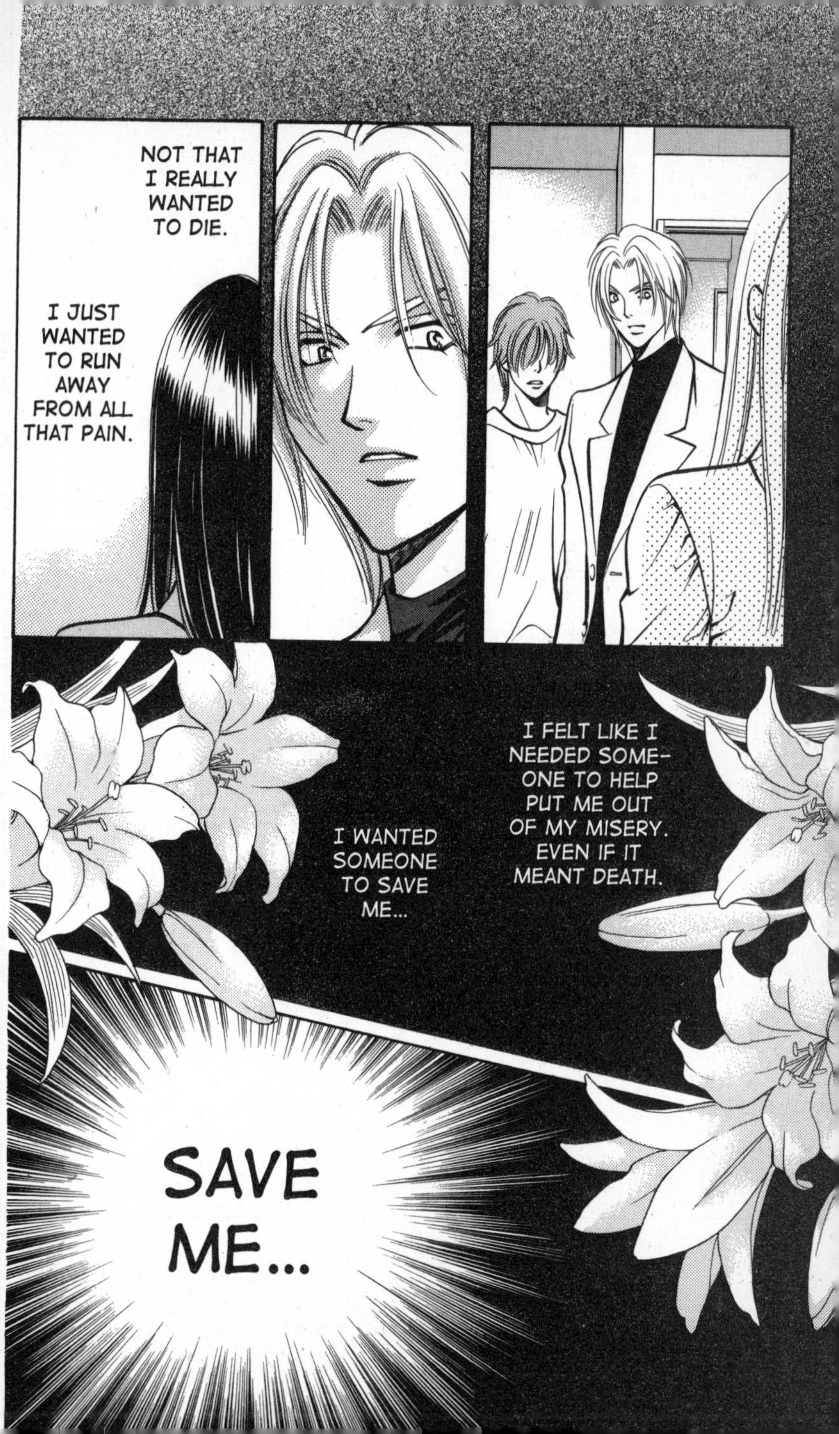
NOT THAT I REALLY WANTED TO DIE.
I JUST WANTED TO RUN AWAY FROM ALL THAT PAIN.
I FELT LIKE I NEEDED SOME-ONE TO HELP PUT ME OUT OF MY MISERY. EVEN IF IT MEANT DEATH.
I WANTED SOMEONE TO SAVE ME...
SAVE ME...

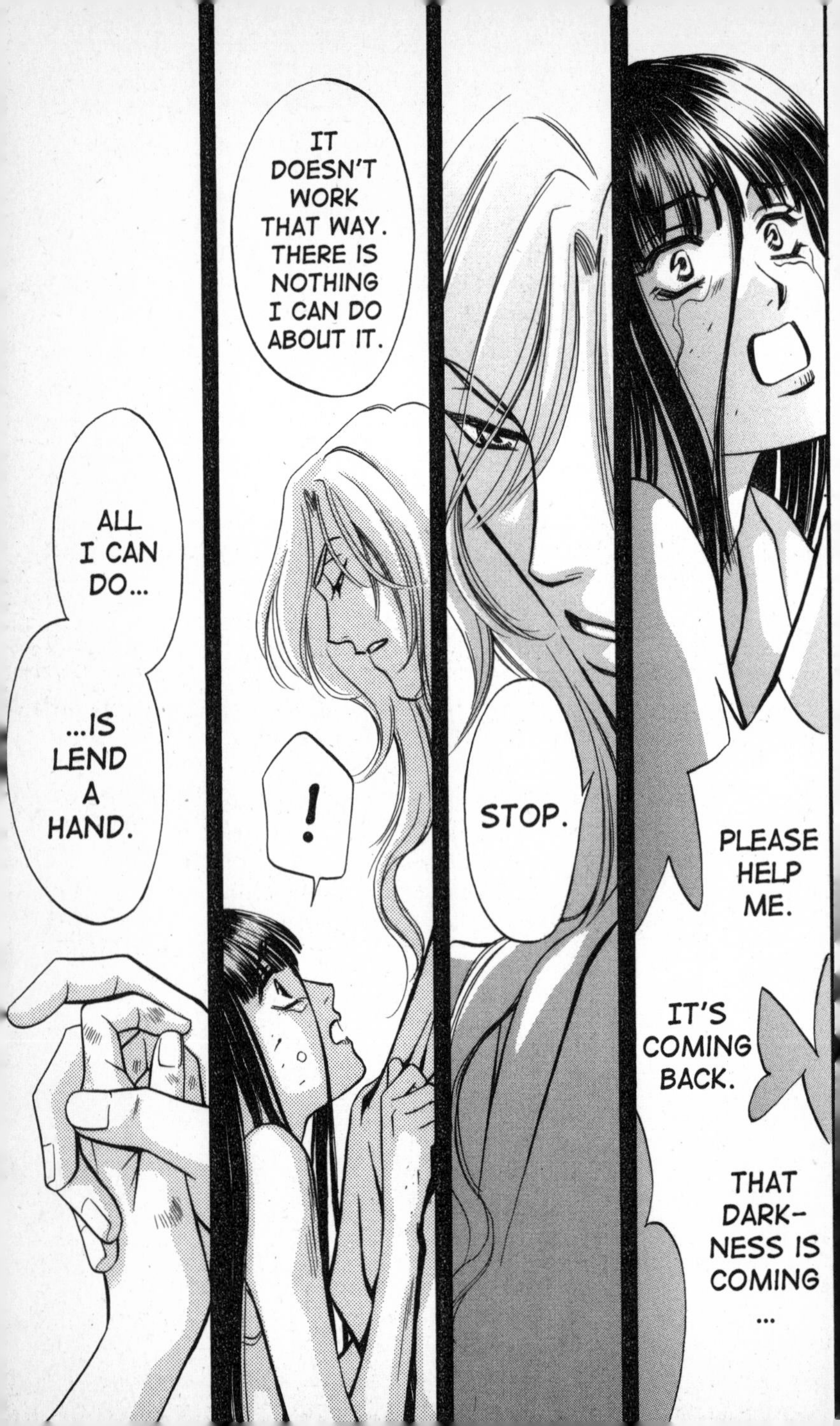
PLEASE HELP ME.
IT'S COMING BACK.
THAT DARKNESS IS COMING ...
STOP.
IT DOESN'T WORK THAT WAY. THERE IS NOTHING I CAN DO ABOUT IT.
!
ALL I CAN DO...
...IS LEND A HAND.

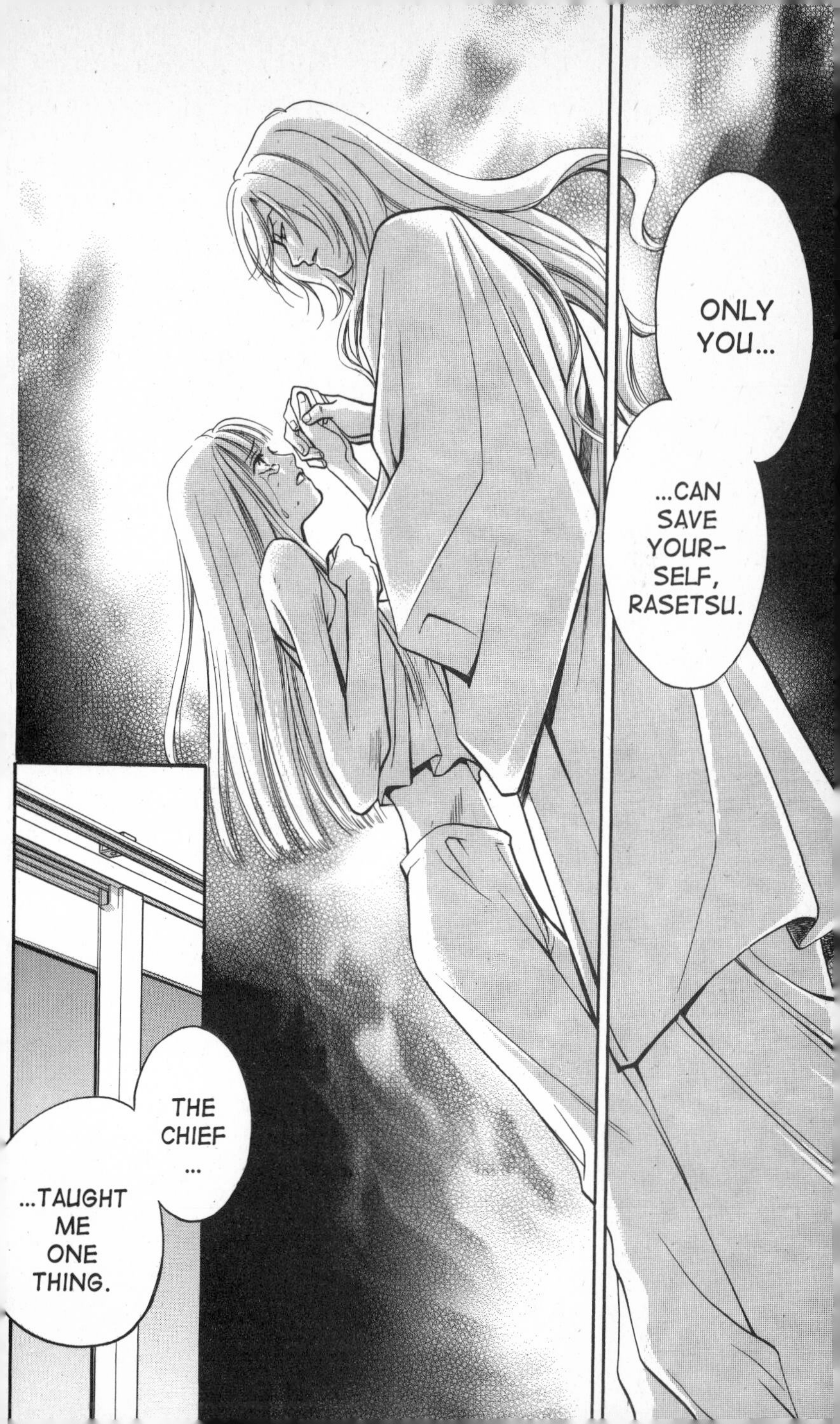
ONLY YOU...
...CAN SAVE YOURSELF, RASETSU.
THE CHIEF ...
...TAUGHT ME ONE THING.

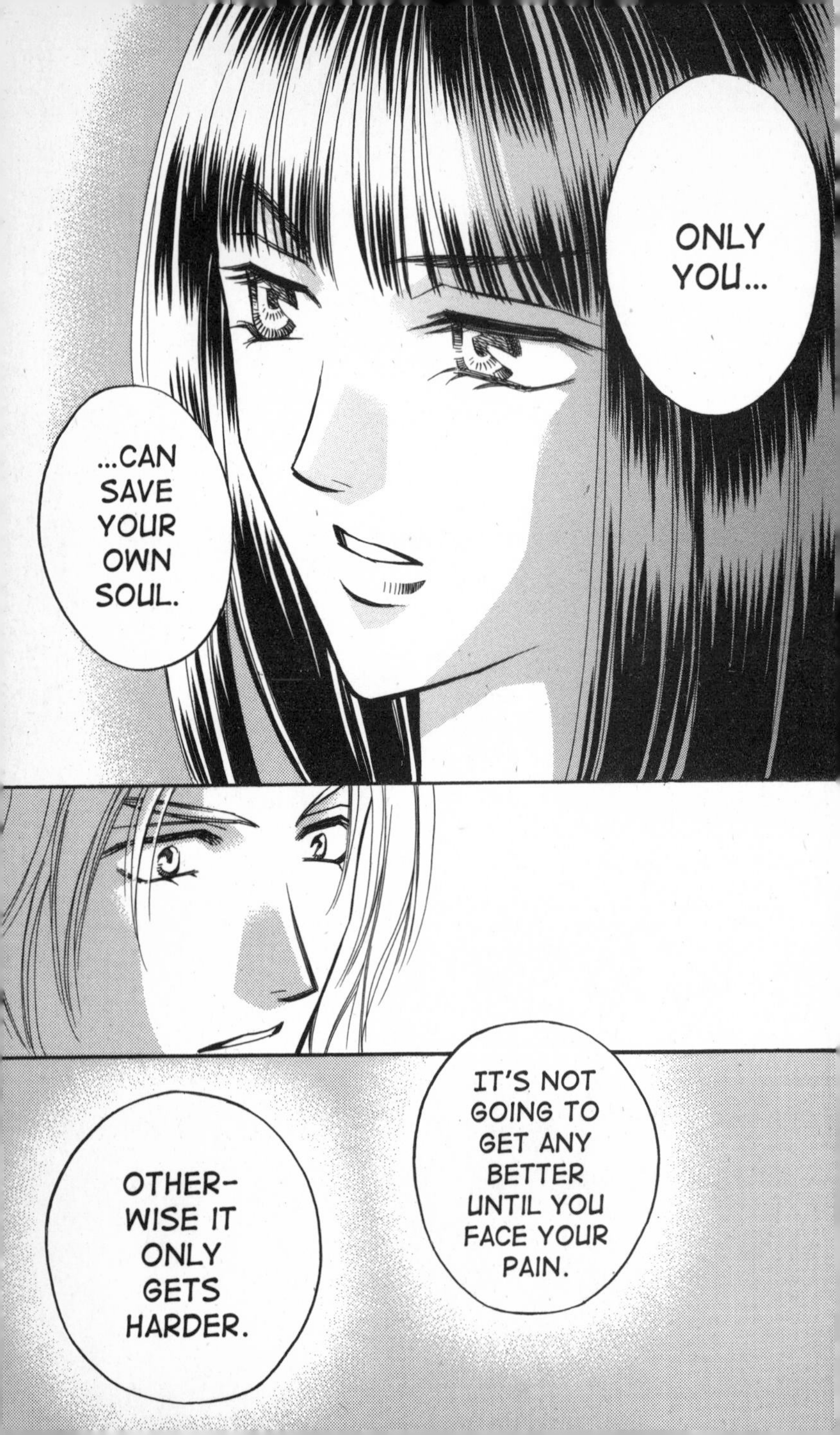
ONLY YOU...
...CAN SAVE YOUR OWN SOUL.
IT'S NOT GOING TO GET ANY BETTER UNTIL YOU FACE YOUR PAIN.
OTHER-WISE IT ONLY GETS HARDER.

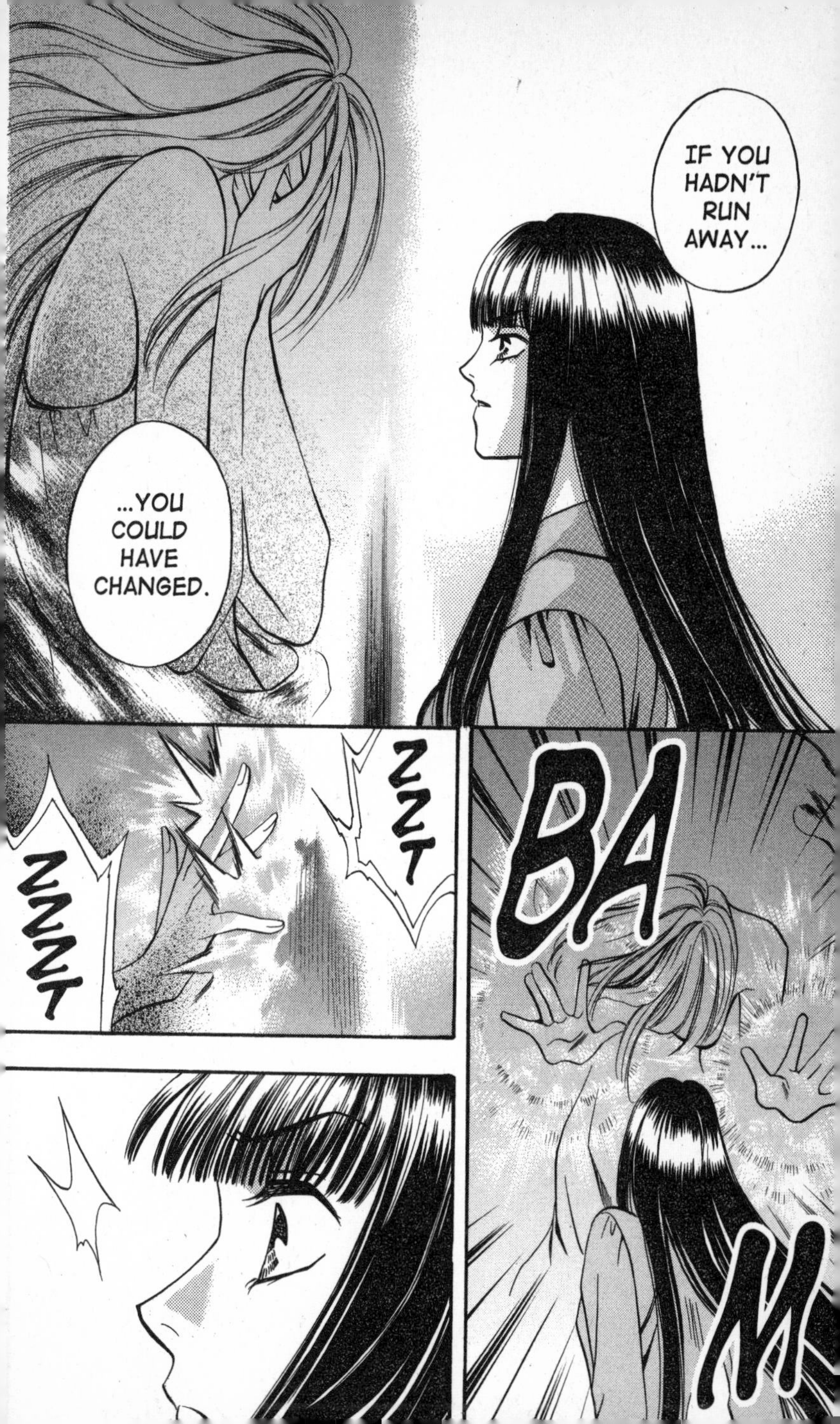
IF YOU HADN'T RUN AWAY...
...YOU COULD HAVE CHANGED.
BA
M
ZZZT
ZZZZT

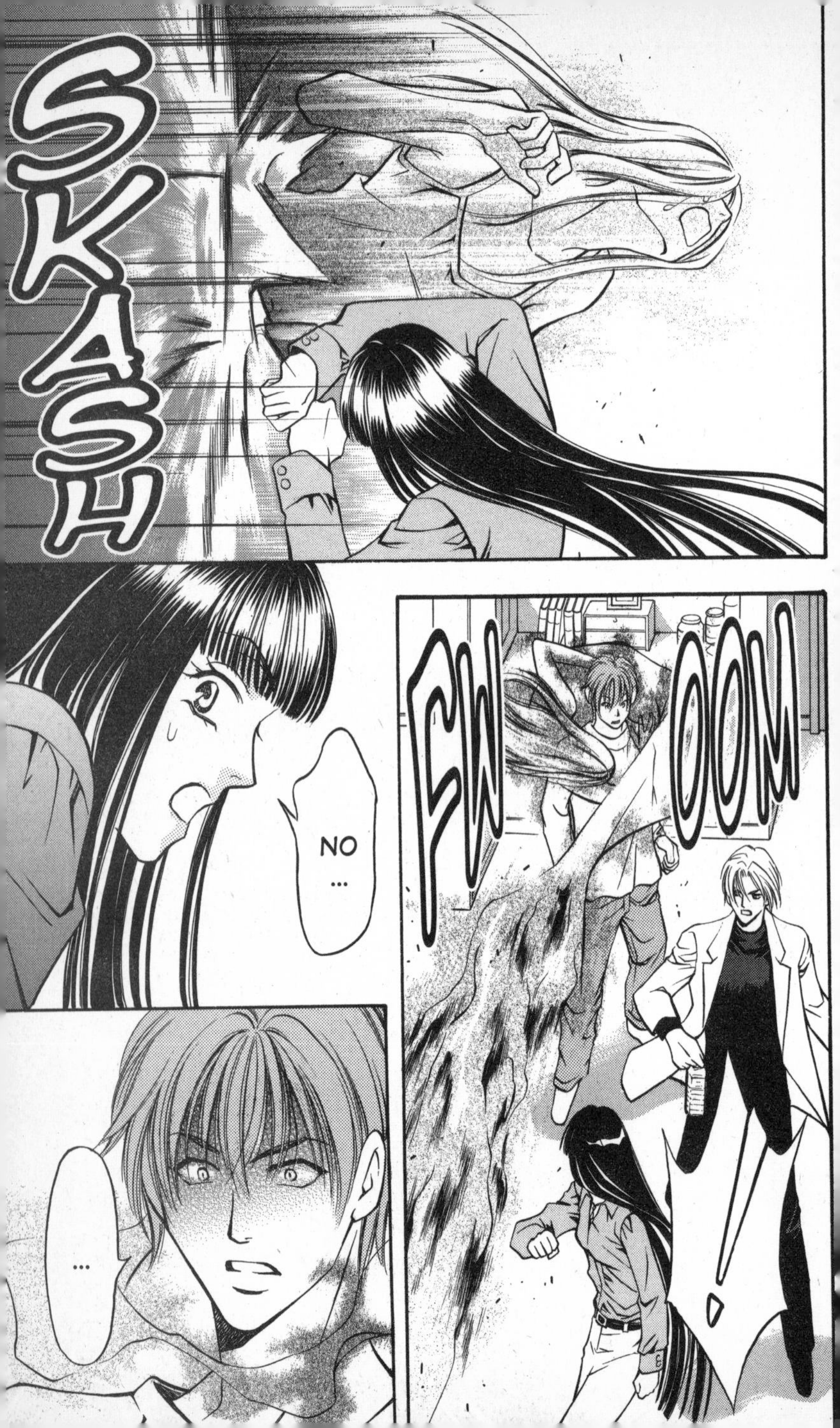
SKASH
FWOOM
!
NO ...
...

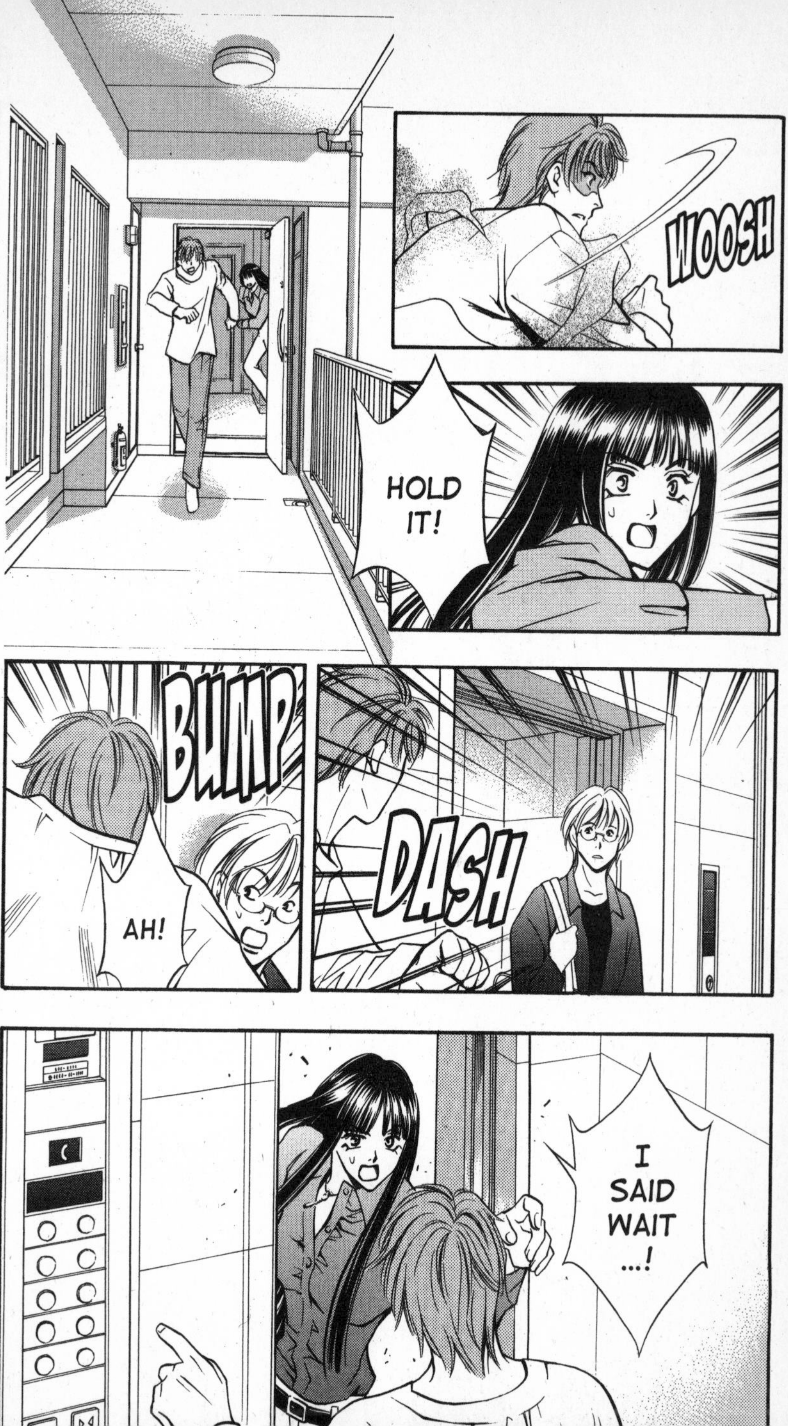
WOOSH
HOLD IT!
DASH
BUMP
AH!
I SAID WAIT ...!

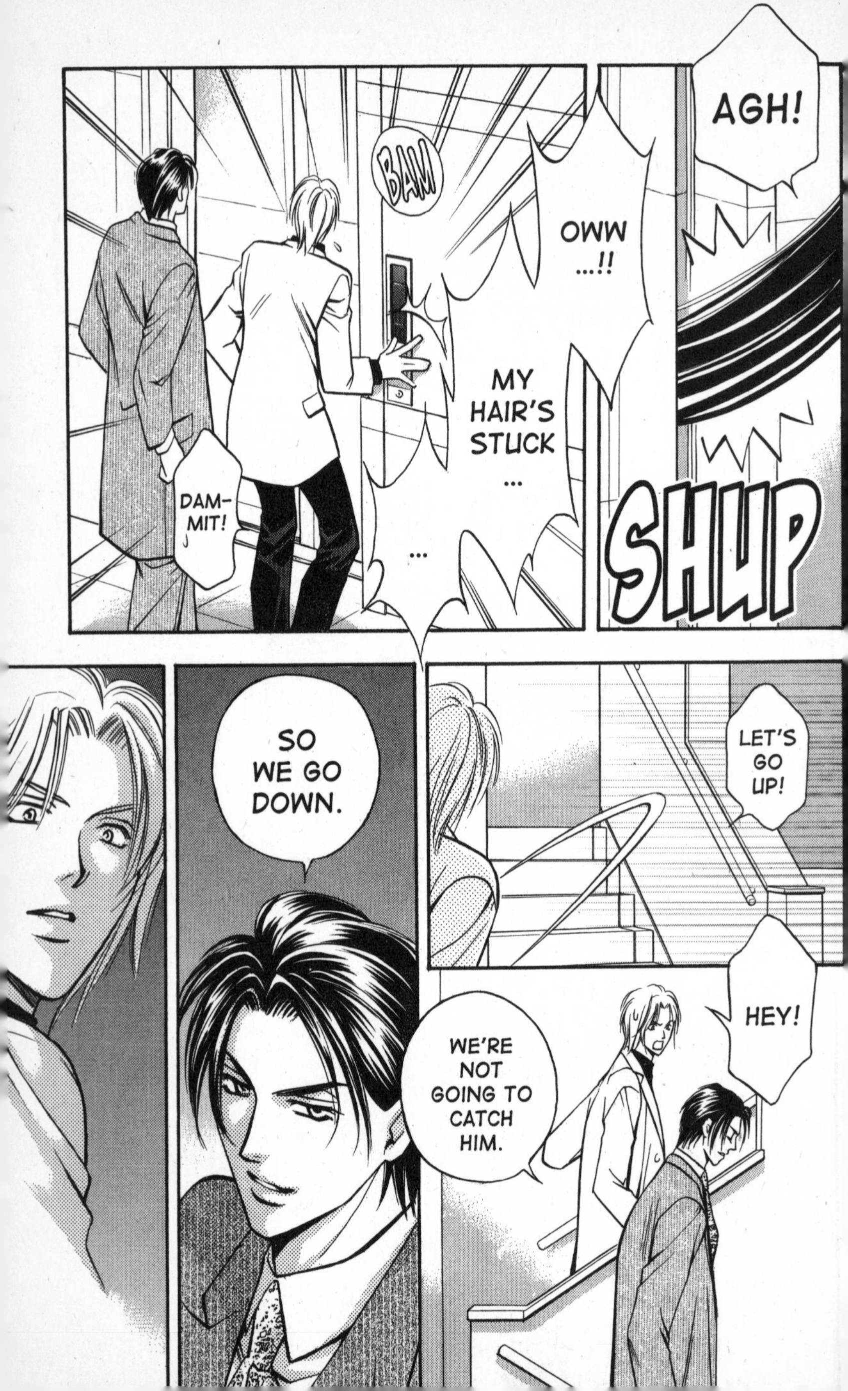
AGH!
SHUP
OWW ...!!
BAM
MY HAIR'S STUCK ...
...
DAM-MIT!
LET'S GO UP!
HEY!
WE'RE NOT GOING TO CATCH HIM.
SO WE GO DOWN.

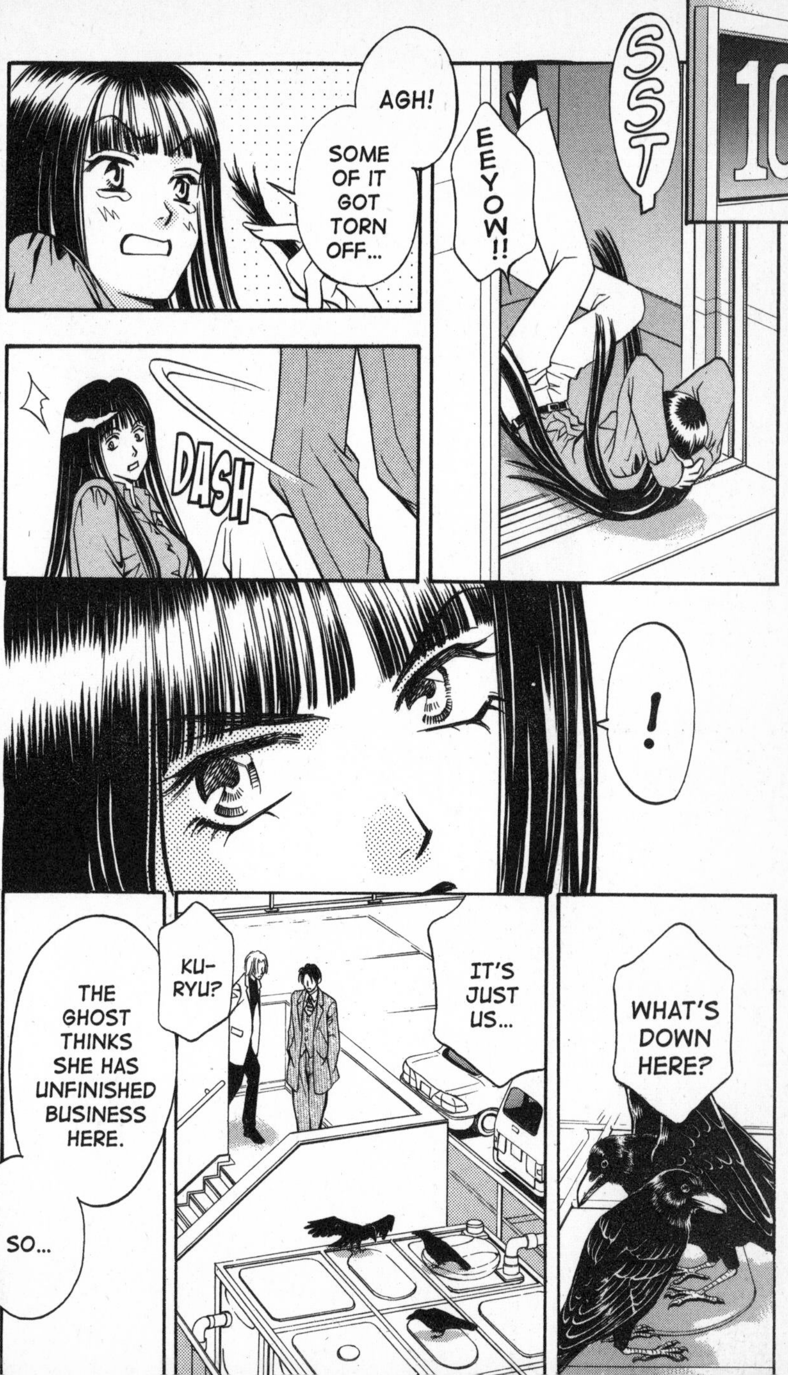

SST
10
EEYOW!!
AGH!
SOME OF IT GOT TORN OFF...
DASH
!
WHAT'S DOWN HERE?
IT'S JUST US...
KU-RYU?
THE GHOST THINKS SHE HAS UNFINISHED BUSINESS HERE.
SO...

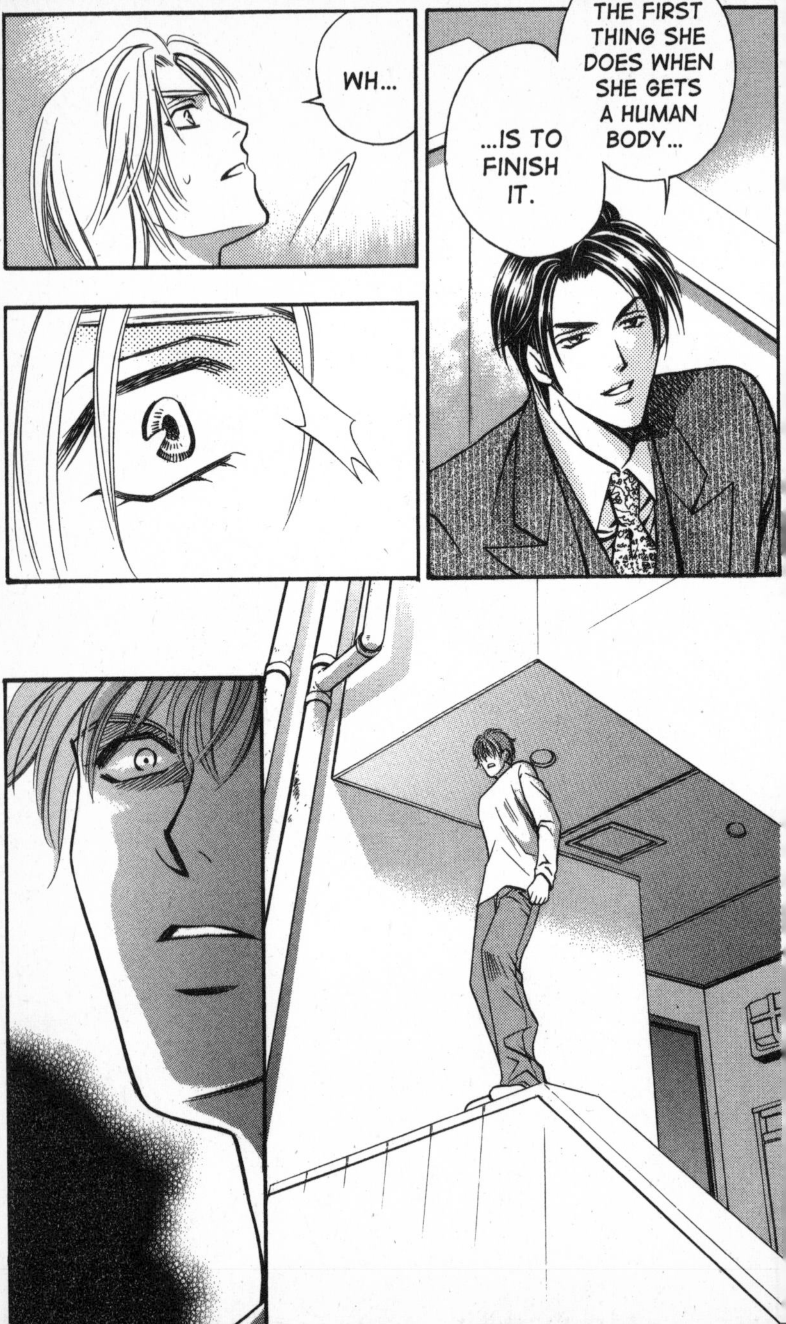
THE FIRST THING SHE DOES WHEN SHE GETS A HUMAN BODY...
...IS TO FINISH IT.
WH...

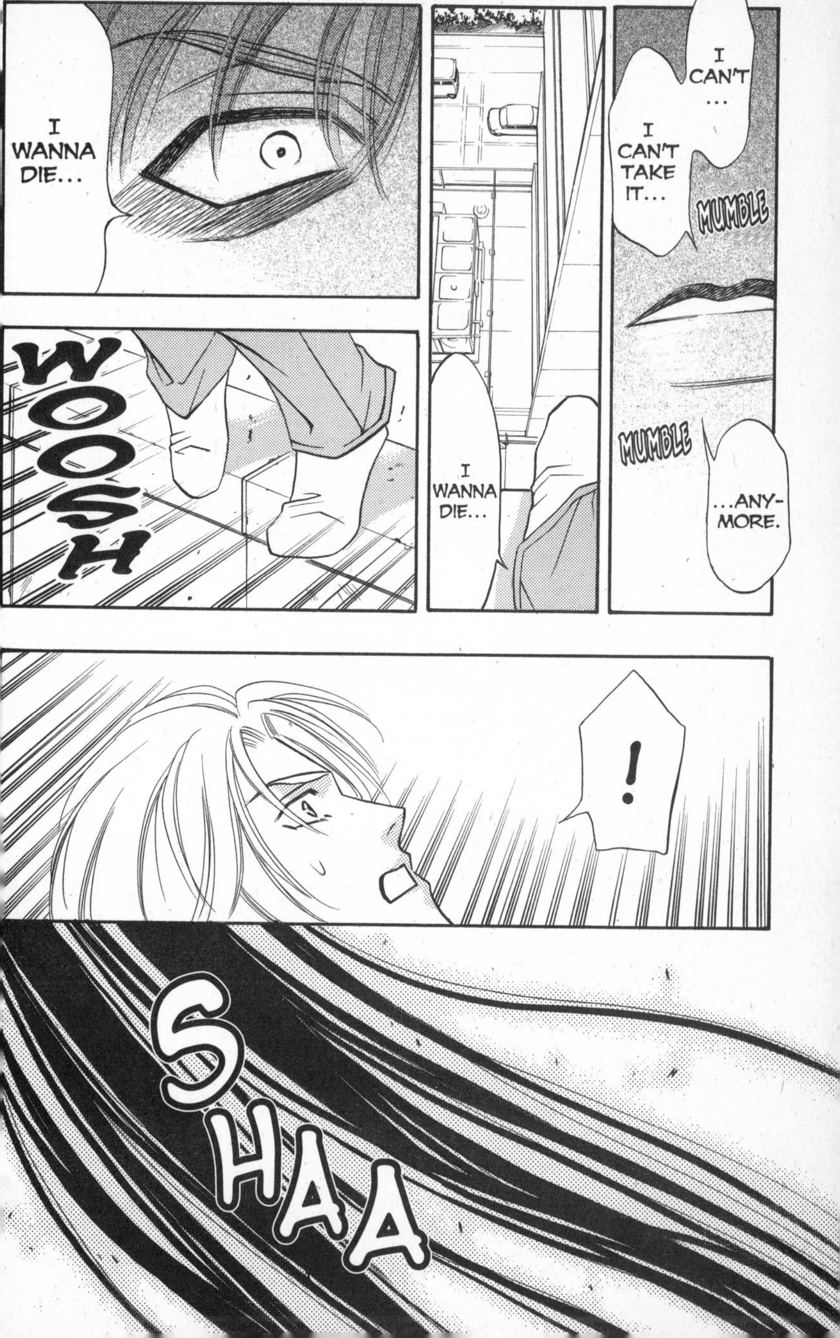
I CAN'T...
I CAN'T TAKE IT...
MUMBLE
MUMBLE
...ANY-MORE.
I WANNA DIE...
I WANNA DIE...
WOOSH
!
SHAA

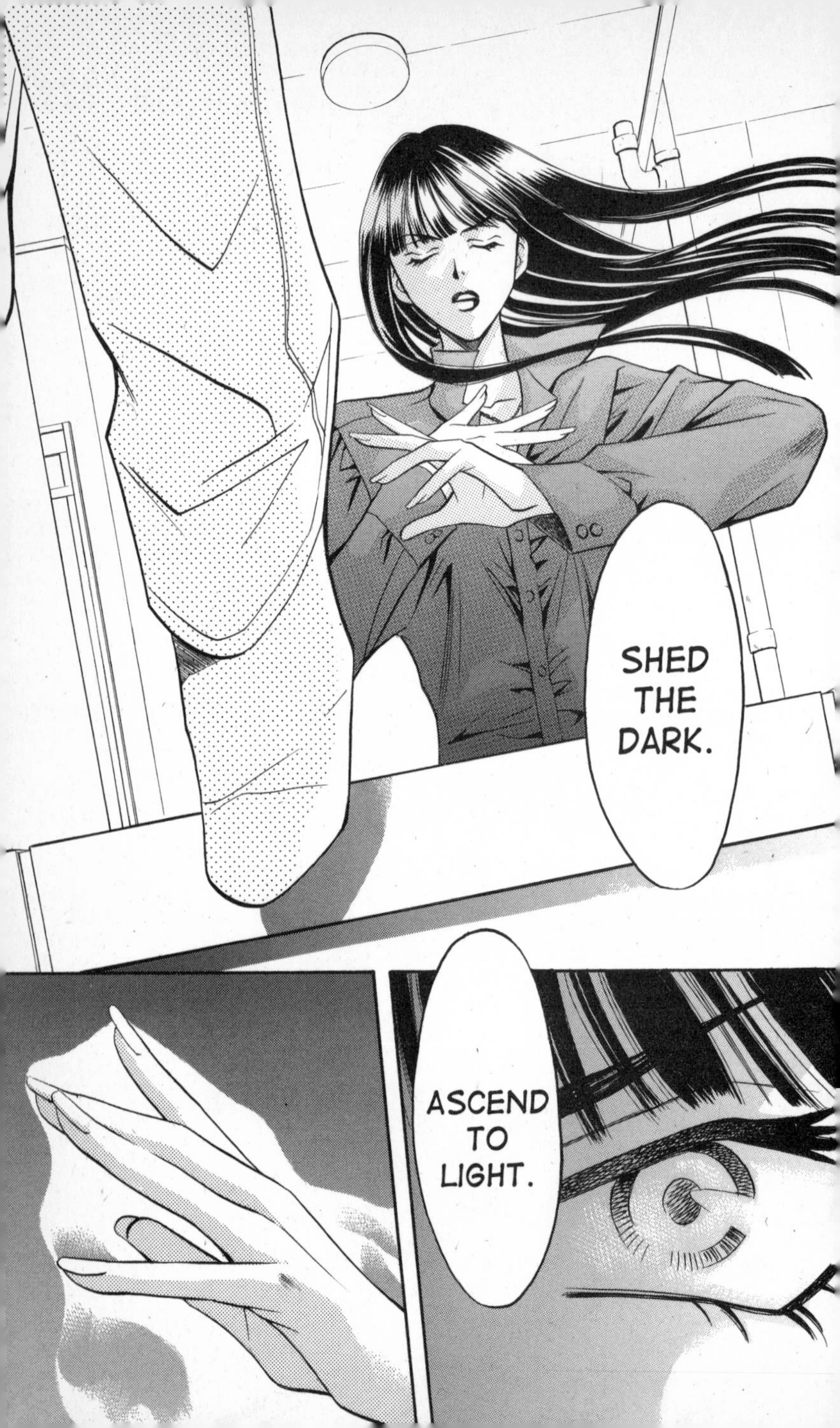
SHED THE DARK.
ASCEND TO LIGHT.

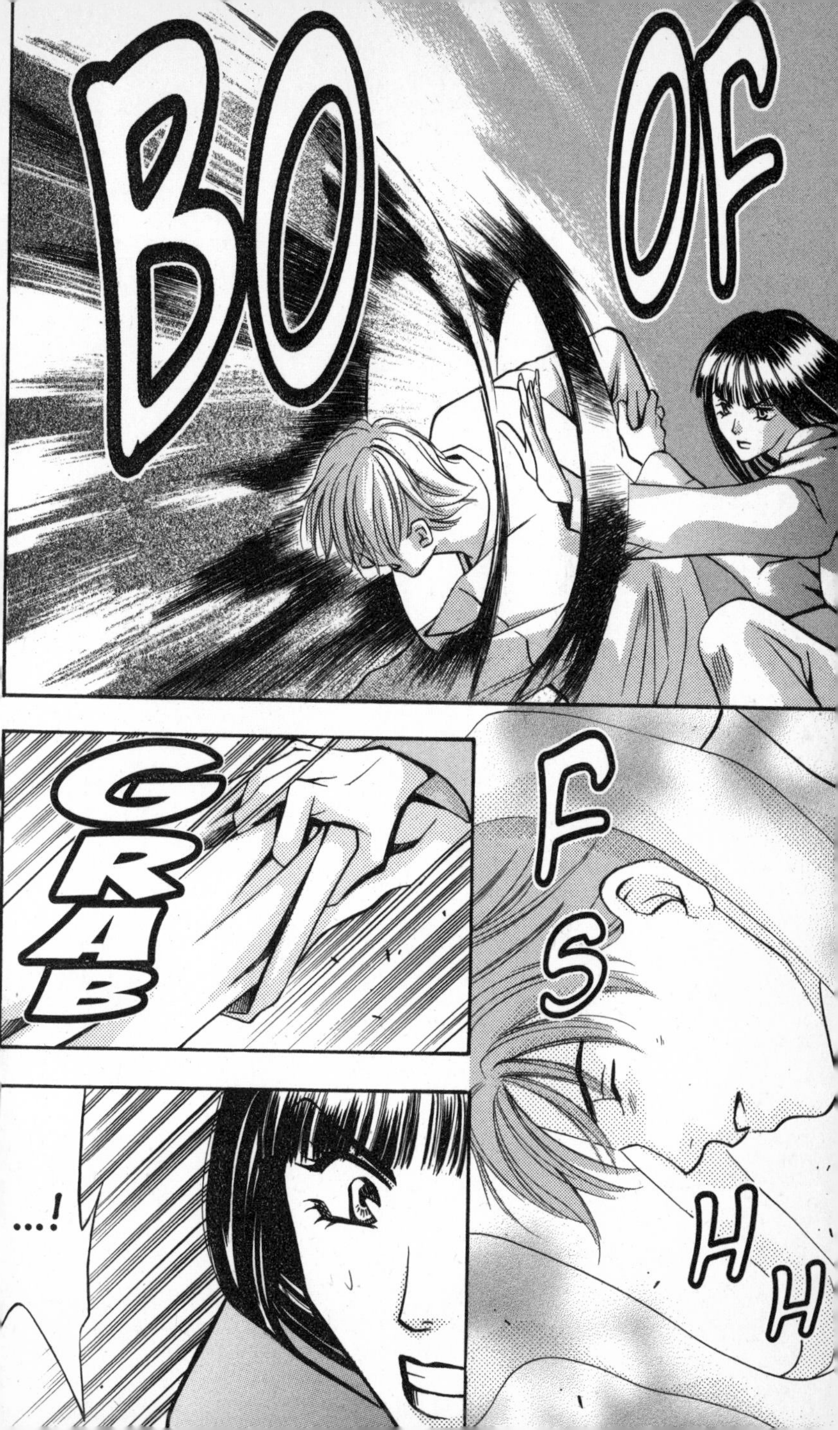
BOOF
FSHHH
GRAB
...!

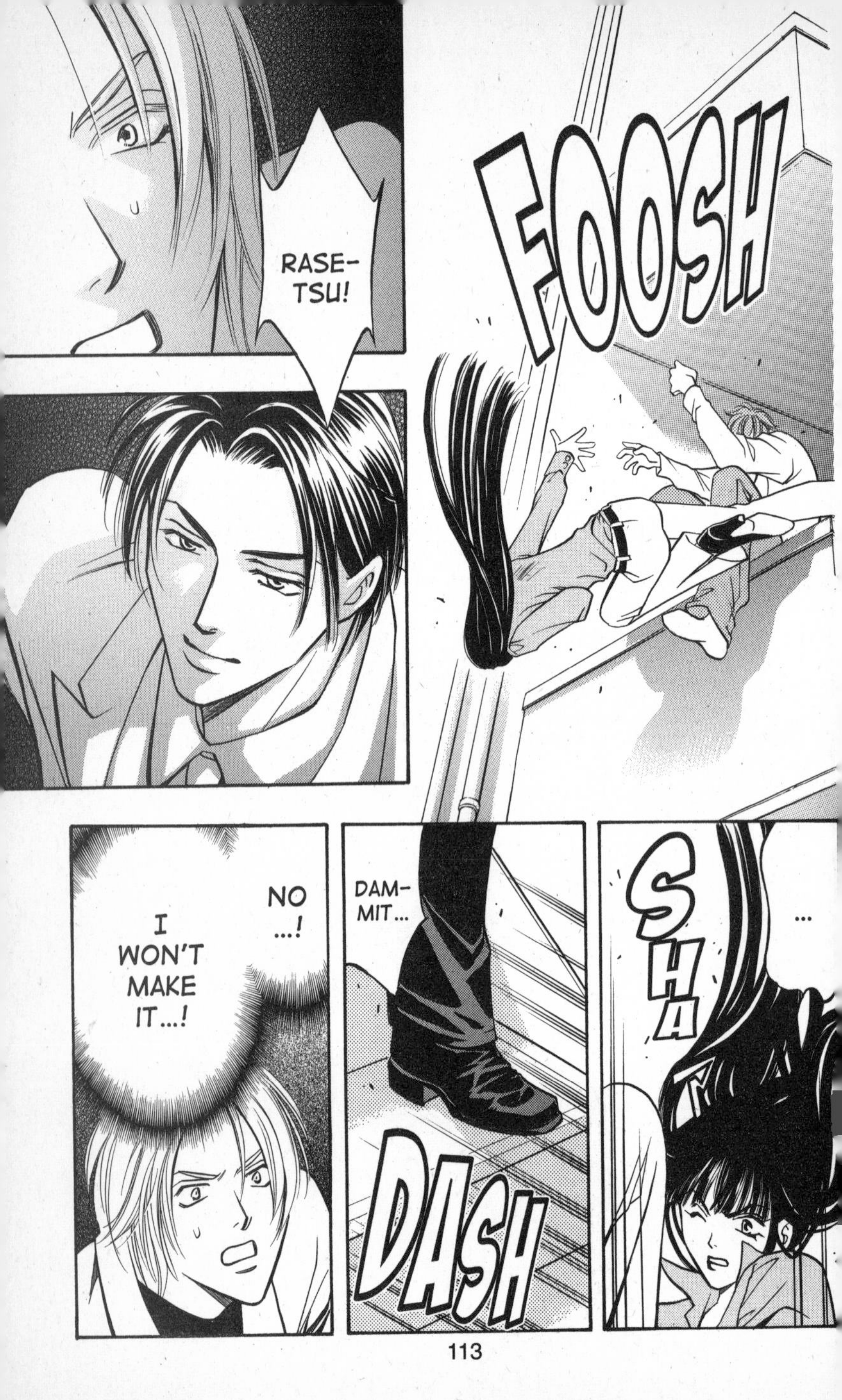
FOOSH
RASE-TSU!
SHAT
...
DAM-MIT...
DASH
NO ...!
I WON'T MAKE IT...!

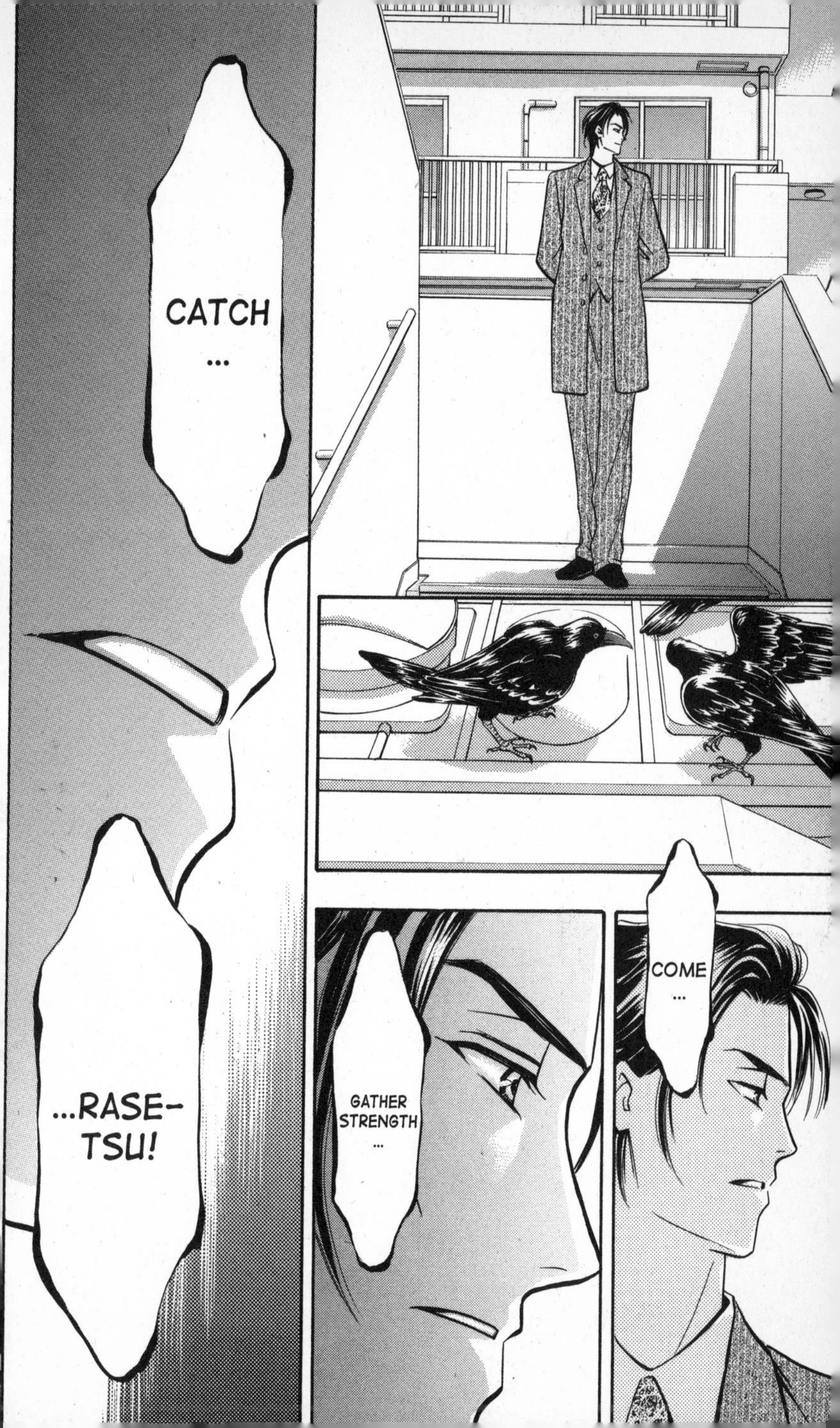
COME ...
GATHER STRENGTH ...
CATCH ...
...RASE-TSU!

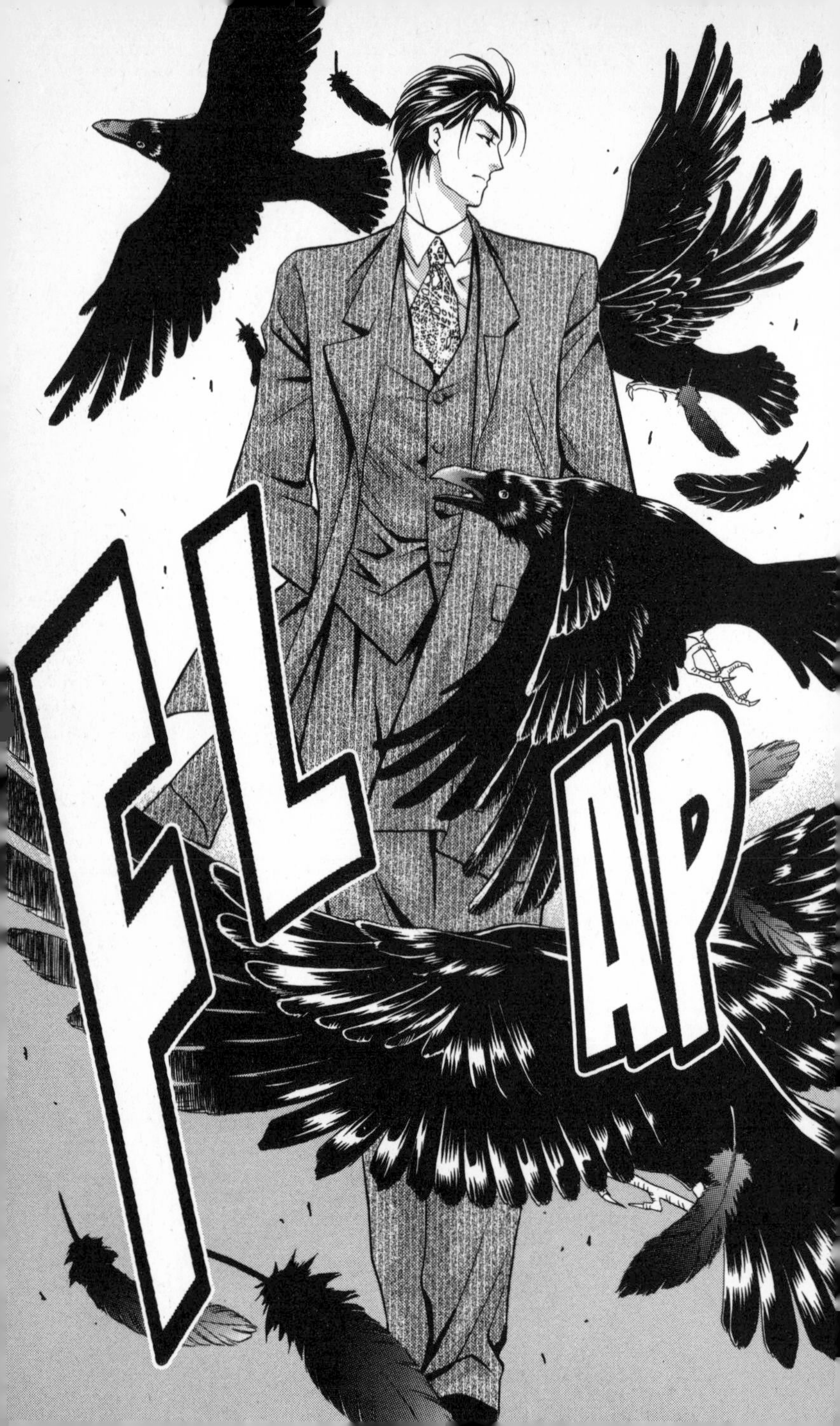
FLAP

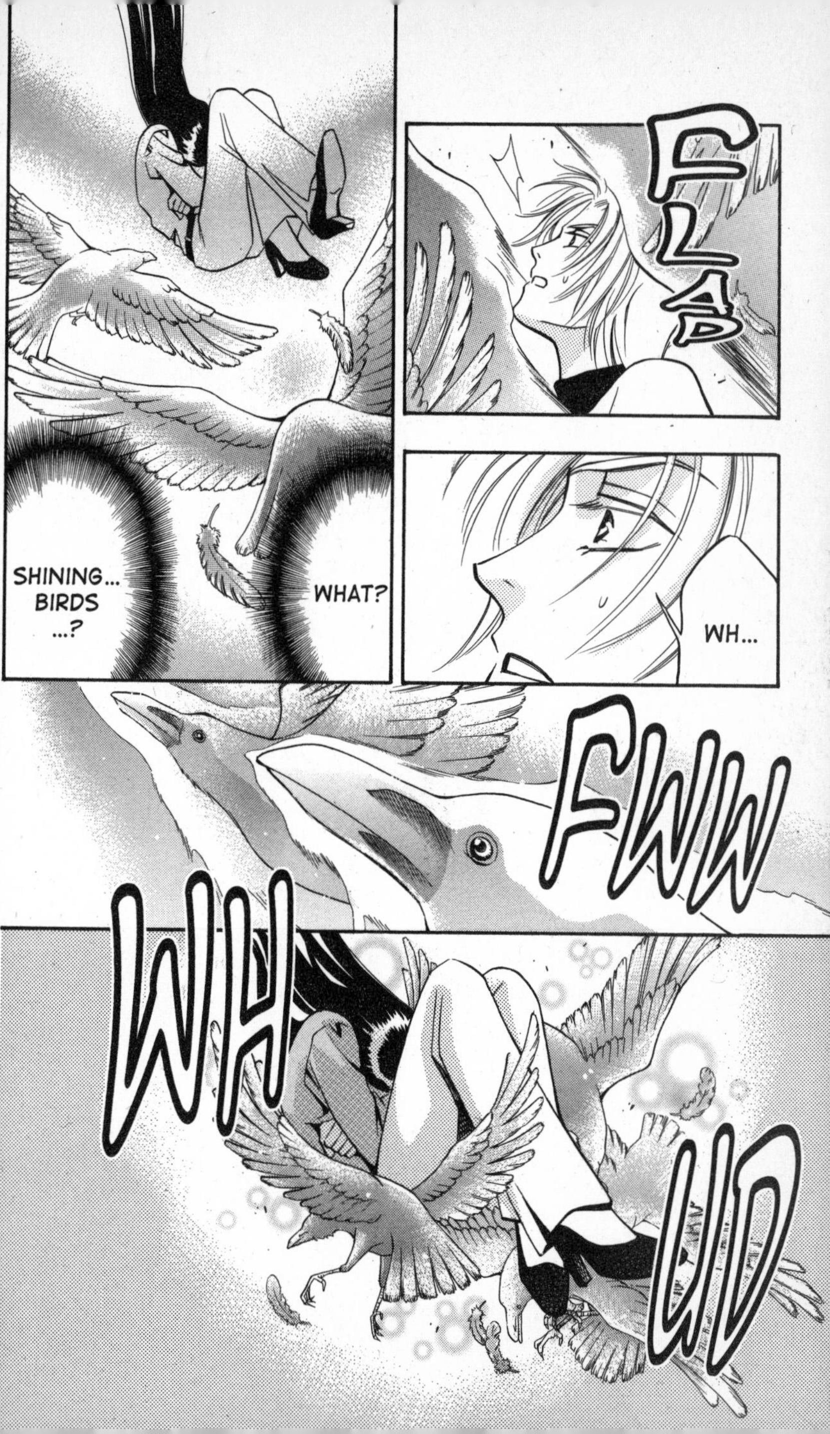
FLAP
WH...
WHAT?
SHINING... BIRDS ...?
FWW
WHUD

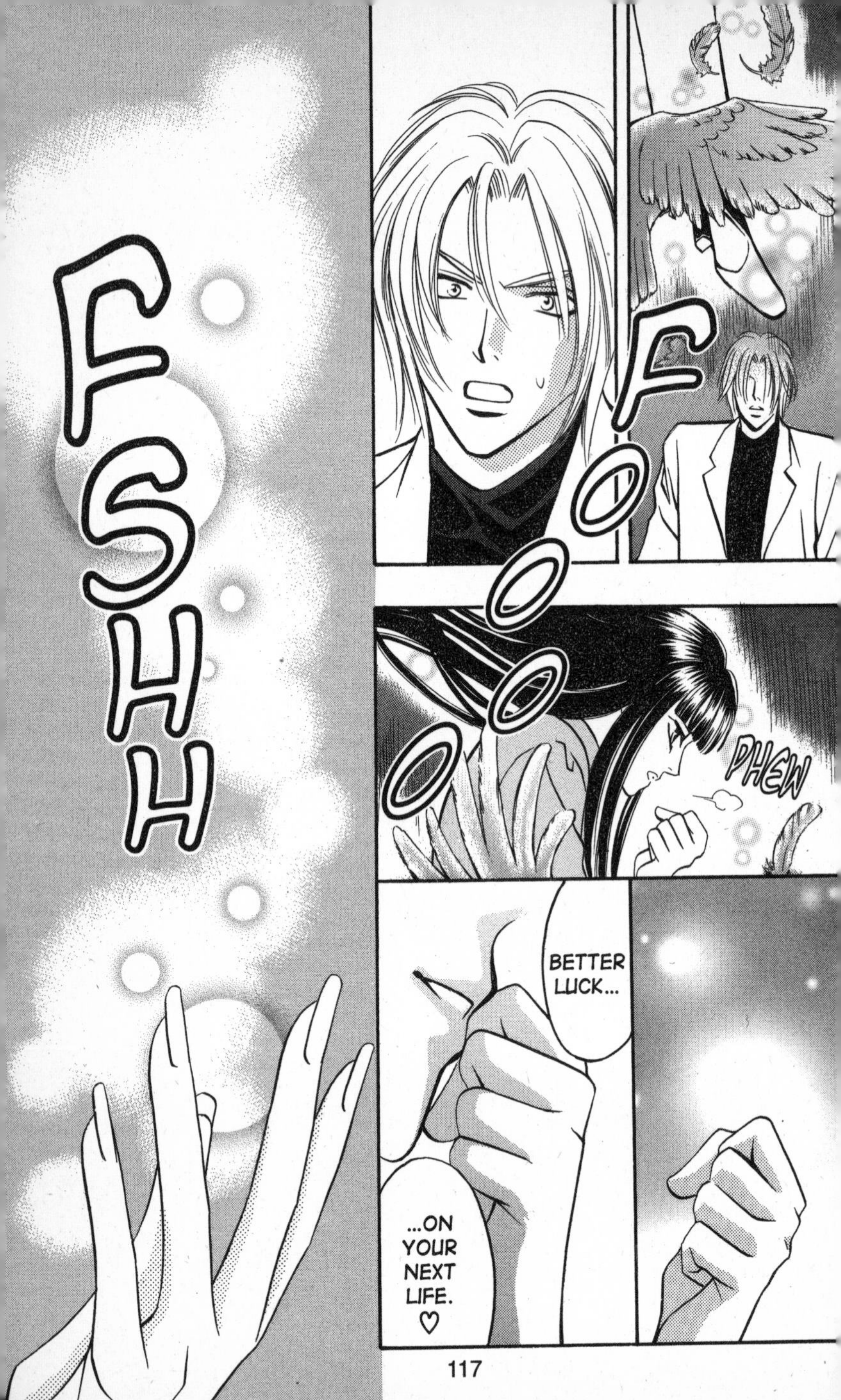
FOOOOO
PHEW
BETTER LUCK...
...ON YOUR NEXT LIFE. ♡
FSHH

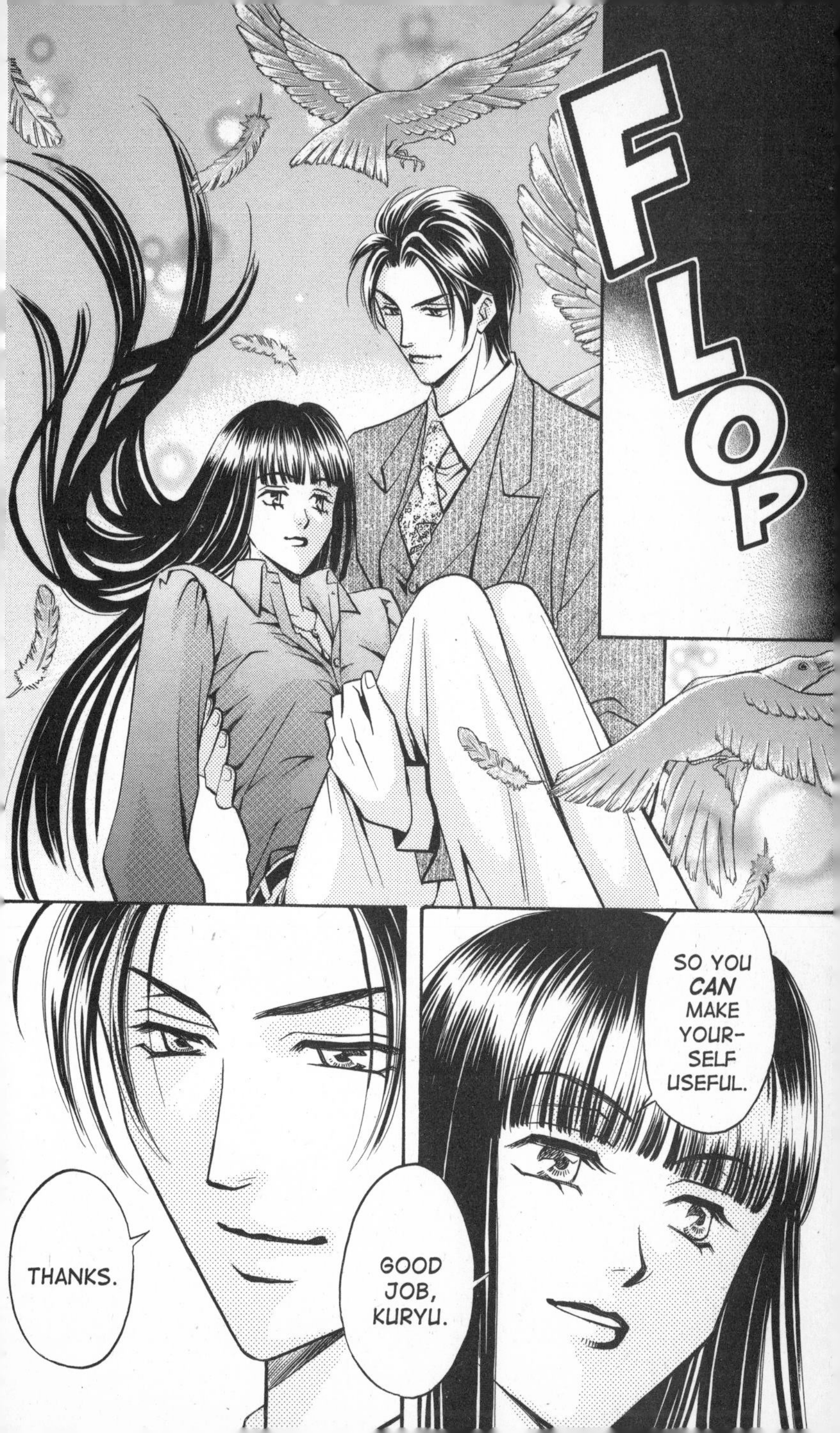
FLOP
SO YOU CAN MAKE YOUR-SELF USEFUL.
GOOD JOB, KURYU.
THANKS.

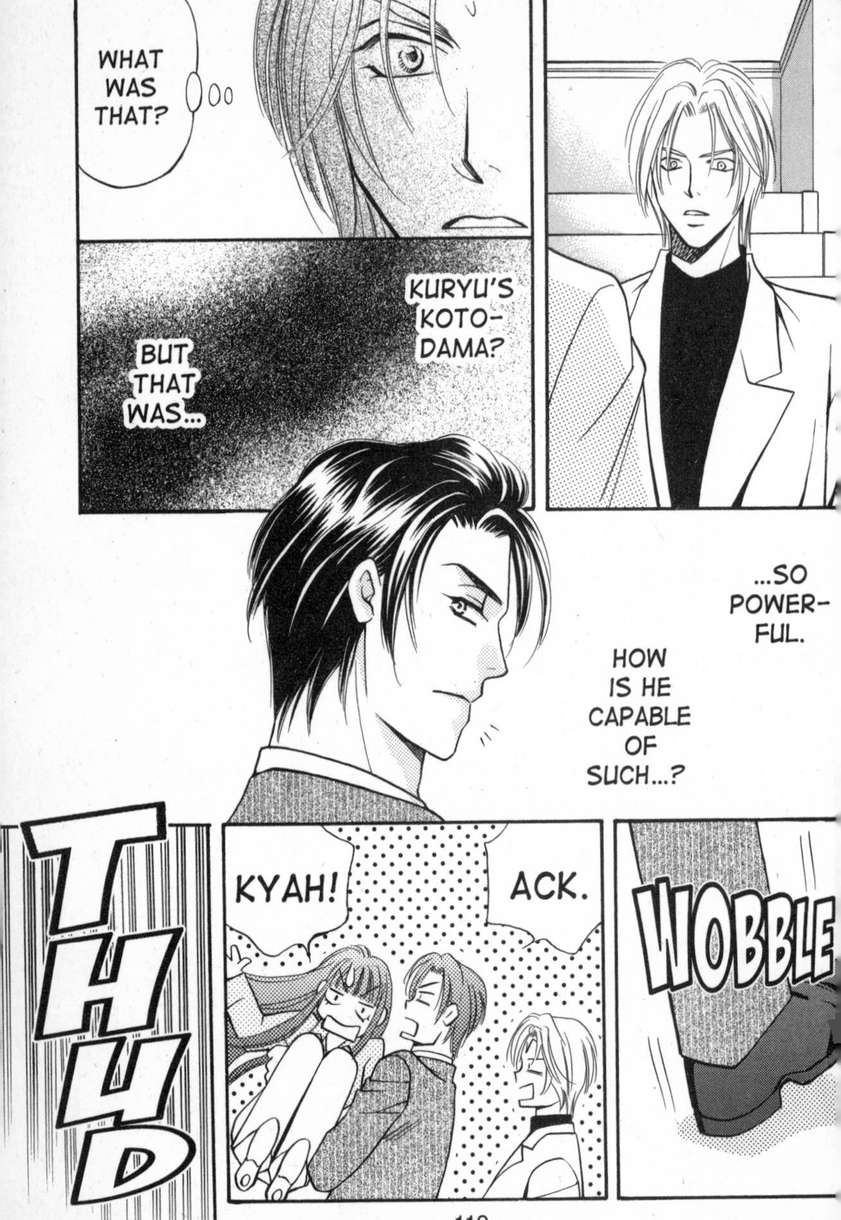
WHAT WAS THAT?
KURYU'S KOTO-DAMA?
BUT THAT WAS...
...SO POWER-FUL.
HOW IS HE CAPABLE OF SUCH...?
WOBBLE
ACK.
KYAH!
THUD

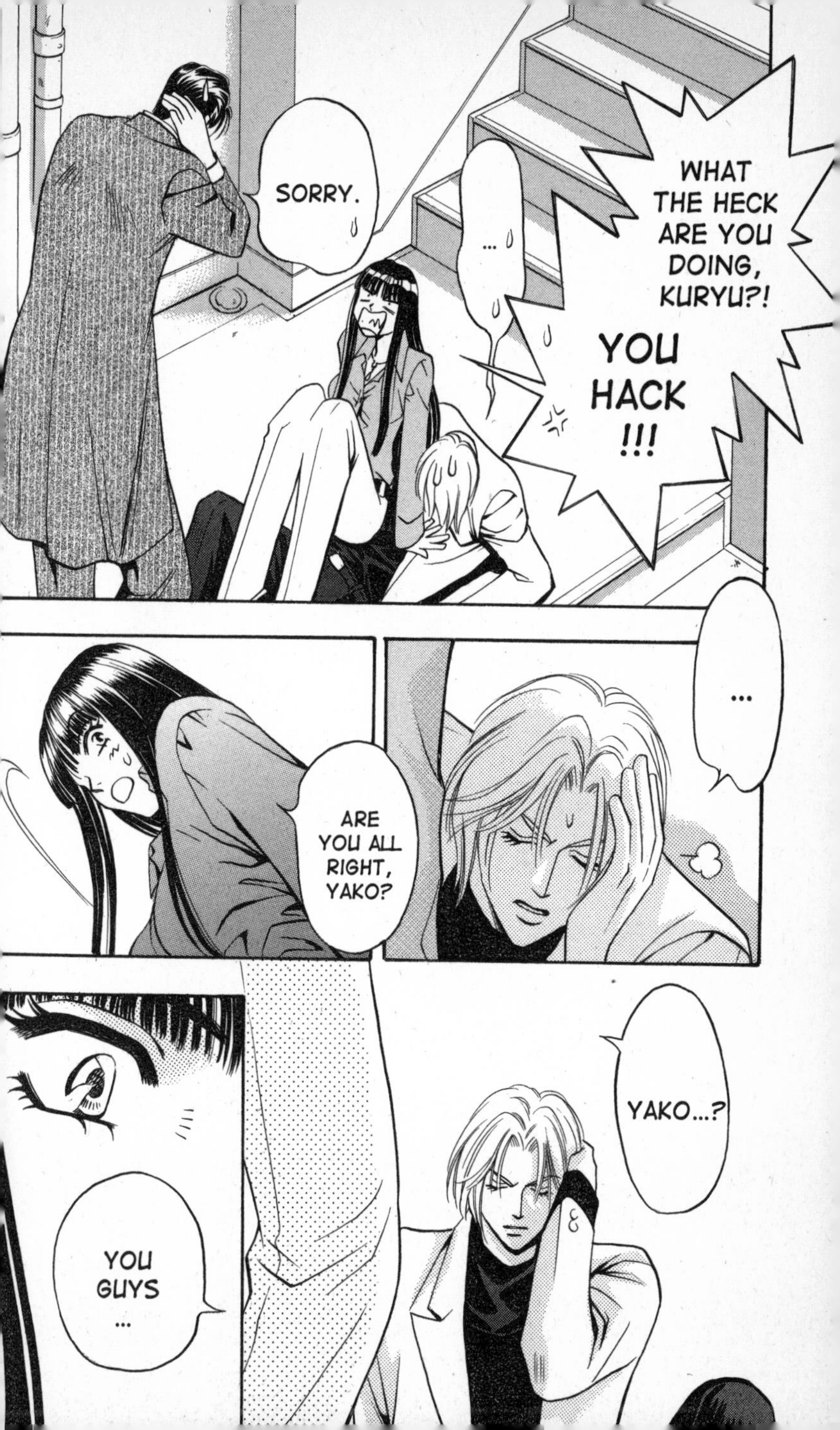
WHAT THE HECK ARE YOU DOING, KURYU?!
YOU HACK!!!
...
SORRY.
...
ARE YOU ALL RIGHT, YAKO?
YAKO...?
YOU GUYS ...

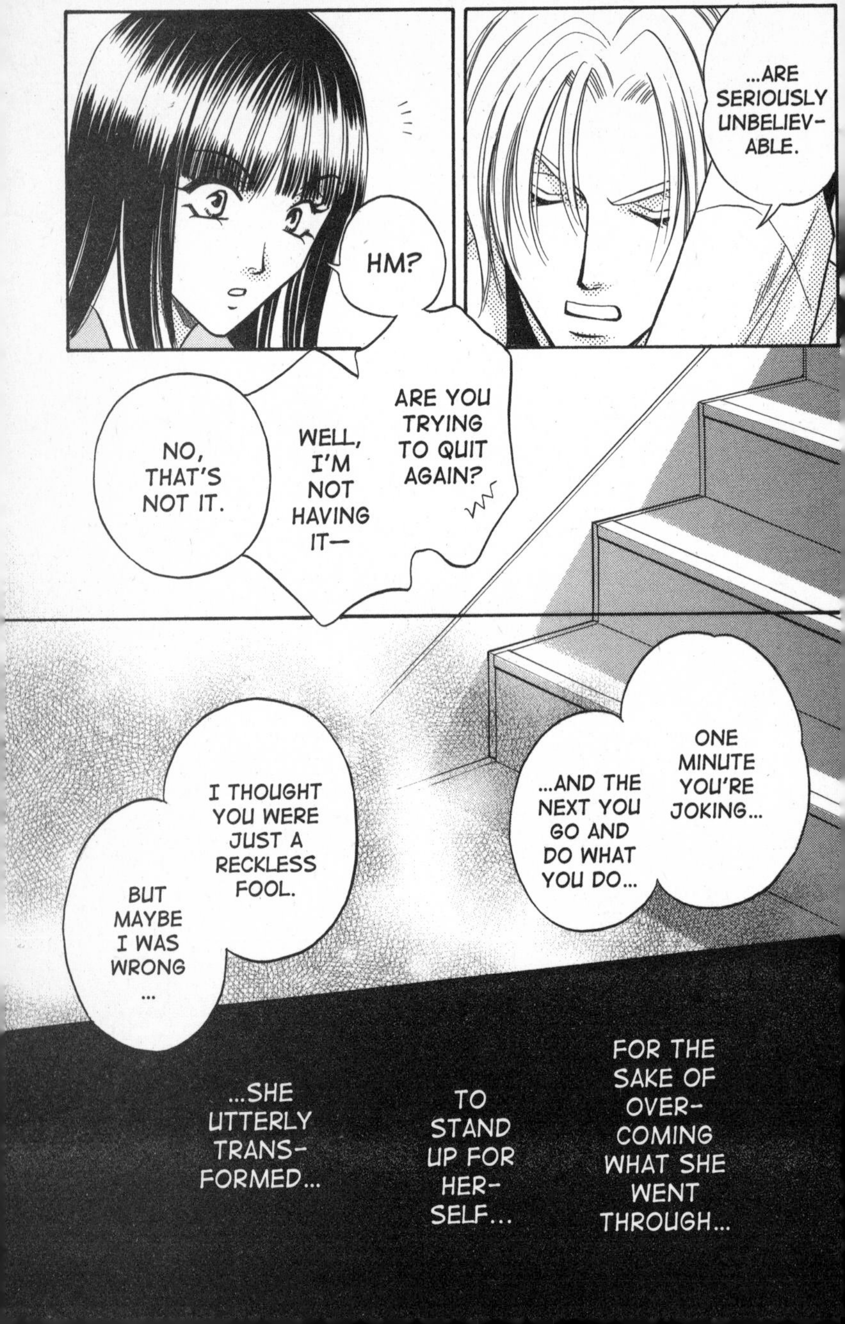
...ARE SERIOUSLY UNBELIEV-ABLE.
HM?
ARE YOU TRYING TO QUIT AGAIN?
WELL, I'M NOT HAVING IT—
NO, THAT'S NOT IT.
ONE MINUTE YOU'RE JOKING...
...AND THE NEXT YOU GO AND DO WHAT YOU DO...
I THOUGHT YOU WERE JUST A RECKLESS FOOL.
BUT MAYBE I WAS WRONG ...
FOR THE SAKE OF OVER-COMING WHAT SHE WENT THROUGH...
TO STAND UP FOR HER-SELF...
...SHE UTTERLY TRANS-FORMED...

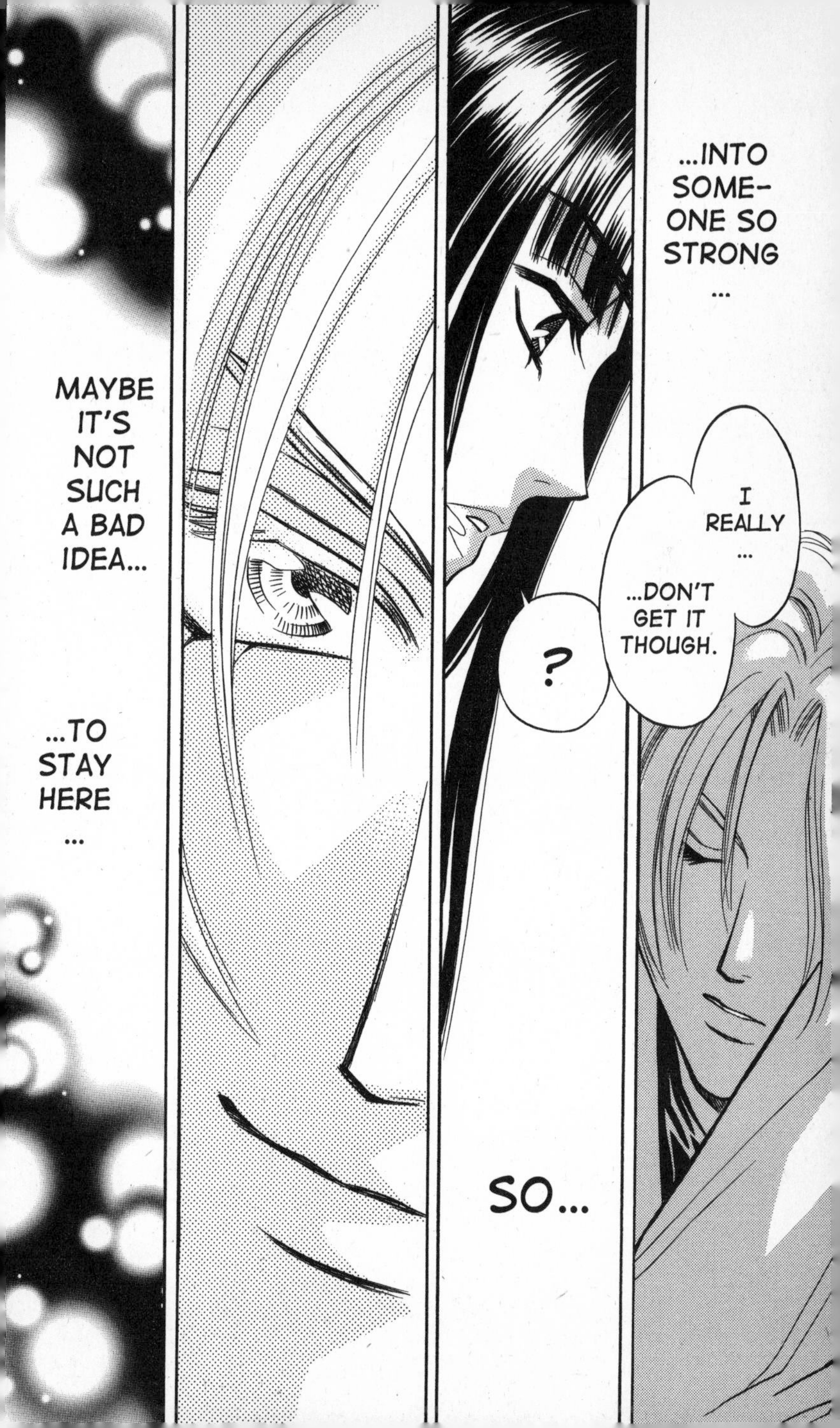
...INTO SOME-ONE SO STRONG ...
I REALLY ...
...DON'T GET IT THOUGH.
?
SO...
MAYBE IT'S NOT SUCH A BAD IDEA...
...TO STAY HERE ...

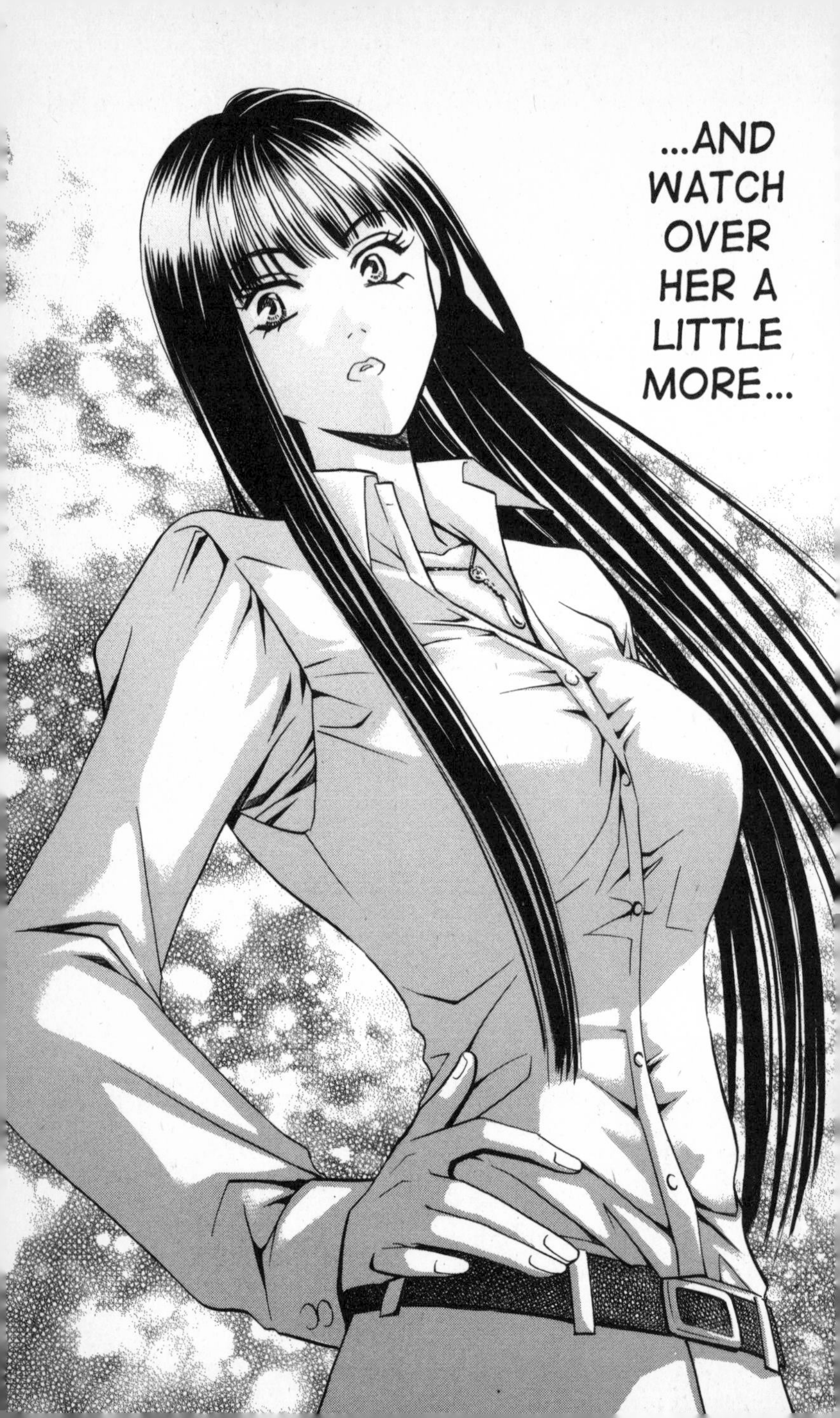
...AND WATCH OVER HER A LITTLE MORE...

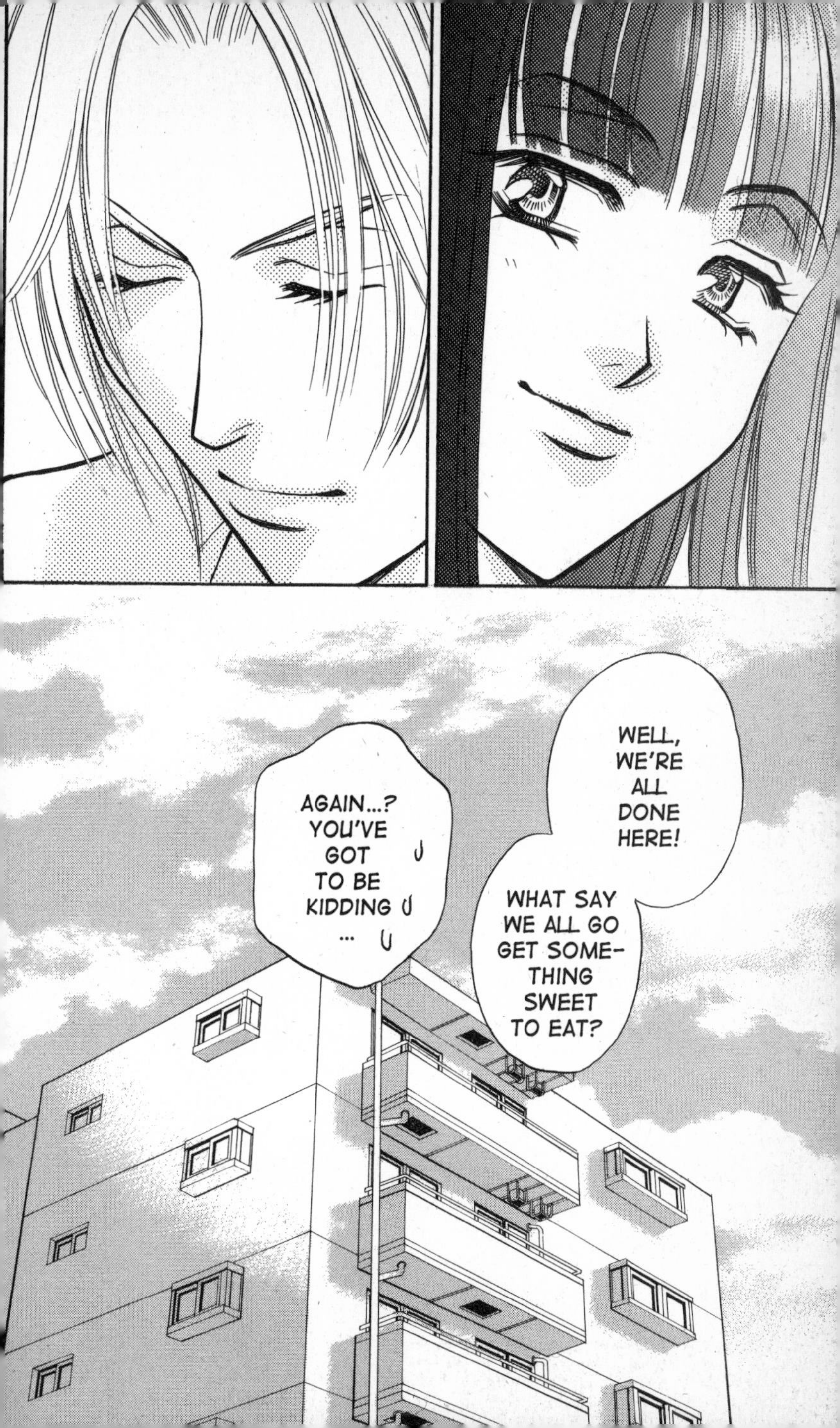
WELL, WE'RE ALL DONE HERE!
WHAT SAY WE ALL GO GET SOME-THING SWEET TO EAT?
AGAIN...? YOU'VE GOT TO BE KIDDING ...

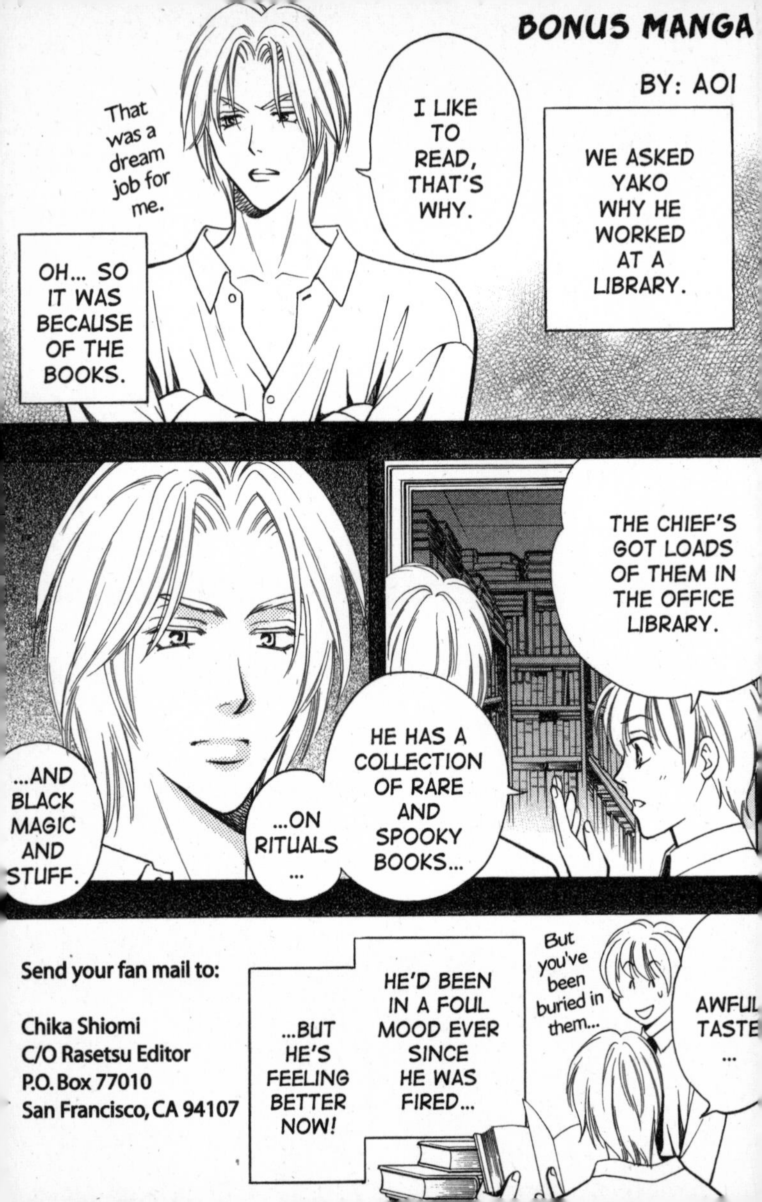
BONUS MANGA
BY: AOI
WE ASKED YAKO WHY HE WORKED AT A LIBRARY.
I LIKE TO READ, THAT'S WHY.
That was a dream job for me.
OH... SO IT WAS BECAUSE OF THE BOOKS.
THE CHIEF'S GOT LOADS OF THEM IN THE OFFICE LIBRARY.
HE HAS A COLLECTION OF RARE AND SPOOKY BOOKS...
...ON RITUALS ...
...AND BLACK MAGIC AND STUFF.
AWFUL TASTE ...
But you've been buried in them...
HE'D BEEN IN A FOUL MOOD EVER SINCE HE WAS FIRED...
...BUT HE'S FEELING BETTER NOW!

Send your fan mail to:

Chika Shiomi
C/O Rasetsu Editor
P.O. Box 77010
San Francisco, CA 94107

Chapter 3

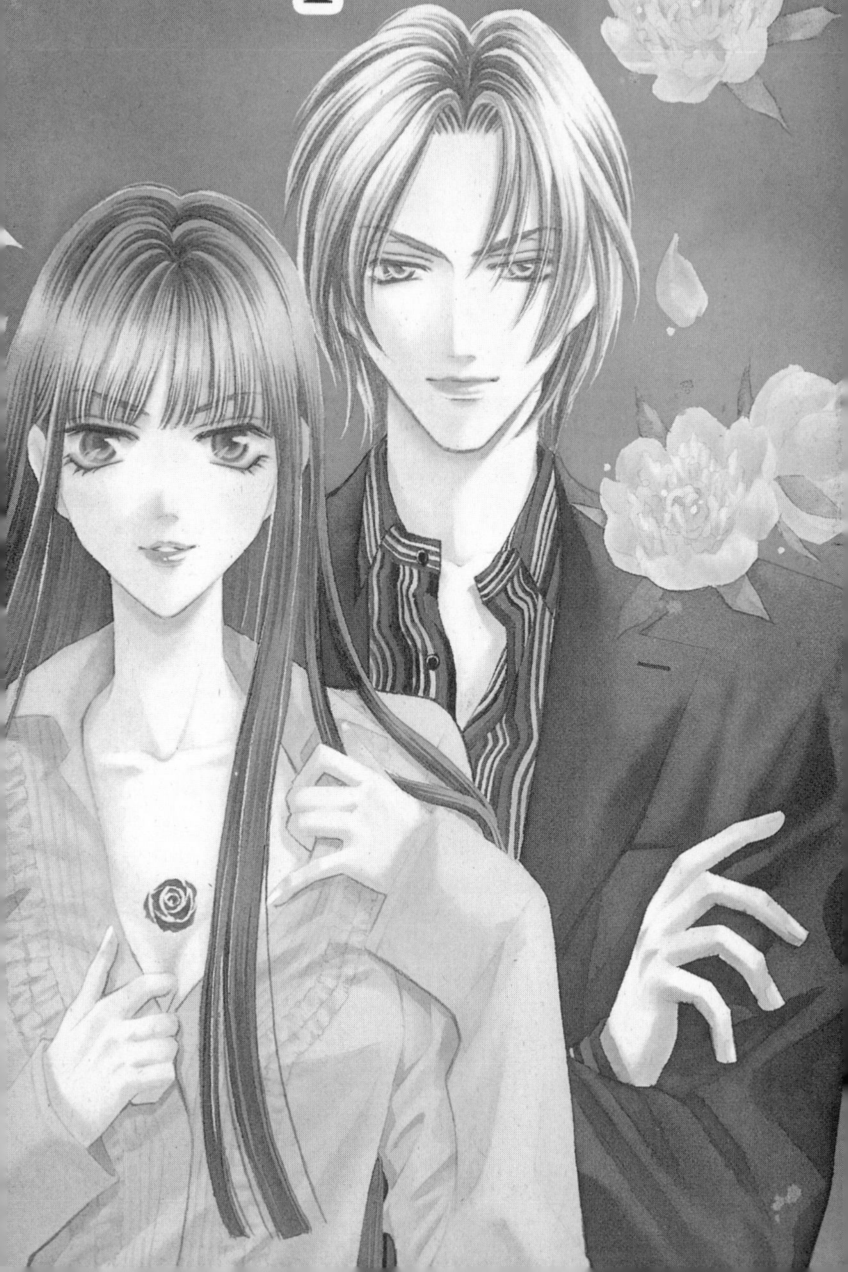

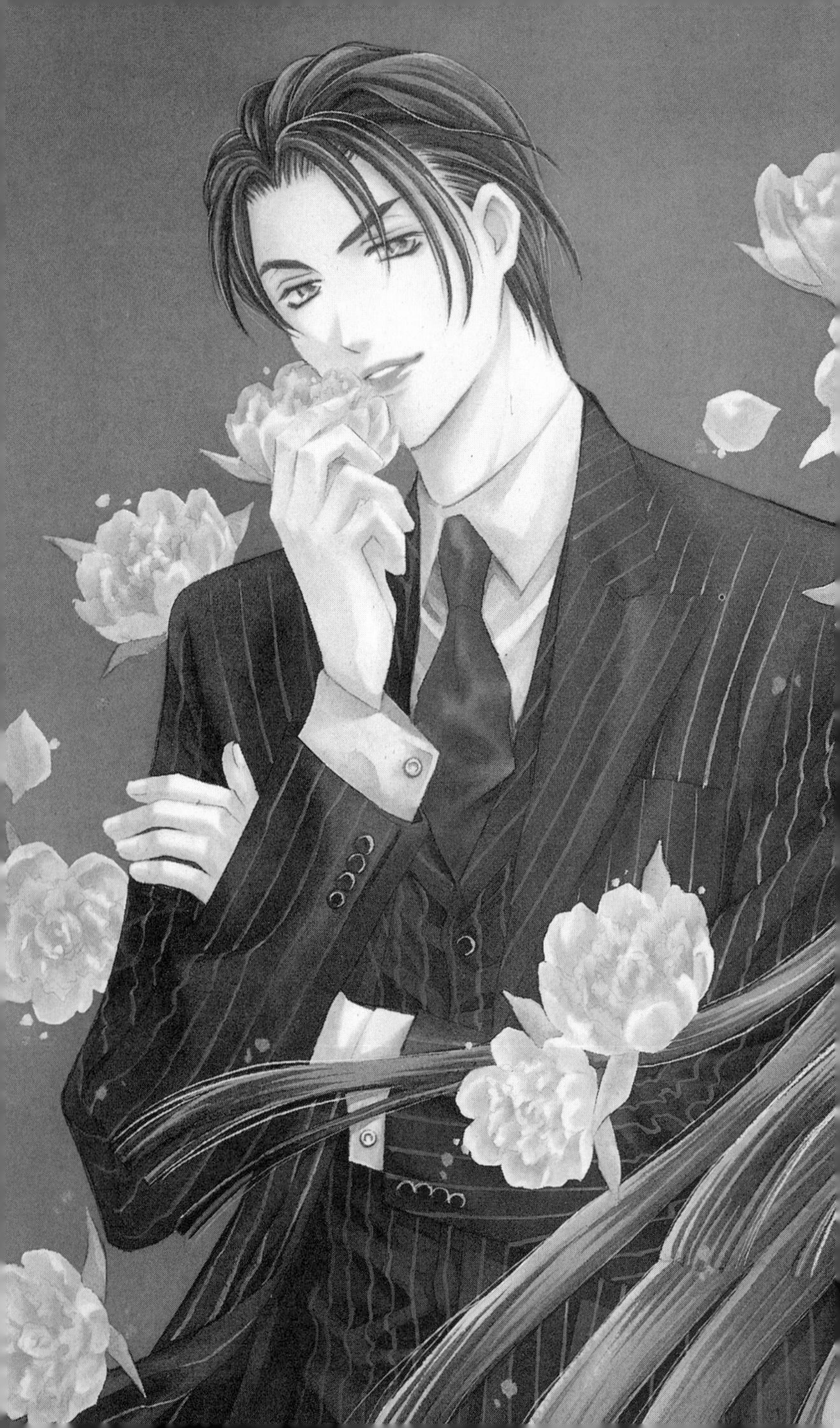

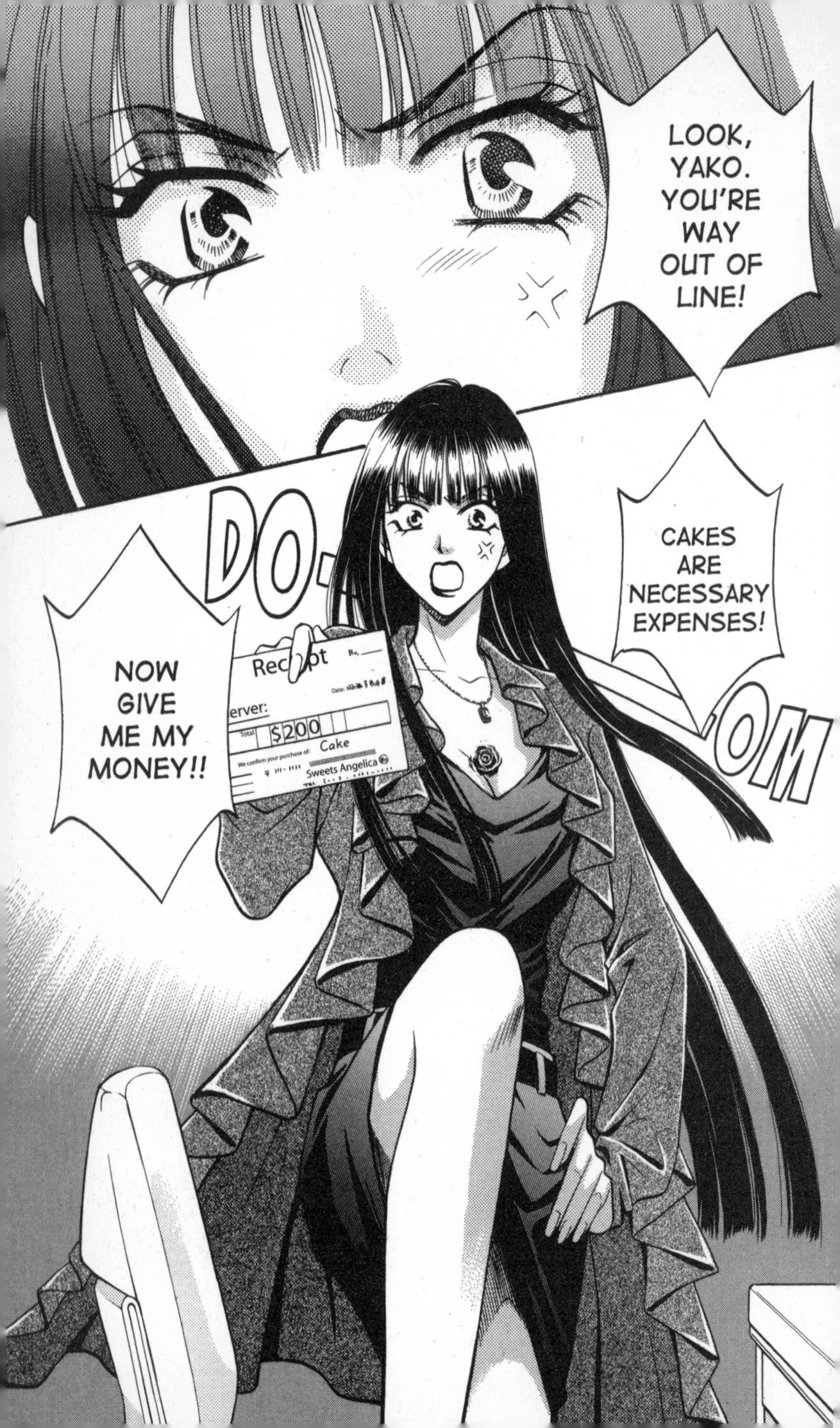
LOOK, YAKO. YOU'RE WAY OUT OF LINE!
CAKES ARE NECESSARY EXPENSES!
DO-OM
NOW GIVE ME MY MONEY!!
Total
$200
We confirm your purchase of:
Cake
Sweets Angelica

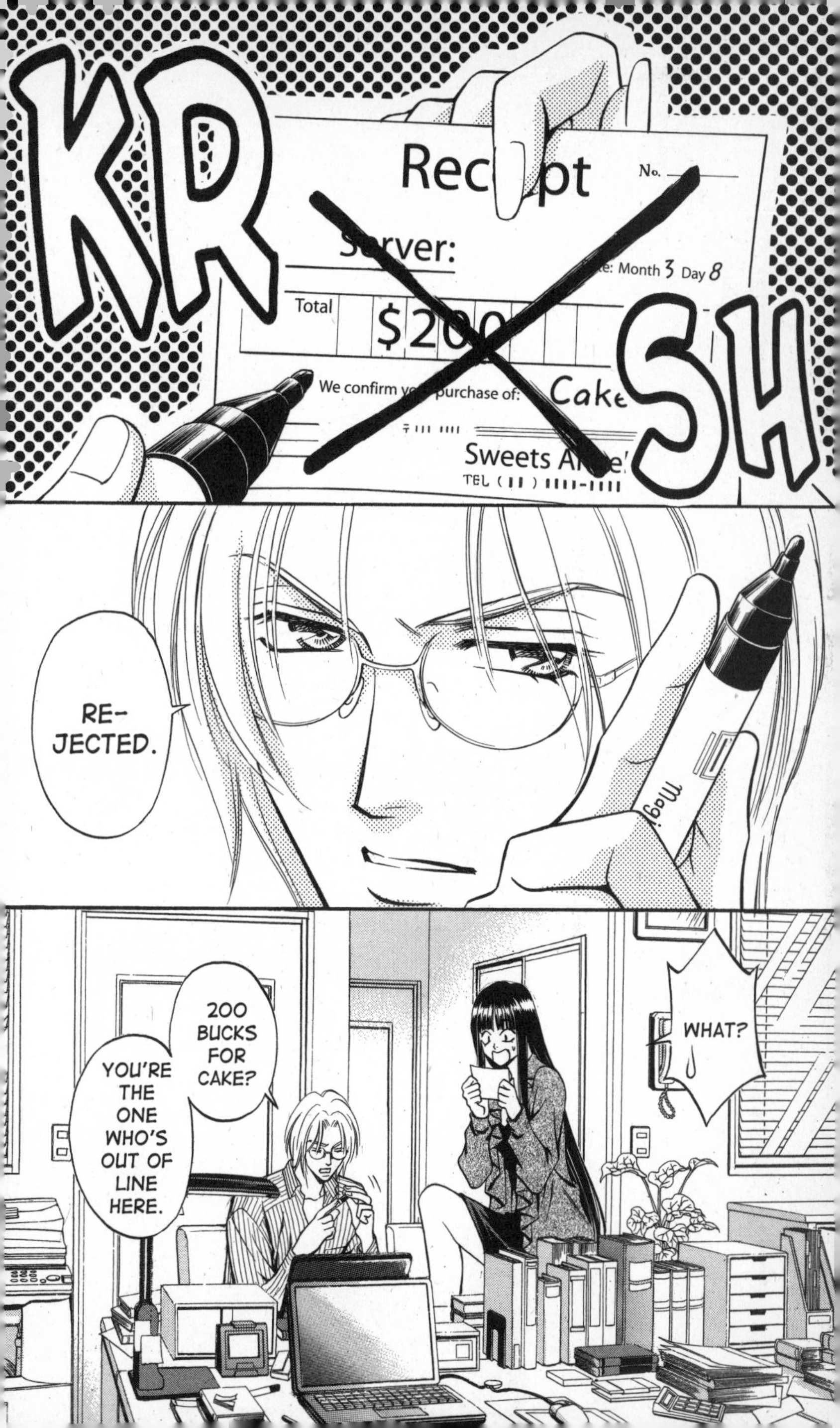
KR
No.
Total
Month 3 Day 8
SH
RE-JECTED.
WHAT?
200 BUCKS FOR CAKE?
YOU'RE THE ONE WHO'S OUT OF LINE HERE.

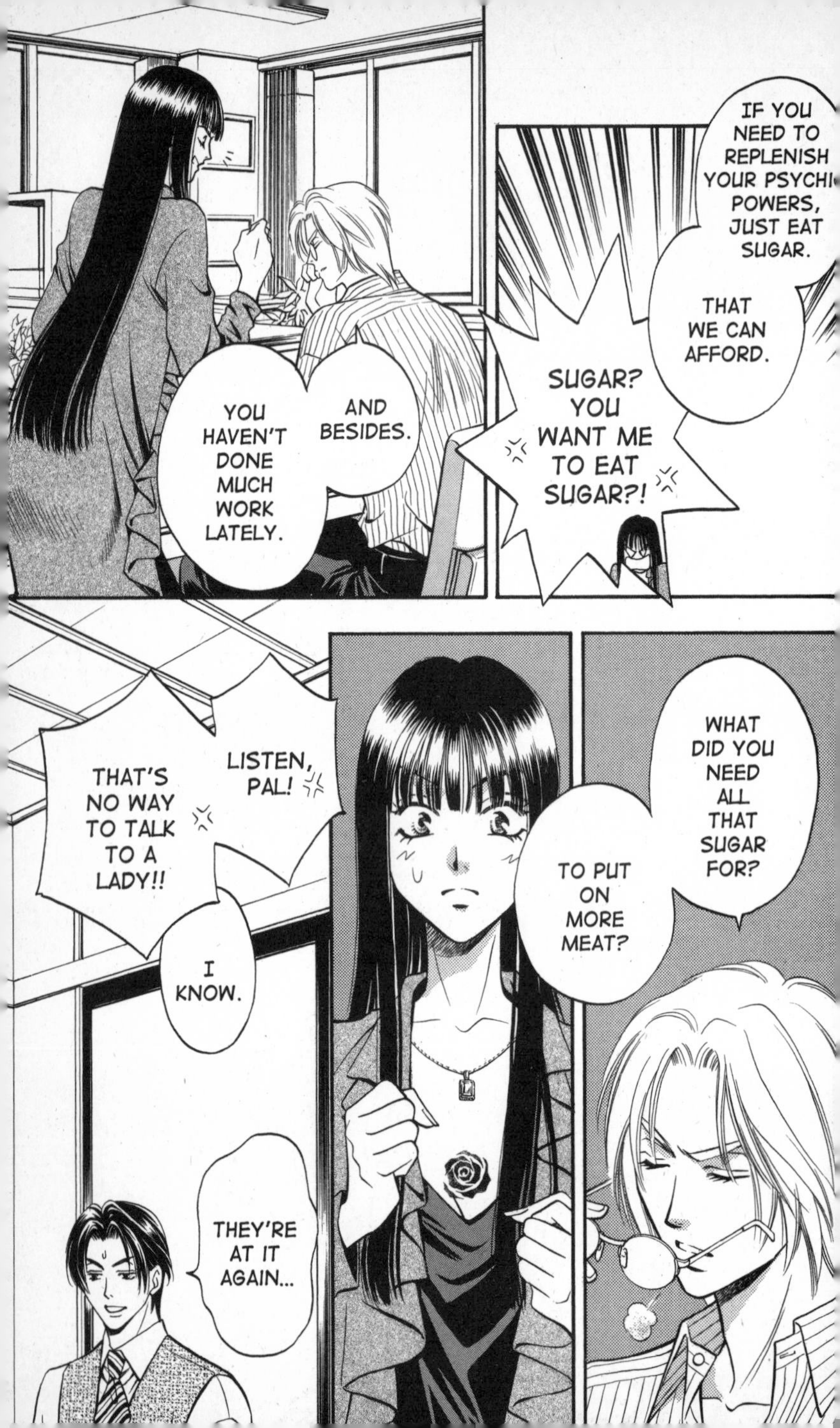
IF YOU NEED TO REPLENISH YOUR PSYCHIC POWERS, JUST EAT SUGAR.
THAT WE CAN AFFORD.
SUGAR? YOU WANT ME TO EAT SUGAR?!
AND BESIDES.
YOU HAVEN'T DONE MUCH WORK LATELY.
WHAT DID YOU NEED ALL THAT SUGAR FOR?
TO PUT ON MORE MEAT?
LISTEN, PAL!
THAT'S NO WAY TO TALK TO A LADY!!
I KNOW.
THEY'RE AT IT AGAIN...

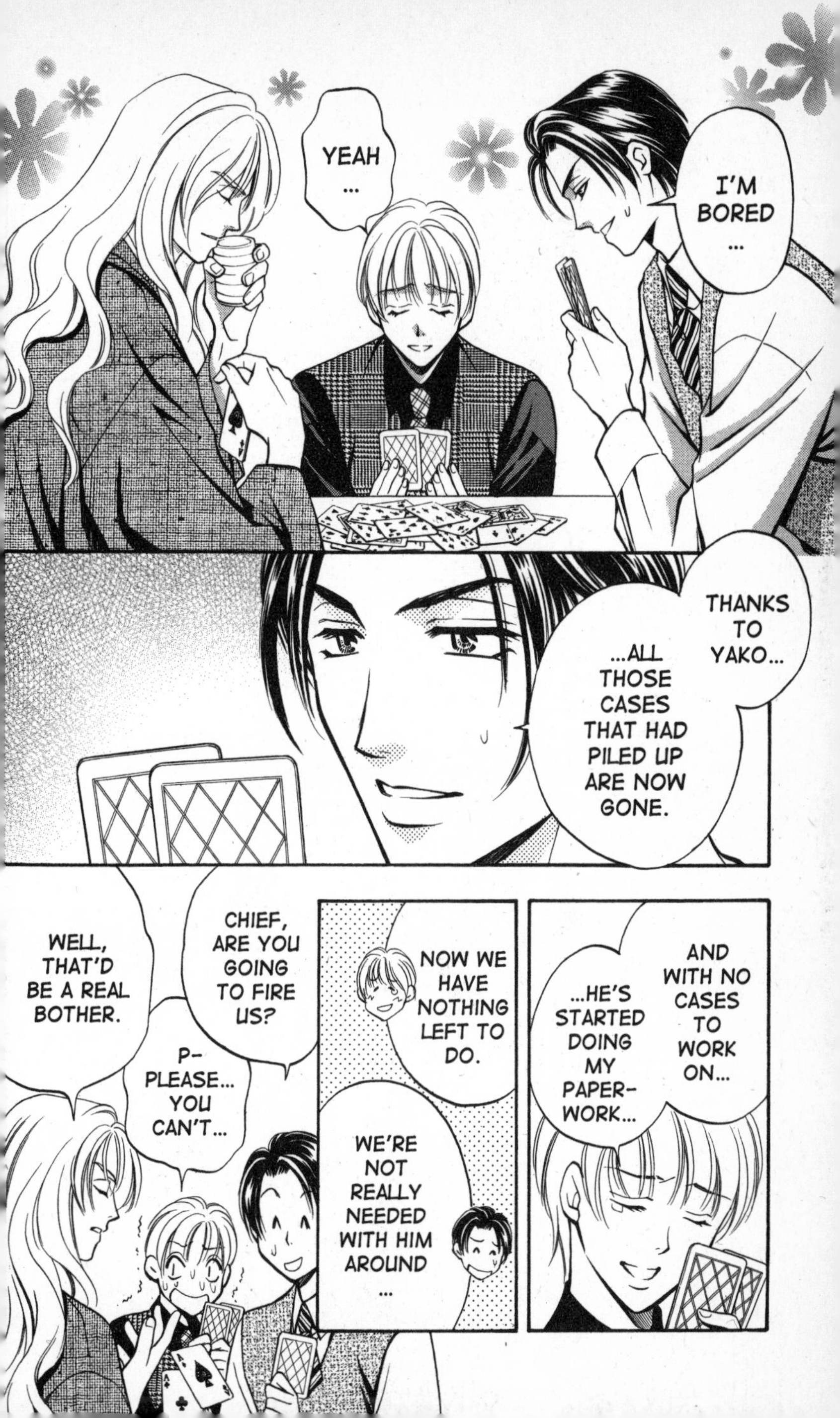
I'M BORED ...
YEAH ...
THANKS TO YAKO...
...ALL THOSE CASES THAT HAD PILED UP ARE NOW GONE.
AND WITH NO CASES TO WORK ON...
...HE'S STARTED DOING MY PAPER-WORK...
NOW WE HAVE NOTHING LEFT TO DO.
WE'RE NOT REALLY NEEDED WITH HIM AROUND ...
CHIEF, ARE YOU GOING TO FIRE US?
WELL, THAT'D BE A REAL BOTHER.
P-PLEASE... YOU CAN'T...

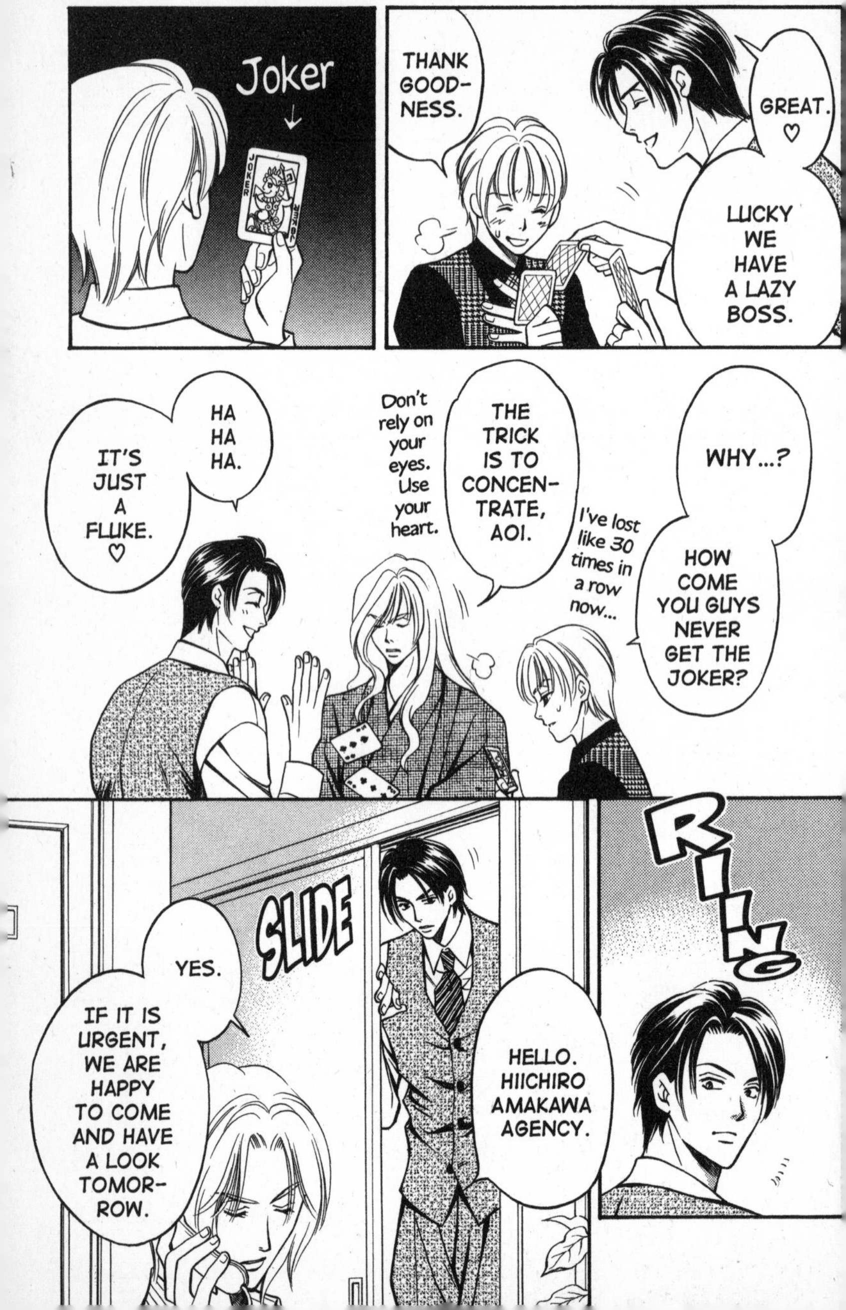
GREAT. ♡
THANK GOODNESS.
LUCKY WE HAVE A LAZY BOSS.
Joker
JOKER
WHY...?
HOW COME YOU GUYS NEVER GET THE JOKER?
I've lost like 30 times in a row now...
THE TRICK IS TO CONCENTRATE, AOI.
Don't rely on your eyes. Use your heart.
HA HA HA.
IT'S JUST A FLUKE. ♡
RING
HELLO. HIICHIRO AMAKAWA AGENCY.
SLIDE
YES.
IF IT IS URGENT, WE ARE HAPPY TO COME AND HAVE A LOOK TOMORROW.

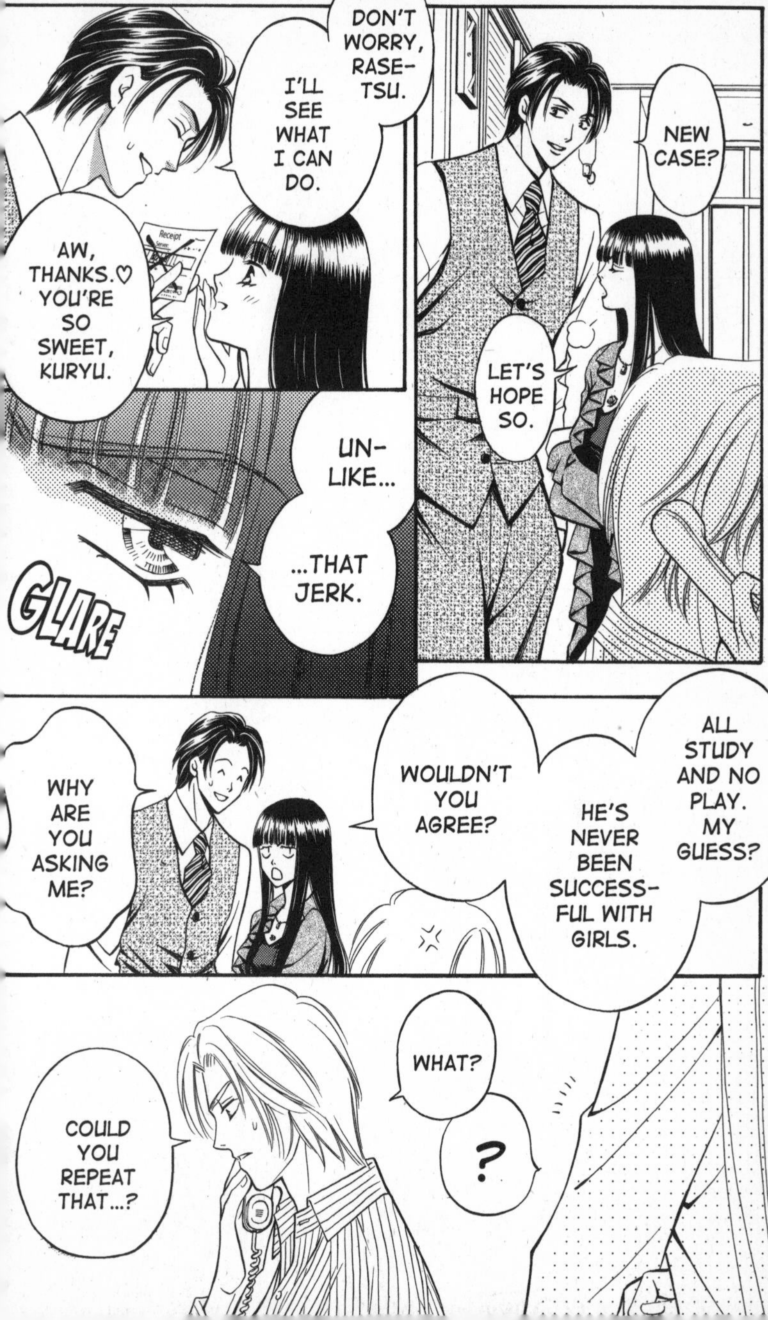
NEW CASE?
LET'S HOPE SO.
DON'T WORRY, RASE-TSU.
I'LL SEE WHAT I CAN DO.
AW, THANKS.♡ YOU'RE SO SWEET, KURYU.
UN-LIKE...
...THAT JERK.
GLARE
ALL STUDY AND NO PLAY. MY GUESS?
HE'S NEVER BEEN SUCCESS-FUL WITH GIRLS.
WOULDN'T YOU AGREE?
WHY ARE YOU ASKING ME?
WHAT?
?
COULD YOU REPEAT THAT...?

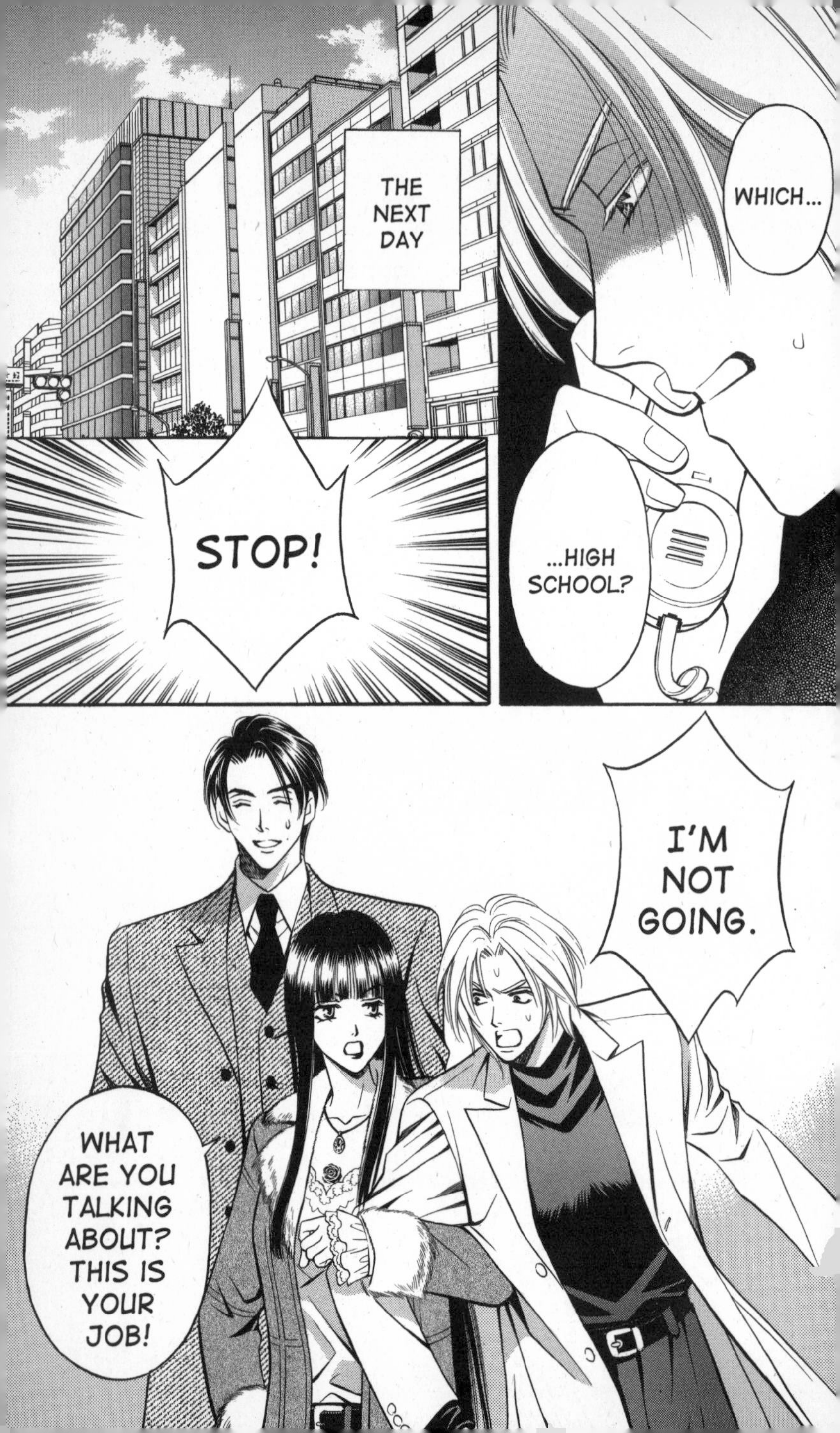
WHICH...
...HIGH SCHOOL?
THE NEXT DAY
STOP!
I'M NOT GOING.
WHAT ARE YOU TALKING ABOUT? THIS IS YOUR JOB!

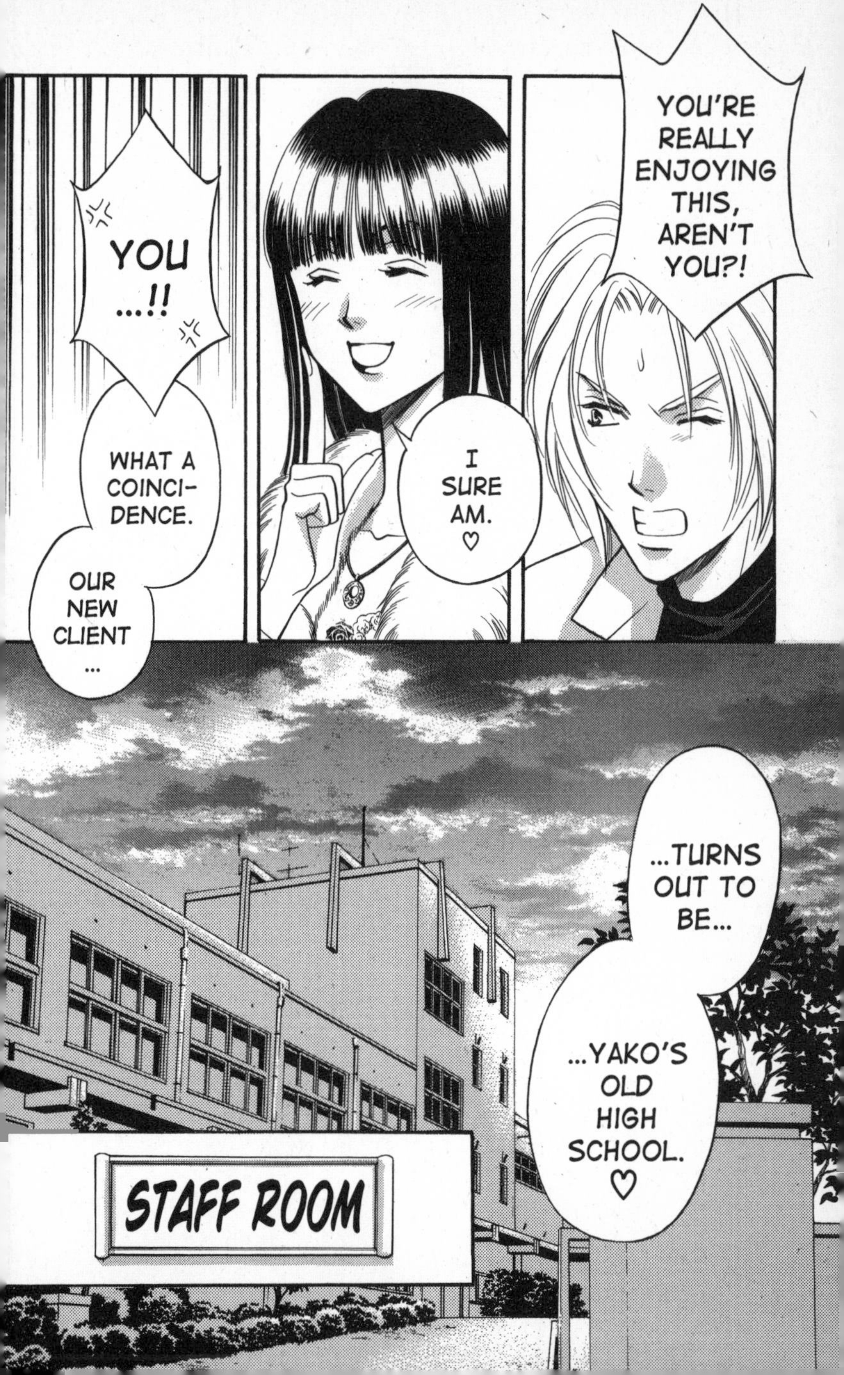
YOU'RE REALLY ENJOYING THIS, AREN'T YOU?!
I SURE AM. ♡
YOU ...!!
WHAT A COINCI- DENCE.
OUR NEW CLIENT ...
...TURNS OUT TO BE...
...YAKO'S OLD HIGH SCHOOL. ♡
STAFF ROOM

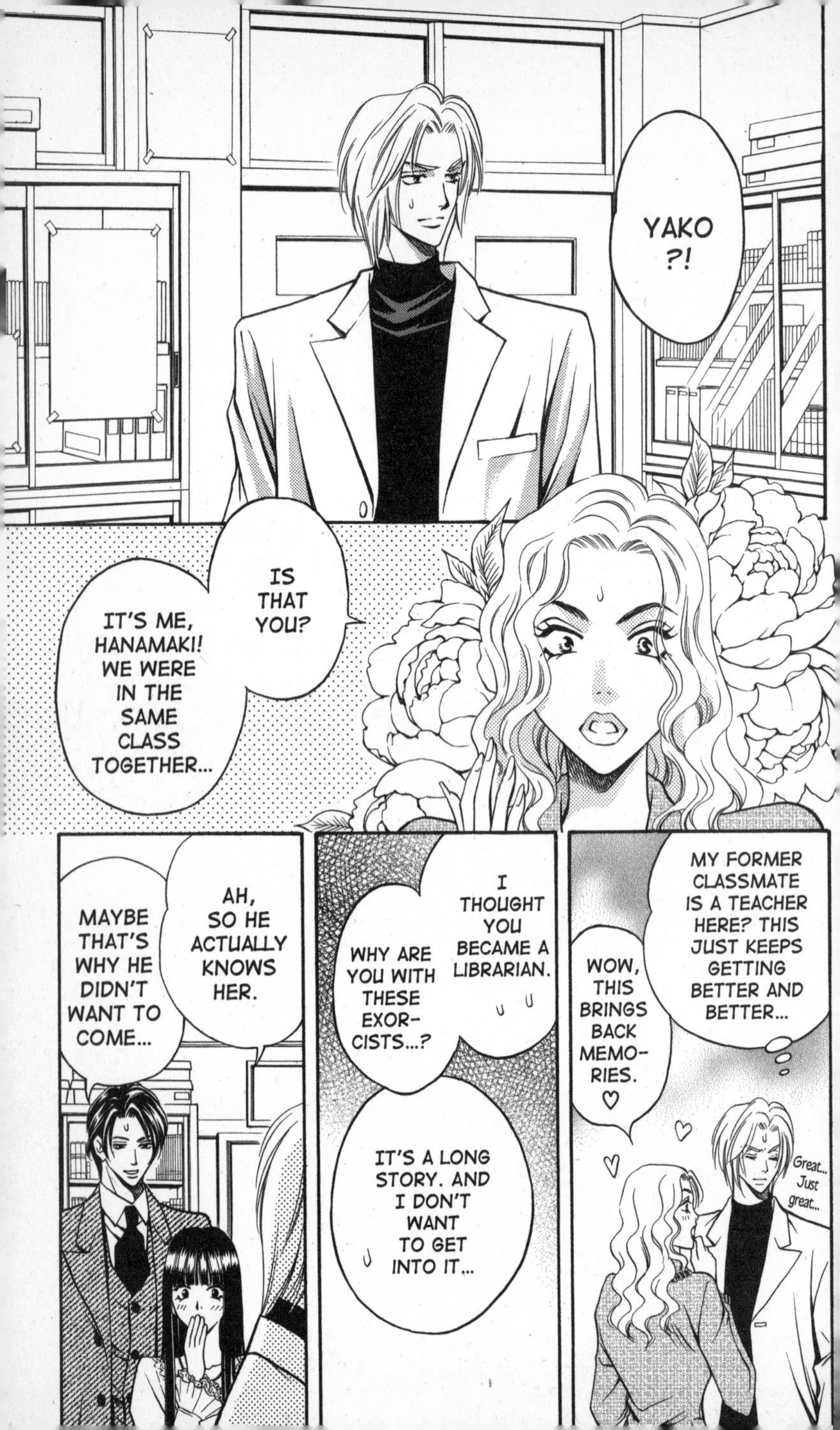
YAKO ?!
IS THAT YOU?
IT'S ME, HANAMAKI! WE WERE IN THE SAME CLASS TOGETHER...
MY FORMER CLASSMATE IS A TEACHER HERE? THIS JUST KEEPS GETTING BETTER AND BETTER...
WOW, THIS BRINGS BACK MEMO-RIES. ♡
Great... Just great...
I THOUGHT YOU BECAME A LIBRARIAN.
WHY ARE YOU WITH THESE EXOR-CISTS...?
IT'S A LONG STORY. AND I DON'T WANT TO GET INTO IT...
AH, SO HE ACTUALLY KNOWS HER.
MAYBE THAT'S WHY HE DIDN'T WANT TO COME...

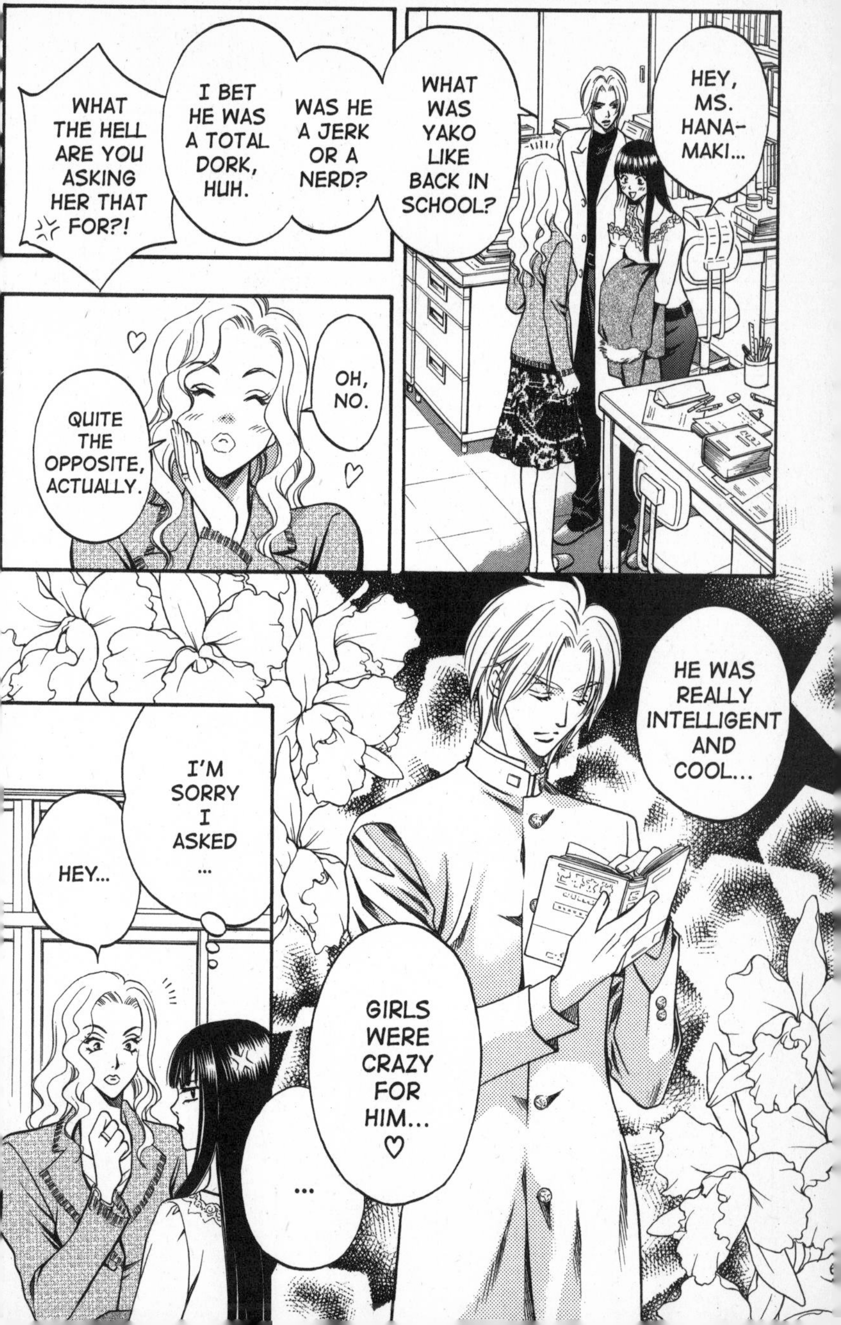
HEY, MS. HANAMAKI...
WHAT WAS YAKO LIKE BACK IN SCHOOL?
WAS HE A JERK OR A NERD?
I BET HE WAS A TOTAL DORK, HUH.
WHAT THE HELL ARE YOU ASKING HER THAT FOR?!
OH, NO.
QUITE THE OPPOSITE, ACTUALLY.
HE WAS REALLY INTELLIGENT AND COOL...
GIRLS WERE CRAZY FOR HIM... ♡
...
I'M SORRY I ASKED...
HEY...

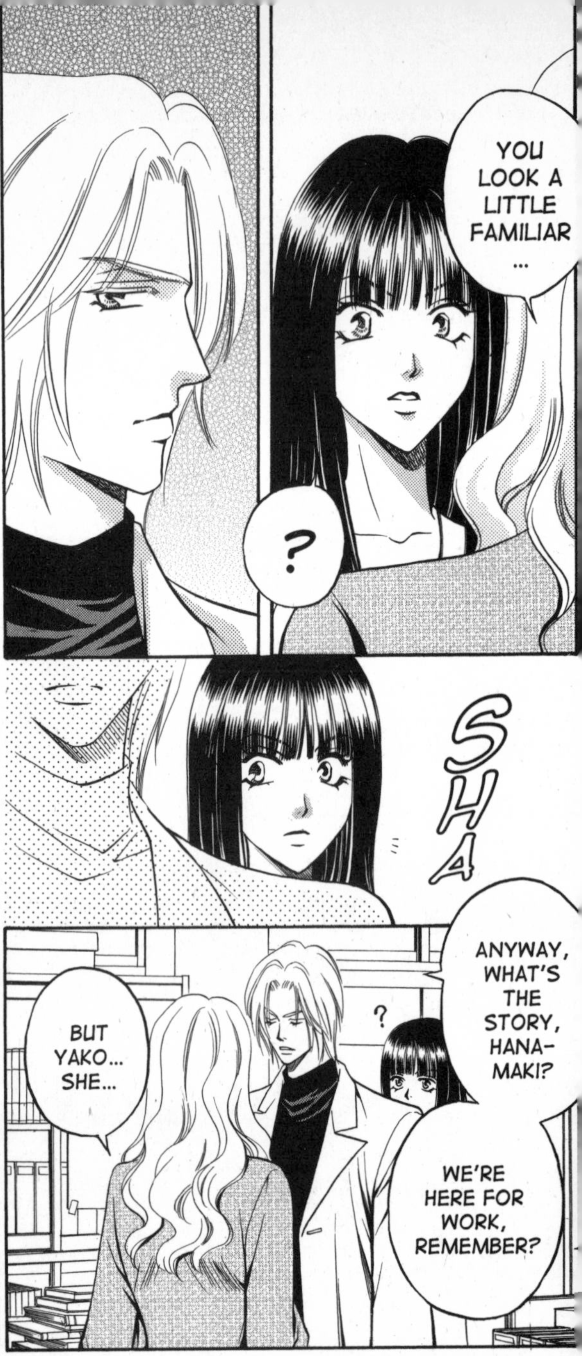
YOU LOOK A LITTLE FAMILIAR ...
?
SHA
ANYWAY, WHAT'S THE STORY, HANA-MAKI?
WE'RE HERE FOR WORK, REMEMBER?
?
BUT YAKO... SHE...

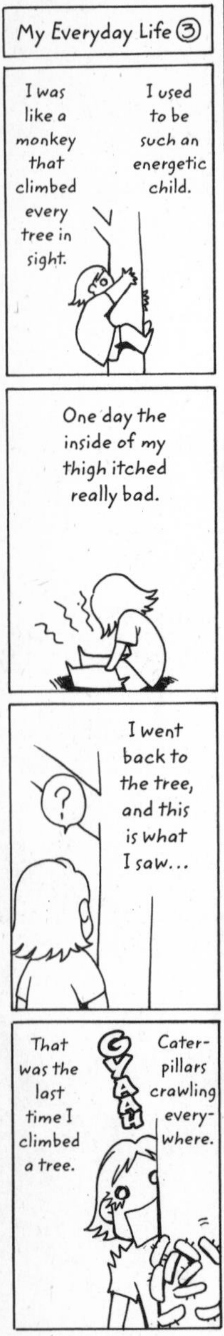
My Everyday Life ③
I used to be such an energetic child.
I was like a monkey that climbed every tree in sight.
One day the inside of my thigh itched really bad.
I went back to the tree, and this is what I saw...
?
Caterpillars crawling everywhere.
GYAAAH
That was the last time I climbed a tree.

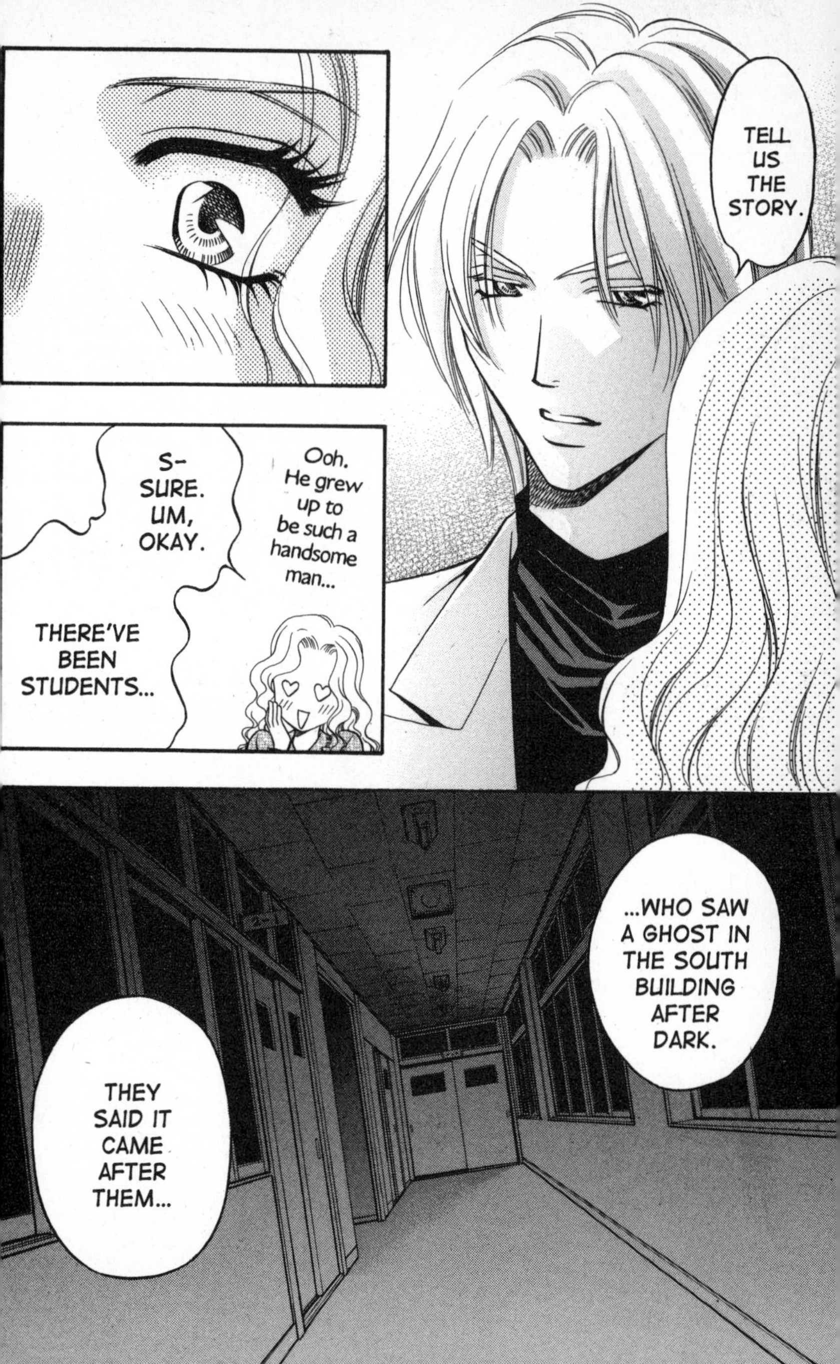
TELL US THE STORY.
Ooh. He grew up to be such a handsome man...
S-SURE. UM, OKAY.
THERE'VE BEEN STUDENTS...
...WHO SAW A GHOST IN THE SOUTH BUILDING AFTER DARK.
THEY SAID IT CAME AFTER THEM...

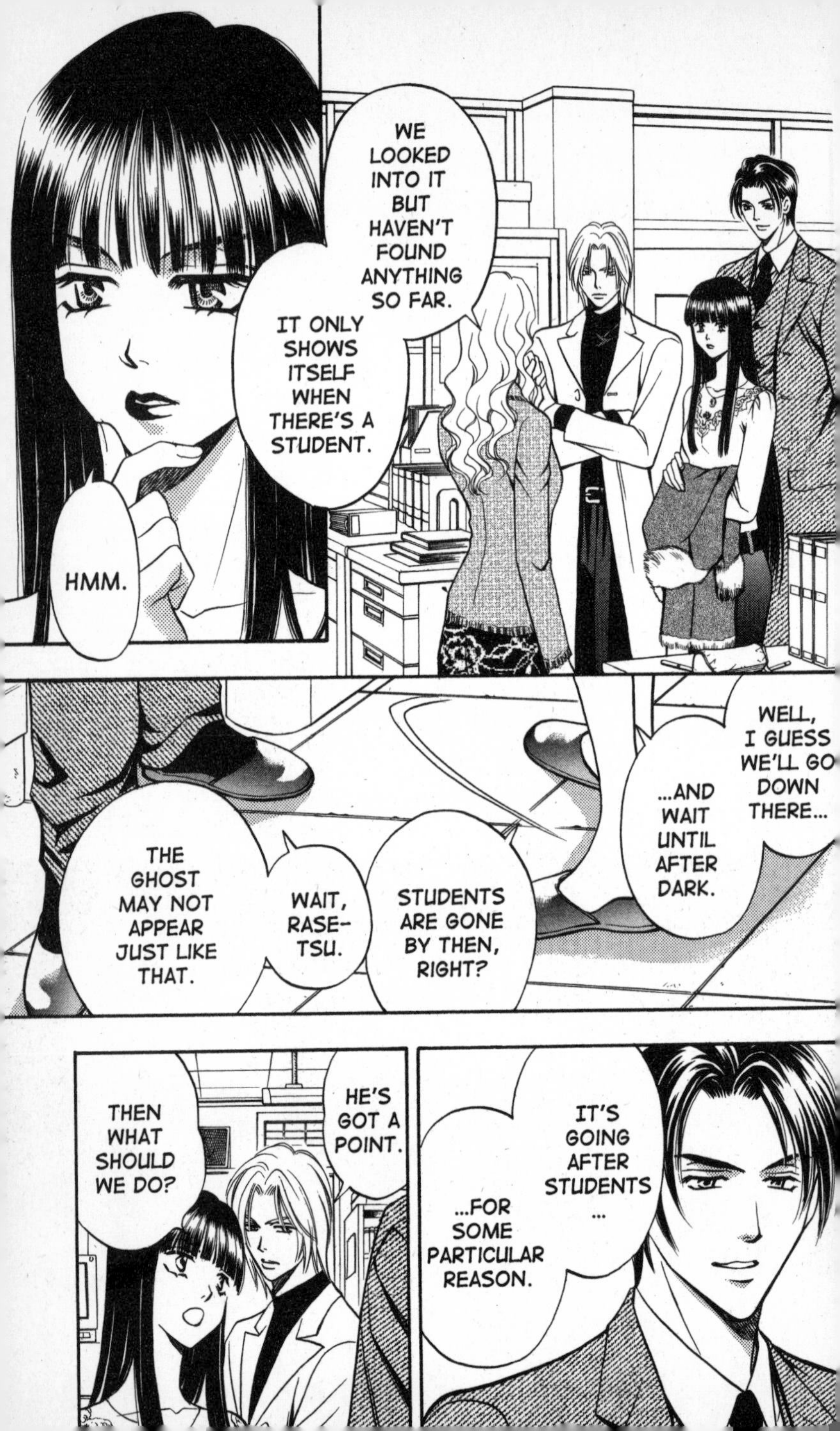
WE LOOKED INTO IT BUT HAVEN'T FOUND ANYTHING SO FAR.
IT ONLY SHOWS ITSELF WHEN THERE'S A STUDENT.
HMM.
WELL, I GUESS WE'LL GO DOWN THERE...
...AND WAIT UNTIL AFTER DARK.
STUDENTS ARE GONE BY THEN, RIGHT?
WAIT, RASE-TSU.
THE GHOST MAY NOT APPEAR JUST LIKE THAT.
IT'S GOING AFTER STUDENTS...
...FOR SOME PARTICULAR REASON.
HE'S GOT A POINT.
THEN WHAT SHOULD WE DO?

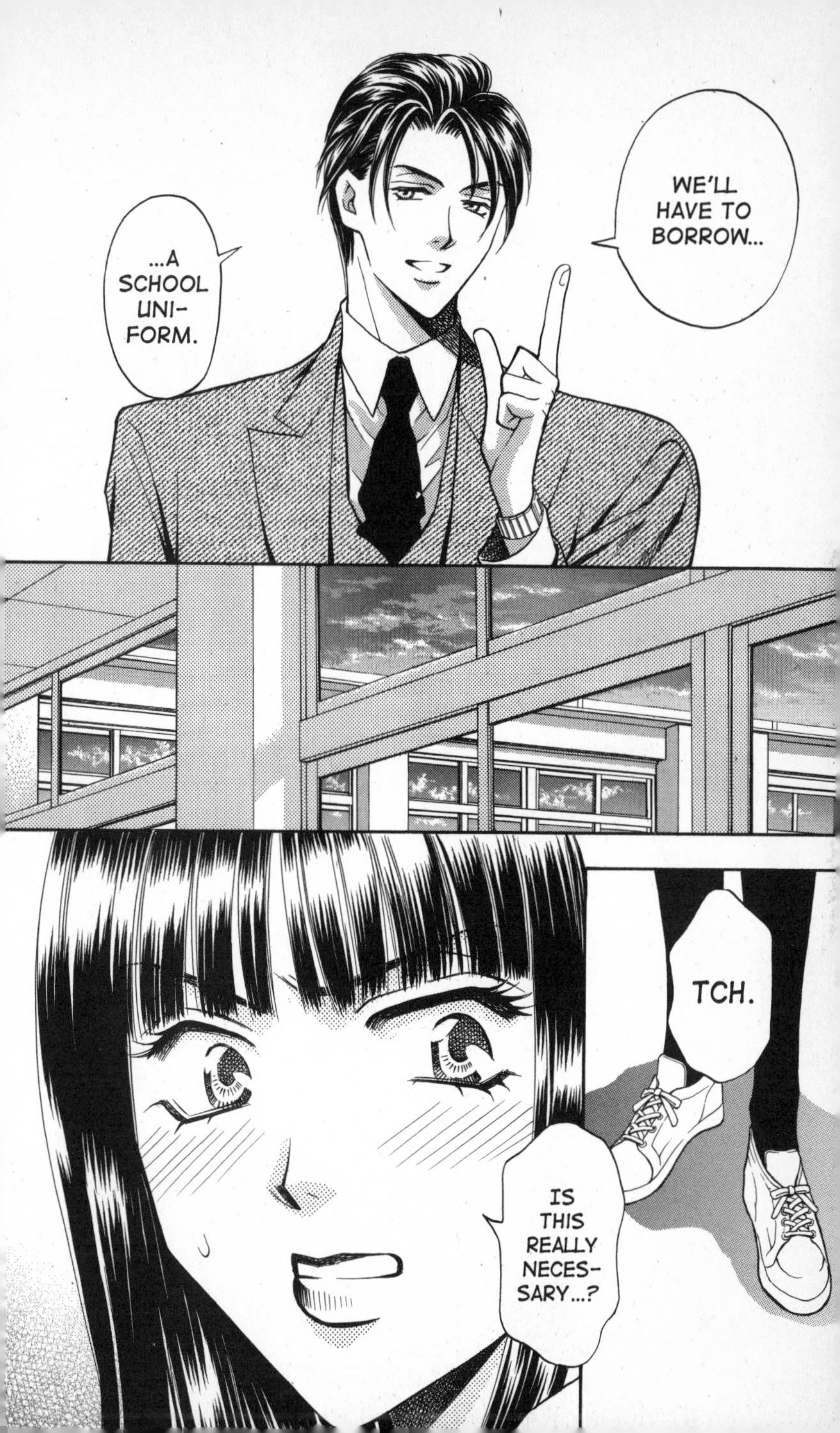
WE'LL HAVE TO BORROW...
...A SCHOOL UNI-FORM.
TCH.
IS THIS REALLY NECES-SARY...?

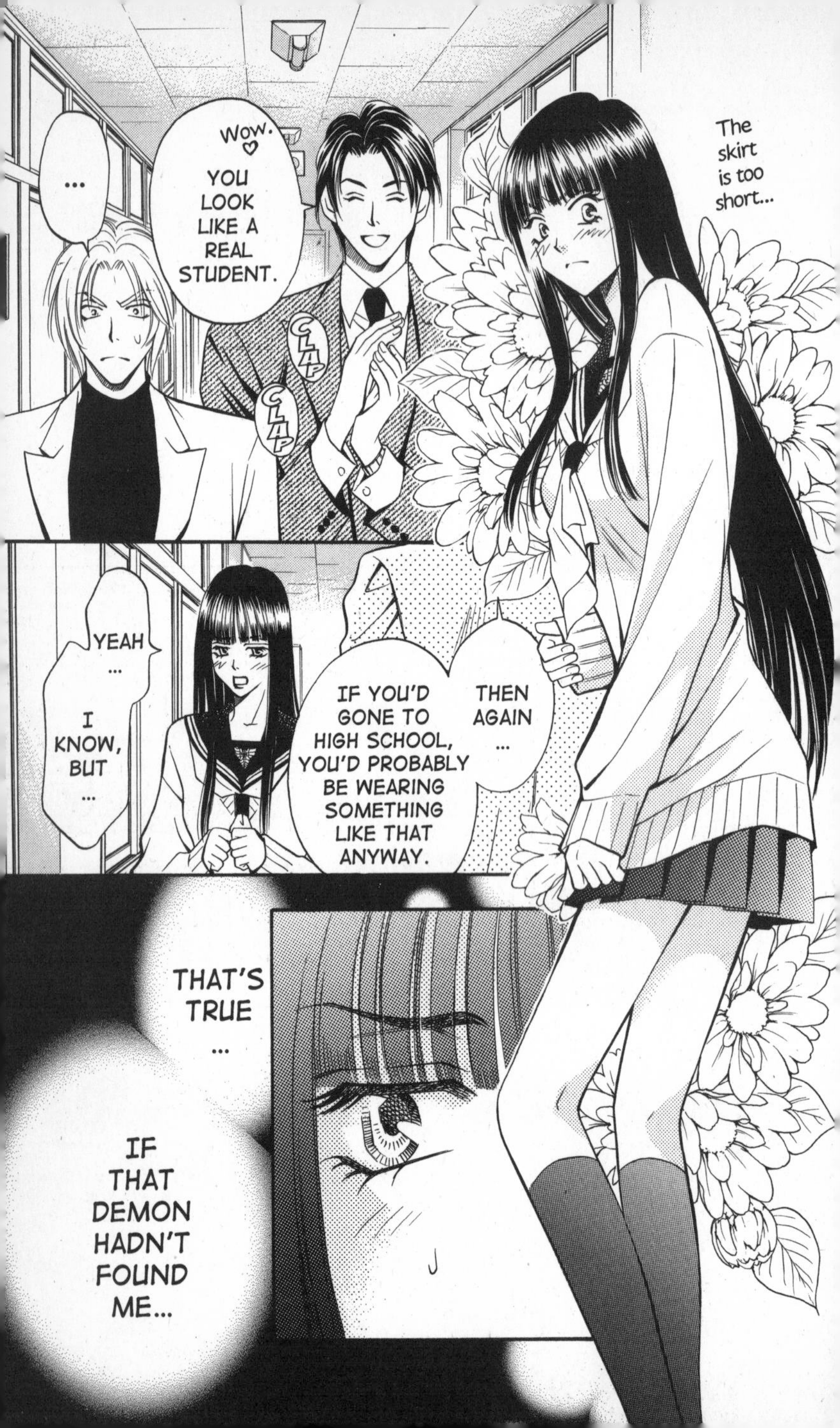
The skirt is too short...
Wow. ♥ YOU LOOK LIKE A REAL STUDENT.
CLAP
CLAP
...
THEN AGAIN...
IF YOU'D GONE TO HIGH SCHOOL, YOU'D PROBABLY BE WEARING SOMETHING LIKE THAT ANYWAY.
YEAH... I KNOW, BUT...
THAT'S TRUE...
IF THAT DEMON HADN'T FOUND ME...

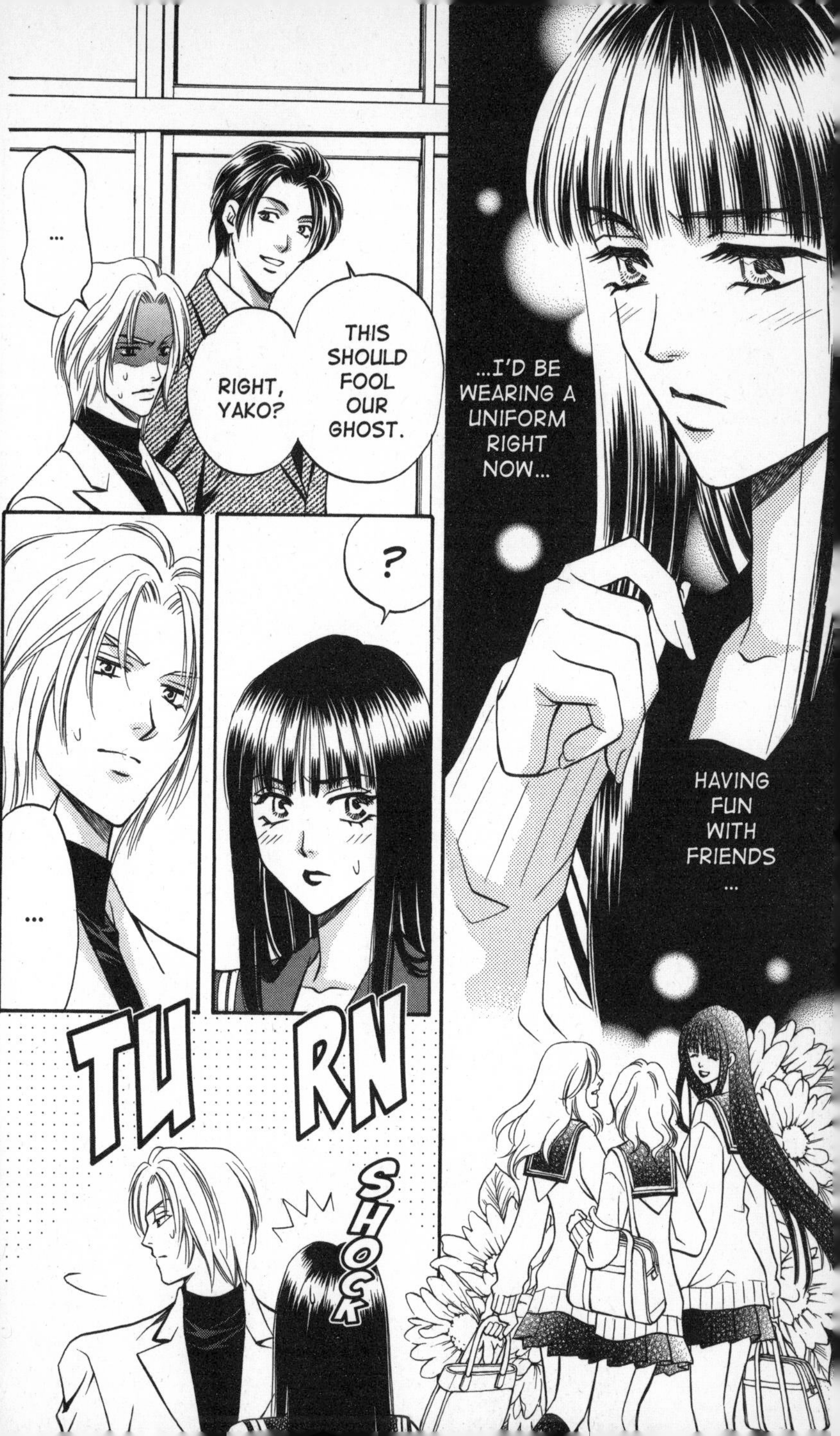
...I'D BE WEARING A UNIFORM RIGHT NOW...
HAVING FUN WITH FRIENDS ...
THIS SHOULD FOOL OUR GHOST.
RIGHT, YAKO?
...
?
...
TURN
SHOCK

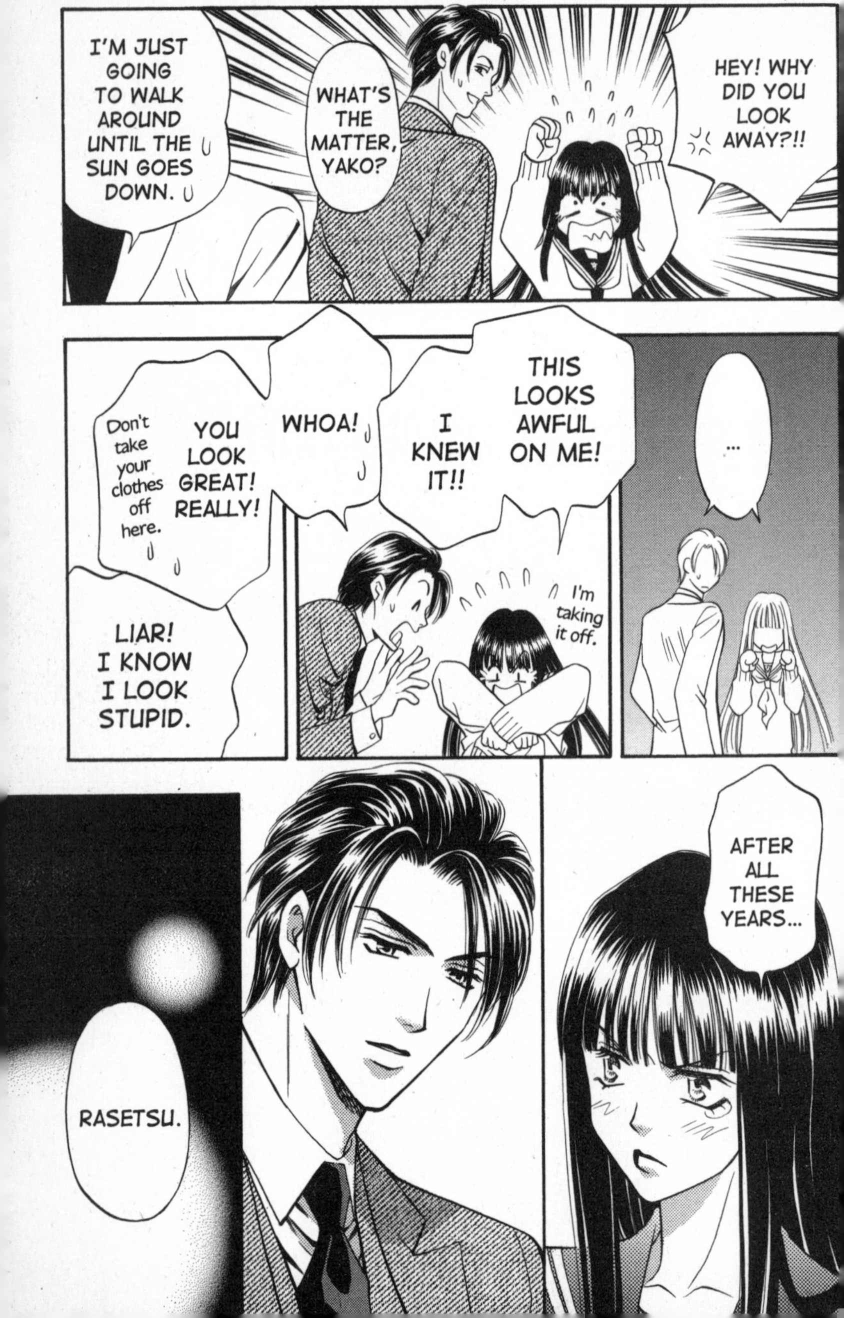
HEY! WHY DID YOU LOOK AWAY?!!
WHAT'S THE MATTER, YAKO?
I'M JUST GOING TO WALK AROUND UNTIL THE SUN GOES DOWN.
...
THIS LOOKS AWFUL ON ME!
I KNEW IT!!
I'm taking it off.
WHOA!
YOU LOOK GREAT! REALLY!
Don't take your clothes off here.
LIAR! I KNOW I LOOK STUPID.
AFTER ALL THESE YEARS...
RASETSU.

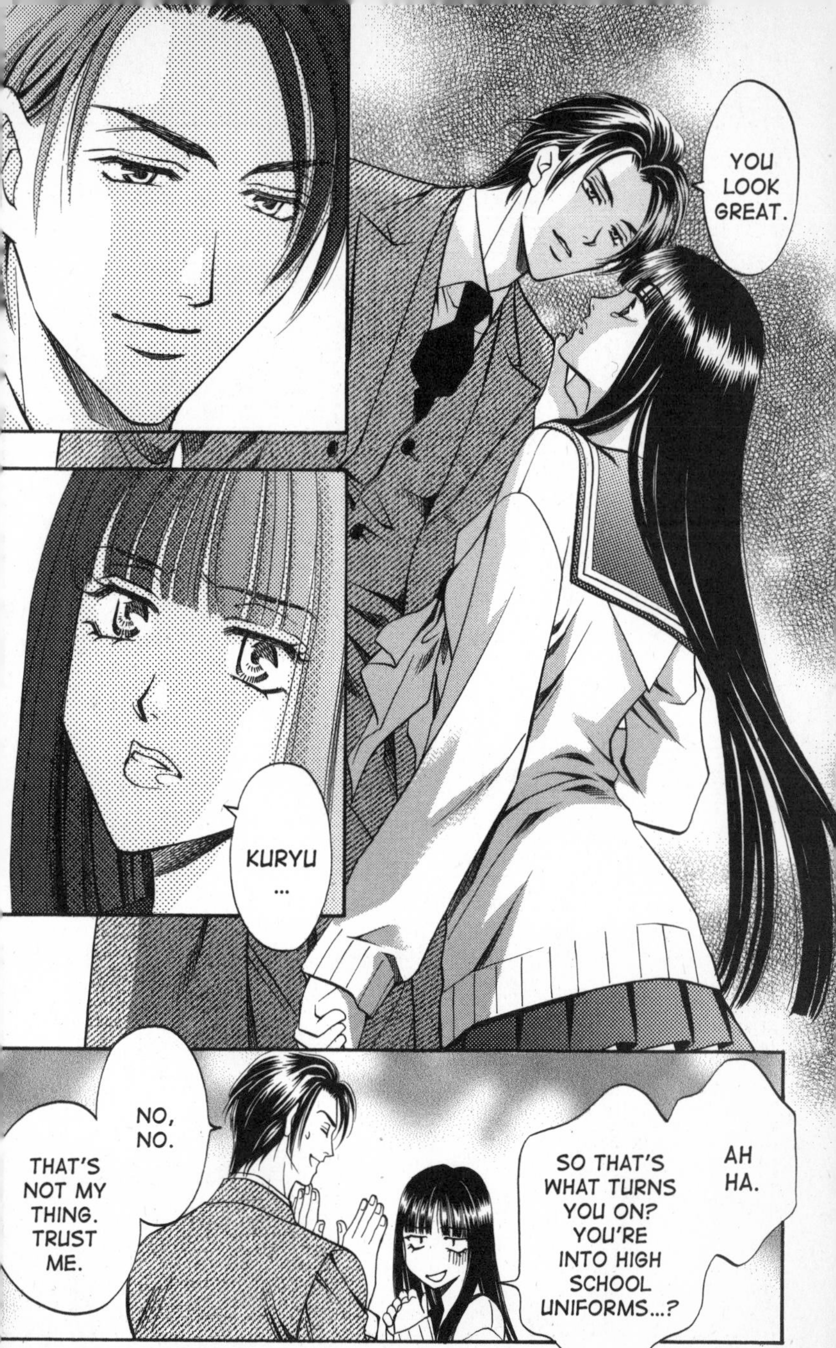
YOU LOOK GREAT.
KURYU ...
AH HA.
SO THAT'S WHAT TURNS YOU ON? YOU'RE INTO HIGH SCHOOL UNIFORMS...?
NO, NO.
THAT'S NOT MY THING. TRUST ME.

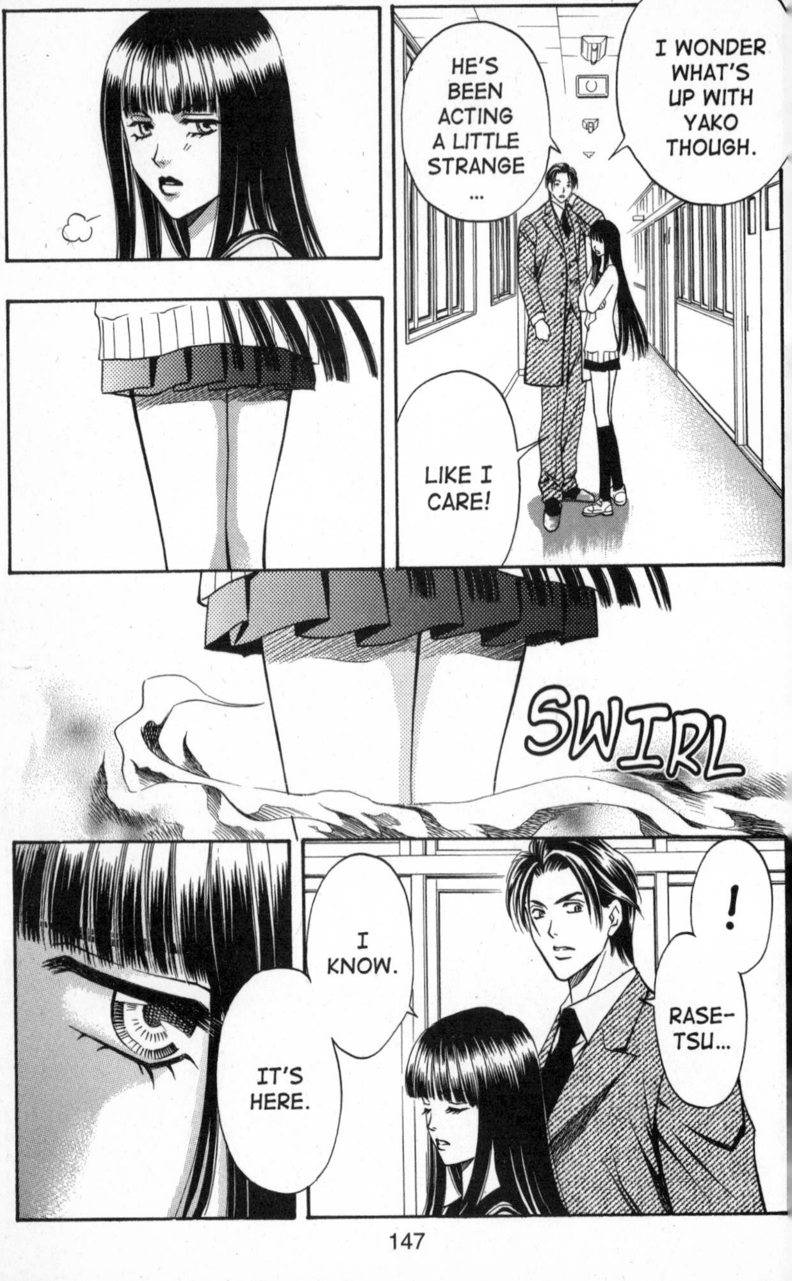
I WONDER WHAT'S UP WITH YAKO THOUGH.
HE'S BEEN ACTING A LITTLE STRANGE ...
LIKE I CARE!
SWIRL
!
RASE-TSU...
I KNOW.
IT'S HERE.

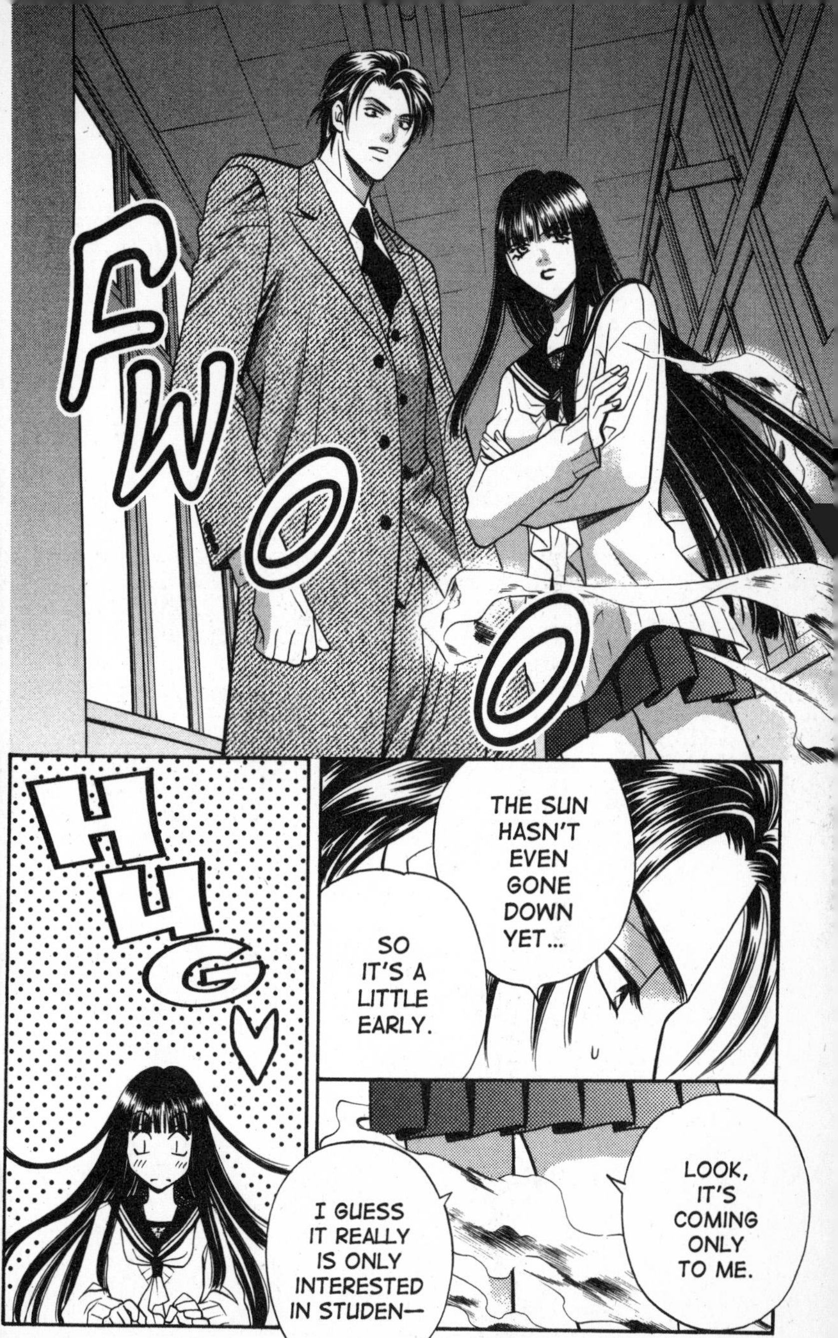
FWOOO
THE SUN HASN'T EVEN GONE DOWN YET...
SO IT'S A LITTLE EARLY.
LOOK, IT'S COMING ONLY TO ME.
I GUESS IT REALLY IS ONLY INTERESTED IN STUDEN—
HUG

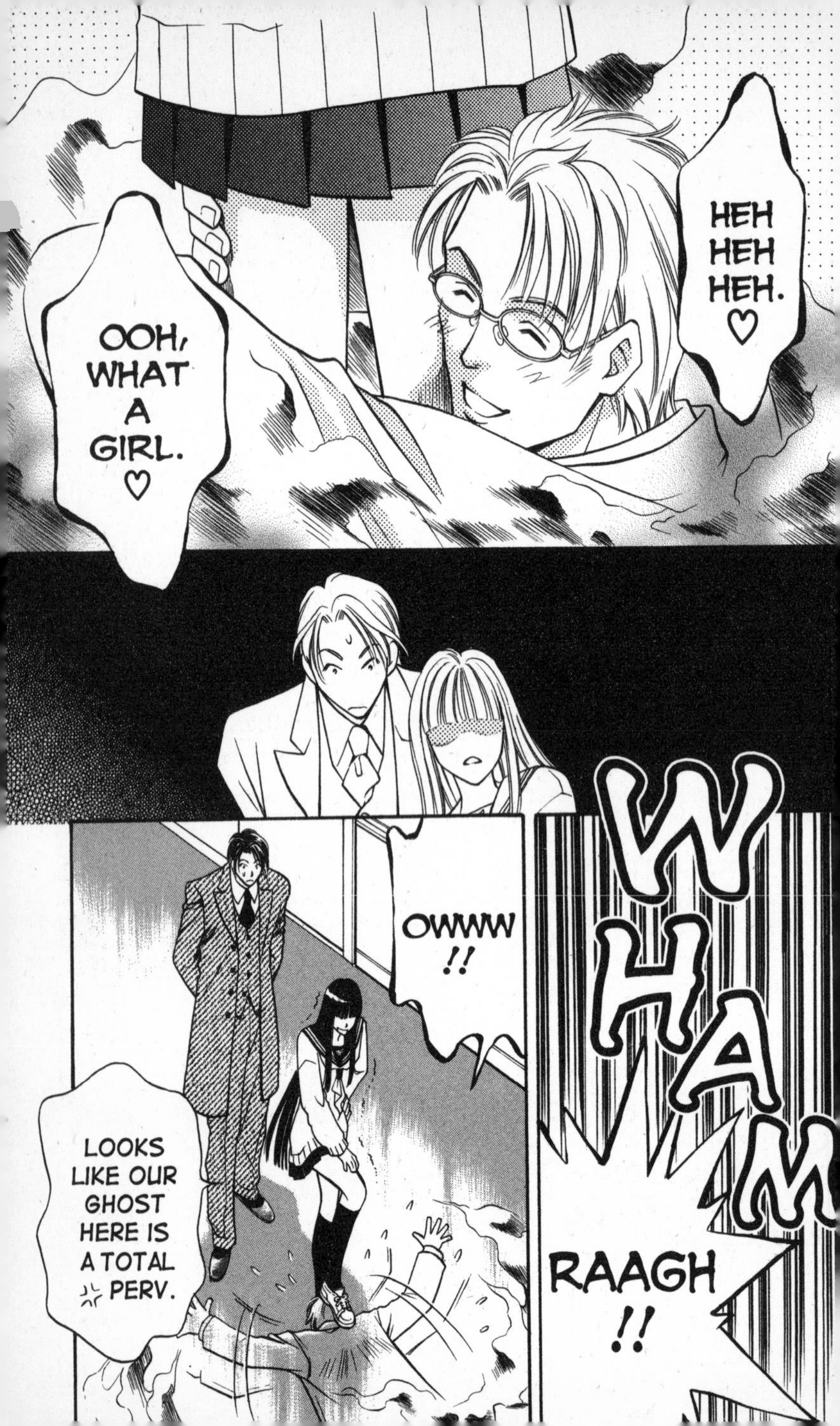
HEH HEH HEH. ♡
OOH, WHAT A GIRL. ♡
WHAM
RAAGH !!
OWWW !!
LOOKS LIKE OUR GHOST HERE IS A TOTAL PERV.

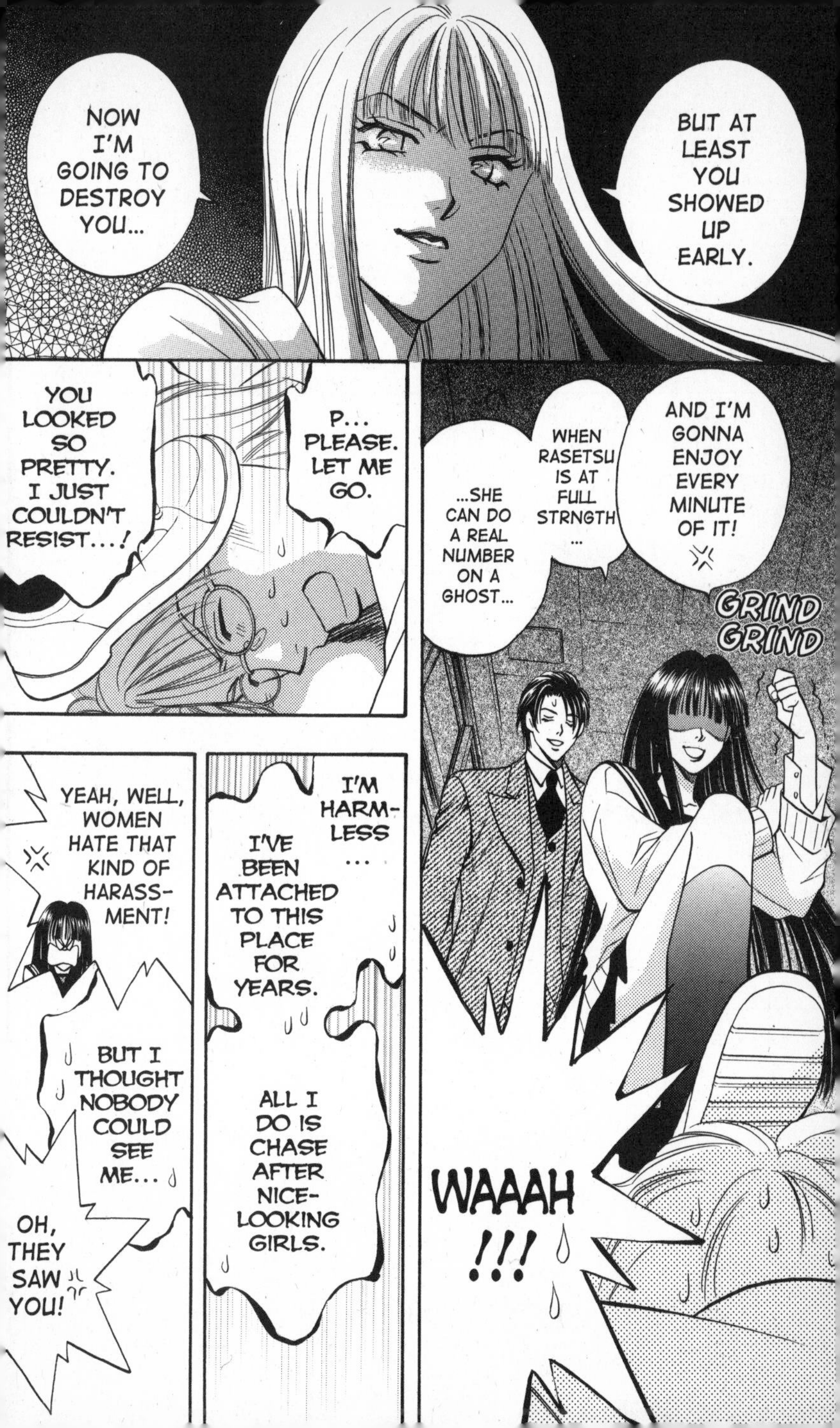

BUT AT LEAST YOU SHOWED UP EARLY.
NOW I'M GOING TO DESTROY YOU...
AND I'M GONNA ENJOY EVERY MINUTE OF IT!
WHEN RASETSU IS AT FULL STRNGTH...
...SHE CAN DO A REAL NUMBER ON A GHOST...
GRIND GRIND
WAAAH!!!
P... PLEASE. LET ME GO.
YOU LOOKED SO PRETTY. I JUST COULDN'T RESIST...!
I'M HARMLESS...
I'VE BEEN ATTACHED TO THIS PLACE FOR YEARS.
ALL I DO IS CHASE AFTER NICE-LOOKING GIRLS.
YEAH, WELL, WOMEN HATE THAT KIND OF HARASSMENT!
BUT I THOUGHT NOBODY COULD SEE ME...
OH, THEY SAW YOU!

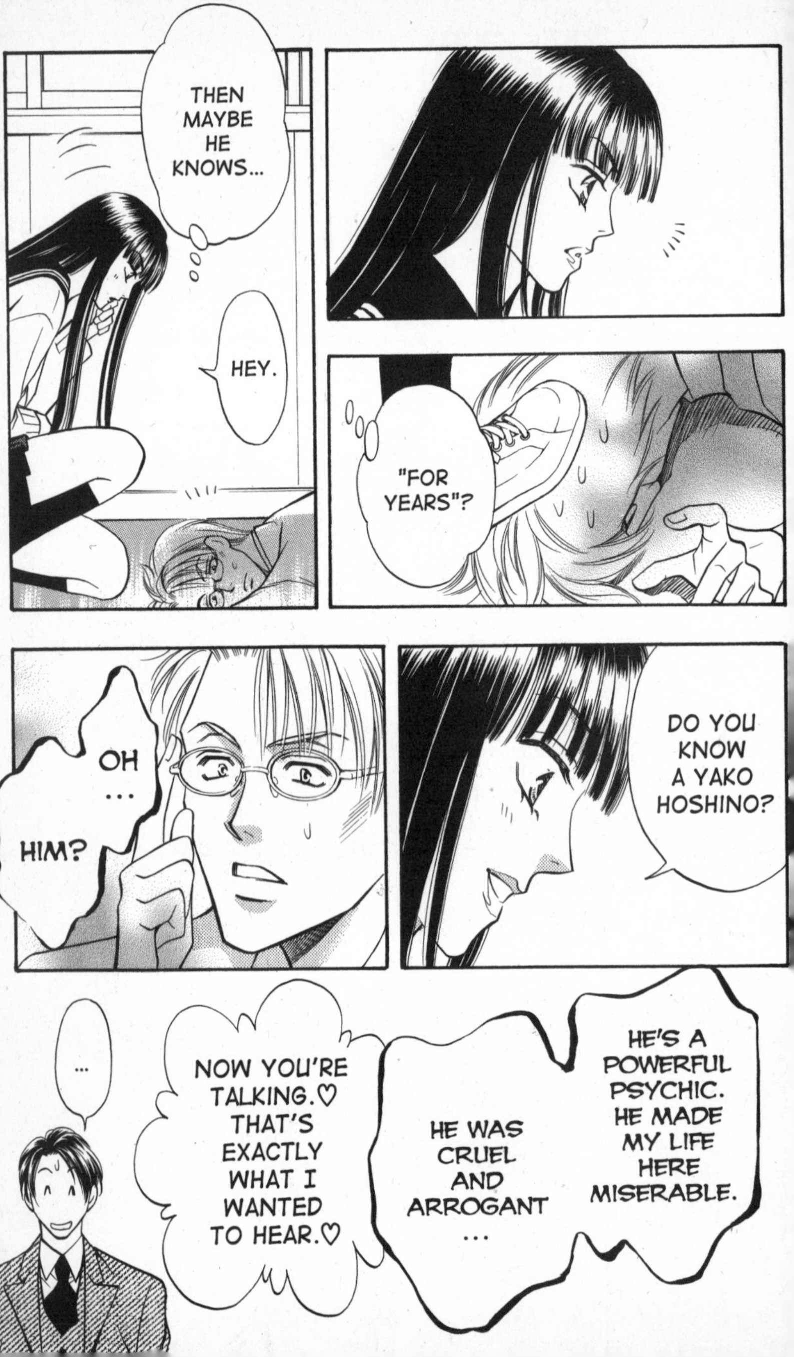
"FOR YEARS"?
THEN MAYBE HE KNOWS...
HEY.
DO YOU KNOW A YAKO HOSHINO?
OH ... HIM?
HE'S A POWERFUL PSYCHIC. HE MADE MY LIFE HERE MISERABLE.
HE WAS CRUEL AND ARROGANT ...
NOW YOU'RE TALKING.♡ THAT'S EXACTLY WHAT I WANTED TO HEAR.♡
...

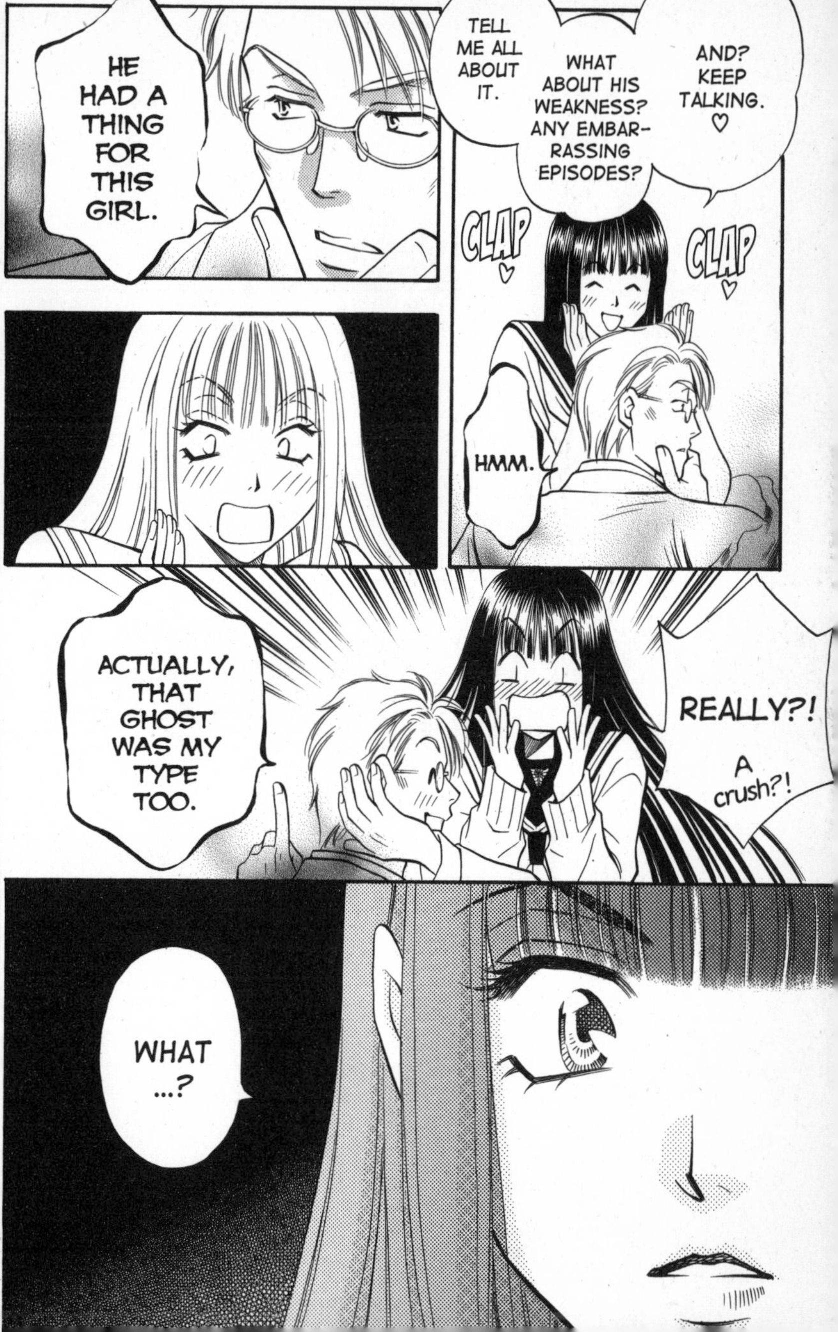
AND? KEEP TALKING. ♡
WHAT ABOUT HIS WEAKNESS? ANY EMBAR-RASSING EPISODES?
TELL ME ALL ABOUT IT.
CLAP ♡
CLAP ♡
HMM.
HE HAD A THING FOR THIS GIRL.
REALLY?!
A crush?!
ACTUALLY, THAT GHOST WAS MY TYPE TOO.
WHAT ...?

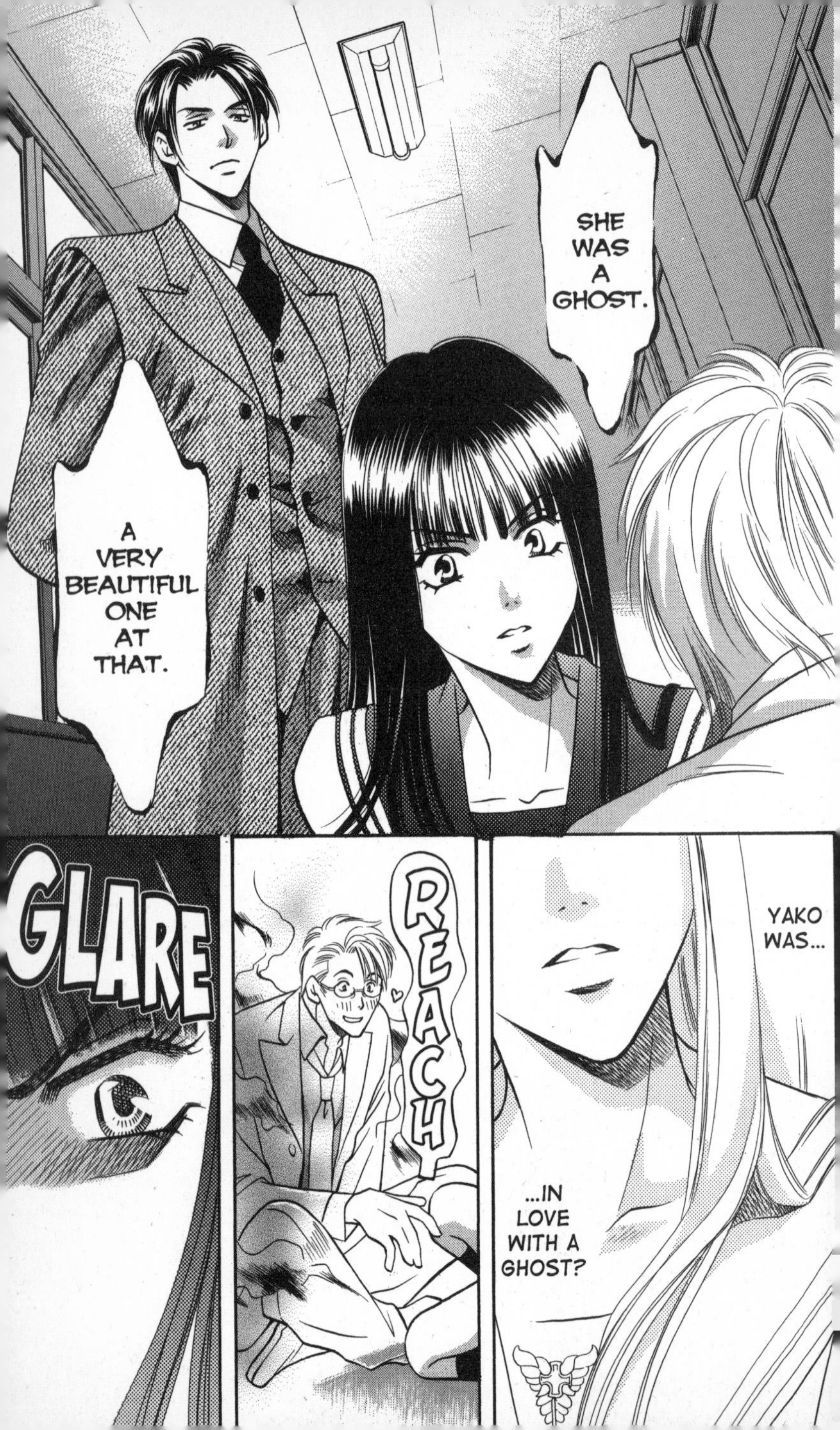
SHE WAS A GHOST.
A VERY BEAUTIFUL ONE AT THAT.
YAKO WAS...
...IN LOVE WITH A GHOST?
REACH
GLARE

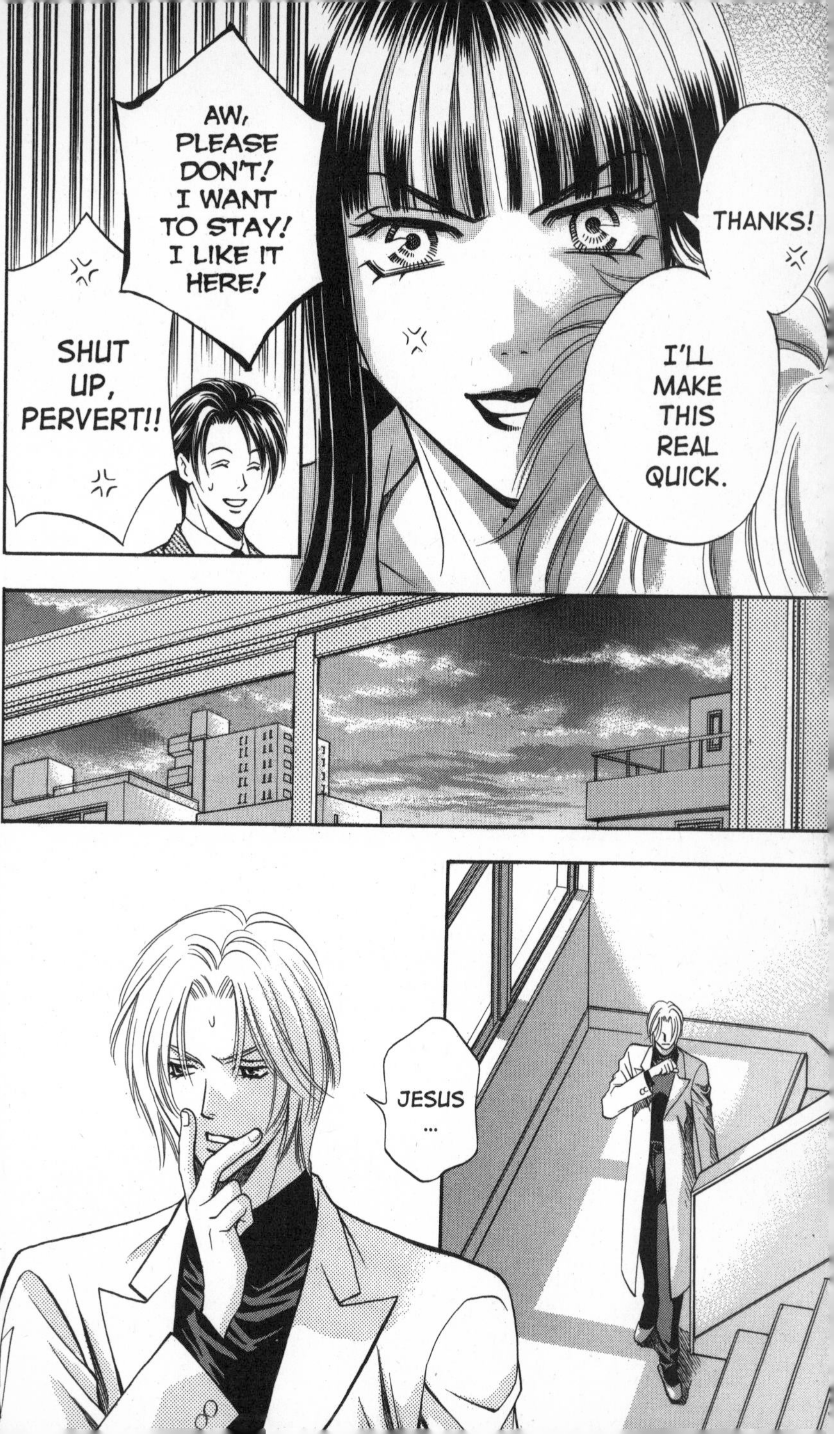
THANKS!
I'LL MAKE THIS REAL QUICK.
AW, PLEASE DON'T! I WANT TO STAY! I LIKE IT HERE!
SHUT UP, PERVERT!!
JESUS ...

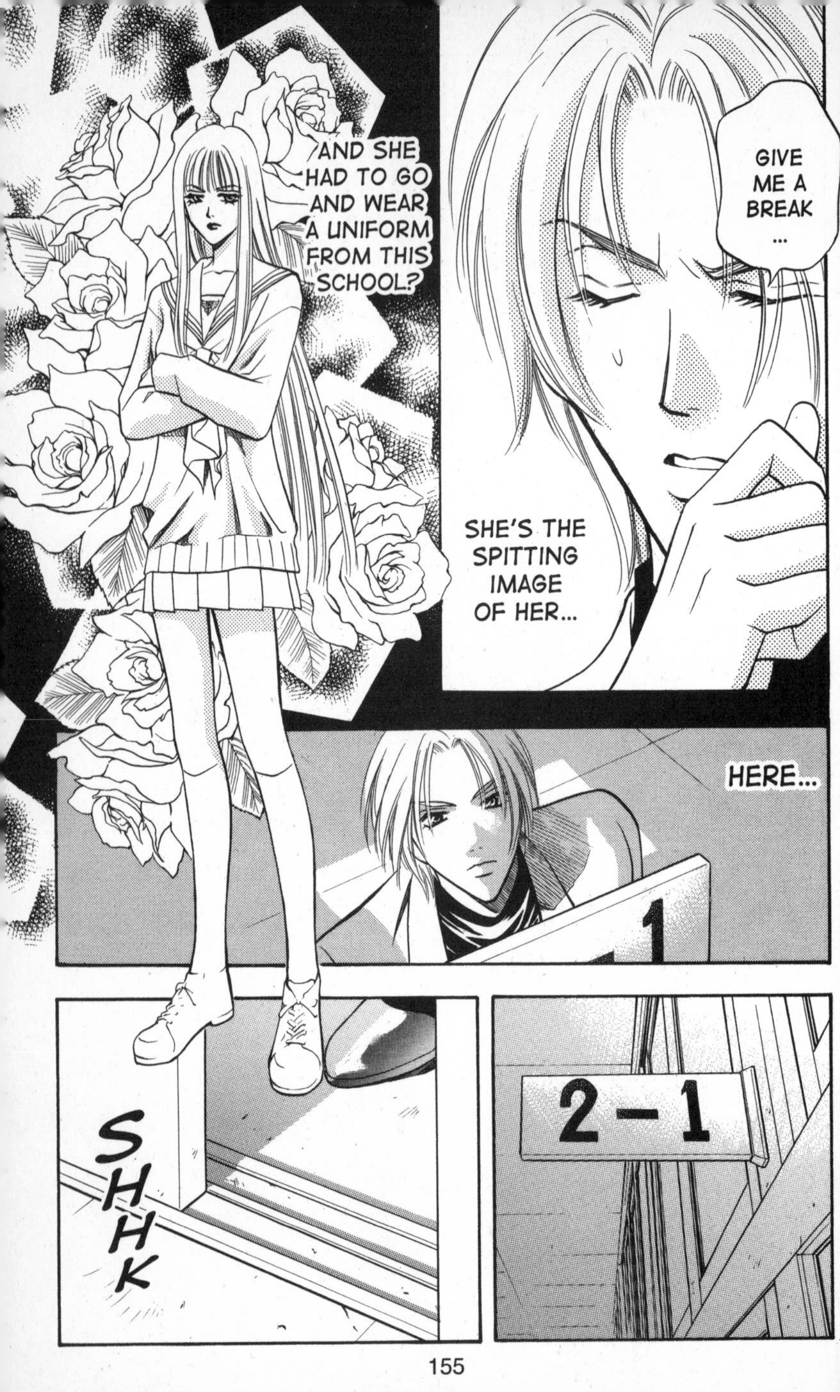
GIVE ME A BREAK ...
SHE'S THE SPITTING IMAGE OF HER...
AND SHE HAD TO GO AND WEAR A UNIFORM FROM THIS SCHOOL?
HERE...
1
2-1
SHHK

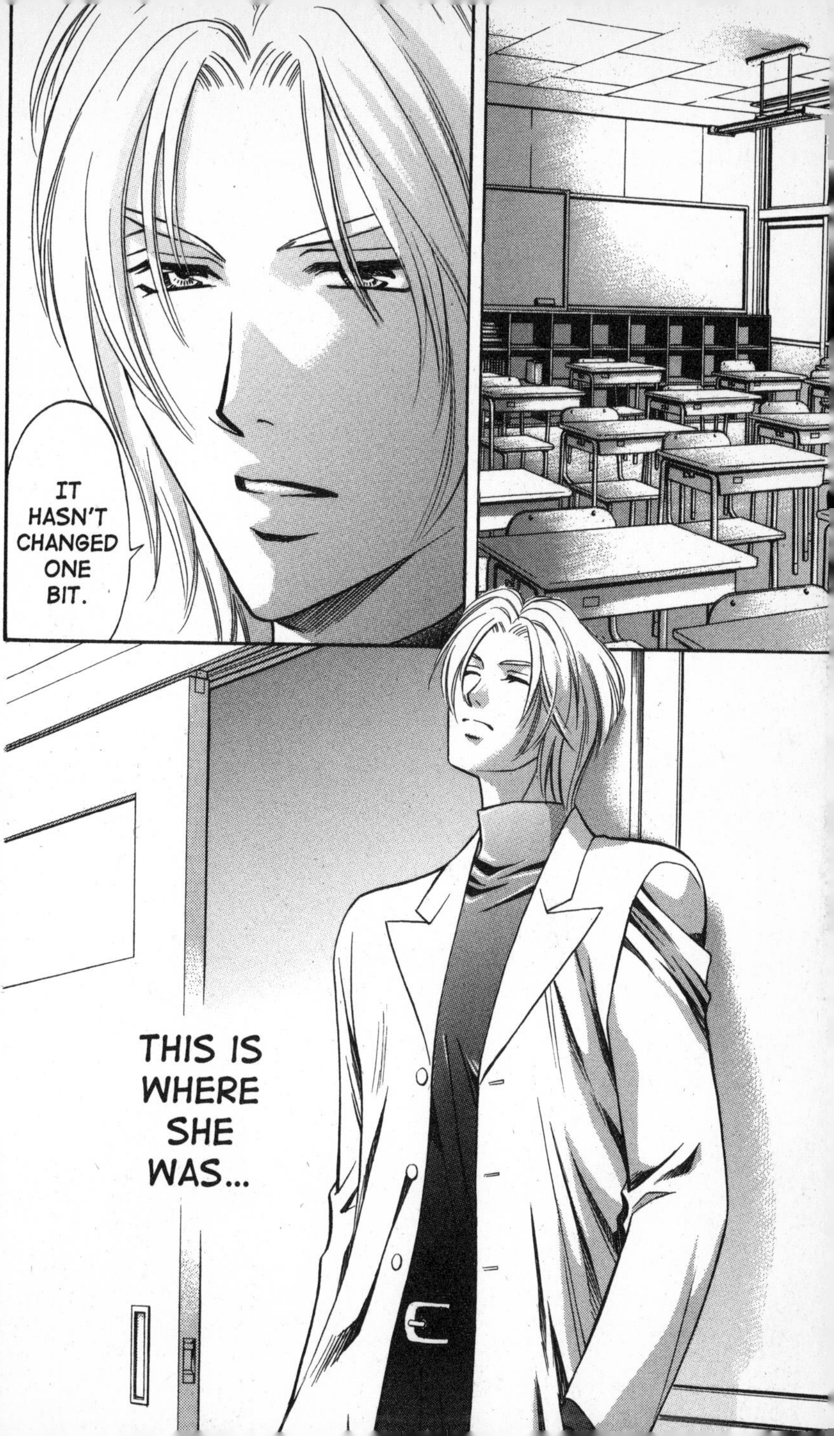
IT HASN'T CHANGED ONE BIT.
THIS IS WHERE SHE WAS...

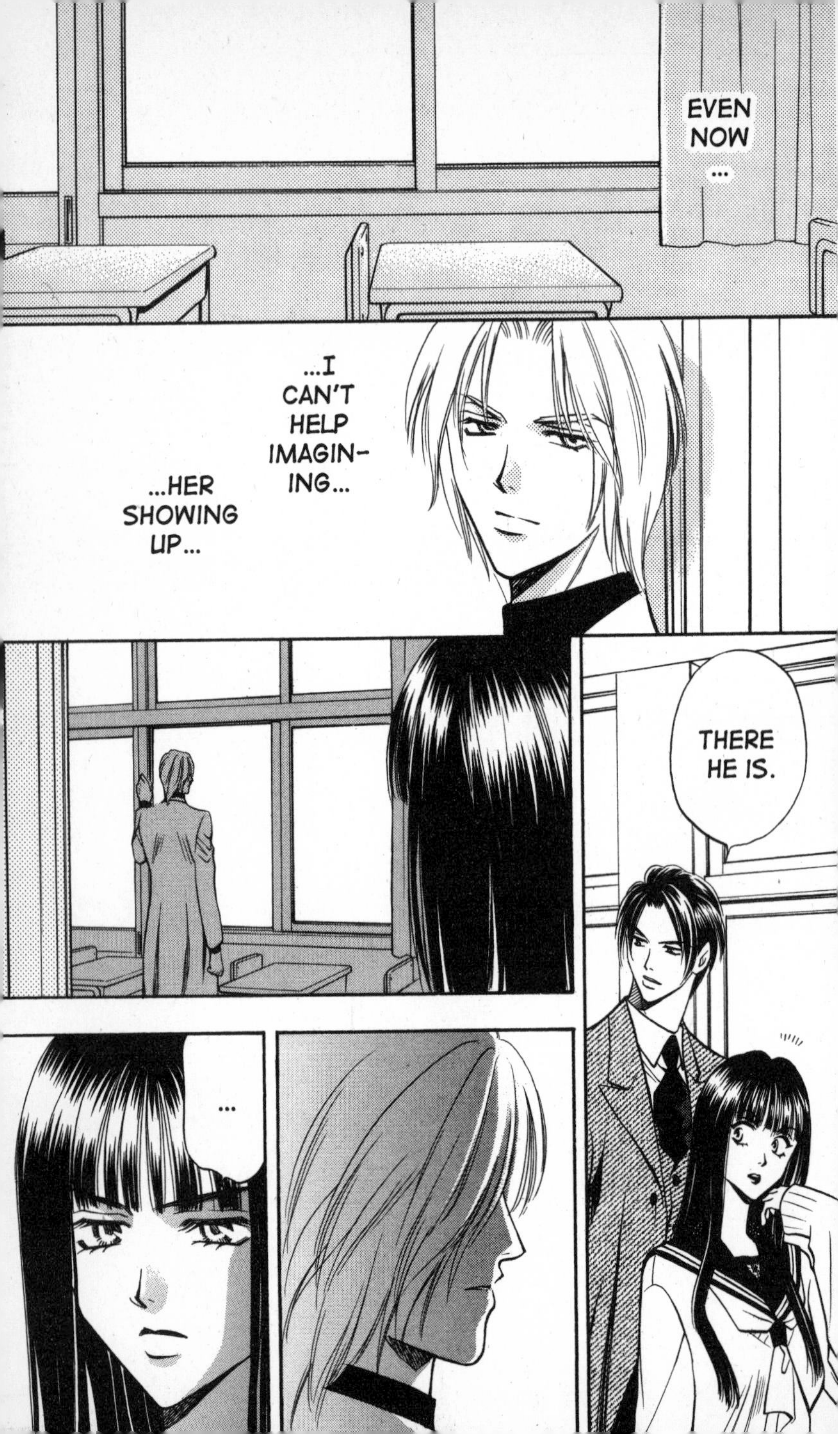
EVEN NOW ...
...I CAN'T HELP IMAGINING...
...HER SHOWING UP...
THERE HE IS.
...

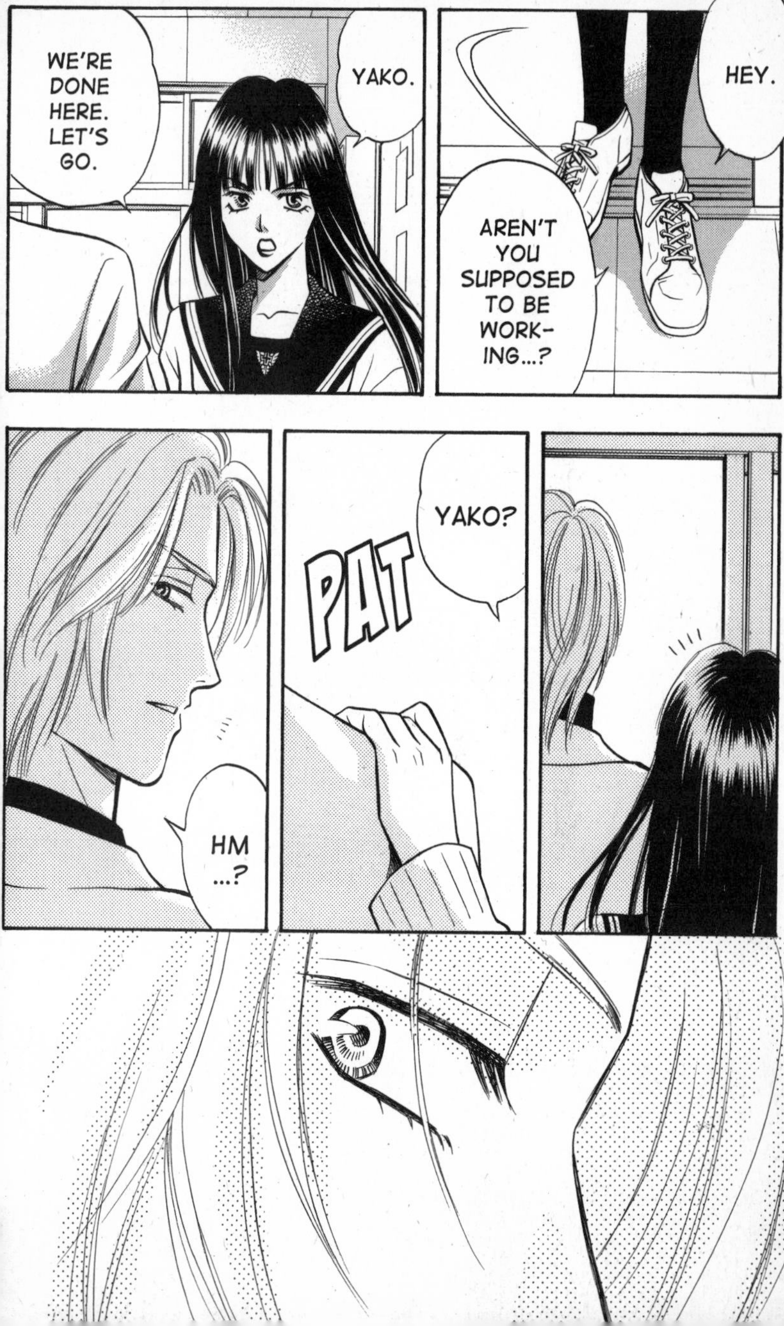
HEY.
AREN'T YOU SUPPOSED TO BE WORKING...?
YAKO.
WE'RE DONE HERE. LET'S GO.
YAKO?
PAT
HM ...?

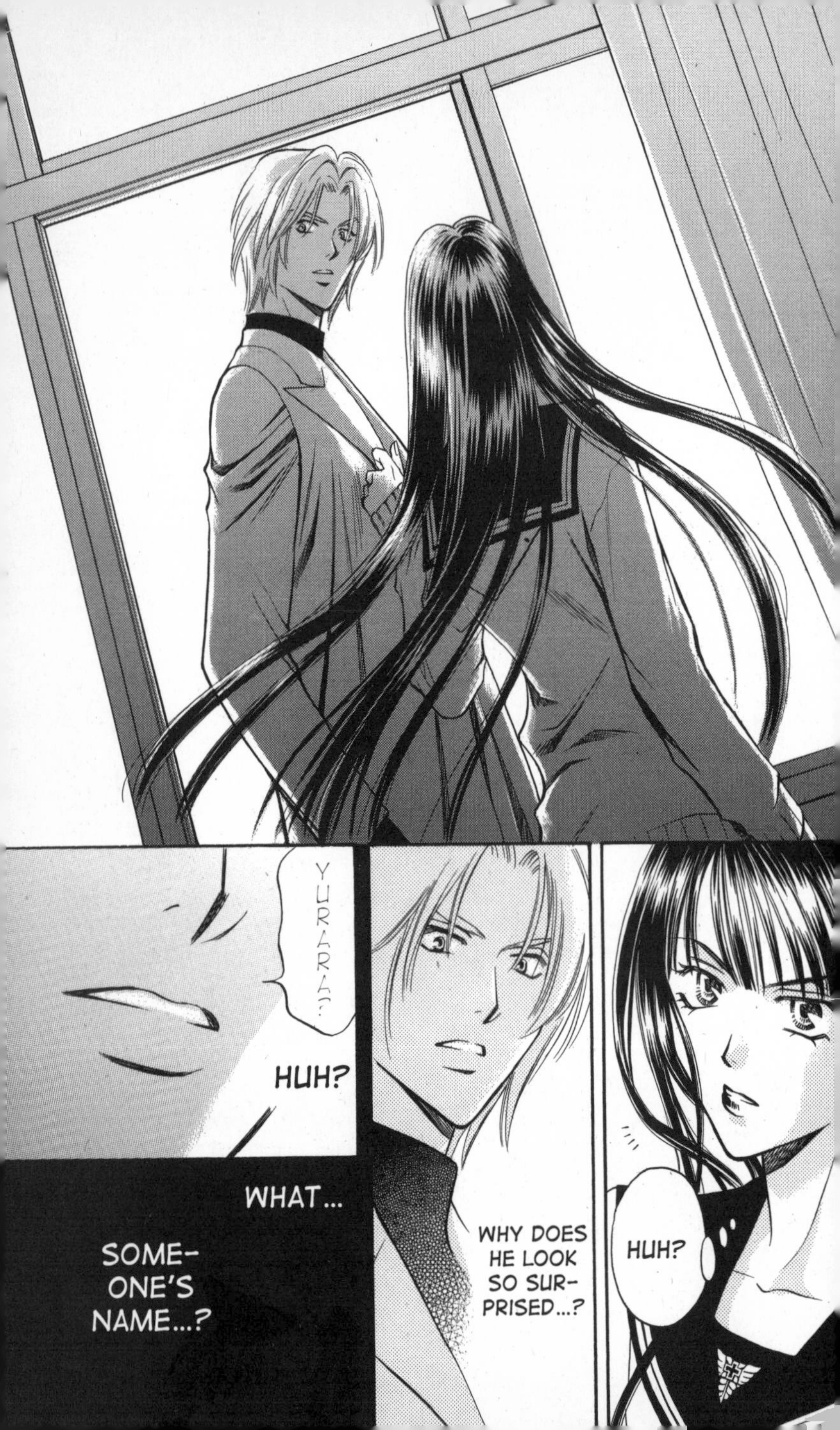
HUH?
WHY DOES HE LOOK SO SUR-PRISED...?
YURARA?
HUH?
WHAT...
SOME-ONE'S NAME...?

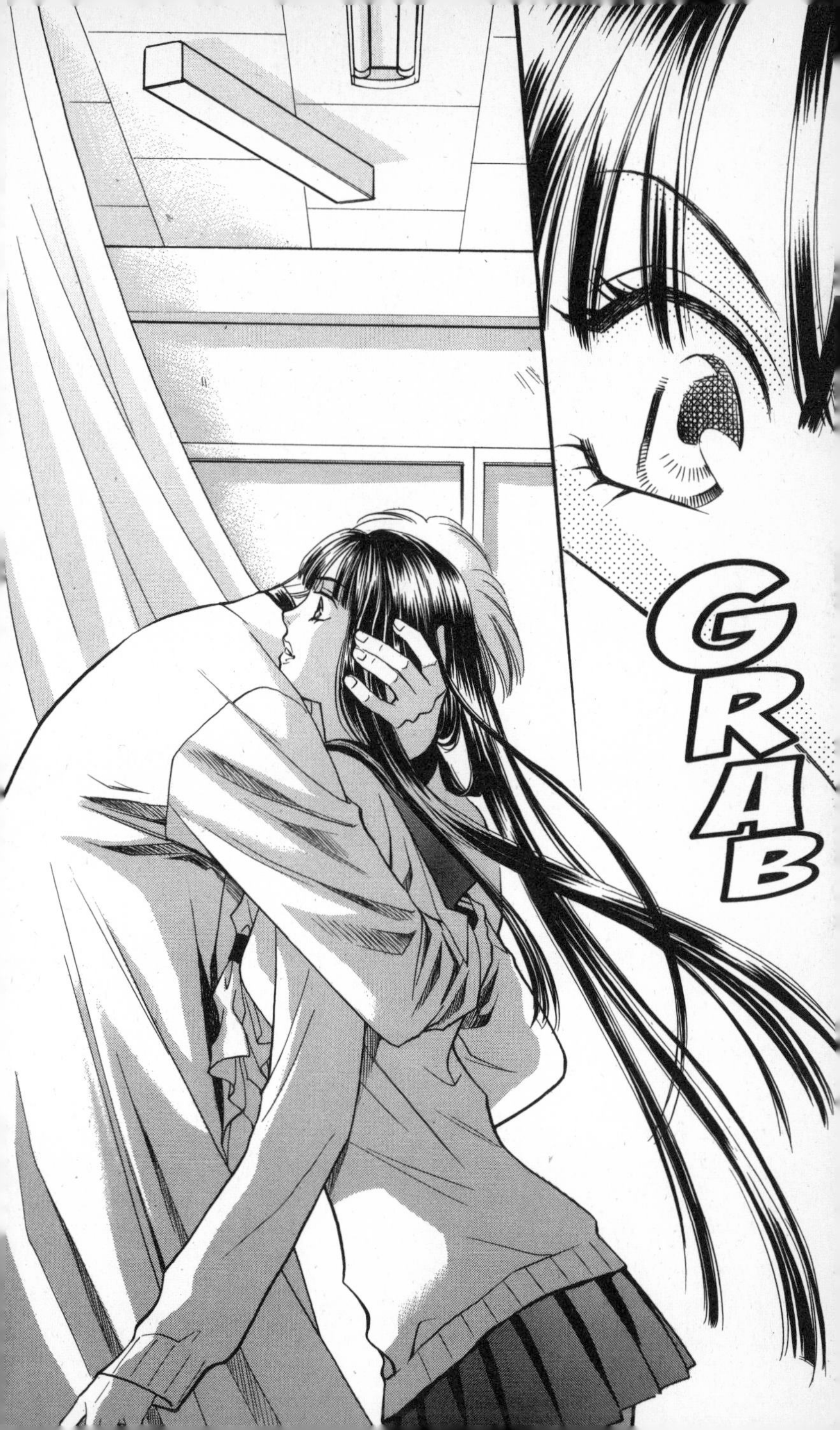
GRAB

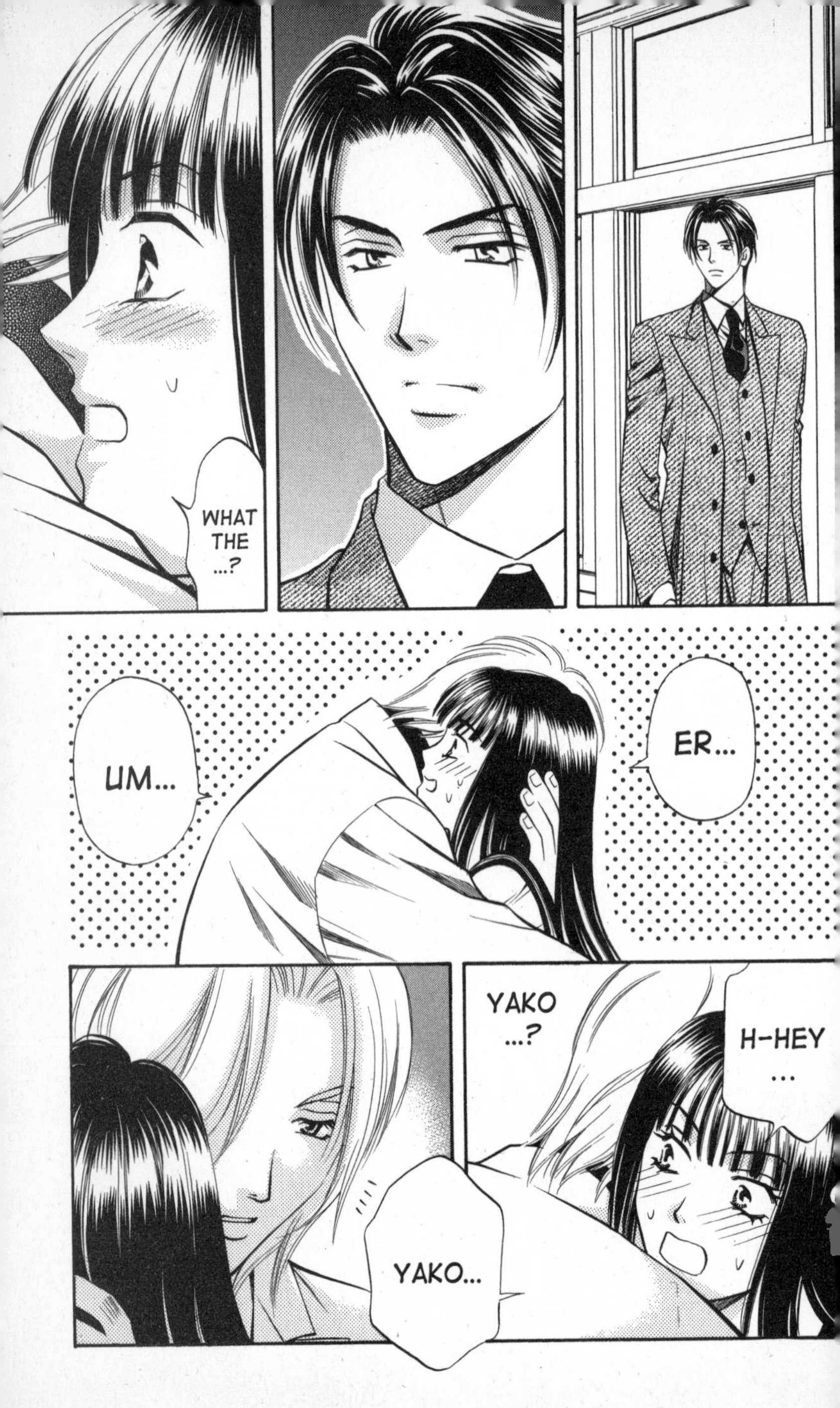
WHAT THE ...?
ER...
UM...
H-HEY ...
YAKO ...?
YAKO...

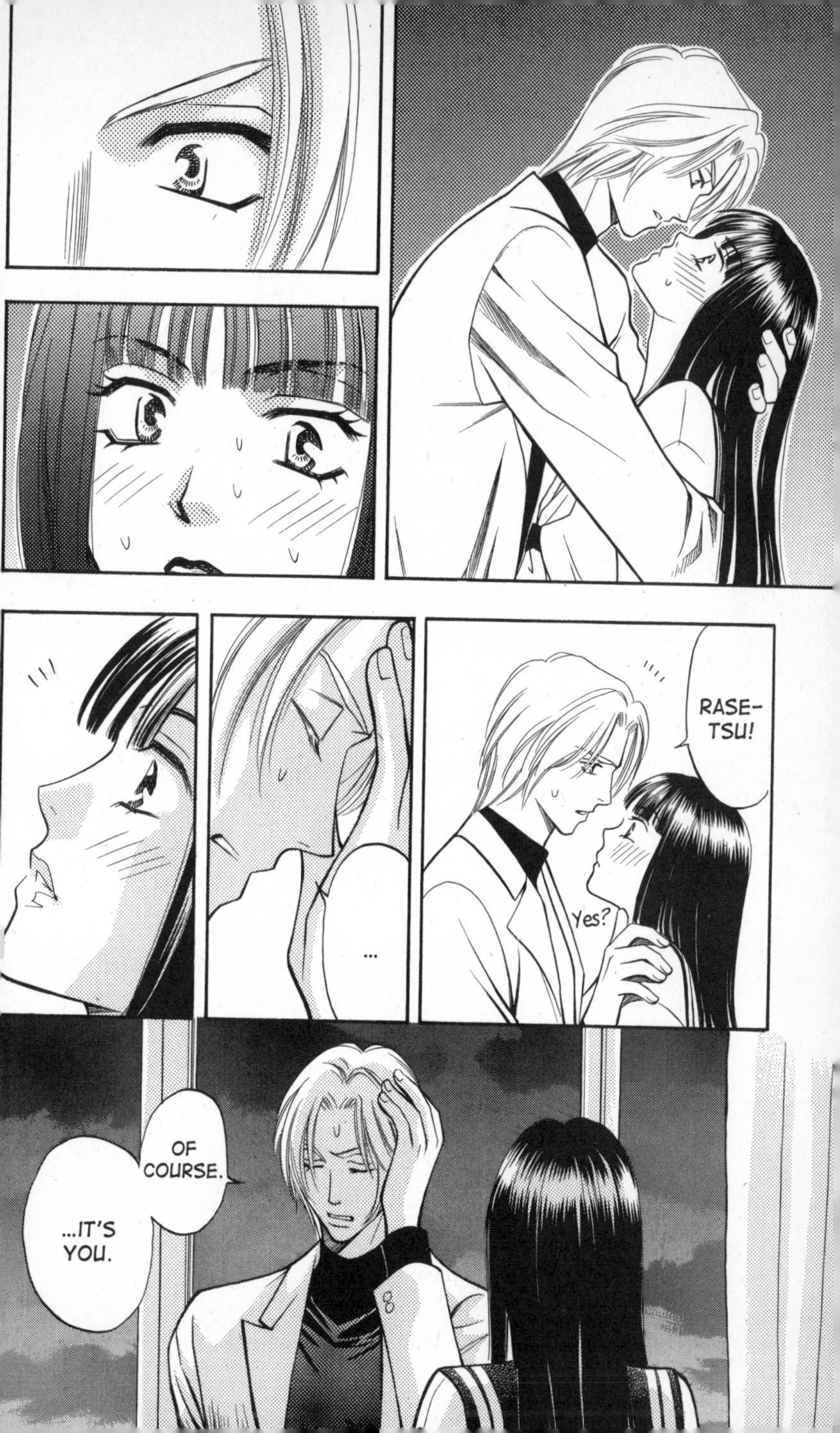
RASE-TSU!
Yes?
...
OF COURSE.
...IT'S YOU.

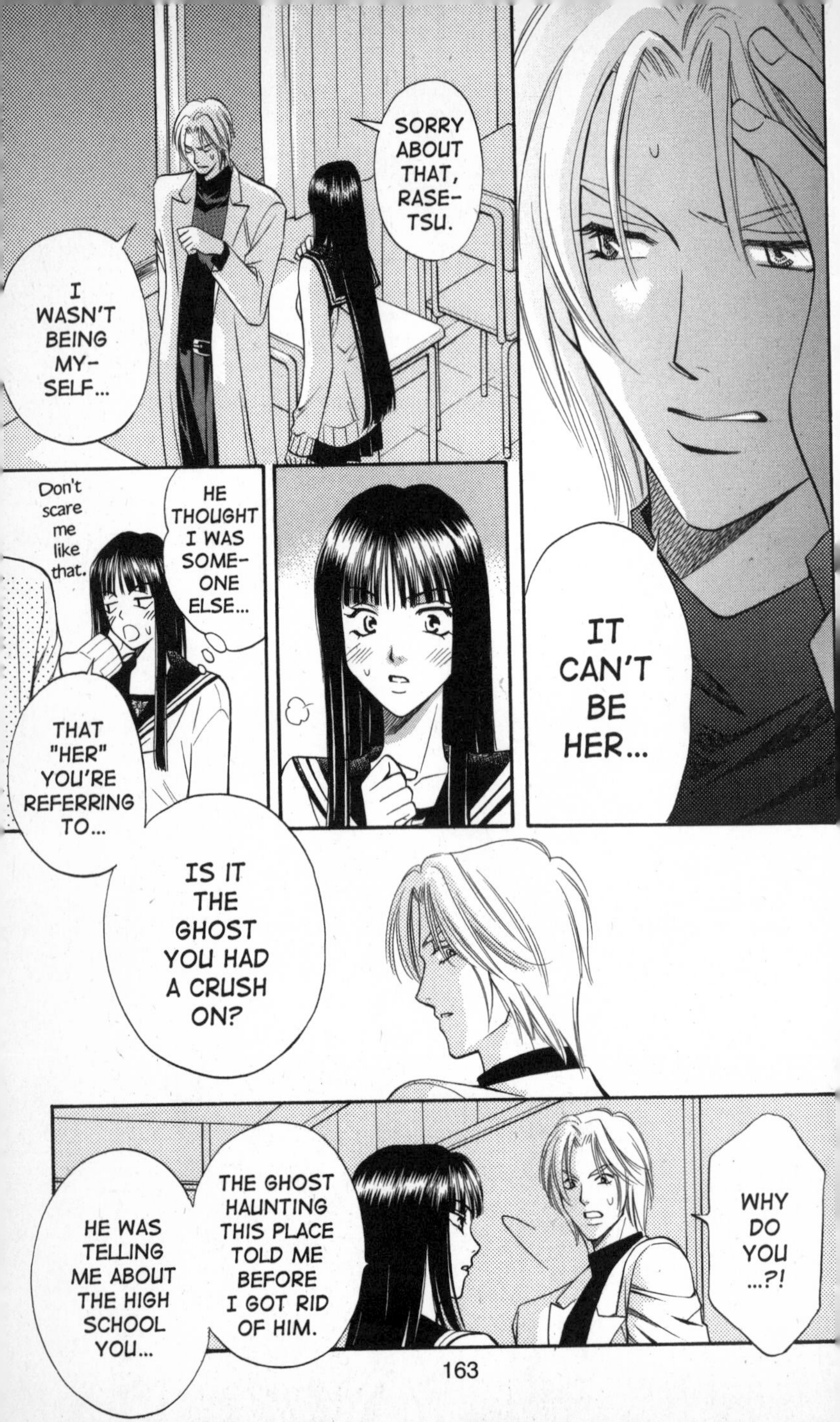
IT CAN'T BE HER...
SORRY ABOUT THAT, RASE-TSU.
I WASN'T BEING MY-SELF...
HE THOUGHT I WAS SOME-ONE ELSE...
Don't scare me like that.
THAT "HER" YOU'RE REFERRING TO...
IS IT THE GHOST YOU HAD A CRUSH ON?
WHY DO YOU ...?!
THE GHOST HAUNTING THIS PLACE TOLD ME BEFORE I GOT RID OF HIM.
HE WAS TELLING ME ABOUT THE HIGH SCHOOL YOU...

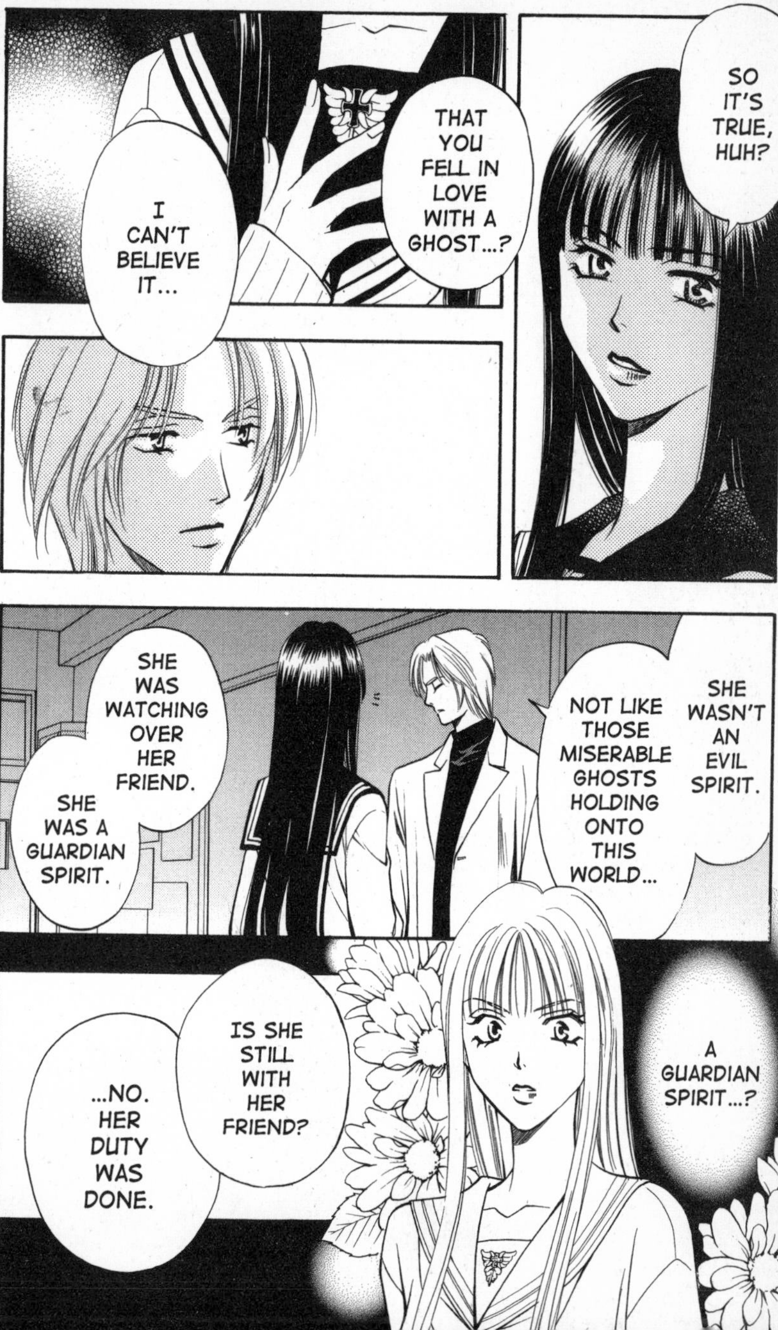
SO IT'S TRUE, HUH?
THAT YOU FELL IN LOVE WITH A GHOST...?
I CAN'T BELIEVE IT...
SHE WASN'T AN EVIL SPIRIT.
NOT LIKE THOSE MISERABLE GHOSTS HOLDING ONTO THIS WORLD...
SHE WAS WATCHING OVER HER FRIEND.
SHE WAS A GUARDIAN SPIRIT.
A GUARDIAN SPIRIT...?
IS SHE STILL WITH HER FRIEND?
...NO. HER DUTY WAS DONE.

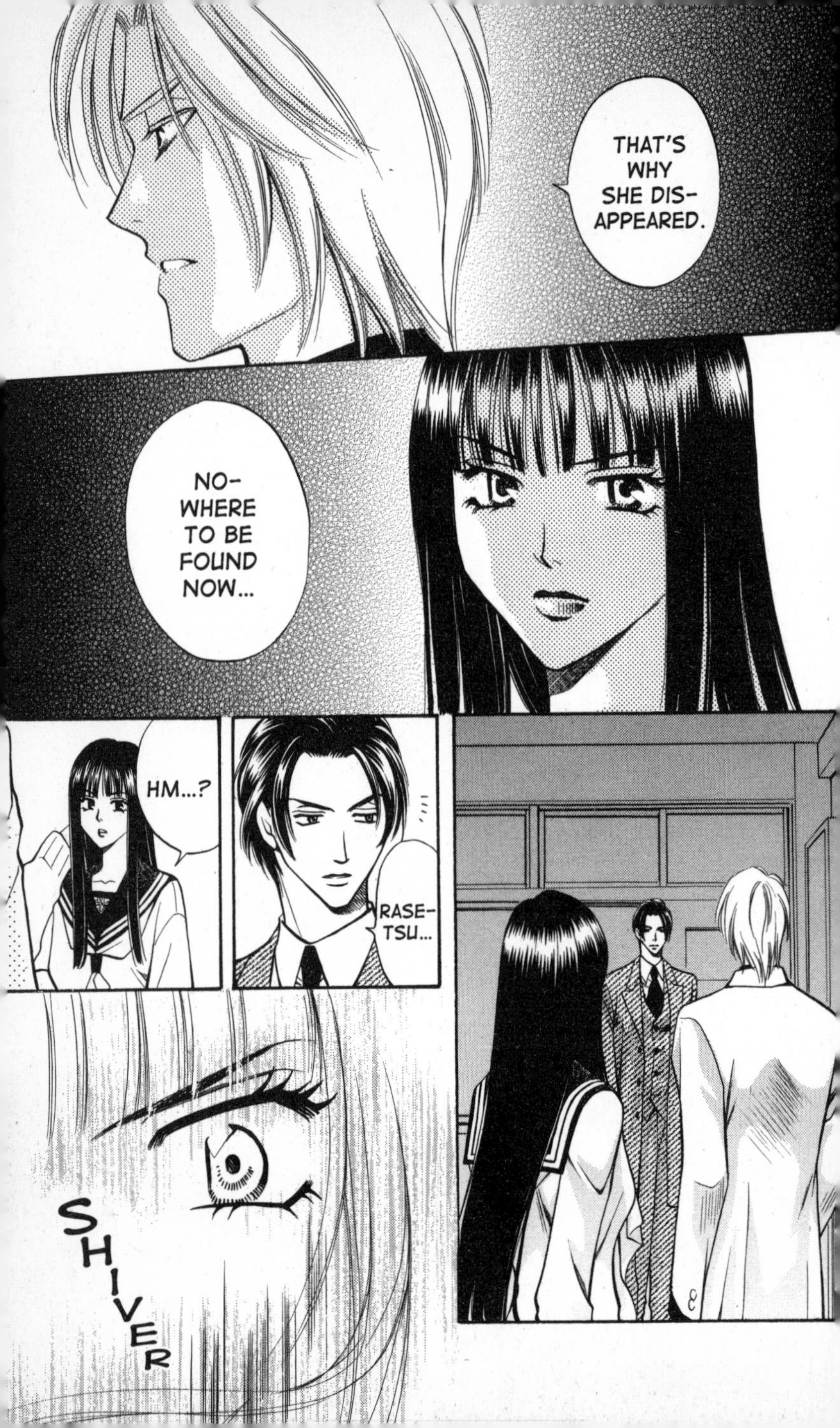
THAT'S WHY SHE DIS-APPEARED.
NO-WHERE TO BE FOUND NOW...
RASE-TSU...
HM...?
SHIVER

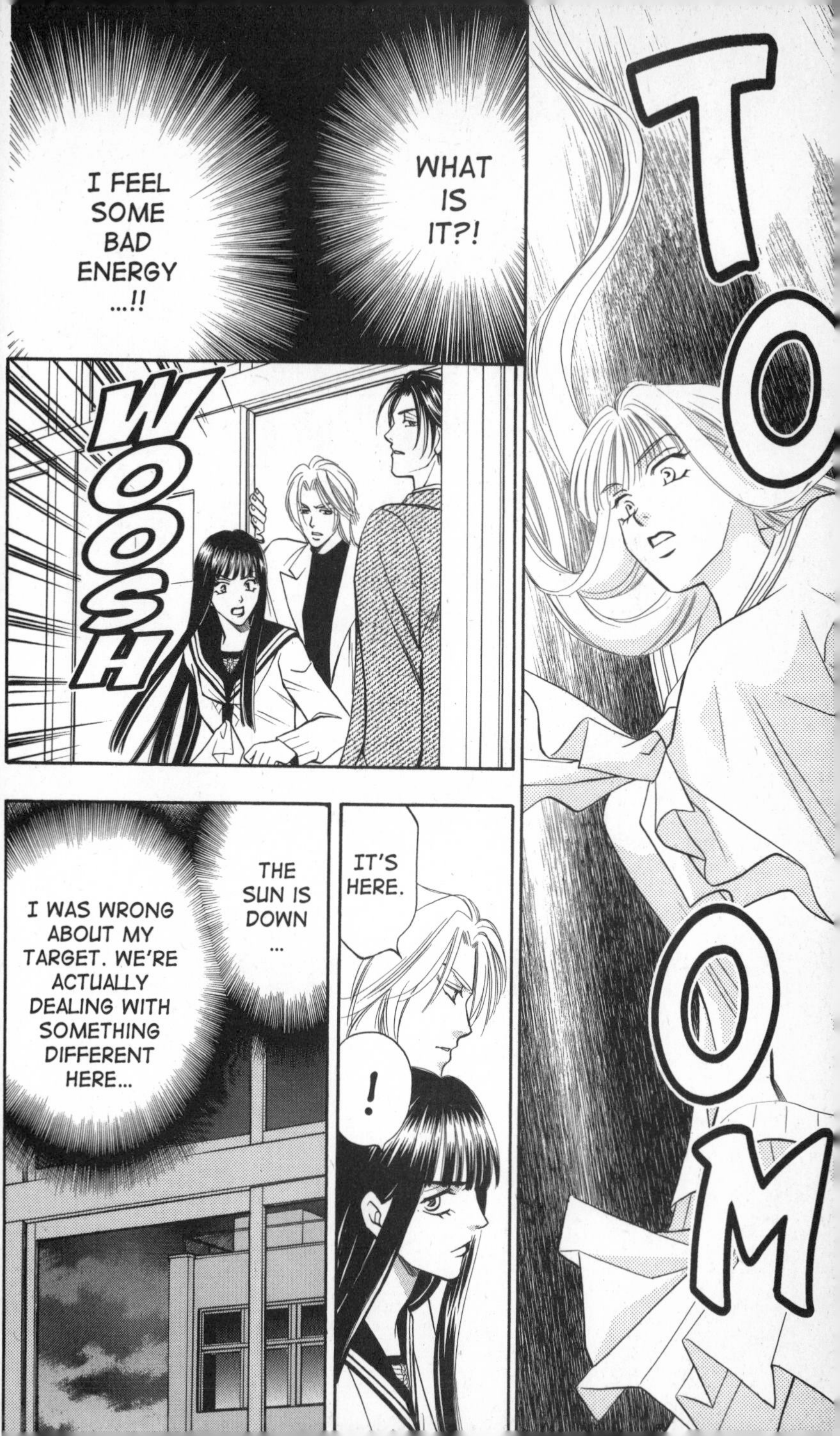
TOOOM
WHAT IS IT?!
I FEEL SOME BAD ENERGY ...!!
WOOSH
IT'S HERE.
!
THE SUN IS DOWN ...
I WAS WRONG ABOUT MY TARGET. WE'RE ACTUALLY DEALING WITH SOMETHING DIFFERENT HERE...

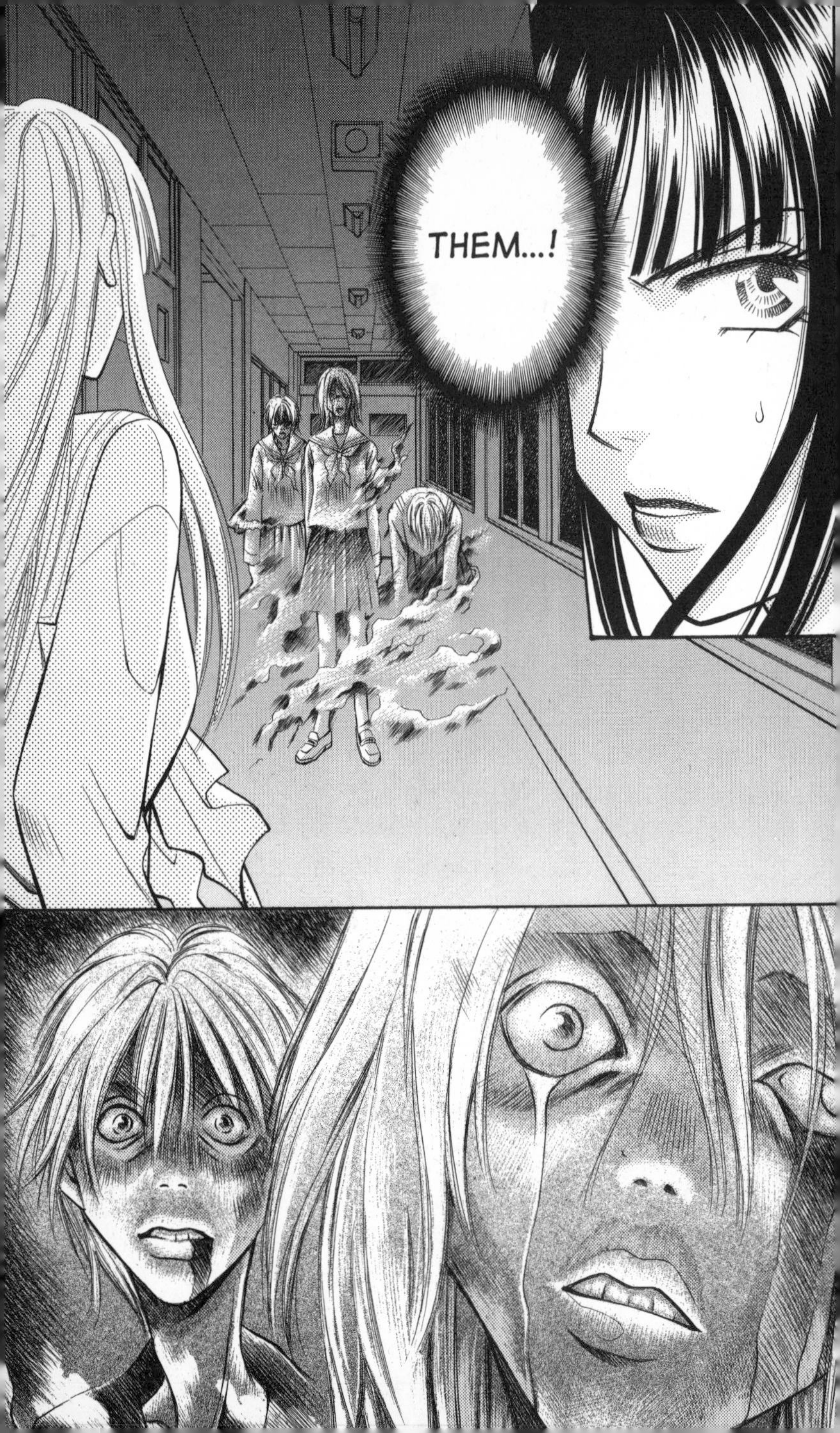
THEM...!

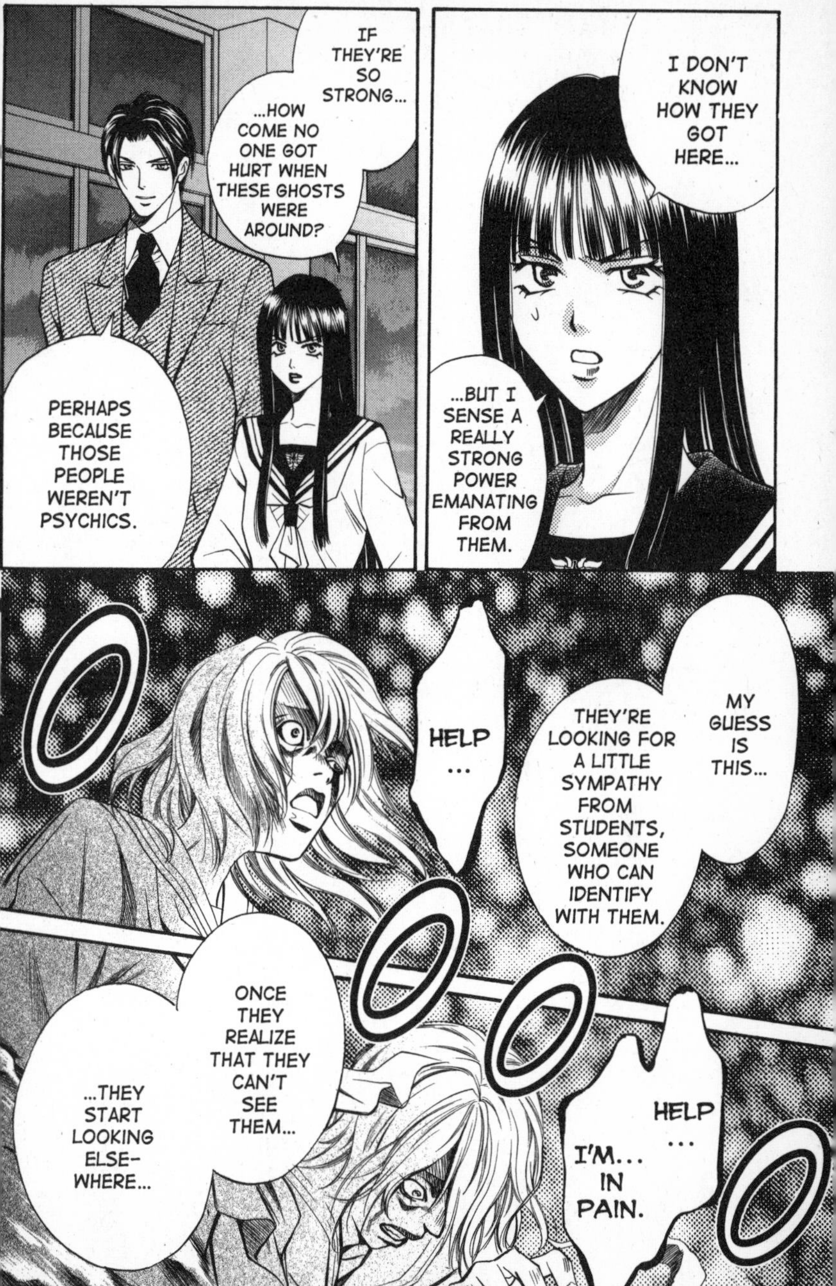
I DON'T KNOW HOW THEY GOT HERE...
...BUT I SENSE A REALLY STRONG POWER EMANATING FROM THEM.
IF THEY'RE SO STRONG...
...HOW COME NO ONE GOT HURT WHEN THESE GHOSTS WERE AROUND?
PERHAPS BECAUSE THOSE PEOPLE WEREN'T PSYCHICS.
MY GUESS IS THIS...
THEY'RE LOOKING FOR A LITTLE SYMPATHY FROM STUDENTS, SOMEONE WHO CAN IDENTIFY WITH THEM.
HELP...
HELP...
I'M... IN PAIN.
ONCE THEY REALIZE THAT THEY CAN'T SEE THEM...
...THEY START LOOKING ELSE-WHERE...

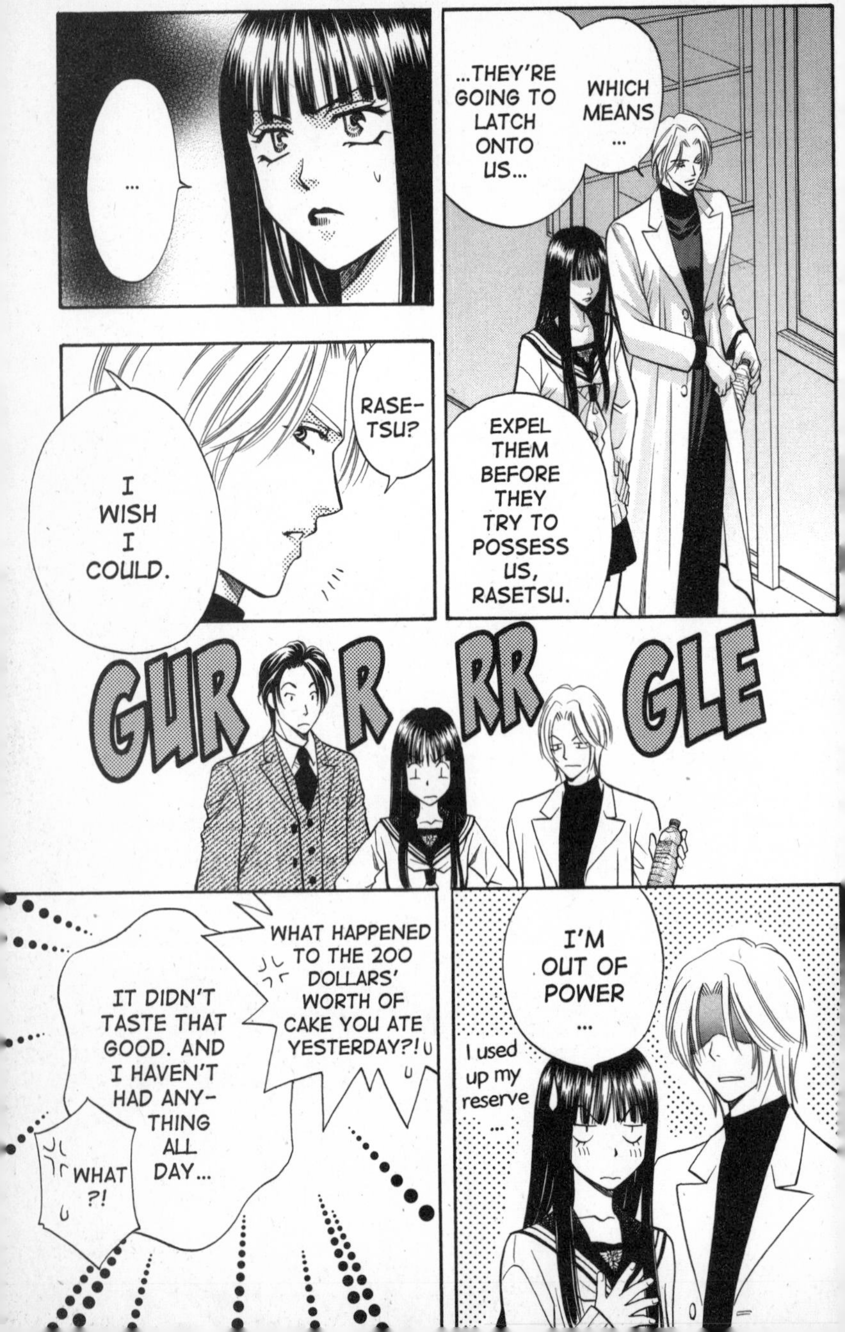
WHICH MEANS ...
...THEY'RE GOING TO LATCH ONTO US...
EXPEL THEM BEFORE THEY TRY TO POSSESS US, RASETSU.
...
RASE-TSU?
I WISH I COULD.
GUR R RR GLE
I'M OUT OF POWER ...
I used up my reserve ...
WHAT HAPPENED TO THE 200 DOLLARS' WORTH OF CAKE YOU ATE YESTERDAY?!
IT DIDN'T TASTE THAT GOOD. AND I HAVEN'T HAD ANY-THING ALL DAY...
WHAT?!

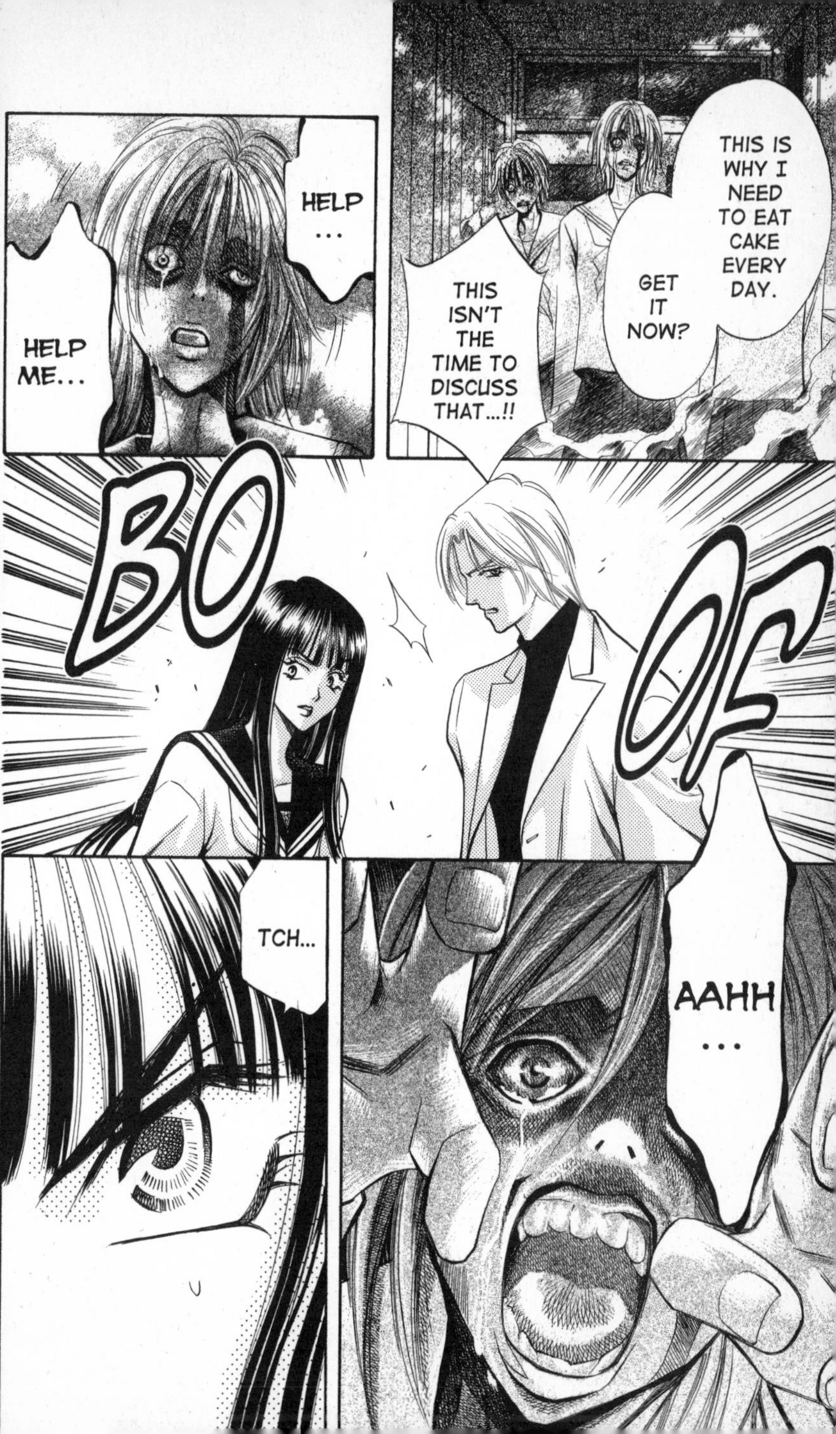

THIS IS WHY I NEED TO EAT CAKE EVERY DAY.
GET IT NOW?
THIS ISN'T THE TIME TO DISCUSS THAT...!!
HELP ...
HELP ME...
BOOF
AAHH ...
TCH...

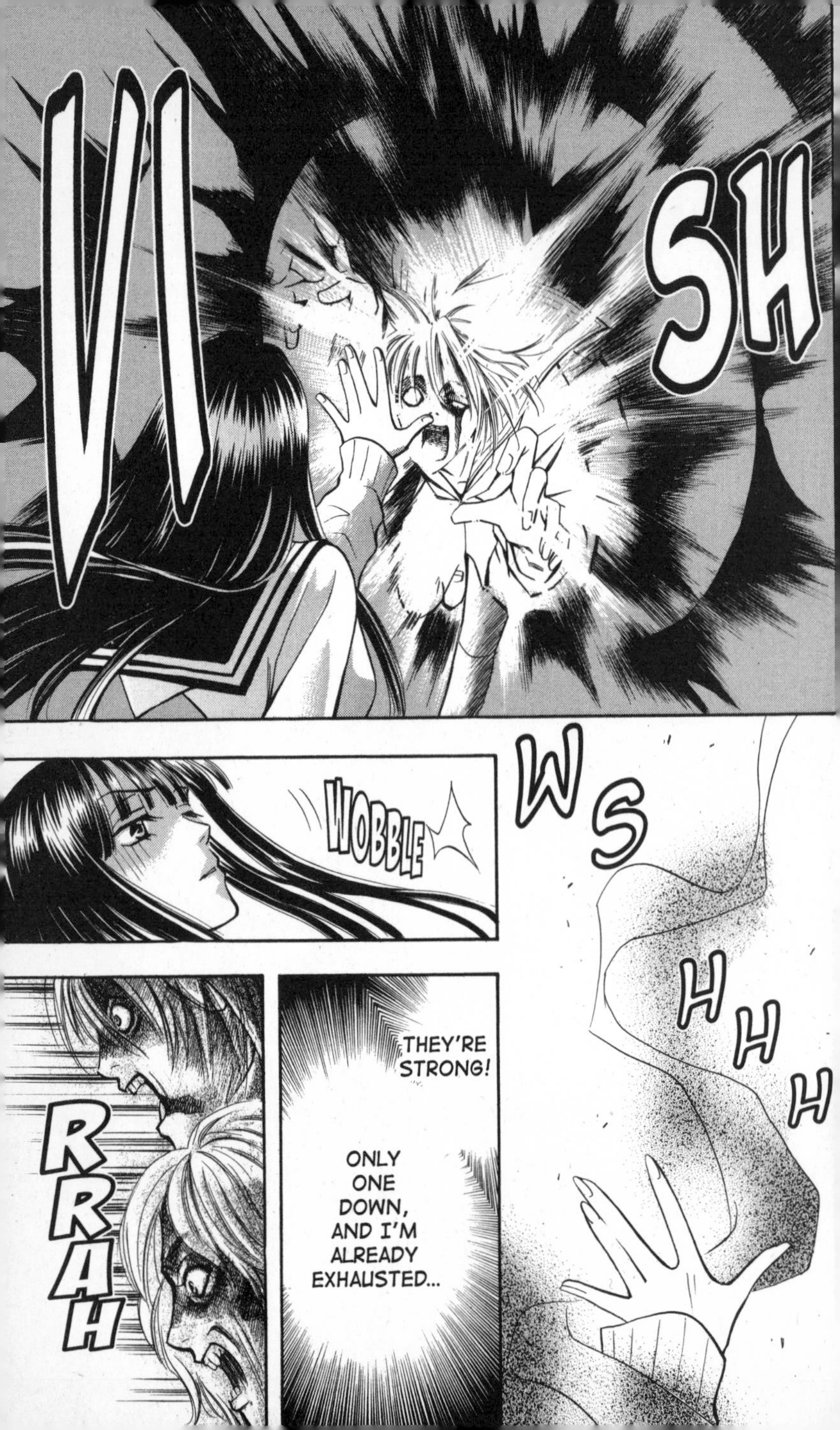
VISH
WSHHH
WOBBLE
THEY'RE STRONG!
ONLY ONE DOWN, AND I'M ALREADY EXHAUSTED...
RRAH

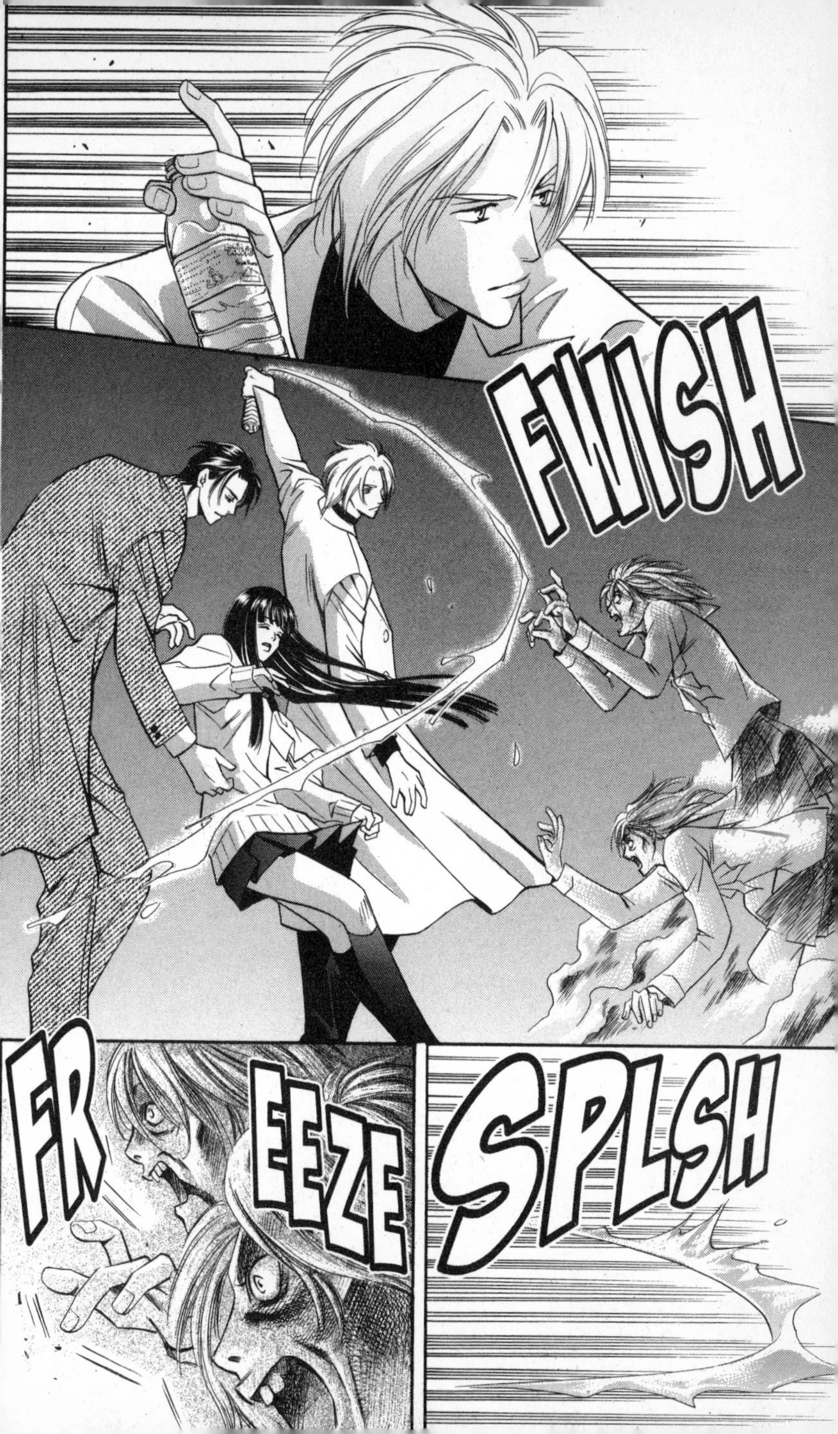
FWISH
SPLSH
FR EEZE

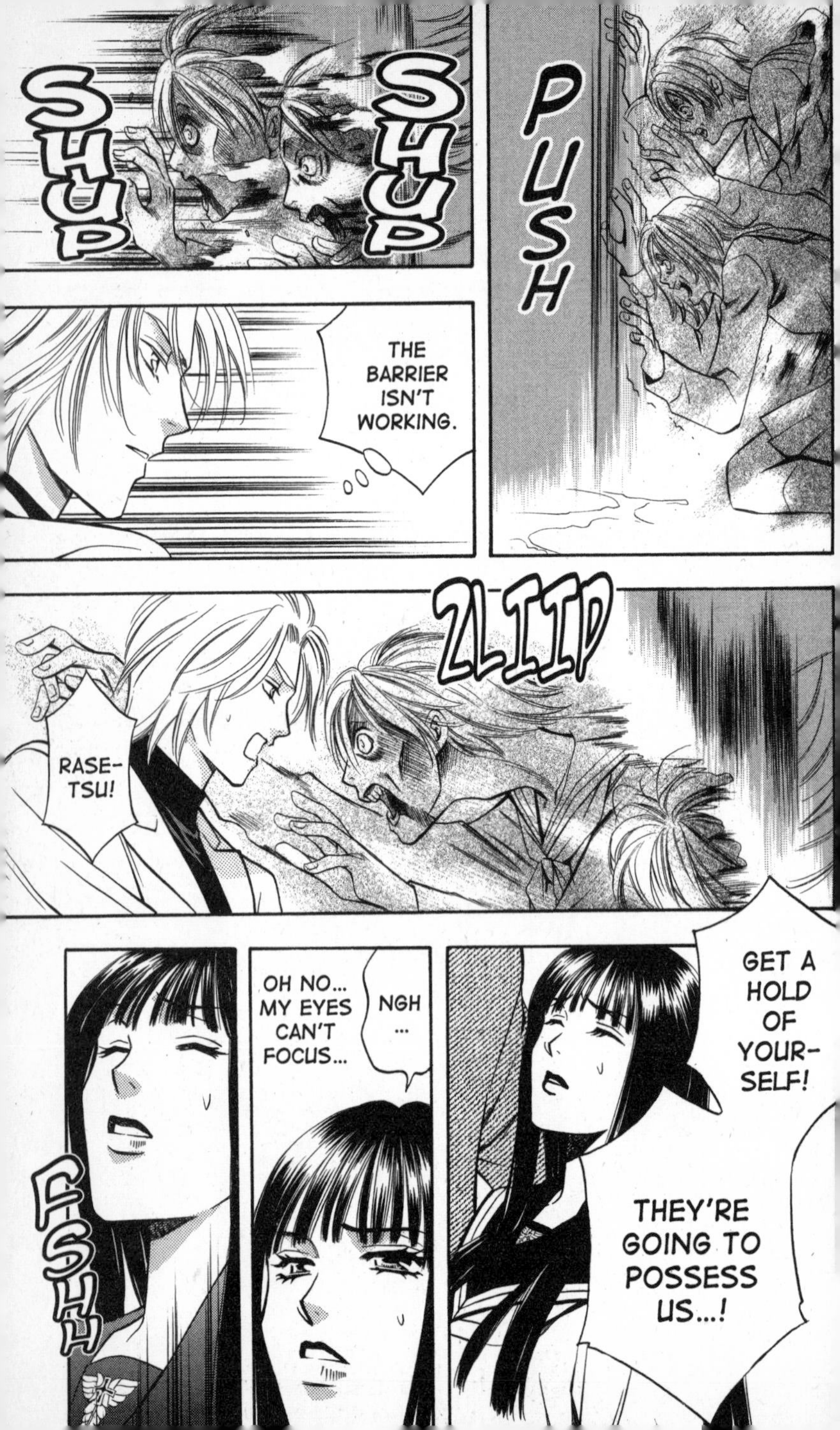
PUSH
SHUP
SHUP
THE BARRIER ISN'T WORKING.
ZLIIP
RASE-TSU!
GET A HOLD OF YOUR-SELF!
THEY'RE GOING TO POSSESS US...!
NGH ...
OH NO... MY EYES CAN'T FOCUS...
FSHH

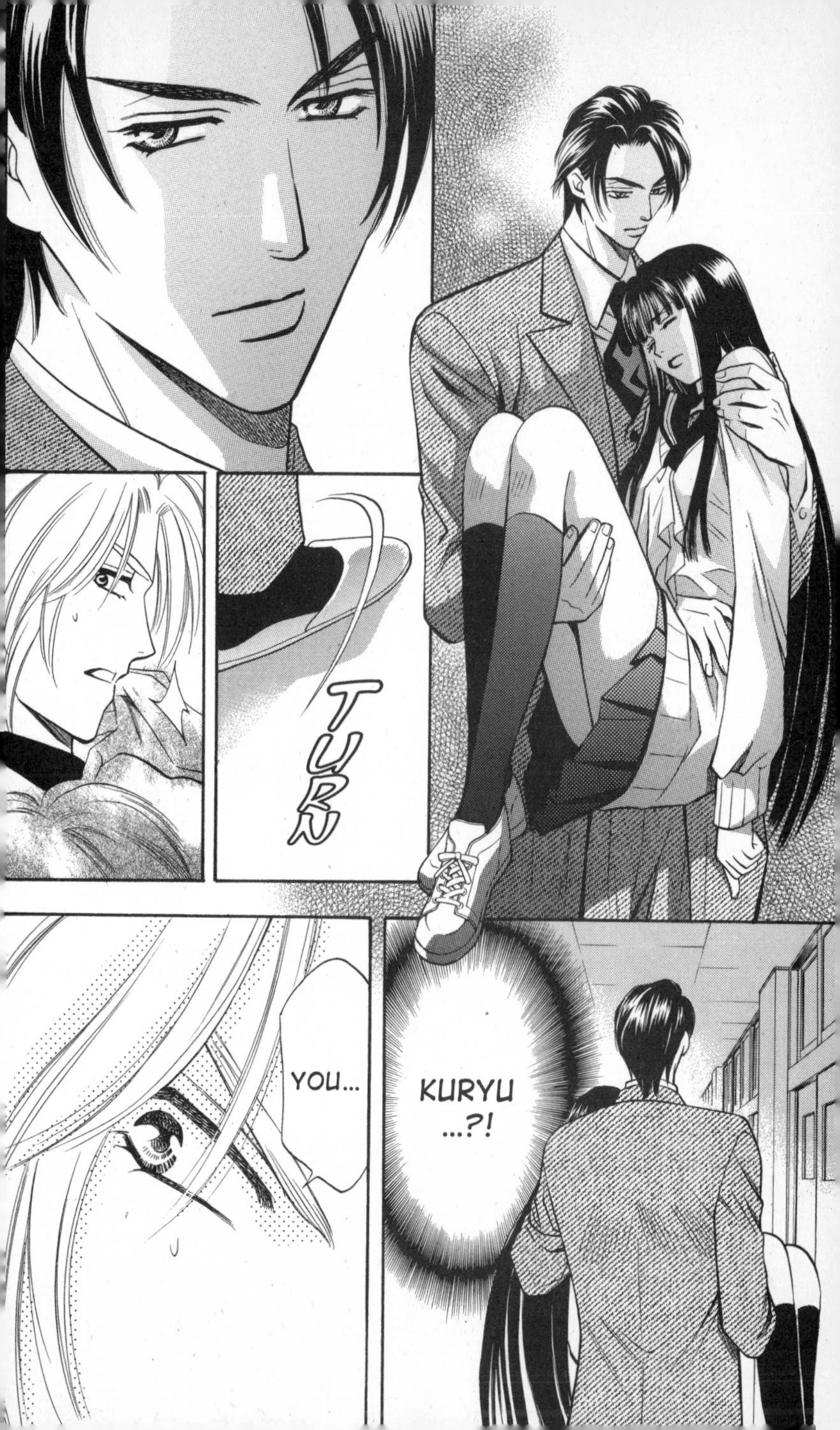
TURN
KURYU ...?!
YOU...

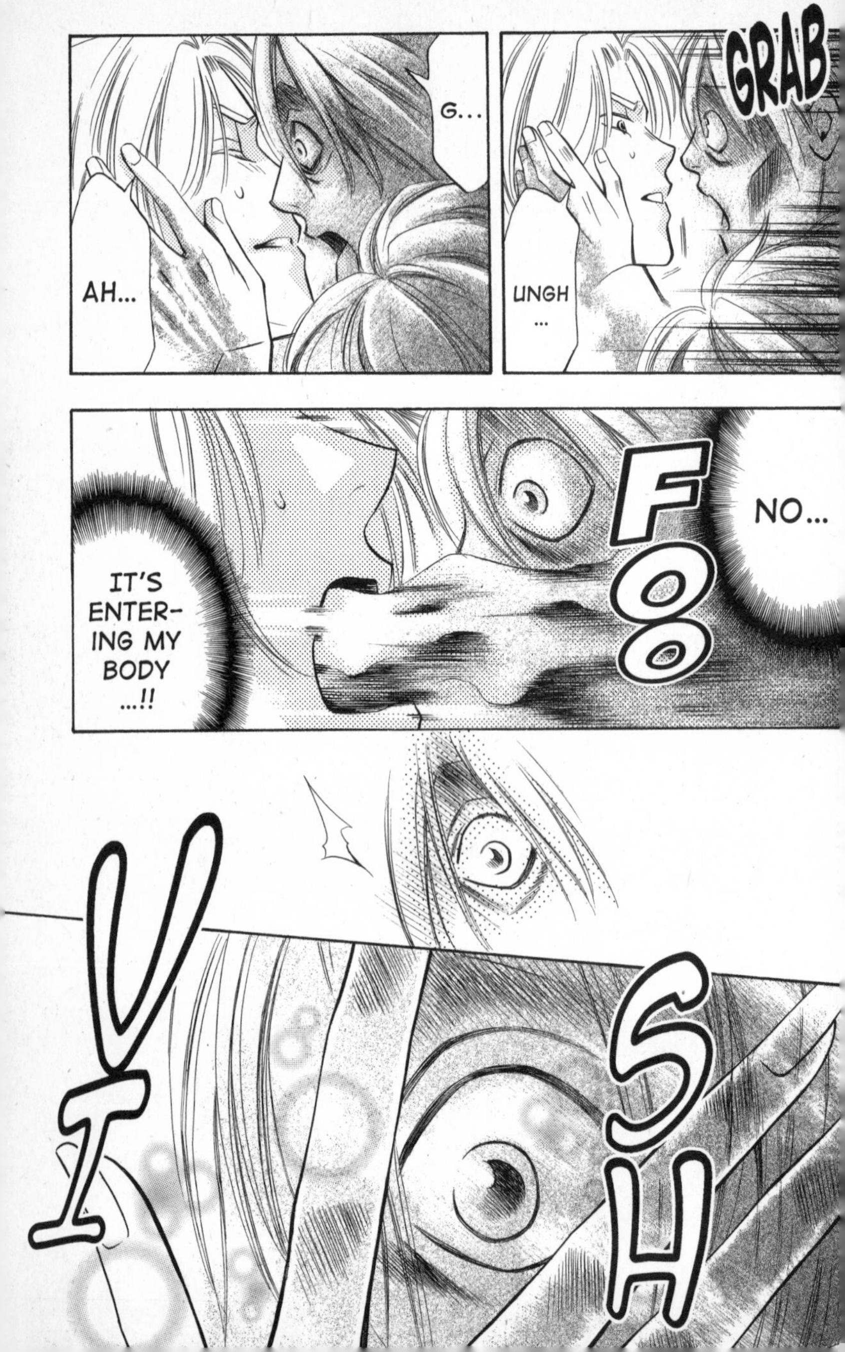
GRAB
UNGH ...
G...
AH...
NO...
FOOO
IT'S ENTERING MY BODY ...!!
VISH

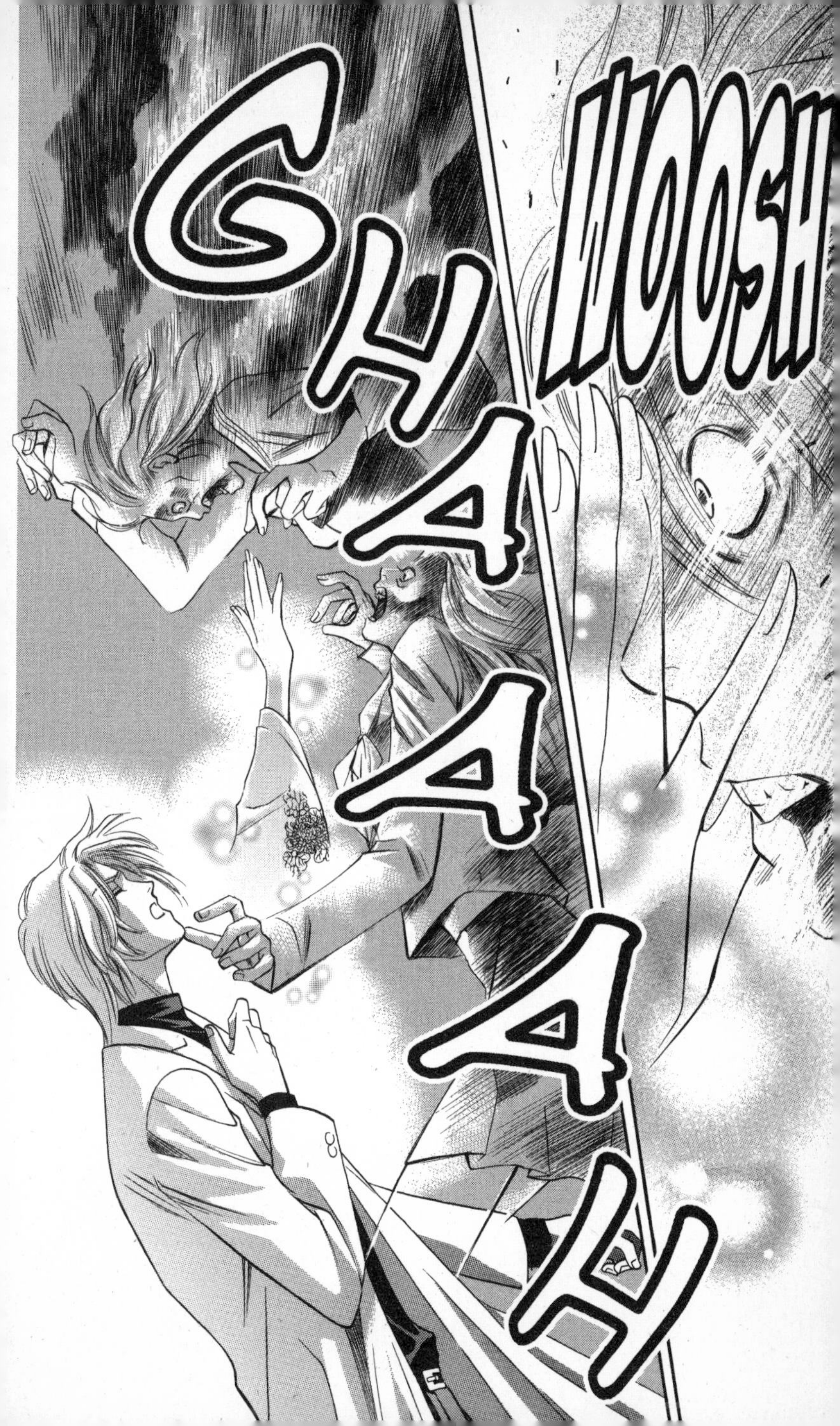
WHOOSH
GHAAAH

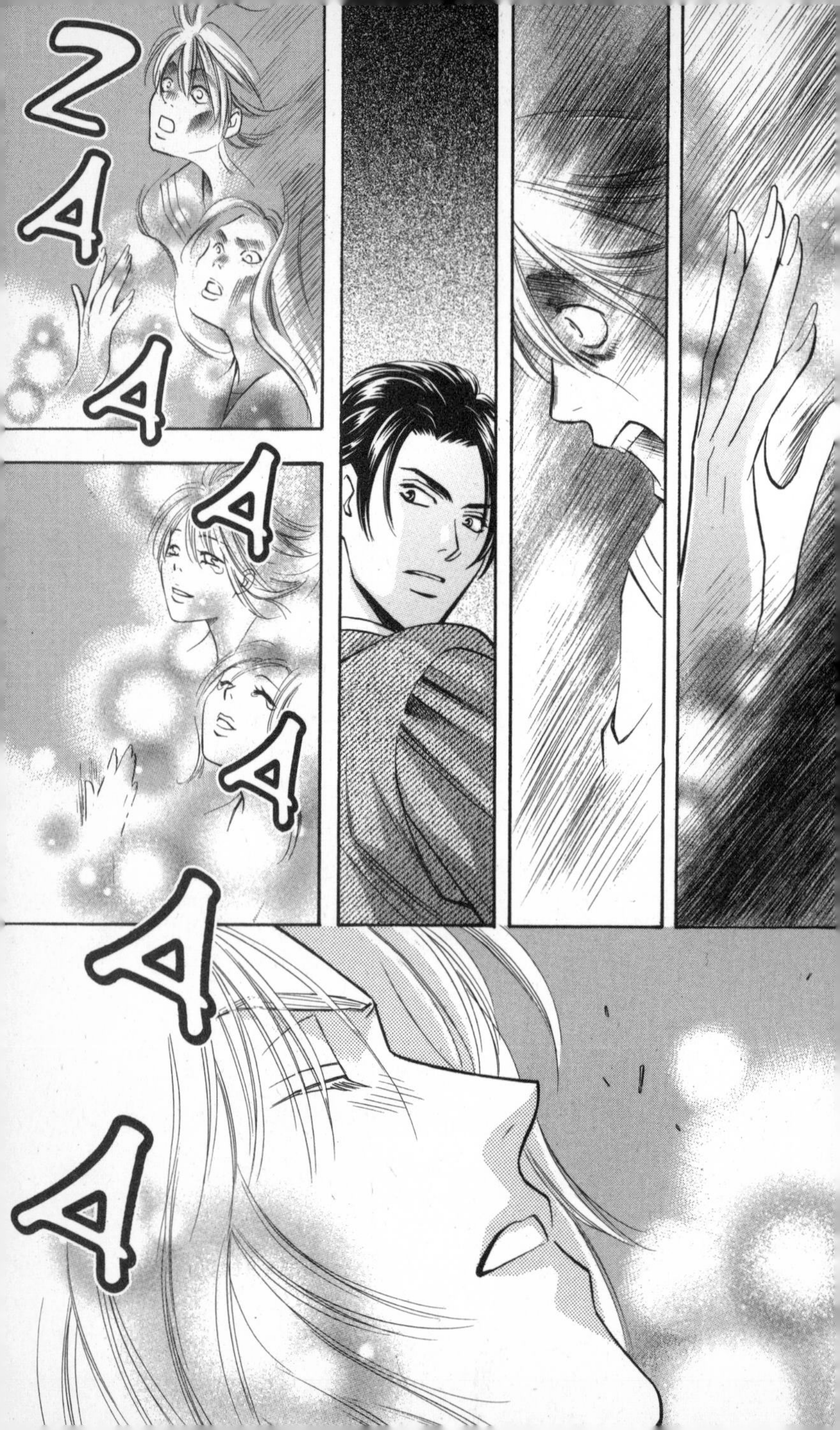
ZAAAAAA

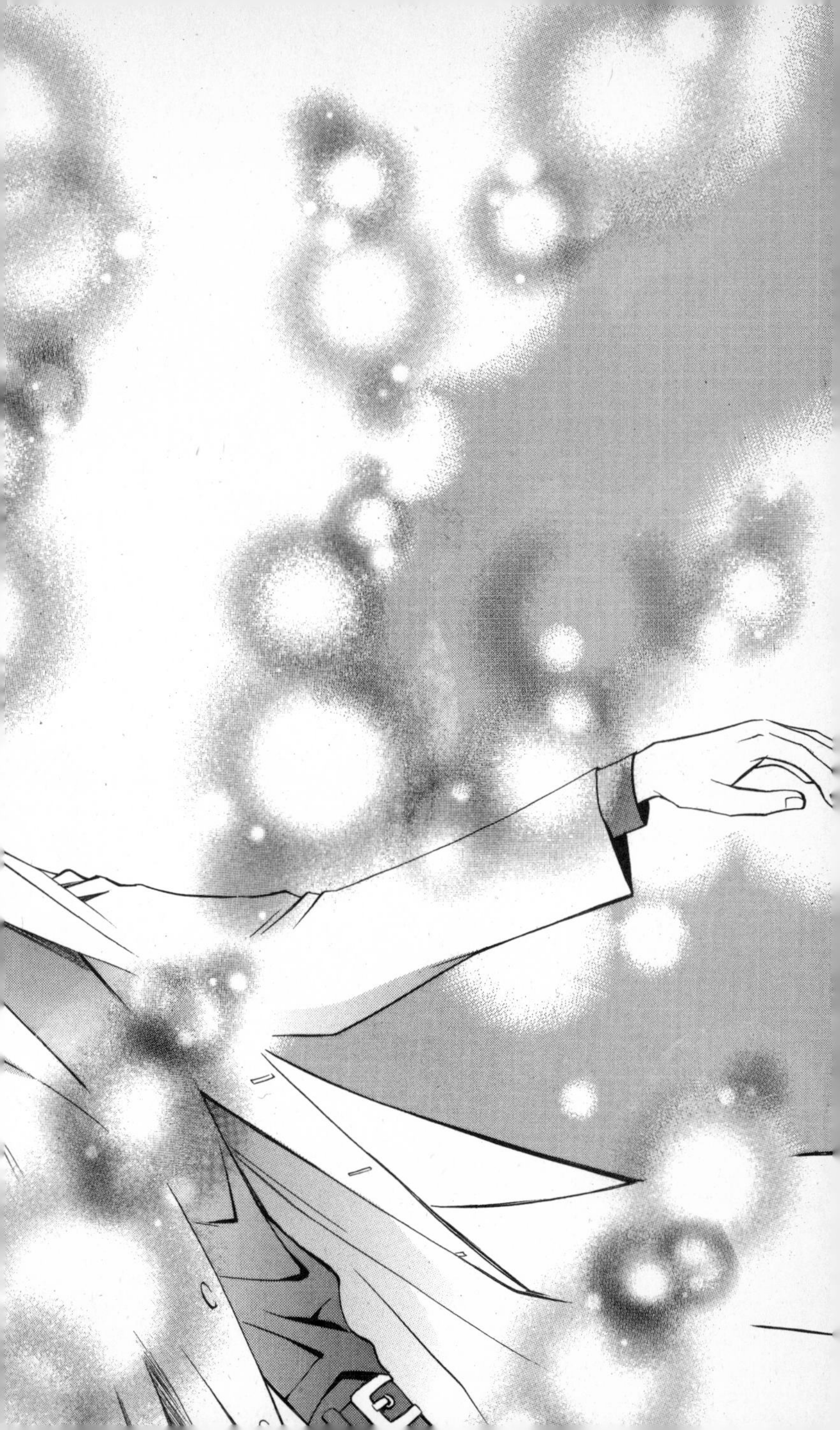

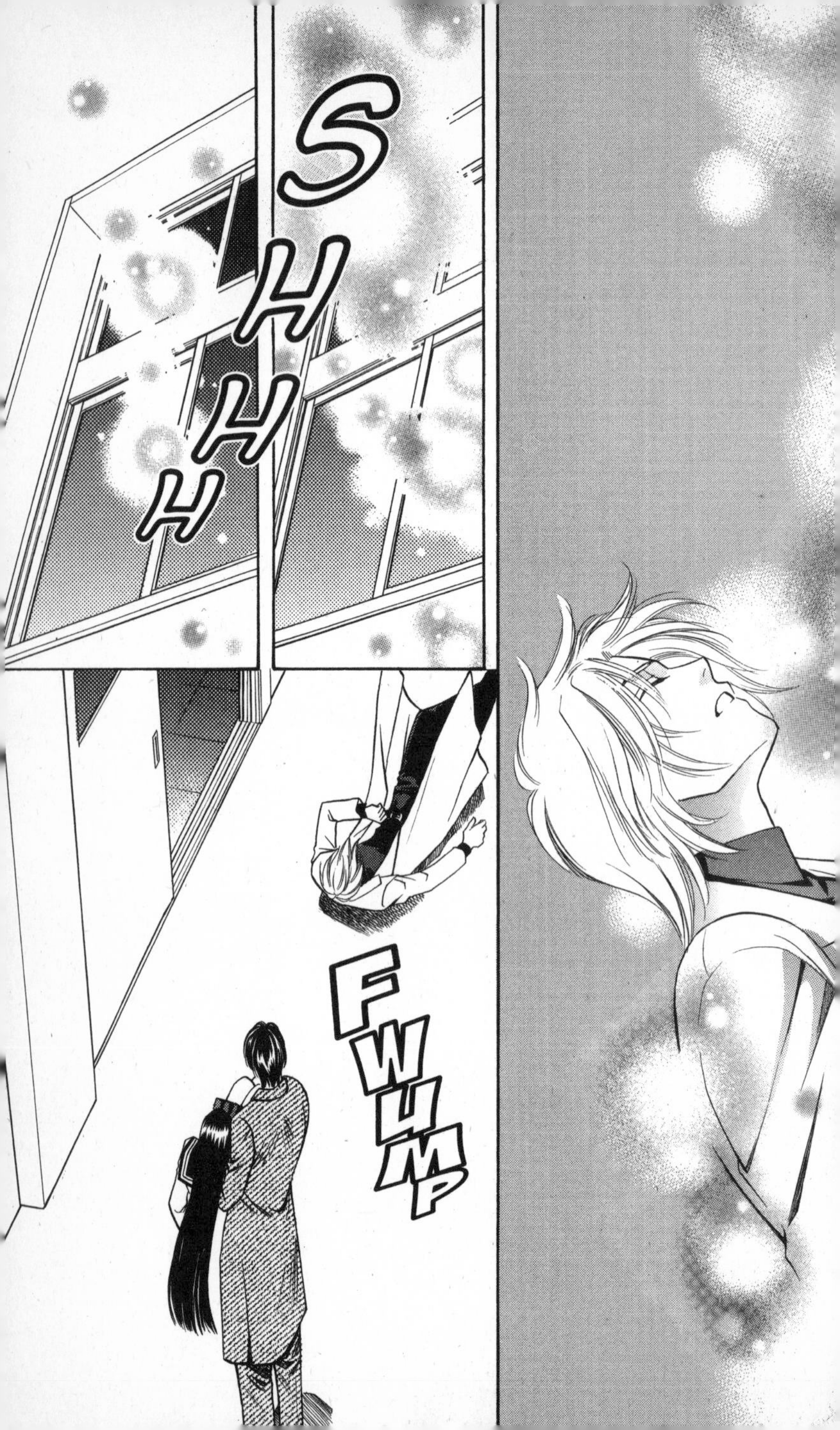

SHHHH
FWUMP

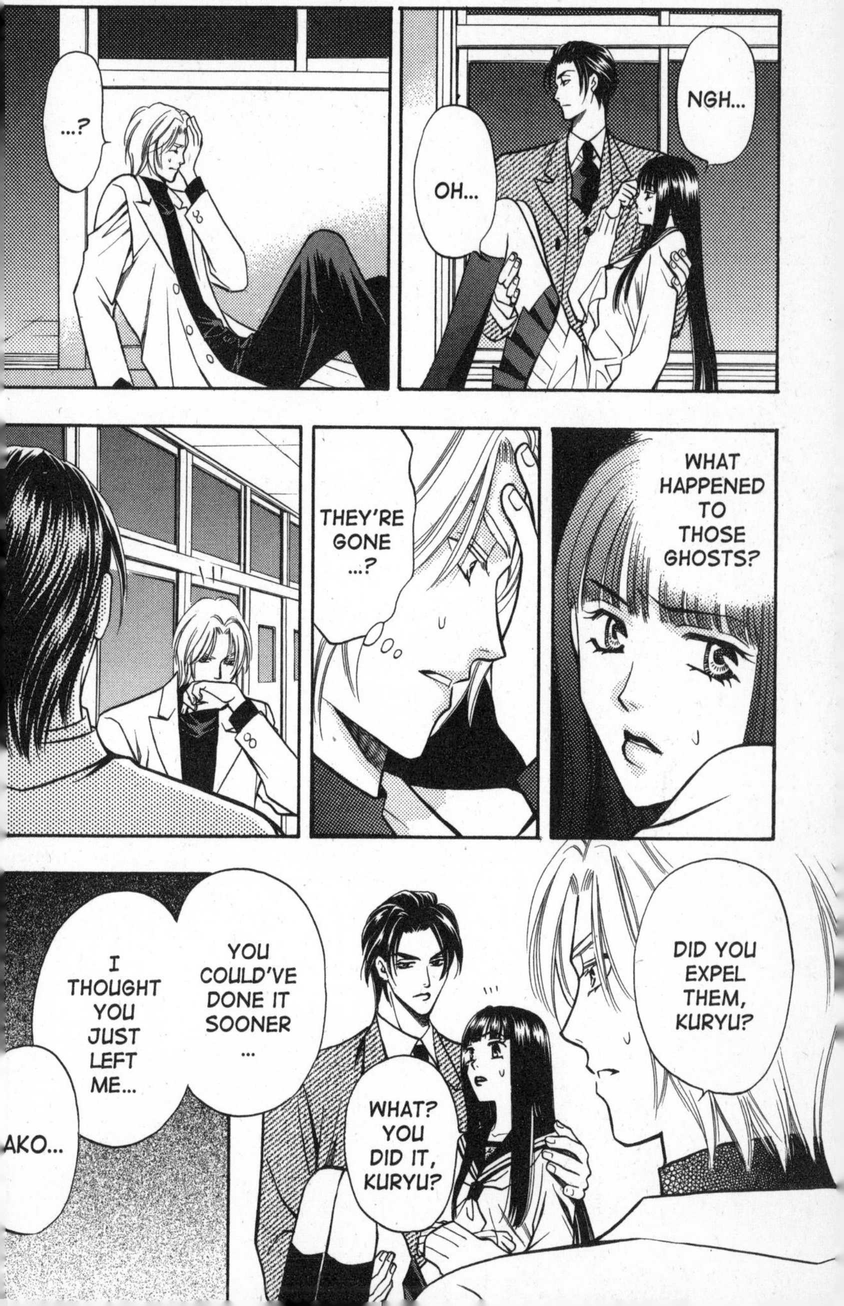
NGH...
OH...
...?
WHAT HAPPENED TO THOSE GHOSTS?
THEY'RE GONE ...?
DID YOU EXPEL THEM, KURYU?
WHAT? YOU DID IT, KURYU?
YOU COULD'VE DONE IT SOONER ...
I THOUGHT YOU JUST LEFT ME...
AKO...

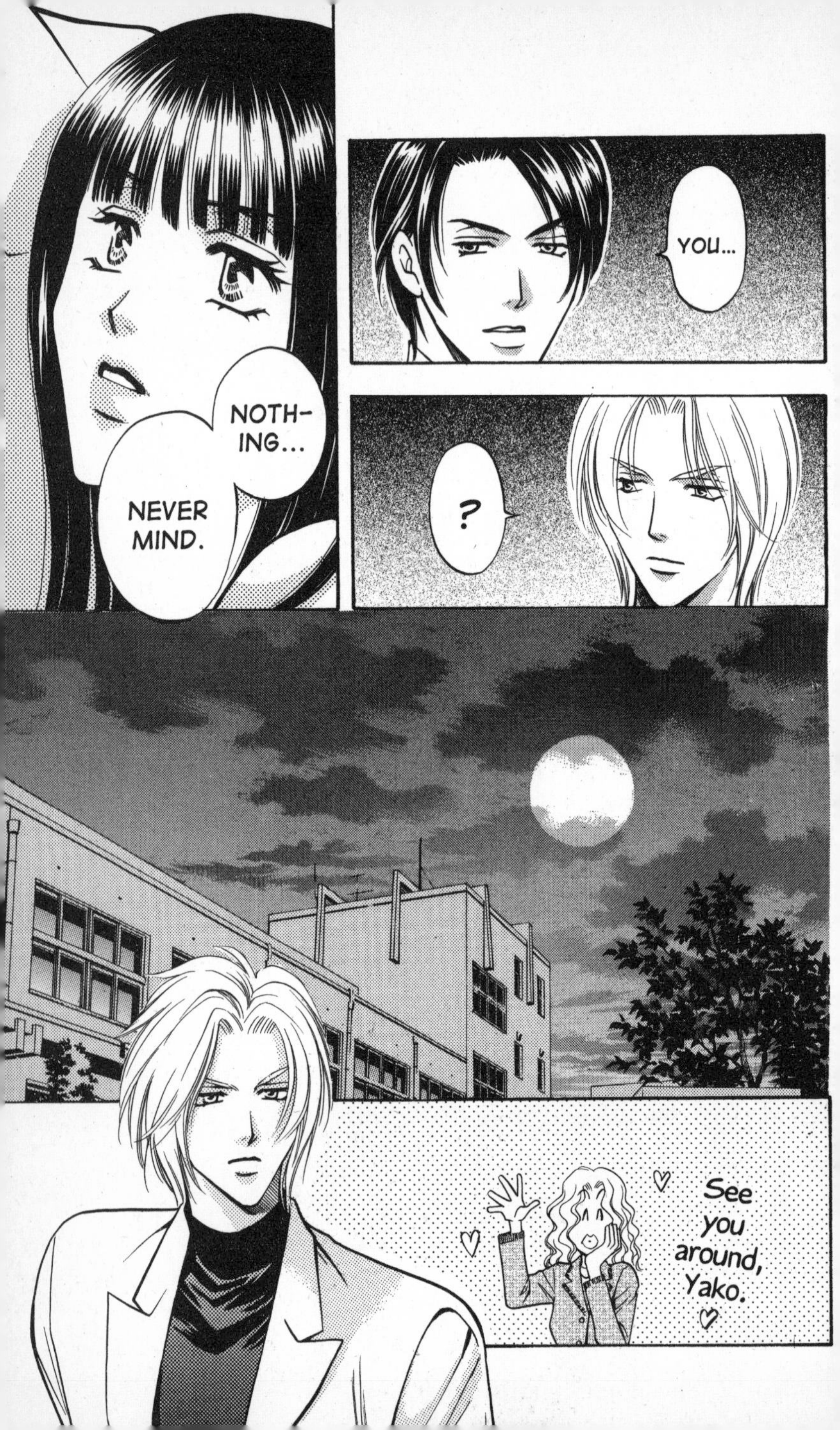
YOU...
?
NOTH-ING...
NEVER MIND.
See you around, Yako.

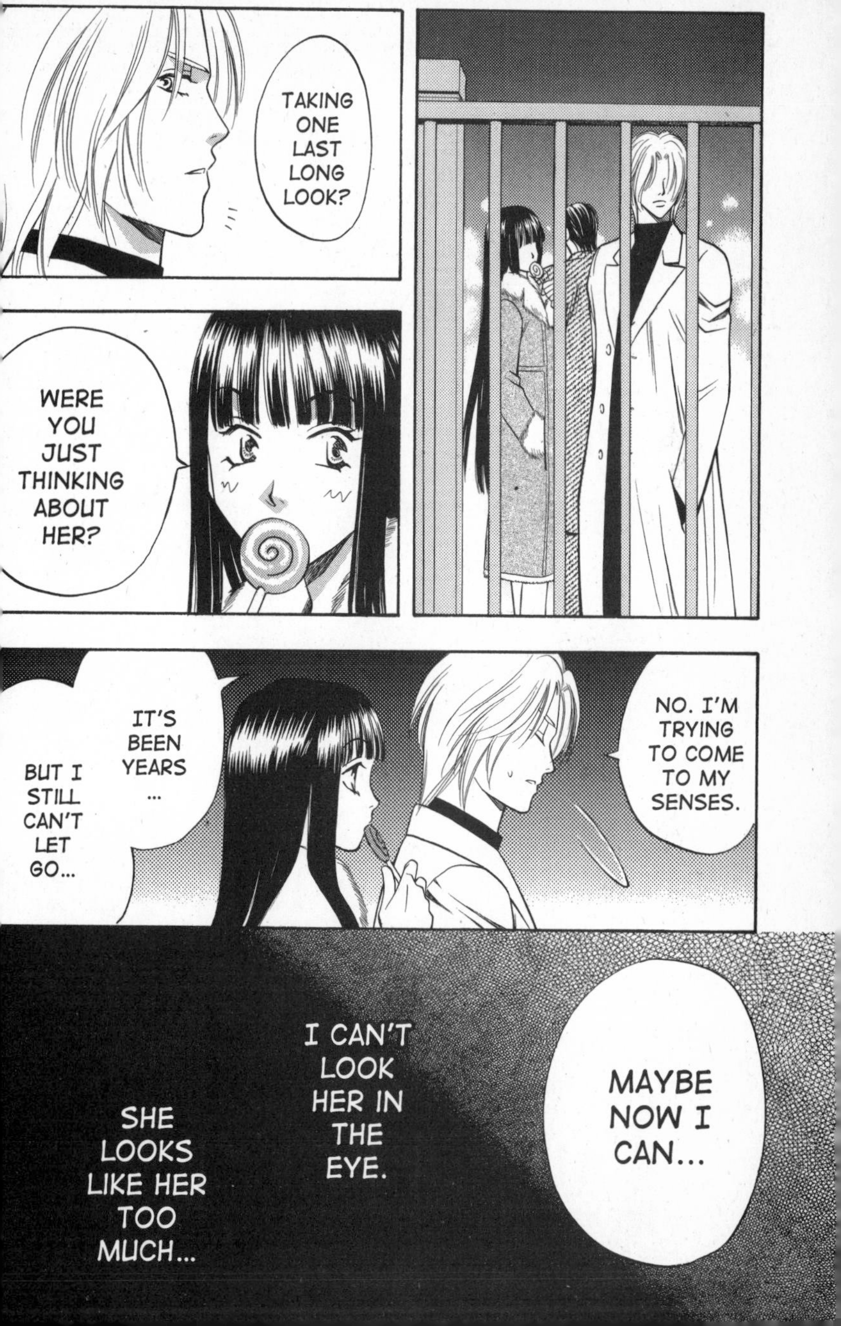
TAKING ONE LAST LONG LOOK?
WERE YOU JUST THINKING ABOUT HER?
NO. I'M TRYING TO COME TO MY SENSES.
IT'S BEEN YEARS ...
BUT I STILL CAN'T LET GO...
MAYBE NOW I CAN...
I CAN'T LOOK HER IN THE EYE.
SHE LOOKS LIKE HER TOO MUCH...

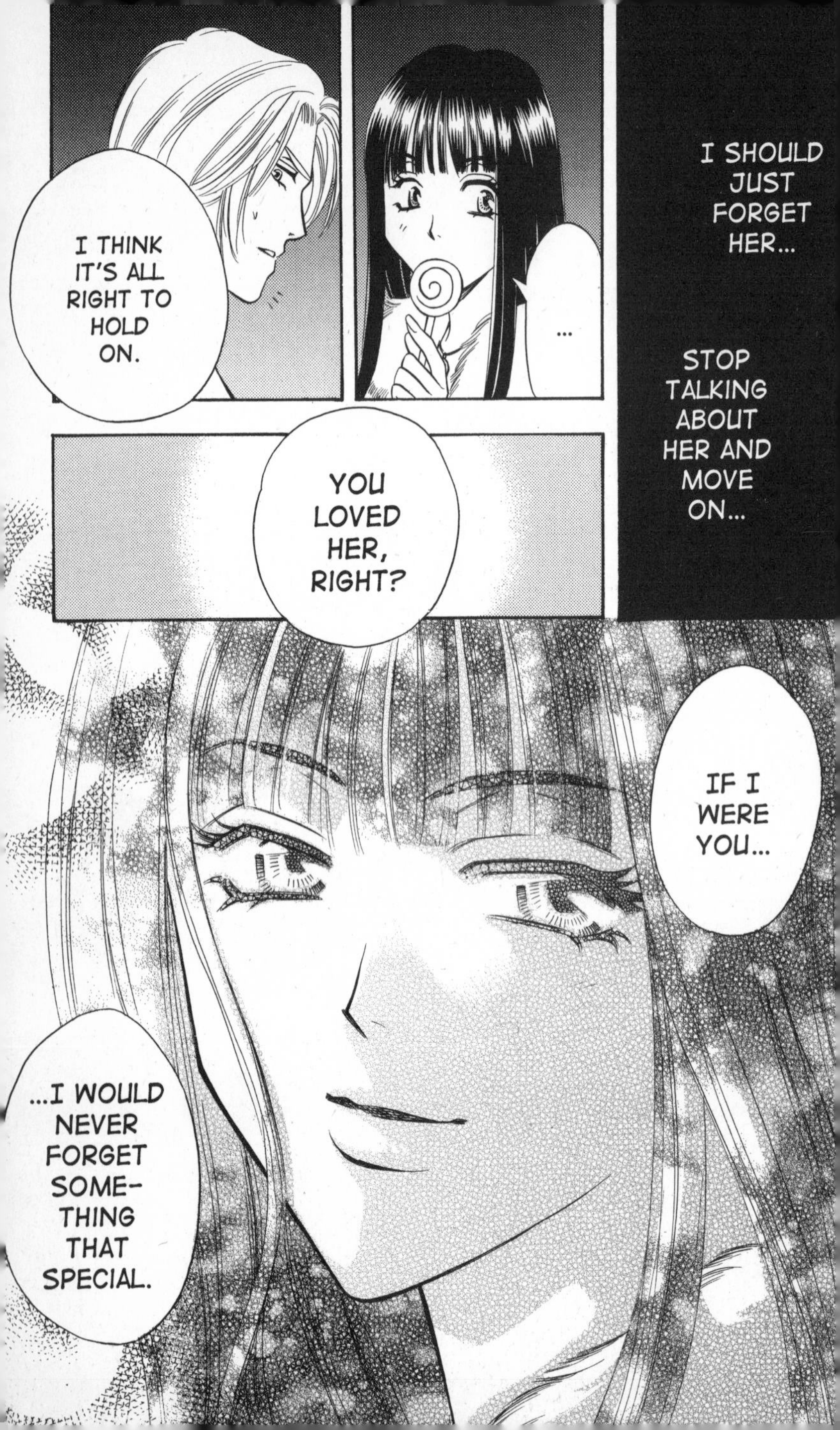
I SHOULD JUST FORGET HER...
STOP TALKING ABOUT HER AND MOVE ON...
...
I THINK IT'S ALL RIGHT TO HOLD ON.
YOU LOVED HER, RIGHT?
IF I WERE YOU...
...I WOULD NEVER FORGET SOME-THING THAT SPECIAL.

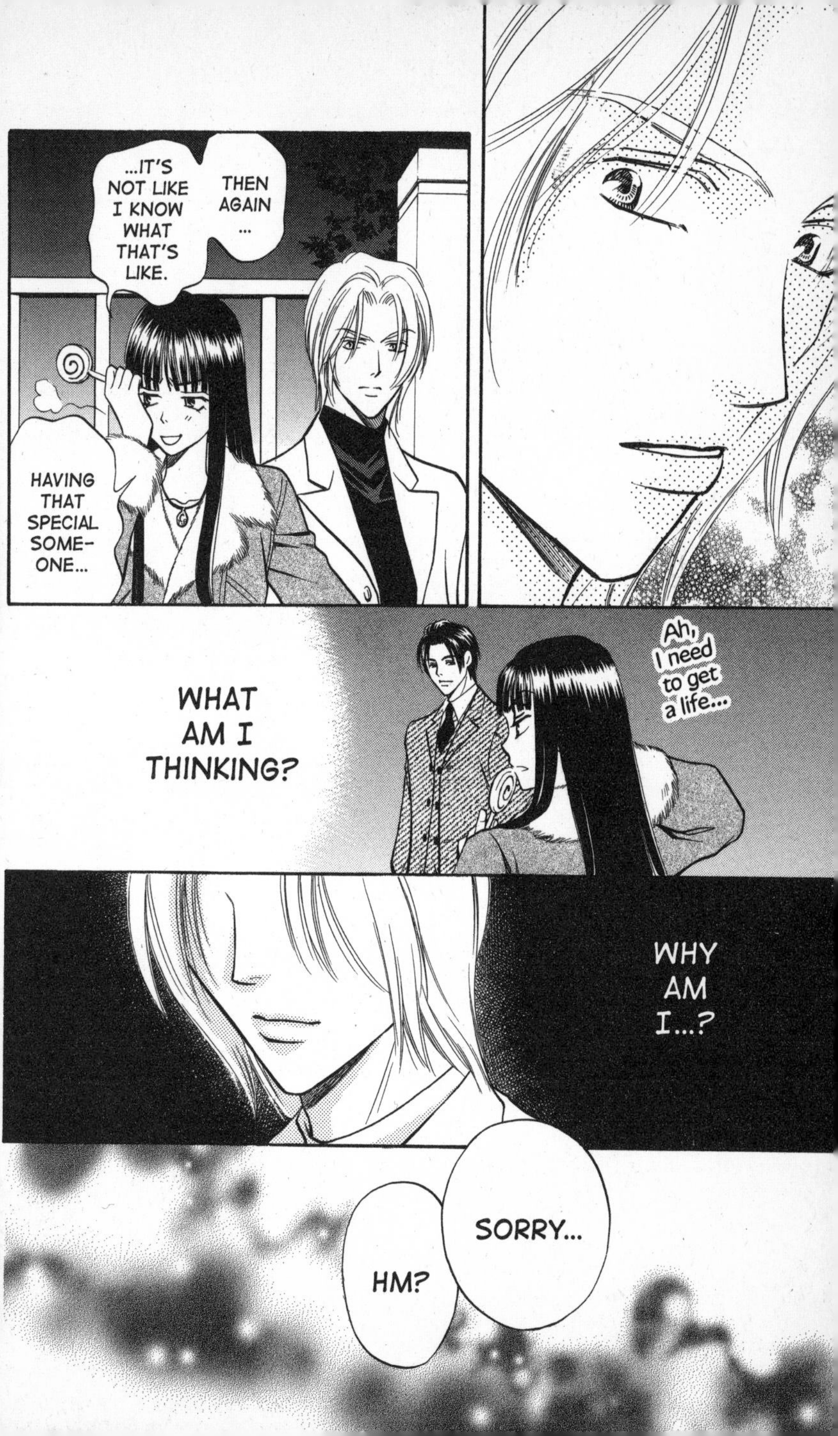
THEN AGAIN ...
...IT'S NOT LIKE I KNOW WHAT THAT'S LIKE.
HAVING THAT SPECIAL SOME-ONE...
Ah, I need to get a life...
WHAT AM I THINKING?
WHY AM I...?
SORRY...
HM?

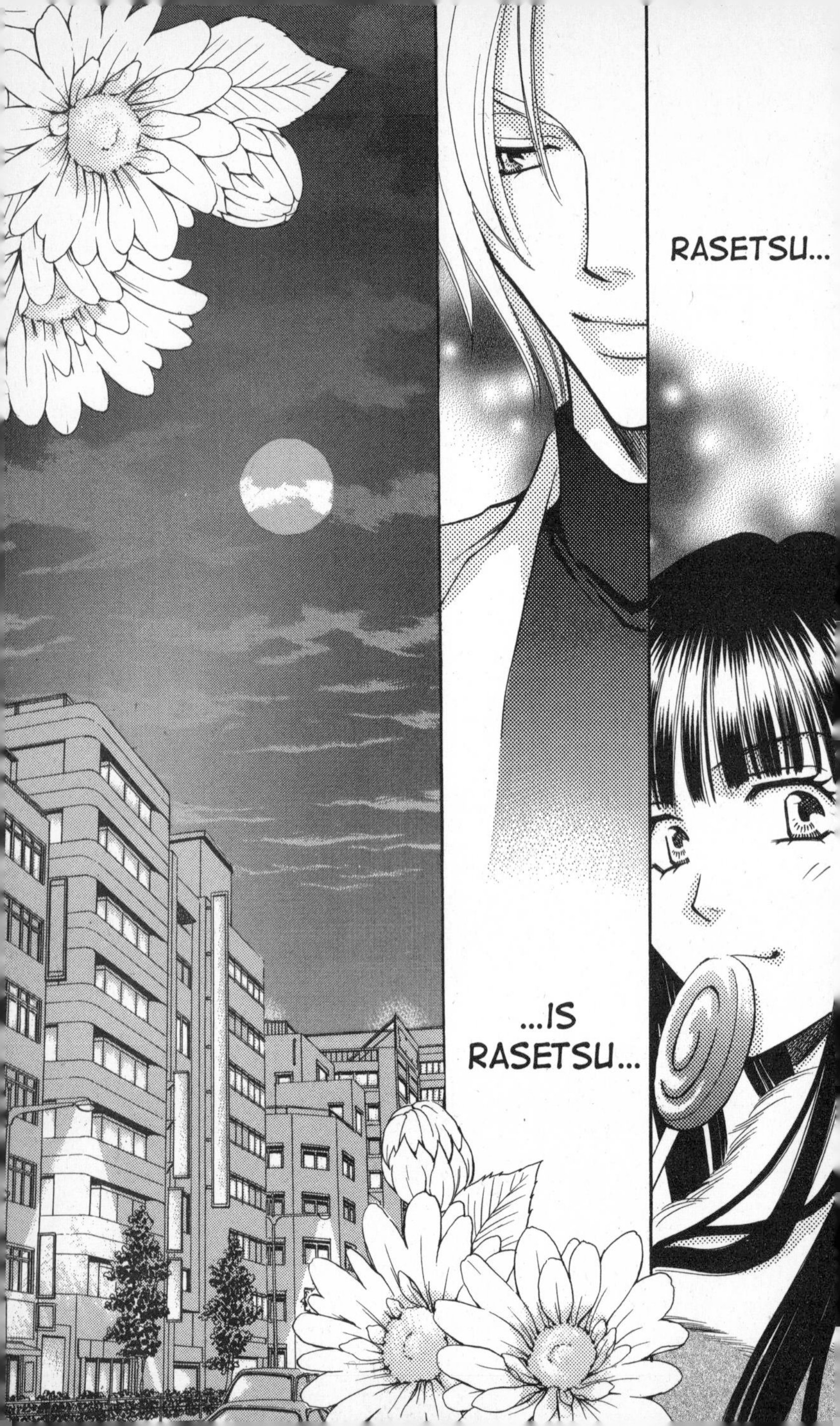
RASETSU...
...IS RASETSU...

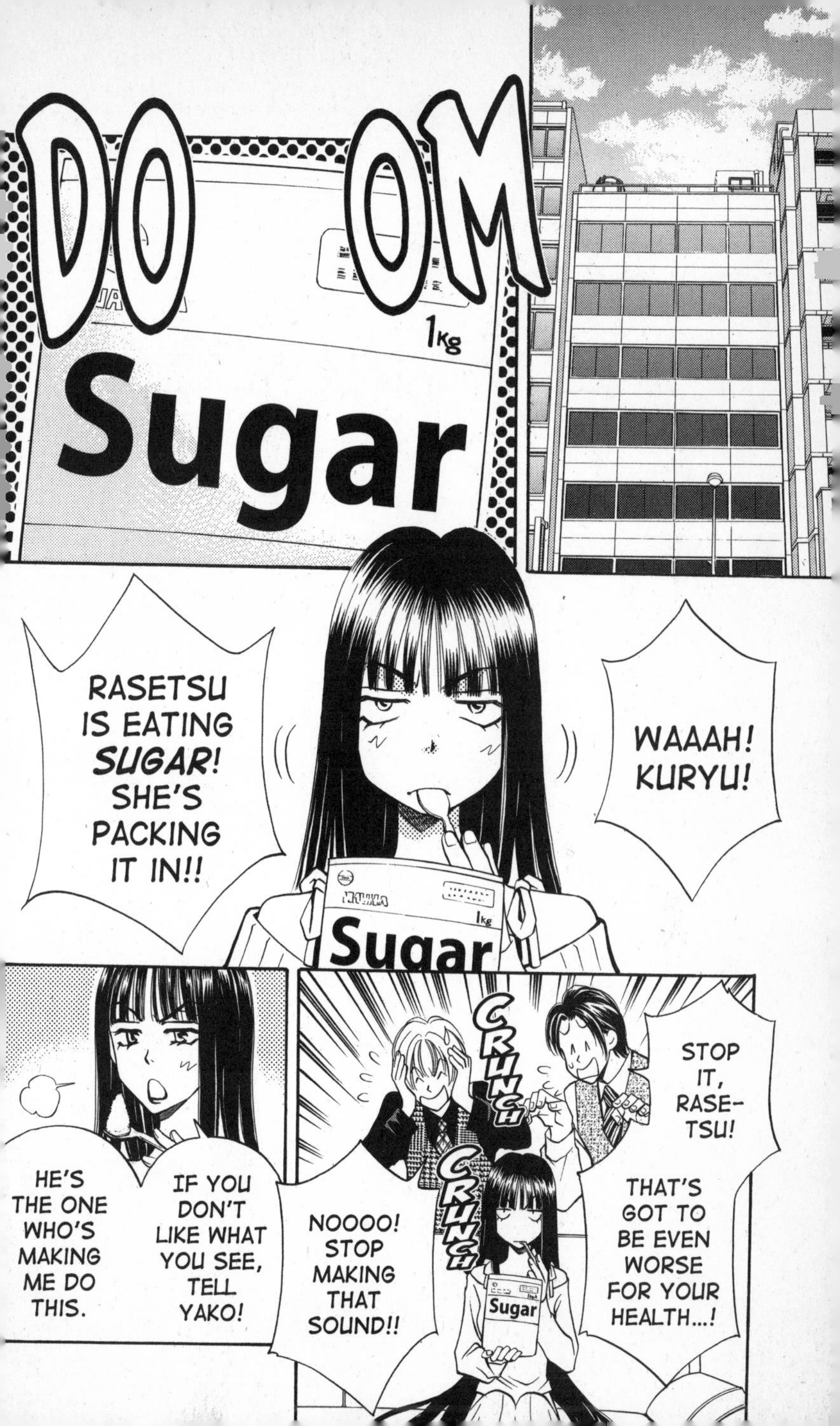
DO OM
1kg
Sugar
WAAAH! KURYU!
RASETSU IS EATING ***SUGAR***! SHE'S PACKING IT IN!!
1kg
Sugar
STOP IT, RASE-TSU!
THAT'S GOT TO BE EVEN WORSE FOR YOUR HEALTH...!
CRUNCH
CRUNCH
NOOOO! STOP MAKING THAT SOUND!!
Sugar
IF YOU DON'T LIKE WHAT YOU SEE, TELL YAKO!
HE'S THE ONE WHO'S MAKING ME DO THIS.

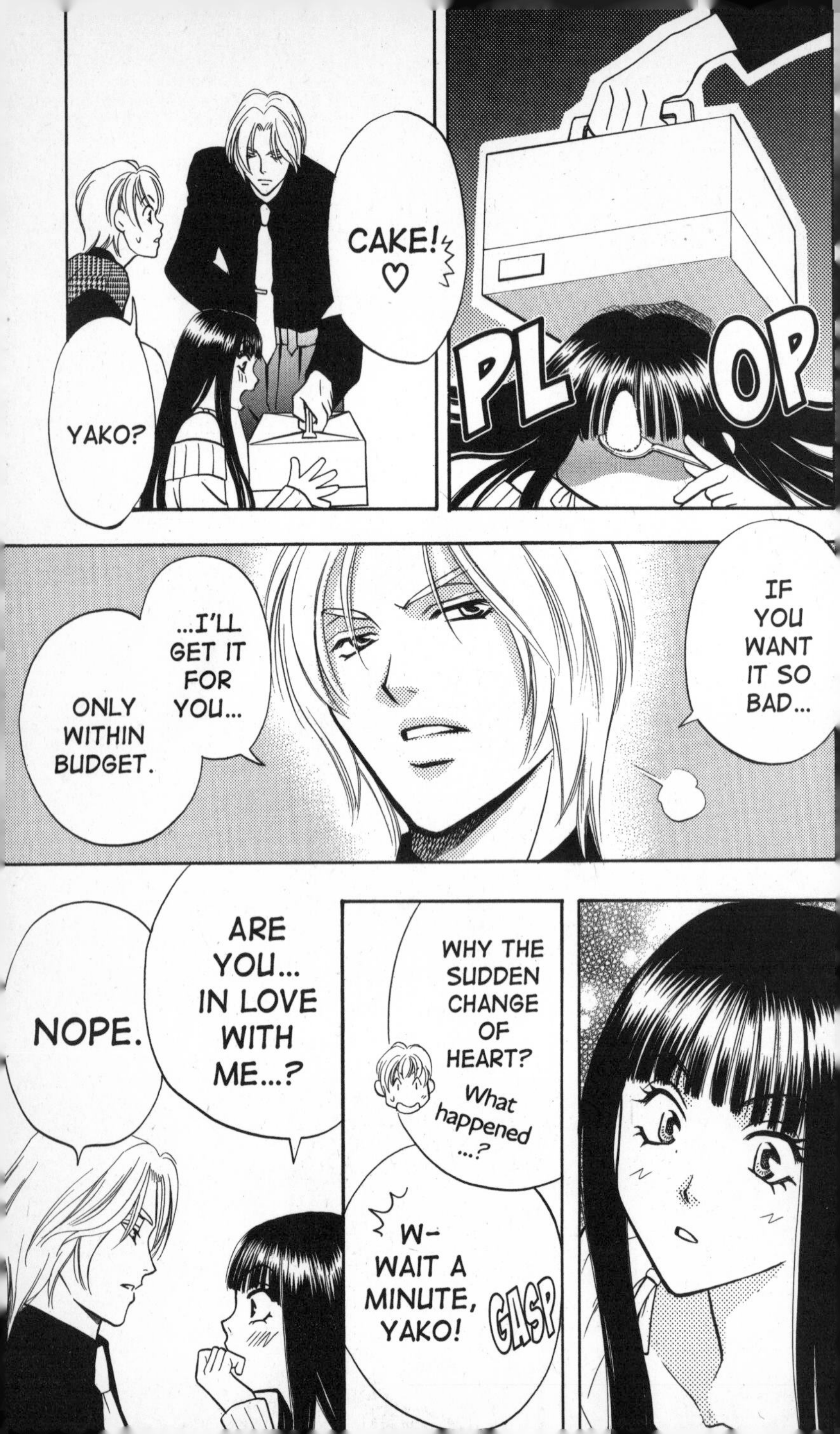
PLOP
CAKE! ♡
YAKO?
IF YOU WANT IT SO BAD...
...I'LL GET IT FOR YOU... ONLY WITHIN BUDGET.
WHY THE SUDDEN CHANGE OF HEART?
What happened ...?
W- WAIT A MINUTE, YAKO!
GASP
ARE YOU... IN LOVE WITH ME...?
NOPE.

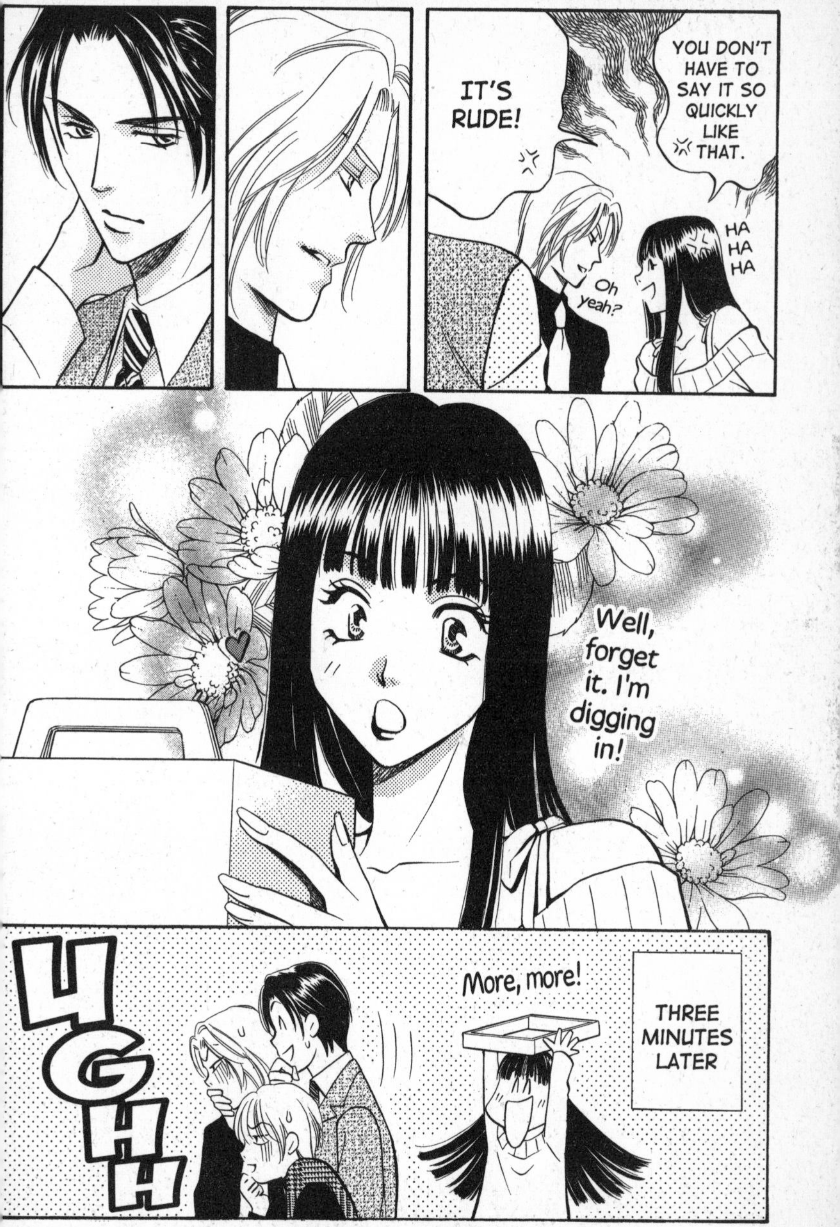
YOU DON'T HAVE TO SAY IT SO QUICKLY LIKE THAT.
IT'S RUDE!
HA HA HA
Oh yeah?
Well, forget it. I'm digging in!
THREE MINUTES LATER
More, more!
UGHH

Rasetsu 1 / The End

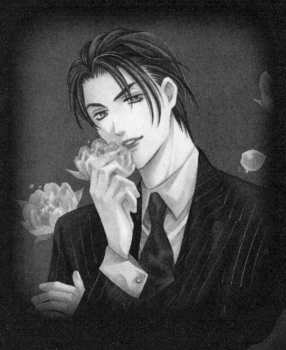

Chika Shiomi lives in the Aichi Prefecture of Japan. She debuted with the manga *Todokeru Toki o Sugitemo* (Even if the Time for Deliverance Passes), and her previous works include the supernatural series *Yurara*. She loves reading manga, traveling and listening to music by Aerosmith and Guns N' Roses. Her favorite artists include Michelangelo, Hokusai, Bernini and Gustav Klimt.

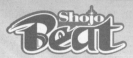

RASETSU
VOL. 1
The Shojo Beat Manga Edition

This manga volume contains material that was originally published in English in
Shojo Beat magazine, May 2009 issue. Artwork in the magazine may have been
altered slightly from what is presented in this volume.

STORY AND ART BY
CHIKA SHIOMI

Translation & Adaptation/Kinami Watabe
Touch-up Art & Lettering/Freeman Wong
Design/Hidemi Dunn
Editor/Amy Yu

Editor in Chief, Books/Alvin Lu
Editor in Chief, Magazines/Marc Weidenbaum
VP, Publishing Licensing/Rika Inouye
VP, Sales & Product Marketing/Gonzalo Ferreyra
VP, Creative/Linda Espinosa
Publisher/Hyoe Narita

Rasetsu No Hana by Chika Shiomi
© Chika Shiomi 2006
All rights reserved.
First published in Japan in 2006 by HAKUSENSHA, Inc., Tokyo.
English language translation rights arranged with HAKUSENSHA, Inc., Tokyo.
The stories, characters and incidents mentioned in this publication are entirely fictional.

Printed in the U.S.A.

Published by VIZ Media, LLC
P.O. Box 77010
San Francisco, CA 94107

Shojo Beat Manga Edition
10 9 8 7 6 5 4 3 2 1
First printing, June 2009

www.viz.com

store.viz.com

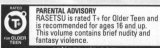

PARENTAL ADVISORY
RASETSU is rated T+ for Older Teen and
is recommended for ages 16 and up.
This volume contains brief nudity and
fantasy violence.
ratings.viz.com